The Streets Belong to Us

Justice, Power, and Politics

COEDITORS
Heather Ann Thompson
Rhonda Y. Williams

EDITORIAL ADVISORY BOARD
Peniel E. Joseph
Daryl Maeda
Barbara Ransby
Vicki L. Ruiz
Marc Stein

The Justice, Power, and Politics series publishes new works in history that explore the myriad struggles for justice, battles for power, and shifts in politics that have shaped the United States over time. Through the lenses of justice, power, and politics, the series seeks to broaden scholarly debates about America's past as well as to inform public discussions about its future.

More information on the series, including a complete list of books published, is available at http://justicepowerandpolitics.com/.

The Streets Belong to Us

Sex, Race, and Police Power
from Segregation to Gentrification

....

ANNE GRAY FISCHER

The University of North Carolina Press Chapel Hill

© 2022 Anne Gray Fischer
All rights reserved
Set in Charis by Westchester Publishing Services
Manufactured in the United States of America

The University of North Carolina Press has been a member of the Green Press Initiative since 2003.

Complete Library of Congress Cataloging-in-Publication Data is available at https://lccn.loc.gov/2021049408.

ISBN 978-1-4696-6504-7 (cloth: alk. paper)
ISBN 978-1-4696-6505-4 (ebook)

Cover illustration: Historic photo of Portland, Oregon, vice squad. Photo courtesy of *The Oregonian*.

For my mother, Robin Fischer (1949–2012)

Contents

Introduction, 1
Built on Women's Bodies

Prologue, 18
White Purity and the Progressive Origins of Police Power

1 Making the Modern City, 26
  Sexual Policing and Black Segregation from Prohibition to the Great Depression

2 Bad Girls and the Good War, 50
  The Nationalization of Sexual Policing in World War II

3 Los Angeles: Land of the White Hunter, 76
  Legal Liberalism, Police Professionalism, and Black Protest

4 Boston: The Place Is Gone!, 107
  Policing Black Women to Redevelop Downtown

5 Atlanta: From the Prostitution Problem to the Sanitized Zone, 138
  Broken Windows Policing and Gentrification

6 Taking Back the Night, 174
  Feminist Activisms in the Age of Broken Windows Policing

Epilogue, 201
These Streets Belong to All of Us

Acknowledgments, 211

Notes, 215

Index, 281

Illustrations and Maps

Illustrations

1.1 "You Give Me Five Dollars," political cartoon, 45

2.1 "She may look clean but . . .," 60

3.1 Black woman and white man, 1965, 99

4.1 White woman in the Combat Zone, 118

5.1 Atlanta antiprostitution protest and counterprotest, 163

5.2 "The Shared Vision," 170

6.1 Combahee River Collective action, 179

6.2 *Gay Community News* street trial images, 181

Maps

3.1 South Los Angeles, ca. 1960, 78

4.1 Downtown Boston, ca. 1975, 108

5.1 Midtown and downtown Atlanta, ca. 1985, 140

The Streets Belong to Us

Introduction
Built on Women's Bodies

∙∙∙

"We are staging out here on Las Vegas Boulevard," Officer Calvin Wandick told a ride-along television crew for *Cops* in 2012. "This is one of the main fairways for working girls. So we're going to be patrolling, and see . . . what kind of crime we can stop." Then Wandick got down to work, pulling two Black women out of the crowd for an interrogation.

His line of questioning concerned the women's age, their clothes, and what was really in the bottles of iced tea they were carrying. One woman was nineteen years old—below the legal drinking age. Officer Raquita Reyes, Wandick's partner, demanded to know how long the woman had been "working," while Wandick rifled through her purse and took out her pepper spray, tactical pen, and condoms. Turning her tools of personal protection into evidence against her, Wandick concluded, "She's out here for all the wrong reasons," even though when the officers stopped her, she had only been engaging in the common practice of underage drinking. Apparently being a poor Black woman in public was enough to constitute "all the wrong reasons."

The woman saw it differently. "I'm a human being just like everybody else," she protested as Wandick cuffed her. "I'm not doing nothing but walking up and down, looking at the lights." Why shouldn't she have the same right to the street as any of the thousands of nightly visitors to the Las Vegas Strip?[1]

Officers routinely apprehend Black women for less. Television shows like *Cops* feature police detaining women for "lurking in shadows," "standing on the street corner," "loitering outside [a] business," or "walking in the street where the sidewalks are provided." When police justify this use of their time for the benefit of the cameras, they claim they're performing a community service. "It's best for her, best for the community, and best for Las Vegas Boulevard that we get her off the street," Wandick said as he led the shackled Black woman into a police van. Every day, poor Black women are arrested simply because of their physical presence on city streets. Audiences might recognize these encounters as regrettable, even unjust, but police logic encourages viewers to dismiss them as mundane casualties of public order—the price of keeping women, families, and cities safe.[2]

Law enforcement has been a crucial mechanism to control Black women's labor and restrict their freedom since Emancipation, if not before then. However, authorities' justifications to legitimize this power have changed over time. When contemporary police deploy the argument—commodified for mass consumption—that public safety and economic growth require the mass removal of poor Black women from city streets, they are simultaneously perpetuating deeply rooted social hierarchies and producing a historically specific vision of gendered criminality.

Across the twentieth century, the boundaries of lawful womanhood—a concept that is an active ideological process, necessarily animated by changing ideas about race, sexuality, and class—were being renegotiated. Urban authorities, social scientists, journalists, reformers, activists, and policed women themselves debated who had a right to public space, what constituted licit behavior and who conformed to it, and whose alleged sexual activity sustained the social order and whose threatened to destroy it. Sexual policing—the targeting and legal control of people's bodies and their presumed sexual activities—played a uniquely powerful role in redrawing and enforcing these shifting boundaries because it defined interlocking hierarchies of Blackness, whiteness, and sexual morality in real time. Through sexual policing, law enforcement helped to create the intertwined social meanings and legal rights of Black and white womanhood.[3]

Officers can approach any woman and arrest her for any reason. But they do not. This book narrates the historical process of how and why different women are made vulnerable to sexual policing. Asking this question showcases how the state recalibrated lethal social inequalities, even as sexual norms underwent dramatic revision; how the enforcement of normative white sexuality generated breathtaking power for urban police; and how sexual policing was foundational to the spatial and economic formation of modern cities.

Officers' everyday power to interrogate and arrest is so normalized in the prevailing understanding of police practices that it conceals the material violence perpetrated against vulnerable women. Sexual policing degrades women's rights to city streets, and arrests trigger cascading repercussions, including lost wages, jobs, housing, and child custody. The extreme power asymmetry between police and targeted women directly enables police to perpetrate gender-based violence such as sexual assault and the extortion of sex in exchange for withholding arrest. By compounding vulnerable women's economic and social instability, sexual policing—rather than serving a function of public safety—makes policed women, their families, and the communities they live in less safe. These harms are not merely the unfortunate side effects of a small corner of law enforcement. Rather, sexual policing is an engine of police power.[4]

......

Women matter in the history of police power.

Men, especially Black men, often stand in as the symbol and subject of the mass incarceration crisis in the United States. Policy makers, pundits, and activists have overwhelmingly focused on the impact of mass incarceration on Black fathers, sons, and brothers. "There is something profoundly wrong when African-American men are still far more likely to be stopped and searched by police, charged with crimes and sentenced to longer prison terms than are meted out to their white counterparts," Hillary Clinton said in a 2015 presidential campaign speech. In this discourse, Black women are the mothers, daughters, and sisters left behind to navigate the free world without male support. There are understandable reasons that this narrative has taken hold—Black men are six times more likely to be incarcerated than white men, for example—but it is nevertheless a patriarchal account that erases the escalating catastrophe of Black women caged in the criminal system. The "free world" does not feel free for many Black women.[5]

In the wake of the murders of George Floyd and Breonna Taylor, participants in the 2020 uprising, marching with demands to "Say Her Name," forced a massive reckoning with police violence and a surging recognition that Black women's lives matter. And yet awareness of Black women's vulnerability to state violence is only a first step toward fully understanding why police target Black women. When we ignore the unique forms of police violence that women confront, we miss a crux of state authority: racialized gender-based policing fuels broad, discretionary law enforcement practices that imperil all targeted people. Across the twentieth century, police served as state arbiters of urban space, and through sexual policing, officers became makers of both gender and race hierarchies as they sorted out which women had a right to the city and which did not, and which women would be criminalized and which would not. *The Streets Belong to Us* demonstrates that it is not enough to say that women are *also* policed or *differently* policed. Women's bodies are an important and overlooked site on which police power—and the modern city—has been built.⁶

Black feminists created the intellectual framework to center gender in analyses of modern state violence. An unbroken lineage of Black activists and scholars—from Ida B. Wells and Fannie Lou Hamer to Angela Davis, Kimberlé Crenshaw, Andrea Ritchie, and Mariame Kaba—have condemned the unique vulnerabilities and violence that Black women experience in the criminal legal system. Historians Kali Gross, Sarah Haley, Cheryl Hicks, and Talitha LeFlouria have documented how state violence targeting Black women was foundational to post-Emancipation modernity. Black feminist insights illuminate disturbing dimensions in the conventional history of twentieth-century police power: gendered anti-Blackness, definitionally contrasted against changing ideologies of normative white womanhood, was a historically specific preoccupation and product of law enforcement. Urban authorities demonized women, both Black and white, as threats to society in different but interconnected ways that provided the political justifications and legal strategies for the consolidation of police power. Racist and eugenic anxieties that "promiscuous" women destroy families, communities, and cities authorized an expanding net of police interrogation, arrests, and incarceration. Within the context of anti-Black exploitation, discipline, and punishment dedicated to the growth of white-dominated wealth, sexual policing played a major role in redefining Blackness, whiteness, and normative sexuality in modern public space.⁷

Women's right to the city has been historically fragile and contested. Across the twentieth century, as Black and white women made distinct claims to public space—to more workplaces, downtown commercial districts, and other formerly white male spaces—police officers adjudicated the deep legacies of the "public woman" and her association with commercial sex. This project took on greater significance after Reconstruction, as urban authorities fought to regain control over emancipated Black women, organizing women workers, and immigrant women to reinforce disrupted urban hierarchies. As a result, a woman's body in city space was never neutral—her social location shaped its meaning and horizon of movement under the police gaze. While criminalized men may be thought to produce individual harm, a woman's presumed deviance was intimately connected to her primary function of social reproduction: her actions threatened to corrode social order and produce a new generation of criminals. Police drew their authority for the surveillance and sorting of humans from the widely held belief that women on city streets were an object of community welfare and, therefore, urgent state interest. Yet the dominant racist logic of *which* women represented the greatest threat to urban order shifted over time.[8]

Within this context, *The Streets Belong to Us* makes three interrelated arguments. Sexual policing was uniquely structured to consolidate discretionary police power in the twentieth century. To justify and expand this discretionary power, urban authorities effectively decriminalized white women's presumed straight, nonmarital sexual practices as they subjected Black women to systematic and intensified police action. In this way, authorities exposed how sexual policing was a factory for making gendered Blackness and whiteness. This battle for increased law enforcement power was grounded in urban political economy: sexual policing made and remade the modern city—first by constructing and fortifying the walls of segregation that ringed Black neighborhoods and later by laying the groundwork for the police regime that enabled gentrification.[9]

Women, as middle-class beneficiaries of state power or its marginalized targets, have been central to the legitimization and legalization of police authority—a dynamic this book traces through the most historically gendered arena of law enforcement: sexual policing. This history begins during Prohibition, when police departments permitted and profited from so-called urban vice—commercial sex, gambling, and liquor—in Black neighborhoods. The scandalous failure of police to suppress vice prompted widespread contempt; police were ridiculed as "stupid, dishonest, incapable," and "one of our national jokes," according to the lead author of a federal commission report on law enforcement in 1931. Criminologists and popular writers alike identified "vice control" as a major source of police corruption and brutality—the "chief menace to police departments." Officers, they argued, should not be responsible for duties "which self-respecting men hate to perform."[10]

Why did police continue to engage in a practice that was widely identified as a waste of law enforcement resources and a dangerous site of police corruption and brutality? Certainly rank-and-file officers jealously guarded the discretionary power, violent gratification, and material enrichment that attended vice policing. However, by World War II, police leaders and their political allies recognized that sexual policing made it possible for urban police forces to achieve a stunning transformation in the eyes of white Americans from corrupt goons to urban saviors. Sixty years after Prohibition, law enforcement exerted tremendous power in urban planning and policy making. Police departments, in collaboration with business leaders and politicians, presided over a regime of mass misdemeanor policing, now referred to as "broken windows" policing, dedicated to clearing "disorderly" people off city streets. Sexual policing, once derided as a wasteful liability, was hailed by the 1980s as a panacea for urban problems—the key to unlocking urban wealth and safety.

Across the twentieth century, sexual policing meant more than simply policing prostitution laws per se, or the narrowly defined exchange of sex for money. In practice, sexual policing amounted to enforcing the dominant priorities of public order. "Public order" in the popular imagination is often assumed to be a neutral and universal social good that equally benefits all who share the city. But public order enforcement draws its meaning and purpose from the social and political context in which it is embedded. Public order policing means enforcing social hierarchies. Seen in this light, when police enforced prostitution-related misdemeanors, they wielded a powerful instrument of urban governance that shaped the lives of all residents—not just the men customarily at the center of twentieth-century police histories. Sexual policing served as a state-sponsored tool to make and enforce modern forms of the color line, women's subordination, and white urban wealth. Moreover, sexual policing was a laboratory for law enforcement authorities and politicians to test novel methods of state power. Zeroing in on sexual policing within its urban context exposes the specific political process in which racist and sexist police violence is laundered into a beneficial public service.*

Policing in the United States has historically meant enforcing the country's founding violence: heteropatriarchy, settler colonialism, and racial capitalism. We can't fully understand modern police power without reckoning with gender and sexuality as an integral link binding these foundational forms of violence together. *The Streets Belong to Us* offers one way to build this analytical framework. It focuses on the sexual policing of Black and white cisgender women for allegedly engaging in straight sexual activities to show how these practices funded police officers' urban takeover, produced normative white womanhood as defined against denigrated Black womanhood, and systematically degraded the rights of Black

---

* While this history focuses on racial segregation, gender oppression, and white economic prosperity as three outcomes of sexual policing, we could add many more items to this list, including the enforcement of ableism, normative gender and sexual binaries, the borders of U.S. citizenship, and the boundaries to access healthcare and other social goods.

women to exist on increasingly capitalized city streets. This is just one piece in the larger complex of gendered and raced state violence. The police enforcement of the gendered anti-Black binary constricted the racial belonging of Indigenous, Asian, and Latina women in distinct ways; these twentieth-century histories are urgently needed. And the discretionary and race-specific enforcement of changing meanings of normativity exposes how race, gender, and sexual hierarchies are constructed through sexual policing; how transgender, queer, and nonbinary people are classified as legal or criminal; and how they are included or violently denied inclusion in the enduring patriarchal, colonial, and capitalist power structure of urban belonging.[11]

・・・・・・

Sexual policing is a form of "morals policing"—also referred to as crimes against public order or against society—a legal category separate from crimes against people or property. Morals policing is a powerful tool for state authorities because it is so slippery: morals violations seem at once obvious while remaining impossibly vague. As a result, they are subject to some of the widest discretion—simply put, authorities' judgment—by police officers and prosecutors across all categories of law enforcement. For example, as of 2021, California law criminalizes "loitering for the purpose of engaging in a prostitution offense," targeting those who act "in a manner and under circumstances that openly demonstrate the purpose of inducing, enticing, or soliciting prostitution." What is the difference between criminal loitering and simply standing on the street—and how can one tell? What is the apparently knowable "manner" or "circumstances" of criminal purpose, and moreover, how can officers police anyone's intentions? Through morals policing, officers have the power to determine whether a woman is hailing a taxi or soliciting motorists for sex, whether a woman is asking a man for the time or for a date. Morals policing transforms a woman's ostensible right to exist on a city street into a criminal act.[12]

Public morals laws have historically included a broad and overlapping set of state and municipal offenses such as, but not limited to, disorderly conduct, vagrancy, loitering, prostitution, common nightwalking, fornication, adultery, or being a lewd and lascivious person. These laws were more or less interchangeable: for example, white women socializing with Black men were arrested for violating vagrancy, disorderly conduct, or fornication laws; and women suspected of promiscuity were charged with prostitution. In the FBI's 1938 Uniform Crime Report, the authors wrote that women suspected of engaging in commercial sex were charged with "vagrancy, disorderly conduct, etc." The authors' casual use of "etc." to round out this list of morals laws offers a hint of just how arbitrary and capacious the laws criminalizing sexually profiled women have been in practice.[13]

The mandate to sexually police women authorized the basic building block of police power: discretion. Sexual policing was (and remains) driven by an officer's discretionary power. Unlike for offenses against property or people, police officers were the primary complainants in public morals enforcement. And a police officer did not have to witness any particular act to make a morals arrest. When giving evidence in court, police testimony typically hinged on a subjective term of art: an observed woman's "arrestable behavior." That shorthand constituted a pliable metric of sexual criminality drawn from the officer's appraisal of a woman's appearance, her reputation, the company she allegedly kept, and the neighborhood in which she was apprehended. As a result, all sorts of women's sexual and social choices—or circumstances—were gathered under the legal category of women's sexual crime.[14]

Women's sexual crime is a legal fiction that has been invented and reinvented through everyday encounters between women and police across the twentieth century. The exercise of discretion has been popularly understood as police officers doing their job. But this misses how police discretion can produce the idea of "crime" itself. Historical interrogations of police practices, like this book, contextualize and denaturalize the exercise of discretion to expose the priorities and logics that structured sexual policing. This work brings us closer to understanding why and how police have deployed their discretionary power against different people over time. As rank-and-file officers and police leaders alike shifted their racial priorities and practices in the sexual policing of women across the twentieth century, they demonstrated a key theme of this book: that the meanings of sexual criminality are historically rooted and politically constructed to satisfy the specific social and economic interests of urban capital.[15]

Morals arrests served—and continue to serve—many purposes, but at bottom, each arrest establishes police authority. Police could decide to press charges with the sole intention of initiating criminal prosecution. But they might also make arrests in order to interrogate or harass people, to gain leverage from potential informants, to sexually extort or assault women, or simply to temporarily remove people from the streets. When the assertion of police authority on city streets was the overriding goal, it was immaterial whether an arrest would hold up in court. Broadly worded, capacious morals laws provided a ready tool for police officers to justify these alternative uses of arrest. In this way, the ability to police the presumed sexual practices of women was constitutive of police power. "The police seem to feel powerless without the authority to arrest offenders for all types of prostitution," one researcher noted in 1986. At multiple turning points, when discretionary police authority was most hotly challenged or defended—for example, during the midcentury "rights revolution" in the law or the broken windows consolidation of the 1980s—these battles were fought on the terrain of women's bodies.[16]

What words can be used to describe the women ensnared in the vague and discretionary legal apparatus of morals enforcement? Certainly some women in this book were arrested while attempting to engage in commercial sex, but to broadly refer to the women arrested in this manner as "prostitutes" reproduces discriminatory police logic and distorts the reality that women were often arrested because of their physical presence on city streets. Some women, after all, were arrested for acts that would not today be considered criminal, such as socializing across the color line or engaging in intraracial, straight nonmarital sex, while still others were arrested while shopping, talking to friends, waiting for a bus or taxi, picking up their children at school, or simply walking down the street. And women who had previously been suspected of, or arrested for, engaging in commercial sex were often police targets regardless of what they were doing at the time of arrest—"A street prostitute on the street is working, where ever she is," one antiprostitution task force argued in 1986—effectively, and unconstitutionally, weaponizing a woman's reputation or past action into an inescapable and constant criminalized legal status. The commonly used phrases to describe women targeted by police are loaded with the taint of criminality. "Sexually suspect," for example, places the burden of guilt on women for allegedly presenting deviant or nonnormative behavior. To remedy this problem, Melinda Chateauvert has helpfully suggested the term "sexually profiled," a phrase that highlights the power of discretionary police to render women suspicious. I use this phrase to refer to women who were surveilled and apprehended by police on morals charges to help us draw connections between sexual profiling and the more publicized forms of contemporary racial, ethnic, and religious profiling.[17]

· · · · · ·

The Streets Belong to Us begins in the 1920s, in a moment of urban flux. City authorities were in the process of implementing a police-managed relocation of red-light districts to Black neighborhoods. At the beginning of the twentieth century, red-light districts had been downtown fixtures. These districts lived at the nexus of urban governance and the raced and gendered social order. They served two political functions: to generate graft that would fund political campaigns and firm political loyalties, and to shield respectable white women and their families against the supposedly irrepressible lusts of men by confining "low" women to specific neighborhoods. Red-light districts were thought to protect the power of political regimes and the moral purity of white homes. During the Progressive era, however, this strategy of containment was replaced by a moral crusade to reclaim white womanhood.[18]

Progressive reformers, marching under the banner of abolishing "white slavery"—whose racist priorities were visible in the very term—mounted a massive campaign to salvage poor white and European immigrant women by shutting down red-light districts. Their agenda depended on a myth of white womanhood as the valorized anchor of sexual morality, the necessary cornerstone of a social order constituted by the white patriarchal household. Black womanhood was accordingly degraded as irredeemably immoral—a naturalized feature of the urban sexual landscape—and Black women were generally absent from this white reform agenda. Spurred on by these moral reform campaigns, politicians and law enforcement authorities vigilantly policed the sexual and racial purity of white women in order to protect the imagined borders of the white home.[19]

Progressives did not win their full repressive demands but rather a tolerable substitute: the relocation of red-light districts to predominantly Black neighborhoods. This inaugurated the defining spatial and racial logics of policing in the twentieth century, as Black people and the neighborhoods they lived in were marked as lawless and sexually deviant. Sexually profiled Black women confined to racially segregated zones of vice were thought to sustain, rather than disrupt, the white moral order. As late as 1964, the authors of a report on police practices wondered why "white women, more than Negro women, are arrested for sex offenses," and they concluded that "the white policeman [is] more offended by sexual promiscuity among white people . . . he 'expects,' and is not annoyed by, such behavior among Negroes." White women, then, remained a police concern in Black neighborhoods well into the postwar period. Their alarming presence in state-sanctioned Black vice districts became the ground on which officers established and enforced racial segregation.[20]

Two seemingly contradictory processes complicated who was arrested and why in the second half of the twentieth century: a gradual liberalization of laws against women's straight, nonmarital sexual practices was accompanied by a redoubling of racial and sexual profiling. By the mid-1960s, the process of liberalization meant that it was no longer considered illegal, either in law or in policing practice, for a woman to have intraracial sex with a man she was not married to—an offense for which white women were routinely arrested in earlier decades. Yet police departments invested, with support at both the urban and federal levels, in a program of broken windows policing, or public-order enforcement, through mass misdemeanor arrests that singled out sexually profiled Black women. This ramping up of misdemeanor policing took root in the same decades during which the law otherwise retreated from regulating nonmarital straight sex.

Beginning in the postwar years and accelerating in the 1960s and 1970s, the urban economic crisis propelled a revision of the pre–World War II fusing of race, space, and sexual policing: white moral purity declined as a key racial function of morals enforcement and the enduring focus on Black containment and banishment surged in urban economic and political importance. Postwar cities reeled from white capital flight, and the property value of urban space became a salient driver of postwar morals policing as cities tried with varying degrees of success to recoup economic losses from departing industry and white homeowners. Within this context, the liberalization of sex laws remade white women's nonmarital straight sexual practices as private and beyond the reach of any public order that police were obligated to oversee. At the same time, blighted downtown districts, once historically white, now became home to new and more explicit commercial sex establishments. As urban politicians set their sights on retail, service industry, and tourist economies, poor and working-class white women moved through downtown vice districts with unprecedented freedom. To be sure, they were still arrested on prostitution charges, but authorities evinced a newfound tolerance of white indoor sex workers and even celebrated them as a useful lure for white consumer dollars.[21]

But when Black women moved into these formerly white downtown spaces that city leaders hoped to recapitalize, they became not only subject to, but also the prime symbol justifying, mass surveillance and policing. Law enforcement authorities, politicians, and business leaders tapped into enduring myths of Black women's violent sexual criminality to target them as a major threat to public safety and a troublesome barrier to economic recovery. The sexual policing of Black women was repackaged by police authorities and their political allies as an essential frontline tactic in a growing arsenal of anticrime programs dedicated to reviving economic growth in postwar cities. The specter of sexually profiled Black women drove political strategies to resurrect status policing (essentially, policing based on people's appearances, which was ruled unconstitutional in 1972) and implement new techniques of mass arrest and banishment.[22]

The simultaneous depolicing of white women and the escalated policing of Black women was no contradiction. They were bound together in a dynamic that unfolded in the context of deepening racial inequality and economic restructuring in the late 1970s and 1980s. Law enforcement solutions circulating in those years offered the tantalizing promise of "reclamation" and "takeover" of urban space from sexually profiled women who were overwhelmingly marked as Black in media accounts and arrest statistics. *The Streets Belong to Us* spotlights the importance of sexual policing to urban battles over gentrification, where an array of stakeholders, from police to real estate profiteers, fought to block Black women's right to the city. In 1981, a white real estate agent in gentrifying Washington, D.C., who led an antiprostitution campaign declared, "We're fighting for turf. . . . We're fighting for the streets." Under these conditions of white urban reclamation—or gentrification—the law enforcement program that would become known as broken windows policing took hold.[23]

Broken windows policing has often been associated with the targeting of Black men. But sexual policing was crucial to testing, legalizing, and enacting this new mass-misdemeanor enforcement regime years before the idea was popularized by criminologists James Q. Wilson and George Kelling in 1982. "Promiscuous and scantily clad prostitutes," in Kelling's phrasing, were just one group in a larger vision of urban decay, but experiments in sexual policing expanded the power of urban police departments and primed broken windows policing for its stratospheric rise after 1982.[24]

Sex and race were fundamental hierarchies around which cities were spatially organized. The twentieth century showcases the uneven and unequal development of women's full social mobility in urban space, as a changing roster of women were marked as threats to social order and economic growth. But the surveillance and policing of sexually profiled women was not just a strategy to regulate women's movement and bodies. Sexual policing justified and facilitated the implementation of racial segregation and gentrification urban policies. Urban public order, and the role of police in securing it, looked very different on either end of the twentieth century.

In the 1920s, white urban order meant the containment of vice to segregated Black neighborhoods. Police officers and politicians profited from the management of vice in Black neighborhoods while vigilantly surveilling white women in order to enforce the racial segregation that made these vice districts politically possible. By the 1980s, however, public order meant the mass clearance of sexually profiled Black women from city streets in order to prepare these urban areas for an influx of white capital. Especially as laws regulating sexual morality and racial segregation loosened over time, the shift in emphasis from white moral purity to systematic Black sexual criminalization helped police achieve expanded social control and political power in distinct legal and political landscapes.

. . . . . .

This book focuses on Black-white power dynamics and, in so doing, dramatizes the police practices that structured life for everyone on city streets. I focus on the interconnected policing practices of Black and white women because twentieth-century law enforcement authorities, criminologists, and reformers thought in Black and white. In police and social science records, Black women were the most frequently imagined racial counterpart to white women. Patricia Hill Collins, Evelynn Hammonds, and Hortense Spillers have taught us why: the meanings of white womanhood were dependent on and constitutive of the meanings of Black womanhood. The presumed purity (and later, normality) of white womanhood was necessarily and definitionally contrasted with the presumed deviance (and criminality) of Black womanhood. The fiction of sexual criminalization depended on the relational construction of Blackness and whiteness to make it real. Drawing on these contrasts, sexual policing has served to engineer and enforce gender and racial inequality, while helping to reproduce the very concept of gendered Blackness and whiteness.[25]

Sarah Haley writes that Jim Crow carceral regimes "produced women every day, and all of the women were white." Tracking the changing meanings of Black and white womanhood amid the acceleration of sexual liberalization, urban capitalization, and feminist and anti-racist politics across the twentieth century throws into sharp relief how women's freedom is not increased linearly or distributed equally—how producing one woman's relative sexual freedom depends on producing another woman's sexual criminalization—and how and why Black women were subjected to intensified surveillance and policing even as poor and working-class white women gained a tenuous right to sexual privacy and public space.[26]

A robust and essential field of scholarship centers queer, trans, and nonbinary lives in the expansion of—and resistance to—police power, exposing sexual policing as a pivotal factor in urban political formations. This work helps us to understand that, much as federal government officials built the "straight state," as Margot Canaday argues, on-the-ground local sexual policing constructed and enforced gender and sexual binaries. To fully reckon with this history, we must also attend to the ways that sexual policing helped to create unequal categories of heterosexuality, which were mapped onto racist definitions of womanhood. As Black feminist scholars Cathy Cohen and Dorothy Roberts have shown, straight-presenting or straight-identifying Black women were not granted the same claims to legitimacy, normality, and legality as white women. Gender conformity and the presentation of heterosexuality were not sufficient to shield Black women from police action in the urban "straight state." By tracing the development of unequal categories of heterosexuality, this scholarship expands our understanding of how gender and sexual binaries were made across the twentieth century.[27]

The power dynamics discussed in this book can be found in cities across the United States. Histories of the modern police are necessarily local *and* national. Urban policing and federal policy are both profoundly shaped by local politics; but police department brass, rank-and-file officers, and city politicians consistently turned to their peers nationwide, as well as federal task forces and funding agencies for strategies, resources, and information. As a result, and even in spite of regional differences, urban police departments demonstrated a remarkable convergence in practice and politics. *The Streets Belong to Us* blends the methods of Elizabeth Hinton and Naomi Murakawa, who focus on the links between postwar federal policy and urban policing, with those of Max Felker-Kantor and Simon Balto, who narrate the national implications of policing in single cities, in order to tell a national story of local policing through key turning points in three regionally distinct cities: Los Angeles, Boston, and Atlanta. Gender- and race-centered analysis delivers a method to uncover the local contexts in which strikingly similar regimes of state repression and violence were built nationwide.[28]

Historians of police must stitch stories together with archival fragments. Where records have not been destroyed, many archives restrict access to what remains. But ironically, the neglect of women in the history of police power made it possible for me to access state archival materials that would have otherwise been restricted or destroyed. In one case, after enduring my repeated requests, a sympathetic and resourceful archivist connected me with a salvaged collection of women's probation records that had fallen through the cracks after it was marked for destruction. As a result, the chapters that follow draw primarily on newly recovered and underused police, probation, and prison records located in city, state, and federal archives. They also make use of the papers of police officers, prison administrators, judges, moral reformers, and politicians who donated their personal records to archives or wrote memoirs. Finally, I rely on national and, when possible, local police arrest statistics to tell a story about police power. These numbers are imperfect and incomplete measures of police practices, but in the fragmented and silenced archives of the state, they offer one way to track and compare police priorities over time.[29]

To uncover what the state will not disclose, I turned to what Kelly Lytle Hernández calls the "rebel archive"—the records of those who fought state power. Anti-racist, civil liberties, and feminist organizations did the necessary work of, first, recognizing the value of women's encounters with, and their responses to, police; and second, saving these records. Feminist activists, lawyers, and journalists involved in the sex workers' rights movement of the 1970s and 1980s generously contributed their time and personal archives, helping this story to be more fully told. And the Black press consistently reported on police practices that were absent in white newspapers.[30]

But how should historians read a rebel archive made by women who were surveilled, interrogated, and policed? Sexually profiled women's voices are often silenced in the archive because they had the least access to public platforms and media, and because their words were mediated by authorities or reporters. Saidiya Hartman has modeled strategies to push past the limits of the archive to affirm the richness, complexity, and authority of dispossessed women's experiences. This book, however, exposes police logics and practices—not the inner lives of sexually profiled women. Inspired by Laura Briggs, I seek to return a measure of dignity and privacy so often denied to women who were at the center of contests to police their movements and their bodies. But like Hartman, I identify sexually profiled women as visionary producers of knowledge. Women who have been repeatedly targeted by police are experts of law enforcement practices. Their memoirs, radio recordings, prison writing, poetry, and personal essays testify to this expertise. Whenever possible, I punctuate moments in the book with sexually profiled women's words. But I do not offer these voices to "prove" authoritative or revealing truths about women's intimate lives. Rather, women's observations, poetry, and protests serve as evidence of their deeply informed appraisals and critiques of state violence.[31]

・・・・・・

The Streets Belong to Us begins with a prologue detailing the Progressive moral reform campaign to abolish "white slavery" through the shutdown of red-light districts and the repressive legal apparatus of morals policing that was built to achieve this end. Chapter 1 then covers the relocation of red-light districts to Black neighborhoods nationwide, and how the enduring commitment to white moral purity that had animated Progressive-era reforms—not to mention the new repressive tools of morals policing—was put to work to cement racial segregation.

Chapters 2 and 3 discuss the recalculation, and gradual decriminalization, of white women's nonmarital straight sexual practices as authorities failed to rein in what became an inescapable twentieth-century trend—sexual liberalization—during World War II nationwide and in postwar Los Angeles. World War II represented the fullest expression of morals policing in the name of white protection: law enforcement authorities puzzled (and panicked) over white women's increasing rates of nonmarital straight sex even as they betrayed ambivalence about enforcing morals laws in Black neighborhoods and interrupting white men's sexual access to Black women. Through this form of morals enforcement, police won new respect from the white public. In postwar Los Angeles, as courts and legislatures relaxed morals laws, white women's sexual practices became a lower police priority and officers, presenting themselves as professional practitioners of the law, deployed their authority to ratchet up their targeting of Black women. Black residents' anger at this deepening racial inequality of sexual policing fueled the Black urban uprisings of the 1960s.

Chapters 4 and 5 track the conjoined development of gentrification and broken windows policing within the context of sexual liberalization, the post–civil rights era, and the urban economic crisis in Boston and Atlanta, respectively. Chapter 4—centered on an experiment to zone an "adult entertainment district" in downtown Boston—shows how the demonized presence of sexually profiled Black women in the city's historically white downtown sparked a realignment of urban capital and local police. As activists, lawyers, judges, and bipartisan politicians fought to dramatically restrict police discretion by decriminalizing so-called victimless crimes, police found their pathway to urban power by conducting mass sweeps targeting Black women downtown with the often explicit goal of readying the city for economic redevelopment. Chapter 5 provides an extended definition and discussion of broken windows policing, offering a study of Atlanta to show how sexual policing made it possible for broken windows policing to take root in liberal, Black-led cities. A consortium of downtown businessmen singled out sexually profiled Black women to force consensus on a new legal and political landscape where law enforcement was seen as the best solution to urban problems of inequality and poverty.

Across the twentieth century, women reformers and, later, feminist activists fought hard to insert themselves into—or demand alternatives to—male-dominated police departments. Returning to a national perspective, chapter 6 discusses how antiviolence feminists in the broken windows era responded to police power. As Black women mobilized to protest a terrifying wave of serial murders and predominantly white women enlisted the authority of law enforcement on behalf of women's protection, feminists disagreed over the question of whether police were the problem—or the *answer* to the problem—of violence against women. Delivering an understudied perspective on the feminist "sex wars" of the 1980s, this chapter also highlights the enduring political traction of white moral protection: as predominantly white feminists fought for expanded police powers to protect women, they launched a revival of the Progressive-era moral reforms discussed in the prologue to fuel the so-called Blue Revolution. Black and multiracial feminist activists crafted new theories of state violence to contest these arguments about the protective value of law enforcement.

Police violence can often seem constant and unchanging. Law enforcement has been foundationally designed to serve patriarchal, white propertied interests, and sexual policing provided a lasting mechanism for this social control. For centuries, police have deployed sexist and racist scripts of white moral protection and Black sexual depravity to enforce elite order, run curbside courts, quell dissent, and clip Black people's freedom. But we ignore what *changed* in sexual policing at our own peril. Across the twentieth century, sexual policing redrew the borders of lawful white womanhood and, in the process, the spatial borders of whiteness itself. Through sexual policing, officers seized unprecedented authority in urban policymaking. And sexual policing catalyzed visionary forms of Black resistance against police predation and violent neglect. Interrogations of modern state violence must start at a key source: sexual policing.

Prologue
White Purity and the Progressive Origins of Police Power

In 1899 white Progressive reformer Charlton Edholm issued a call to arms: "There is a slave trade in this country, and it is not black folks this time, but little white girls—thirteen, fourteen, fifteen, sixteen, seventeen years of age—and they are snatched out of our arms, and from our Sabbath-schools and from our communion tables." Edholm crusaded against "white slavery," the rallying cry of a generation of Progressive moral reformers who fought to abolish prostitution in the name of its white victims. This "new abolitionism" marked a stunning feat of historical erasure: The "old" abolitionists of the antebellum era had made the sexual assault and exploitation of enslaved Black women a hallmark of their antislavery campaigns. But now, amid the blood-soaked reign of Jim Crow terrorism, abolitionists turned their rescue work onto "white girls."[1]

The American tale of white slavery was forged in the industrial city as bosses feasted on the cheap labor of immigrants, poor whites, and African Americans. White slavery wore its racial politics on its face. This was a crusade to reclaim poor white women, freshly arrived to the city in search of work, who—in a morality play that was staged and restaged in films, dime novels, pamphlets, and reports—had been seduced, tricked, coerced, or captured by predatory immigrant, Jewish, Black, and Chinese men. As repetition spun the white slavery tale into truth, the afterlives of legal slavery were shunted into obscurity. White slavery was built on reconstructed racisms.[2]

Black women's ongoing vulnerability to sexual violence was banished from the white moral imagination. For those whites who still remembered, the mark of slavery stained Black women's innocence and rendered them ineligible for any moral crusades. "Negro women [were] expected to be immoral and [had] few inducements to be otherwise," reformer Frances Kellor wrote. Instead, Progressive reformers, afflicted by what Emma Goldman called an "epidemic of virtue," fixated on the "unattached" poor white and European immigrant women living in the anonymous tumult of the racially mixed city. Without the moral and economic anchor of father or husband, these free-floating white women, adrift and at the mercy of exploitative bosses or worse, were a "moral hazard"—a lurking threat to the white Christian moral order rooted in white women's domesticity and economic dependence on men.[3]

But Progressive reform was not merely a warmed-over revival of Victorian evangelical woman-savers who handed out bibles and offered shelter and domestic training to "friendless" women. This new generation of moral reformers was committed to deploying the power of the state and yoking the reclamation of white womanhood to repressive legal machinery. A Progressive alliance "of evangelicals, feminists, business leaders, and medical experts" assembled to demand the "immediate and unrelenting" criminalization of prostitution. They started by training their sights on the urban fixture of red-light districts—where, they believed, "young girls are ruined, sold and hired, and kept in hopelessness and hideous slavery." The project to abolish red-light districts swelled to become one of the most coordinated and comprehensive reform campaigns the new century had yet seen.[4]

In a cruel twist of history, the white slavery tale and the Progressive crusade to save white womanhood triggered the twentieth-century construction of a carceral apparatus that would come to systematically target Black women.

• • • • • •

Red-light districts did not just spring to life, spontaneous and unplanned. Before reformers mobilized to abolish red-light districts, historian Mara Keire reminds us, "first they created them." Real estate developers, downtown business owners, and other urban elites had fought to establish a localized site of "necessary evil." Some saw the red-light district as "a necessity like a sewer," as one Arkansas banker argued, which contained human filth and prevented it from polluting the entire city. Others appealed to the protection of "decent women," claiming that "segregated" sex districts—as they were called at the time—provided a safety valve for men's lustful impulses. The authors of a 1916 vice report in Bridgeport, Connecticut, wrote that a "segregated district is really a protection to the morality of the womanhood of the city, for without it rape would be common and clandestine immorality would increase."[5]

At the turn of the twentieth century, red-light districts sat at the spatial and political center of the city. Brothels, bars, and gambling parlors ringed the downtown commercial district, offering convenient access for men, typically the only permitted clientele, in town on business or other manly errands. Early twentieth-century cities, then, were physically mapped to accommodate two male domains: business and play. Politicians and police departments were deeply invested in these so-called segregated districts. Police officers harvested bribes from red-light operators and donated a cut of these funds to the reigning mayoral administration or election campaigns in order to fortify political allegiances. In this way, the policy of segregated vice greased the machinery of urban politics. By fusing together politicians, police, and elites, prostitution policy was the connective tissue of early twentieth-century urban government.[6]

Segregated districts were social "kaleidoscopes," as historian Mark Wild writes, and a variety of racial and class combinations were present at every turn. In some cities, downtown districts bordered or overlapped with Black neighborhoods or Chinatowns. Houston's red-light district—established in 1908 with "An Ordinance Colonizing and Segregating Houses of Ill Fame"—mandated racial *and* reputational segregation. But elsewhere, white and Black women, as well as other women of color depending on regional populations, worked together. Individual establishments were sites of nested segregation, stratified by race and class, and with the exception of elite houses that trafficked in "exotic" racial encounters, the poorest establishments generally featured the most interracial contact. A patchwork of restrictions may have prevailed—forbidding workers who were women of color or customers who were men of color—but white men held exclusive access throughout the district. Red-light districts were organized to "[maintain] the dominance of white men over all other social groups," as historian Thomas Mackey writes.[7]

White women in segregated districts had been an object of evangelical reformist concern before the Progressive era, but large-scale efforts to rescue "ruined" women would mean doing away with the segregated districts—and perhaps ruin the city itself. The prospect of white women's salvation was not compelling enough for city authorities to risk unleashing vice throughout the city. Indeed, segregated districts made a necessary sacrifice of "low" white women in order to deliver protections to respectable white women and the white city more broadly. By raising their banner on behalf of errant and exploited white womanhood, Progressive reformers dramatically disrupted this prevailing white consensus.

It was absurd to suggest that segregated districts protected white women, Progressive reformers argued. On the contrary, they endangered the virtue of white women and, in turn, the moral white family. The corruption of white womanhood that took place in red-light districts—which, not incidentally, was directly connected to the political corruption that sustained them—threatened to degrade the basic functions of democratic society. As one reform committee wrote in 1922, "Even if promiscuity could be made hygienically safe, yet prostitution and sexual immorality would continue to be a most serious menace to our civic life."[8]

The social purity that guided Progressive reforms was bound up with visions of white purity. Antiprostitution reformers regarded segregated districts as a form of "race suicide," and they were in close conversation with proponents of eugenics. Paul Popenoe, a eugenicist and prominent advocate of forced sterilization, argued in the pages of the dominant antiprostitution reform periodical, the *Journal of Social Hygiene*, that "suppression of prostitution" must be included as a "eugenic measure that will tend to raise the level of the race and reduce the number of feeble-minded and feebly-inhibited persons born." The Women's Christian Temperance Union issued a resolution supporting the abolition of segregated districts, committing itself "to promote such measures as will suppress prostitution with its attendant results deteriorating to the moral and physical health of the race." Black moral reformers engaged in distinct forms of rescue work on behalf of Black womanhood, but given the dominance of white people in this reform movement, it is reasonable to assume that these white reformers had one specific "race" in mind.[9]

White women were targeted, both rhetorically and materially, in the drive to shutter segregated districts. An older Victorian evangelical portrait of the "fallen woman," which emphasized white women's vulnerability to male exploitation, certainly underwrote Progressive-era reforms. But as Progressive reformers worked to purify white womanhood, law enforcement became just as important as the Bible. Frederick Whitin, a lead member of the Committee of Fourteen, New York City's antivice organization, argued that in the fight against prostitution, the policeman is "the community's most necessary agent." Middle-class white women debated the value of bending the state to this project of moral reclamation. In her memoir, Progressive-era policewoman Mary Sullivan described an exchange with her cousin. "I do not see how you can bear to shut a cell door on a woman," the cousin remarked. Sullivan replied, "It is often a way of protecting her as well as the community at large. You wouldn't hesitate to plunge a knife into a woman if you felt that you were saving her from invalidism or death."

In this way, defenders of coercive, state-powered moral reform like Sullivan articulated what was at stake in women's sexual practices and the sacrifices that were necessary to save women and "the community at large."[10]

As reformers fought state authorities to advance their white purity agenda, their red-light battle swelled into an all-out war on prostitution. They lobbied hard to build a sprawling legal infrastructure of morals laws, police and probation programs, and reformatory prisons designed to protect white women through the cleansing power of law enforcement. Eugenicist allies justified the sexual criminalization of white women in order to stop the social circulation of "mental defectives" and the "feeble-minded." And a venereal disease panic, which fueled a massive crackdown on women during World War I, significantly boosted reformers' efforts.[11]

In the campaign to abolish segregated districts, reformers won the creation of a new legal category of morals laws that upgraded nonmarital straight sex from a public disgrace to a crime. This category of morals crime became well established in a remarkably short window of time. By 1930 there was little legal distinction among the varieties of women's nonmarital straight sex: prostitution and promiscuity blurred into a single legal category. In fourteen states, prostitution was defined as "giving or receiving the body for indiscriminate intercourse with *or without hire*." In forty states, "engaging in prostitution" was "a more general term implying common repute." The ambiguity of the legal definition of prostitution extended to a full suite of vague, sexualized misdemeanors that police officers could draw on to arrest women on city streets: vagrancy, disorderly conduct, lewdness, or simply "suspicion." Criminologist Eugenia Lekkerkerker concluded in her 1931 survey of women in the American legal system that "through [the] broad formulations" of these morals charges, they "can truly be considered as a kind of penal masterkeys for all sorts of petty transgressions against public order and decency."[12]

With this new slate of laws, police officers were empowered to arrest women suspected of engaging in any form of straight, nonmarital sex—commercial or otherwise. Police officers exercised broad discretion in enforcing these ambiguous laws. In 1925 George Worthington and Ruth Topping, social hygienists who studied legal processes in Chicago, Philadelphia, New York, and Boston, concluded that until a social scientist "devises tests for determining moral levels [of arrested women], for gauging degrees of reformability in units of moral responsibility, judges and probation officers must continue to grope among probabilities and content themselves with 'sizing up' delinquents." While Worthington and Topping were describing discretion in the courts, they must have also recognized that a "pinch of science and a dash of common sense must still remain the formula for a verdict" on the curbside courts over which police presided.[13]

These new morals laws were backed up by a mushrooming network of legal institutions designed to control women's presumed sexual behaviors. Women reformers in particular—wealthy philanthropists allied with probation officers, social workers, and policewomen—deployed their wholesome, maternal authority to build legal infrastructures that promised to protect (through punishment) their preferred targets for moral rescue: poor native-born white and European immigrant women. These new institutions blended social welfare programs with criminal interventions and included policewomen who conducted "protective" work targeting women; jail diversion programs headed up by female probation officers; and woman-led reformatory prisons. As Worthington and Topping wrote, these reformist legal institutions could be "punitive or reformative."[14]

In their work, Progressive women labored to establish a clear line between "punitive" and "reformative" legal interventions. Indeed, the "classification and segregation" of offenders to determine appropriate legal "treatment" was a reformist mantra, celebrated as the pinnacle of modern, scientific, and humane rehabilitative criminology. Baked into this mantra was a sometimes explicit, sometimes implicit racial hierarchy. The sheer force of rehabilitative criminological consensus on the need for "classification and segregation" muted the undeniable influence of eugenic thought and Jim Crow practices, hiding the operation of racism in plain sight. Because Progressive reformers drew on racial visions of salvageable white womanhood to justify the moral value of their efforts, everyday decisions and practices within the legal structures they built were freighted with racist logics. As a result, white women were more likely to access the reformative innovations, which were nonetheless enmeshed in forms of legal punishment. The Minnie Barton Training Home in Los Angeles—a reformatory jail founded in 1917 and superintended by Minnie Barton, a probation officer for the Los Angeles Police Department—restricted admission "only [to] members of the Caucasian race (including Mexican)." One white probation officer in Detroit explained, "Our difficulty is that we are taking the same type colored girl as white without the same facilities in the community to help us, which makes supervision for the colored girl more difficult." A Black probation officer in New York City lamented, "Where there is protection for the white girl, there is not so much for the Negro."[15]

But because both punitive and reformative institutions were administered through the same system of policing, surveillance, and incarceration, the ostensible boundary dividing the two was frequently compromised. Policewomen's interventions often ended with jailing the very women they aimed to protect. Probation supervision heightened police officers' attentions and left women vulnerable to rearrest. And reformatories, touting moral, educational, and occupational rehabilitation, devolved into the same punitive, custodial regimes reformers had originally opposed. By grafting legal institutions onto the project of rehabilitating white womanhood, reformers effectively (if, for some, unintentionally) consolidated the punitive power of law enforcement. Ultimately, as historian Anya Jabour writes, "By the end of the Progressive era, it was increasingly apparent that the specialized legal apparatus that had been instituted to address the problem of prostitution had become a problem for prostitutes." The reformist legal institutions that were founded to promote the moral rehabilitation of white and European immigrant women expanded the scope of law enforcement interventions targeting all women. By the passage of the Volstead Act and the enactment of Prohibition—another fruit of moral reformist lawmaking—a sprawling network of police, probation, jails, and prisons was established with a legal mandate and an enlarged capacity to target the presumed sexual behaviors of women.[16]

・・・・・・

Bowing to the overwhelming public pressure whipped up by Progressive reformers, and backed up by new legal structures, political and law enforcement authorities conceded that the downtown segregated district must be retired. As historian Emily Remus argues, downtown business owners in Chicago came around to supporting the shutdown of the city's red-light district because they wanted to pave downtown streets with respectability for middle-class white women on shopping excursions. This move was not without protest: predominantly male defenders of segregated vice would call for a revival of red-light districting through World War II. Despite the enduring support for segregated vice, by the close of World War I, big-city reformers declared that red-light districts had been vanquished.[17]

However, the Progressive-era shuttering of downtown districts did not break up the partnership between politicians and police. Urban authorities continued to treat vice as a lucrative source of political and material profits, a relationship further incentivized by the criminalization of alcohol sales. As a result, segregated vice districts were not "closed," as so many triumphantly claimed. They were merely shoved into Black neighborhoods, ushering in a modern era of urban racial segregation that was enforced with a Progressive-era repertoire of new legal tools. At the beginning of the twentieth century, "the ghetto was not yet a foregone conclusion," as Saidiya Hartman writes. But within a matter of years, sexual policing would make it so.[18]

1 Making the Modern City

Sexual Policing and Black Segregation
from Prohibition to the Great Depression

• •

During the 1920s Black residents in the urban North bore witness to a perplexing—and infuriating—development: even as the borders of segregation hardened around them, more whites were streaming into their neighborhoods. After red-light districts were shut down, Black journalists reported with outrage that their neighborhoods were becoming "infested with these loose white women." White men indulged in nightly invasions too. But it was the white women who roused police attention as officers enforced racial segregation. During Prohibition, the injury of segregationist policing was added to the insult of white defilement of the spaces where Black residents lived, learned, and worshiped.[1]

In 1924 an editorial in the Black-owned *Chicago Defender* decried this state of affairs with a dispatch from the city's white press. "Secret service operatives and the city police joined forces," the editorial's author quoted from a white daily. "They struck through the [predominantly Black] near South side to end exploitation of white girls by Negro resort keepers." White Progressive reformer Jessie Binford, a Hull House resident and director of the Juvenile Protective Association, had sounded the alarm on the alleged "exploitation of white girls" on Chicago's South Side. The *Defender* editorial protested Binford's selective concern for "white girls" and her indifference to "girls NOT white, those of brown and yellow skin." Binford shared the prevailing priorities of too many other white reformers, which the *Defender* author sarcastically summed up as follows: "Save the white girl—to hell with all OTHER girls."[2]

Sexual policing in the 1920s was driven by an abiding preoccupation with rescuing white womanhood that increased the vulnerability of Black people, and in particular Black women, to violence by white men and police officers alike. "THE WHITE GIRL!" the *Defender* author wrote. "Around her is thrown the armed protection of civilization." By 1924 this "protection" was literally armed with a blackjack, a gun, and a badge.[3]

Police of the 1920s were the beneficiaries of Progressive-era moral crusades to expand legal infrastructure on behalf of white purity. Reformers who had fought to abolish red-light districts in the first two decades of the twentieth century empowered police departments with the legal tools to repress—rather than merely manage—urban prostitution. Despite their expanded repertoire of morals laws to shutter red-light districts, police officers and politicians were loath to relinquish this lucrative source of shared payoffs. But the reformers' onslaught was too intense to be ignored, so authorities conceded—with a catch. The resulting "shutdown" of segregated districts during the Progressive era amounted to a relocation of red-light districts to Black neighborhoods.[4]

Law enforcement authorities exploited racial inequality to project an image of repression while maintaining moral enforcement's profitability. Police deployed their discretionary power to channel the flow of an urban faucet, permitting the inundation of white men into Black neighborhoods, aggressively policing white women's interracial sociability, and erratically targeting Black women for morals offenses. Police had helped to erect Black vice districts, and now they enforced morals violations (or withheld enforcement for a fee) on the same streets, creating a doubled segregation: segregated vice and racially segregated Black residents. This transformation—more advanced in cities like Chicago and New York, but soon to become the national policy—set the twentieth-century logic and practice of urban policing in motion.[5]

Morals policing became the terrain on which authorities enforced racial segregation and the boundaries of race in modern cities. Officers, vigilantly patrolling the color line in the new segregated vice districts, determined which women were deserving of their "armed protection" and which were not—a project of race-making as much as it was of gender-making. Even as the moral force of reform waned during Prohibition and poor white women were increasingly scorned as "problem girls" rather than victims, the enduring preoccupation with white female purity necessarily had an impact on the ways that Black women were policed. Indeed, the criminalization of white women, particularly those engaging in interracial socialization, brought the full weight of the Progressive-era criminal apparatus to bear on Black neighborhoods.[6]

The relocation of segregated vice districts to racially segregated Black neighborhoods cemented the relationship between police and Black residents in the twentieth century. On the one hand, police practiced violent neglect: they permitted, and profited from, vice activities in Black neighborhoods, and this neglect communicated to the city that Black neighborhoods were sites of sexual deviance and lawlessness. On the other hand, police practiced violent action: they erratically and aggressively targeted Black communities for morals violations. Black women were at once vulnerable to arrest while also profoundly unprotected from the depredations of white men turned loose on the city's vice playground. The protests of Black residents like the author of the *Defender* editorial made these developments visible by persistently calling out the white hypocrisy and state force that rendered their neighborhoods vulnerable to a toxic combination of police neglect and arrests. Morals policing exemplified a pattern of police action and abandonment in segregated Black neighborhoods that would reign across the twentieth century.[7]

Prohibition ended in scandalous failure, leaving police publicly discredited and widely reviled. Police departments were called to account for long-standing practices of lawlessness, extortion, and brutality in the enforcement of morals laws. From the rubble of Prohibition, police leaders mobilized to reclaim the authority of besieged law enforcement. They found redemption by rebranding officers as muscular, punitive "crime fighters." Led by national figures like the FBI's J. Edgar Hoover, law men trumpeted "scientific" data gathering and cutting-edge weapons and surveillance technologies. The effectiveness of crime-fighting policing was measured in high arrest rates, which the FBI started to collect, standardize, and circulate in 1930.[8]

Crime-fighting proponents had little to say about sexually profiled women, preferring instead to rivet the public's attention with the capture of high-profile gangsters. But their newly collected statistics spoke louder: police departments leaned on sexual policing to shore up their crumbling legitimacy, kicking morals enforcement into overdrive. During the economic crisis of the Depression, women were arrested at a much faster rate than men and increasing numbers of women were raked into the law enforcement machinery. The rates of arrest for Black women during the Depression were wildly haphazard from city to city and, in a single city, from month to month. Intensifying police action, especially in Chicago and New York, foreshadowed the systematic arrests that Black women would ultimately confront on city streets nationwide.[9]

As police departments emerged from the scandal-ridden aftermath of Prohibition, the arrest rates of women became a key measure of police activity and power. And despite fluctuations in arrests, the framework for this new post-Prohibition police regime was firmly in place by the 1930s:

future morals enforcement policies would be enacted on a racial urban landscape that police had created with a combination of violent force and neglect. Vice districts were confined to Black neighborhoods, and through these urban sites, police enforced racial segregation in cities nationwide. In the interwar decades between Prohibition and World War II, sexual policing to enforce white purity created the conditions of urban Black repression—and Black protest—that would propel the future of twentieth-century cities.

From Segregated Vice to Racial Segregation

In the early 1900s, when Progressive-era reformers mobilized to shut down red-light districts, they issued their demands on behalf of exploited white womanhood. Segregated red-light districts were downtown fixtures in post-bellum cities that served an important political function: the graft they generated funded election campaigns and sealed political loyalties. Responding to the massive shutdown campaign, police and politicians met reformers halfway: instead of abolishing vice districts, they routed them to Black neighborhoods, which housed residents with the least political power in the city. The reformers' preoccupation with white purity and the presumption of Black immorality made this a tolerable relocation. Sociologist Walter Reckless described this trade-off in his study of Prohibition-era prostitution in Chicago: while he found that commercial sex had moved deeper into the Black Belt, he felt it was nevertheless "important to note that in the twenty years of public suppression there were relatively few underworld invasions of good residential areas."[10]

The new segregated vice districts served the same function as earlier red-light districts: money trees for political machines. During Prohibition, a cut of police payoffs continued to be funneled into municipal election slush funds in cities from Los Angeles to New York. So even as reformers congratulated themselves on their victory over vice, police still managed, rather than stamped out, the business of sex, gambling, and liquor. But now, Progressive-era legal reforms designed to repress prostitution delivered to police departments the mandate—and broad discretion—to arrest virtually any woman on city streets deemed sexually suspect.[11]

The question of which women would be collared under these new conditions was another matter. Though urban authorities would not settle on a systematic urban policy until after World War II, the informal policy in the interregnum would define the relationship between police and Black residents throughout the twentieth century. Three dynamics characterized the Prohibition-era relocation of vice to Black neighborhoods. First, as police routed vice into these neighborhoods, they played a key role in cultivating the image of Black neighborhoods as sites of—and Black residents as agents of—sexual deviance and lawlessness. Second, as police, politicians, academics, and the white press circulated this prevailing myth of Black sexual immorality and criminality, they justified residential segregation and naturalized spatial hierarchies of race, lashing Jim Crow logics onto local police practices. And finally, the creation of racially segregated vice districts contributed to the material degradation of Black neighborhoods, justifying further and more aggressive police action. In other words, police officers erratically and aggressively enforced morals violations in Black neighborhoods that they themselves permitted. Black residents consistently protested that vice policing simultaneously created violent conditions of state neglect and criminalization in their neighborhoods.[12]

Black residents were now forced to confront a new invasion in their neighborhood: white people. "Most of the vice complained of by these so-called protectors of white morality, if there be such a thing, is imported into the ward by white outsiders," a *Chicago Defender* editorial wrote. In 1922 a Black politician flipped the script on Black deviance and white respectability by arguing that "the Negro suffers more from imported vice than from domestic vice" as white people descended on the Black neighborhood "to degrade and demoralize our section." Certainly poor and working-class Black residents worked in sex, gambling, and liquor businesses to compensate for the discriminatory and exploitative licit job market. But Black leaders, predominantly (though not exclusively) elite and middle class, angrily condemned the transformation of their neighborhoods into police-sanctioned red-light districts.[13]

This white influx mainly consisted of so-called slummers. These were mostly middle-class white men visiting Black neighborhoods for what one Black newspaper derided as a "moral holiday" only to return to their "good residential areas" with their respectability untarnished. Black residents especially resented what a *Defender* journalist referred to as "white men streaming in and out of the place in a continual parade." While middle-class white women occasionally accompanied men for a thrill, Black vice districts (like their red-light predecessors) were policed to limit these sites to male pleasure. As one bar manager noted in 1927, he was "given friendly advice by coppers . . . that they will let me run this place and . . . there will be no trouble as long as I keep the women out." The slummers who came to Black neighborhoods to solicit women for sex degraded Black women by presuming every woman's sexual availability and harassing them. "White men drive up and down Central Ave and molest women and young girls to and from church," one man wrote from a Black neighborhood in Los Angeles. "Oh God please give us a decent place for our women and children to live in." By treating Black neighborhoods as their personal vice playland, white men helped to define Black neighborhoods as "synonymous with immorality and license," the editors of the *Pittsburgh Courier* protested.[14]

A national realignment was under way. In many southern cities, segregated vice districts had been located in Black neighborhoods since at least the turn of the century. The relocation of red-light districts reflected a convergence of North and South. "It has long been the policy of southern cities to leave the colored part of the town 'wide open' and in addition to that to center in the colored portion much of the vice of the white population," Arthur Spingarn, a Jewish leader in the National Association for the Advancement of Colored People (NAACP), wrote in 1918, describing what ultimately became the reigning policy nationwide. "When a southern city was 'cleaned up' it has meant too often that the dregs were simply swept from the white into the colored section." Urban prostitution policy became racially segregated nationwide—and even in southern cities where the segregated vice district had already been situated in Black neighborhoods, the Progressive-era wave of repression hardened the urban color line. According to one journalist, in Baltimore "both white and Negro girls [had] worked" in the legal red-light district; its closure in 1915 had "forced the separation of white and black prostitutes." The processes to enforce the relocation of vice from downtown business districts to Black neighborhoods may have looked different from South to North, but the regionally distinct policies produced the same result: Jim Crow nationwide.[15]

As more Black refugees from the Jim Crow South moved North, interracial sex became a key pretense for escalating enforcement of Black segregation. Police turned their attention in particular on white women in the company of men of color. White men and Black women were erratically policed, signaling a dominant police presumption of white male sexual license and the sexual depravity of Black women. Black residents clearly understood these dynamics even if urban authorities did not explicitly state their purpose. One Black reporter wrote that "white women [are especially]

Making the Modern City 31

warned to steer clear of Harlem, regardless of their missions here." Through these police practices, the article concluded, "the police [are] determined to make a jim crow section out of" Harlem.[16]

Interracial nightspots, particularly those where Black men and white women were likely to meet, commanded the bulk of police scrutiny. At the same time, as historian Douglas Flowe writes, clubs frequented by mostly Black people "went uninvestigated." And when interracial clubs were the target of prolonged antivice lobbying and police surveillance, Black women who worked as hosts or dancers did not always arouse legal concern. Baron Wilkins, the owner of a Harlem "black and tan," was ultimately convicted for running a dance hall without a license and liquor law violations. But at Wilkins's trial, "even though one of the colored entertainers gave a sample of her dancing on the witness stand and let love of her art overcome any desire she might have had to protect her employer," policewomen Mary Sullivan wrote in her memoir, the court stopped short of ruling the club "disorderly." Whether or not the judge subscribed to the prevailing naturalized vision of hypersexual Black womanhood, he was not willing to punish Wilkins for the presence of such displays in his bar—nor even, apparently, in the judge's court. The greater concern was white womanhood, which interracial sociability threatened to corrupt.[17]

At a time when interracial sex was considered inherently deviant, law enforcement authorities had little need for miscegenation laws to police urban sociality. "There is no law making interracial association unlawful," the Baltimore police commissioner admitted. Even so, he continued, police make discretionary arrests because "it is assumed that the persons are together for some unlawful purpose, mostly prostitution." In 1925 the general secretary of the Committee of Fourteen, New York's antivice organization, explained that "there is nothing on our statute books which makes it a crime for an adult white girl to live with a Chinaman. Of course, girls who do so may be assumed to be prostitutes."[18]

Even in the absence of formal sanctions outlawing interracial socialization, police during Prohibition had broad discretion to enforce capacious Progressive-era morals laws. They used this power to bright-line racial segregation, participating in a larger project of race- and gender-making. In a typical episode, when police observed a racially ambiguous couple, officers harassed the woman to resolve the problem of the couple's racial profile. A 1925 *Chicago Defender* editorial protested that "young women [are] made to suffer the lewd epithets of police hirelings instructed to weigh blood, mark color, to say who is who and what, by the gods, is what!"

Women were "accosted at pleasure by police" who demanded to know their racial identity. And if less melanated women were "escorted by young men of darked hue," they were treated to even greater police malice. A year later, another editorial reported that police "are still stopping couples on the streets and questioning them because they are not certain of the woman's race." The author added, "If she is white, they are both arrested." Because the prevention of interracial socialization, especially socialization involving white women, was such a demonstrably high state priority, when police engaged in morals enforcement, they necessarily made gendered and racial determinations: in this way, as police affirmed and enforced urban racial segregation, they became crucial arbiters—and therefore makers—of racialized womanhood.[19]

Black operators of commercial sex ventures were well aware that white women increased their risk of police action. When a Black undercover investigator in New York visited a house asking "to find a white girl," he was refused. "We wouldn't have any white girls because they get you in too much trouble," the woman managing the house said. "They take a fellow inside and take his money from him and when he goes out the first thing you know a cop would come back." In this explanation, the manager reversed the prevailing narrative that Black women baited white men for sex and robbed them. The policy of excluding white women could represent a financial loss for the house, where, given the dominant racist pricing structure, the operators could have charged a premium for white women. But the unwanted involvement of the police in a Black-managed business that catered to Black men surely firmed the manager's commitment to refuse such a request from potential customers. Her male associate agreed: "I got strict orders when I came in this house that I couldn't have any white women around and I don't want them." Regardless of whether there were miscegenation laws on the books, white women observed with men of color were sure to attract the otherwise lax attentions of police in Black neighborhoods.[20]

Especially in northern states like Massachusetts, interracial policing exposed a peculiar exception to the reign of lynching terror that preyed on Black men and women. When authorities centered white women in the enforcement of racial segregation, they produced a situation where white women involved with men of color received the larger share of punishment. White women's punishment did not match the extralegal brutality that Black people confronted, nor the legal brutality of railroaded convictions and executions. But it proved to be one more segregation enforcement tool in states that practiced a form of white supremacy distinct from that of the Jim Crow South.[21]

Segregationist sexual policing endured well past the Prohibition era. In 1937 twenty-year-old Marjorie, a poor Irish Catholic woman, was arrested for idle and disorderly conduct in Boston while she was on parole from a state reformatory because police had observed her "frequenting various taverns . . . while in the company of a Negro." Although the arresting officer noted that there was "no direct evidence of immorality," the fact of Marjorie's interracial socializing was "enough to constitute an arrest." It was Marjorie's fourth arrest in two years: previously she had been charged with lewdness and common nightwalking after being observed by police "in company with Negroes" or "with a colored man." While Marjorie spent these two years in and out of prison, being arrested and rearrested for her association with Black men, on only one occasion were her companions arrested with her.[22]

Marjorie confronted a multiplying thicket of law enforcement and rehabilitative interventions. White women reformers, operating in legal institutions established during the Progressive era, proved as zealous as police in confining her. During Marjorie's first prison term at the Reformatory for Women in Massachusetts, the standard-bearer of rehabilitative incarceration, case workers diagnosed Marjorie's problem as a "definite infatuation with Negroes." After Marjorie's fourth arrest and her subsequent return to the reformatory, Miriam Van Waters, the celebrated reformist superintendent, delivered Marjorie's rehabilitative prospects in much blunter terms: "If she is going to leave here . . . she has got to stop associating with Negroes." Marjorie was just one of many poor white women imprisoned and criminalized in this fashion. Progressive-era reformism and Prohibition-era segregationist policing had joined together to strengthen punitive instruments of the state in service to white purity.[23]

In the South, segregationist prostitution policing served as yet another tendon to flex the enforcement of Jim Crow. Even though miscegenation laws had been upgraded to a felony in North Carolina in 1921, white authorities in Charlotte took advantage of police reports "that white prostitutes are frequently found with Negro men" to buttress residential segregation laws. A grand jury recommended "zoning to separate the races . . . in order to reduce vice and prostitution." It was at this point that Black reformers confronted the limits of the strategy to protest the presence of white people in their neighborhoods: protesters were forced to challenge the invasion of white vice in their communities while at the same time resisting the stranglehold of racial segregation. Woods Morgan, chairman of the Negro Citizens Investigating Committee, affirmed that "we are greatly troubled with these [white] prostitutes all over the Negro section." But, he added, "it is questionable whether segregation of whites and Negroes will solve the problem of prostitution between the two races."[24]

Black residents who wanted to reclaim their neighborhoods from segregated vice appealed to urban authorities' proven preoccupation with white purity. They sought to spur political action using a double-voiced strategy that emphasized their own respectability and white women's deviance. In 1916 a Black journalist reported from Saint Louis that "lewd white women invade[d]" the Black neighborhood, "catering to race men." In Atlanta, columnist Hattie Crooms was furious that "Sunday church goers are compelled to visualize some of the most daring, dastardly, brazen acts of immoral conduct by white women." And an informant from a Black neighborhood in Los Angeles pleaded for help from a white antivice investigator, writing, "Many white girls are in these dens. Some are young. This is a hell hole out here." Black residents highlighted white women's participation in the segregated vice district with a dual purpose: both to force a response from urban authorities and to resist a "broader indictment" against Black life and morals, as historian Stephen Robertson writes, by emphasizing the "dastardly, brazen" acts of white women and the moral rectitude of besieged Black women and men. They shrewdly played to the politics of white purity while also exposing the myth of pure white womanhood.[25]

But during the interwar period, an important shift was taking place among white authorities and reformers. The narrative power of white women's victimhood, which had driven moral reform campaigns, flagged. As the "fallen woman" became the "girl problem," the balance tilted away from poor white women's vulnerability and toward their menace. In law enforcement, social science, and popular discourse, criminological accounts of white women increasingly emphasized criminality over victimhood. "Many years ago, when 'white slave' crusades were at their height, we heard many sensational stories of young girls being drugged, kidnapped, and forced into a life of shame," policewoman Mary Sullivan wrote in her memoir, referring to the moral panic around "white slaves"—or white women allegedly sexually trafficked by predatory immigrants and men of color—that rocked the anglophone world in the early 1900s. White slavery crusades had been fueled by fears of soiled white womanhood rather than actual evidence. Within two decades, after Progressives had built a massive law enforcement infrastructure to reclaim white women, legal authorities began to dismiss the white slavery frenzy as a fiction. "Very few of these [white slave] stories would bear investigation," Sullivan wrote. "They made a good excuse for girls who went into the business voluntarily, and they were frequently offered as a defence by women arrested for prostitution." Sociologist Walter Reckless concluded that by the early 1930s, sexually profiled white women were no longer viewed as "virtuous victims" but were instead considered criminals.[26]

Popular audiences who had avidly consumed tragic tales of white slaves during the 1910s increasingly dismissed the sympathetic portrait of white women's sexual victimization. As the upheavals of World War I and Prohibition troubled social boundaries, public longing for stability found satisfaction in a punishing attitude toward women. In his popular accounts of crime in America, journalist Courtney Ryley Cooper, who worked in close association with FBI chief J. Edgar Hoover, argued that even the most victimized white women still harbored sexual criminal tendencies. Of a racially unmarked woman caught in a vice raid, he wrote, "Even though it be granted that she was beaten, that she was held captive, that she was forced by physical threats or physical fear to give herself to men, a logical viewpoint would be that there was some other compelling motive . . . which began it all, some willingness on her part to at least skirt the edges of prostitution." Two years later, Cooper wrote that people he interviewed "with wide experience in prostitution insist that there is no such thing as a true white slave," laying to rest the emblem of white female exploitation and victimization that had guided an enormous amount of Progressive-era reform energy. The term "white slavery" was still widely used as late as the 1930s, but it became primarily a euphemism for interracial sex between white women and men of color.[27]

White authorities still reached for the old white slavery script when they turned up interracial socialization during Prohibition—but white women were now rebranded as sexual criminals. For example, in 1928, two white investigators for the Committee of Fourteen, the antivice reform organization in New York, surveilled the Kewpie Doll, an interracial Harlem bar. They observed a white woman with "a very fair complexion, claiming to be a southern girl," dancing with a "colored man," and believed that "she seemed to be completely in [the] control" of her "colored manager." Perhaps a decade or two before, reformers would have celebrated her rescue after an unwitting descent into the Black underworld. But in this case, reformers and police answered the white slavery narrative with criminalization: despite the presence of "colored prostitute-inmates," when the Kewpie Doll was raided, only white women were arrested along with three racially unmarked men.[28]

After the relocation of vice to Black neighborhoods, Black residents were left in a bind. Rather than delivering the shutdown of vice, the politics of white purity instead brought the full weight of Progressive-era legal infrastructure to bear on Black neighborhoods. Just as Progressive urban reform had advanced under the banner of white female salvage, so too would the specter of interracial sex—chiefly white women with men of color—drive Prohibition-era urban law enforcement. Sexual policing in Black neighborhoods did not repress vice as residents demanded; rather, it was put to work to enforce racial segregation in cities nationwide. One Black reporter recognized the policy that developed in the Prohibition era: "The 'wide open' character of most urban Negro communities hurts our reputation . . . and tightens the walls of segregation about us." Black women, absent from most white reformist concerns, would come to experience the most harmful repercussions of white purity policing.[29]

Violent Police Neglect Black Women

When segregationist police work in vice districts was turned on Black neighborhoods, the outcomes were inconsistent but laced with the danger of violence. Police managing the new segregated districts operated on the racist white myth that Black women were inherently licentious. As a result, Black women confronted a terrible paradox: they were simultaneously disregarded by police even as they lived under the threat of arrest. Segregationist sexual policing produced material harm in Black women's lives—and through this violence, officers made race, by determining which bodies could exist in which urban spaces; and gender, by determining which woman's virtue was worthy of state intervention and restoration.

White urban authorities often dismissed behaviors in Black women as natural that they would have found deviant in white women. "I have seen many . . . colored women who are boisterous and who speak to almost any man for no other reason than childish good nature," one policewoman wrote, revealing a notable indifference to the moral protection of Black women. A police chief in Atlanta recalled that during the Prohibition era "there was very little concern [about Black prostitutes] by the white police or white community." But this lack of concern swiftly turned into violent police action whenever arrests were politically useful, perhaps during an election year, after a fresh revelation of police corruption, or when police inaction would be most glaring to white audiences. As one study found, "It is a noticeable policy of the Detroit police to arrest colored girls almost exclusively on week-ends, when business is most brisk." In this way, police treated Black women with what amounted to violent neglect, ignoring them when they weren't harassing or arresting them.[30]

Men on a "moral holiday" in racially segregated vice districts caused extremely dangerous situations for Black residents. One woman in Los Angeles lived near "two verry disrespectable women" with "men going in all day and nite long." She was so alarmed after the house "was set on fire" while visitors were over drinking that in 1939 she wrote to Earl Warren, the state's attorney general. "I asked the owner why he did not prosicute [the tenant] and get her made . . . she [might] burn the whole place down[.] so you see every one is scaired of the damige she can do." The woman reported the house to multiple authorities, but "nothing has been done," and "one state officer said she was aloud to have her boy friends." Life in these unprotected zones of police-protected vice was fraught with offenses to residents' dignity and fears for their physical safety.[31]

White men exploited their full access to Black neighborhoods to terrorize residents. In Pittsburgh, five white men broke into Eva and Ike Bolden's apartment "allegedly seeking a house of prostitution." Roused by the noise and frightened to find five strange white men in her home, Mrs. Bolden grabbed a knife to defend herself against "the intent of the white men." She was soon joined by her husband and, "in the ensuing melee, windows were broken and chairs smashed." Far from facing legal consequences, the white attackers instead pressed charges against Eva and Ike Bolden, who were both arrested for aggravated assault. In this way, police-sanctioned vice—itself a blanket statement about the police disregard for the integrity of Black homes and Black lives—produced domestic terror and Black criminalization.[32]

Black residents were well aware that their neighborhoods' safety and integrity were being sacrificed for others' gain. They knew that police were "lulled into indifference by the 'yallah' money of dive keepers and their political henchmen," according to a 1929 editorial in the *Pittsburgh Courier*. "Prostitution, gambling dens, and bootleg joints dispensing the most poisonous brands of illicit liquor are boldly flaunted and the police not only ignore these conditions but like many politicians, actually profit from them," another *Courier* editorial declared that same year. A Brooklyn resident wrote that in the "black belt . . . police pay no attention and act dumb as they receive their deuce ($2) daily from each girl to keep moving. . . . The police are getting their's or this could never go on so long." In Los Angeles, a police officer who opposed these morals enforcement practices explained, "I know the pay-off men, I know the go-betweens; but what can I do when it's sanctioned by city politicians?"[33]

The Black press brimmed with accounts of police collusion and political corruption as Black neighborhoods' dignity and safety were traded for white men's pleasure and profit. "Criminals, corrupt police and rascally politicians [are] working hand-in-hand to mulct and demoralize the neighborhoods in which we live and in which our children must be reared," the *Pittsburgh Courier* fumed. "There has been too much acquiescence in the practice of city administrations of segregating vice in our sections in order to spare other parts of the cities, while continuing to collect their tribute off human degradation." NAACP leader Walter White wrote a letter to the *Chicago Defender* explaining that "it was reported to us on good authority that the police had been given instructions to close up [vice] in down town New York but to lay off Harlem and let white people go there to do whatever they wished." A Black investigator in Harlem reported that "a number of high officials," including the warden of Welfare Island and a "high police detective," regularly visited the white-owned Sheep Club.[34]

Black neighborhoods had become the go-to sites for morals arrests, but those arrests were not designed to repress vice, to say the very least. It was widely known among Black residents that police either ignored or profited from commercial sex, gambling, and drinking in segregated vice districts. And when white moral outrage periodically flared up, particularly when Prohibition-era scandals exposed the prevalence of police corruption, police quelled reformers with crackdowns on Black neighborhoods. "A large number of arrests of Negro women 'pad' the records," as Paul Kinsie, a social hygienist, wrote, "and tend to show police activity." This became a distinctly post-Progressive feature of twentieth-century policing. Writing about Chicago, sociologist Reckless dubbed this pattern the "vice situation cycle," where white reformers and the white press exposed vice-enforcement corruption and the police redirected public outrage by leading urban "clean-ups" in Black neighborhoods. In 1924 George Brown, a Black vice syndicate operator in Los Angeles, said, "It has always been the custom here . . . when the town gets too bad . . . to go over to Central avenue and clean up the negroes. That always satisfied the longhairs," he noted, referring to moral reformers. "And the blow has fallen where there is least resistance—on those who have the smallest chance of a comeback."[35]

Black women bore the brunt of these morals crackdowns, though the intensity varied from city to city. During the 1920s the mass morals arrest campaigns that would become the core of urban policing had not yet been racially systematized nationwide. Though Black women faced morals law arrests disproportionate to their population, the severity of this disproportion rose in some cities and decreased in others across the decade. In Chicago and New York—major destinations in the interwar period for Black refugees from the South—the overrepresentation of Black women arrested on morals laws dramatically increased. "If the percentage of colored women in the total load of the Morals Court continues to increase," Reckless wrote of Chicago, "the court will in a few years become practically an agency dealing with Negro female sex delinquents." Though Black people accounted for just roughly 4 percent of Chicago's population in 1920, by the middle of the decade, Chicago police arrested a numerical majority of Black women. In New York the general secretary of the antivice Committee of Fourteen puzzled over the high numbers of Black women hauled into courts and jail on morals charges, and he reasoned that "expenses incidental to the arrest of colored women"—namely, the expense of securing evidence—"are comparatively small." In other words, police were required to provide less (if any) evidence to make an arrest on a Black woman that would stick in court.[36]

Yet in cities where Black women already represented a clear majority of arrests, the disproportion swung widely from month to month. In March 1925 nearly half of all women facing the New York Women's Court on morals charges were Black; in April, a slower month for arrests, that number sank to less than 20 percent. "This shows," the Committee of Fourteen general secretary concluded, "that when the police are particularly active, the proportion of negro cases increases." When police were pressured to rack up arrests, they aggressively netted Black women; otherwise, as a Black reporter in Harlem wrote, police "were found to be enacting the roles of wooden Indians insofar as driving the women off the streets is concerned."[37]

In cities outside of Chicago or New York, white women remained an enduring focus of police and white public concern. In Los Angeles, for example, white women would represent a numerical majority of morals arrests until well after World War II. And the proportion of morals arrests for white women rose in the late 1920s from 58 percent to 62 percent, while the proportion of such arrests for Black women fell from 28 percent to

24 percent. (Latina women were also disproportionately arrested relative to their urban numbers, but Black and white women represented the bulk of arrests for morals laws in Los Angeles.) In Pennsylvania a researcher studying women in urban jails found that Black women were most disproportionately sentenced to jail for crimes of violence "out of all proportion to the white"; however, "in offenses involving sex, there seems to be no significant or definite cleavage between the races." Black women were disproportionately vulnerable to arrest—but police neglect was as salient a force in their lives as police action.[38]

The fact that Black women were violently targeted *and* neglected by police was not a contradiction. According to prevailing racist and sexist police logics, it would make as much sense to accept a sexually profiled Black woman as a natural feature of the urban landscape as it would to consign her to jail. Nor should violent neglect be confused with occasional lenience. On the contrary, these conditions only heightened the precarity and danger in Black women's lives.[39]

The wild unpredictability of morals policing fostered a climate of fear and widespread resentment of police corruption. While sentenced to the Reformatory for Women in Massachusetts, Eleanor, a Black woman, wrote a poem called "Underworld Parlance," describing the violence embedded in urban policies of protected vice and unprotected women:

> The cops are too stupid to catch a big crook,
> So they run after you and me.
> If by mistake they pull in a crook
> And find he has influence or cash,
> The unlucky cop is duly chastised,
> And fined for being so rash.
> So we hear a great deal
> About their crusades on vice,
> But these cases we hear almost nothing about
> Are the ones they chalk on the ice.[40]

As Prohibition limped toward repeal, scandals would make public awareness of police corruption all but inescapable. White audiences were forced to recognize what Black residents had experienced for years: the corruption and brutality inherent to morals policing. To recover their authority, police would rebrand the same systems of segregated vice they had previously exploited for profit.

Fallout from Prohibition: The Making of "Crime-Fighting" Policing

Prohibition left police departments mired in a crisis of legitimacy. Throughout the 1930s police were plagued by revelations of endemic brutality, and urban vice scandals broadcast the collusion of police with gambling, liquor, and prostitution syndicates. When Herbert Hoover convened the National Commission on Law Observance and Enforcement, or the Wickersham Commission, to reckon with the failures of Prohibition, the lead author, criminologist August Vollmer, drew a conclusion in his 1931 commission findings that would be virtually unimaginable for modern readers to encounter in a federal report: "Law enforcement is one of our national jokes." Ernest Hopkins, a Wickersham Commission member, wrote in his popular chronicle of the commission's investigation, *Our Lawless Police*, that "in no previous period of our national life has a general popular antagonism toward public authority, and distrust of it, been more prevalent through the United States." The Massachusetts Special Crime Commission, one of many state-level investigations inspired by the Wickersham Commission, concluded, "There is a serious breakdown of the law enforcement agencies. . . . [The] time has come when it will no longer suffice to attempt to patch up and repair the existing machinery."[41]

The popular indictment against police forces emphasized two charges: first, that the police were not enforcing laws; and second, that when police *did* enforce laws, their performance was lawless, brutal, and incompetent. Morals policing was the site where both charges against police most glaringly converged. In the torrent of reports and articles that circulated during the Depression, women made fleeting but nevertheless powerful appearances as victims of the tandem operation of police neglect and brutality. For example, in New York's 1931 Seabury investigation, a sprawling study of corruption in the state's criminal system, one racially unmarked woman testified that she was "beaten, stripped, and criminally assaulted by two vice squad policemen who had been drinking in her apartment." Morals enforcement exposed the fusion of violent neglect *and* violent action endemic to policing practices, to which all poor and working-class women were vulnerable in distinct ways. However, it was the experiences of white, European immigrant, and racially unmarked women that typically attracted white attention during this period of outrage.[42]

Undercover officers faced no consequences for sexually exploiting or assaulting women in the course of gathering evidence for morals charges. In

New York an editorial in a Black newspaper wrote that "the public was shocked to hear that officers of the law were ordered to play the part of agents provocateurs and cohabit commercially with prostitutes in order to secure evidence against them." One study of prostitution argued that "the officer's participation in the illegal act almost to the point of consummation" undercut police authority and "the interests of society, both in controlling prostitution and in upholding respect for law and its enforcement."[43]

Even the collection of supposed "evidence" was found to be a sham. At a meeting between municipal judges and the New York Police Department commissioner in 1931, the assembled authorities agreed that even the most common piece of evidence—marked bills submitted by officers to the courts to "prove" the transaction, which were widely understood to *not* be the actual bills used in the setup to arrest women on morals charges—was, as one judge declared, a "ridiculous performance." Police also frequently hired "stool pigeons" to frame women, handing over their own marked bills to "prove" the women's guilt just before detectives rushed in for arrest. One white stool pigeon confessed that he averaged over one hundred dollars a week doing this work for police. The New York investigations disclosed that "absolutely guiltless women are now in prison, convicted of prostitution."[44]

To set up their arrest-for-profit schemes, police and their decoys exploited the racial segregation that policing had established and enforced. When one stool pigeon, Chile Acuna (who was racially marked as white), testified against his former employer, he admitted that if New York Police Department officers "were short of arrests, they sometimes went up to Harlem, where they would walk into colored houses and make arrests." The *Amsterdam News* reported that Black women were more vulnerable to arbitrary raids and frame-ups "on the theory that colored women would have less chance in court than white women." And white male stool pigeons were useful because interracial socialization remained a useful pretext for police raids: For example, Acuna would raid a Black apartment, and the police would charge in after him. Then the officers would demand to know, "What is this white man doing here?" The residents, stunned by the invasion, "did not know what to say." The Black women were arrested and subsequently convicted, all because a white man working for the police had invaded their apartment.[45]

In the wake of Prohibition scandals, morals policing was singled out as a law enforcement "disaster." A 1934 Harvard survey of the Boston Police Department called "vice control" the "chief menace to police departments."

The reigning practices of morals enforcement—which easily accommodated police abuse, sexual assault, entrapment, collusion, frame-ups, and shakedowns of women—sapped the credibility of police departments. "This set of activities, besides being at times a source of political scandal and high cost of tribute, frequently exceeded lawful bounds," Wickersham Commission member Hopkins wrote, concluding that "the 'moral issue' was a major, and perpetual, distraction to law enforcement."[46]

The vice squad officer was a particular object of popular derision—"as vile as a vice cop" was reportedly a popular Depression saying—and dramatically undermined police authority with his violent and lawless practices. Journalist Courtney Ryley Cooper conceded, "No doubt there are honest men on vice squads," but he argued that "the whole business is so filthy with corruption, with bribe-taking, with double-crossing and petty extortion that clean men do not want the assignment." Importantly, police corruption was not an individual practice, but rather—as many Black residents well knew—it was baked into the structures of urban governance. For example, one grand jury report in Chicago found that police extorted "huge sums" from prostitution and policy, or gambling, operators to fatten an election slush fund for the "America First ticket"; another grand jury in San Francisco reported that police collected over $1 million annually in graft. These accounts sparked outrage, not only because of officers' lawlessness but also because they were enriching themselves during a period of severe economic hardship (see figure 1.1).[47]

At this nadir of police authority, many investigators agreed that police should not perform morals enforcement at all. Leonard Harrison, lead author of the Harvard survey of the Boston Police Department, argued, "It would be much better to enlist volunteers than to continue the present [practice] of detailing patrolmen [to vice]." Short of abolishing the police vice squad, however, Harrison and his team recommended the complete quarantine of this "morally hazardous" work in order "to remove from the main body the extreme danger of corruption" and to "elevate the service by freeing it from tasks which self-respecting men hate to perform." A former Department of Justice agent who served as a grand jury investigator in San Francisco said that the "unenforcibility [sic] of laws against prostitution, gambling, and other alleged vices" inevitably bred corruption.[48]

Law enforcement had foundered on the shoals of morals policing; under a mounting assault, police leaders were charged with crafting new models of policing that would reassert the authority of law enforcement. A new generation of reformers emerged from the internal ranks of police brass,

FIGURE 1.1 Political cartoon, 1935. After the scandalous failure of Prohibition, sexual policing was reviled as a corrupt and lawless liability. "White slaves" endured in the popular imagination as both victims and criminals, though the balance steadily tilted toward criminals after the Progressive era.
© Daily News, L.P. (New York). Used with permission.

rather than the external private organizations characteristic of the Progressive era. Instead of fixating on white purity, as the Progressive-era reformers had, police reformers leading this new movement were "driven by . . . their concern about the low status of big-city police," as historian Robert Fogelson writes. Rescuing police authority, rather than white womanhood, was their most pressing priority. At a 1932 National Crime Commission conference, the solicitor general flatly rejected the wholesale overhaul of law enforcement in the United States as the solution to the challenges of urban police departments. Instead, he recommended strategies to "combat lawlessness by strengthening the machinery of law-enforcement and mobilizing opinion in support of law-enforcing agencies."[49]

At this crucial turning point, police leaders mobilized to restore authority and legitimacy to embattled urban law enforcement. They rebranded themselves as officers of the "crime-fighting" school of policing, a label that explicitly presented police as *not* the criminals that so many reports had shown them to be. The crime-fighting model relied on "scientific" methods of police efficiency, cutting-edge weapons technologies, and the primacy of masculine police authority. High arrest rates were the metrics of this model's success, ostensibly proving the vigor and efficacy of a functioning police department. Local police forces doubled down on instruments of violent suppression and surveillance; police departments were caught up with what Samuel Walker calls a "weapons fetish"—for service revolvers, machine guns, and tear gas—"that rivaled the obsession with fingerprints."[50]

The crime-fighting regime got a powerful boost as the federal government fell in line behind J. Edgar Hoover's FBI-led "War on Crime" to reassert the political legitimacy of police. Throughout the 1930s Hoover lobbied hard for what he called a "machine-gun school of criminology," pushing forward a tough policing agenda rooted in rigorous police training, mass surveillance, and arrest-heavy practices. With the election of Franklin Roosevelt, the federal state swiftly ratified Hoover's program to consolidate and expand police power. In 1934 Congress passed a meaty Omnibus Crime Bill that, among other changes, empowered federal law enforcement agents to conduct armed investigations across the country. Federal police were seen as the capable, efficient, and honorable counterpart to disgraced local police. Ironically, despite the New Deal's legacy of expanding the welfare state, federal criminal policy in the Depression "prioritized criminalization and enforcement over social intervention," as historian Claire Potter writes.[51]

A Depression-era crime panic, which Hoover vigorously stoked, proved useful for local police forces. The actual existence of a crime epidemic was doubtful. In their 1933 "Crime and Punishment" contribution to the President's Research Committee on Social Trends, criminologists C. E. Gehlke and Edwin Sutherland concluded, "No support is found for the belief that an immense crime wave has engulfed the United States." Statistics pointing to increased crime, then as now, depend simply on the number of police arrests—statistical compilations that were in fact first compiled and published by the FBI in 1930. Indeed, through the FBI's national project to collect and circulate national arrest statistics, arrest rates became a key measure (however dubious) of police efficiency and accountability. Rising rates of arrest did not prove a rise in crimes committed but rather only demonstrated "a broader definition of deviant behavior and a tougher pattern of law enforcement," according to Fogelson. An increase in arrests did not index actual "crimes" committed but served to deliver a powerful message. America's federal police organization was centralizing and expanding, and a consolidating alliance of police leaders was determined to claw back authority by exporting the FBI's aggressive, arrest-heavy policing program to local departments.[52]

The crime-fighting school did not focus on the sexual policing of women. Police leaders of the era preferred to trumpet their effectiveness by catching high-profile gangsters and bank robbers. But in the wake of Prohibition scandals, police departments inherited Progressive-era legal structures to broadly repress alleged prostitution and promiscuity across the racial spectrum. And when they fought to recapture their authority during the Depression, they put these laws to work through the mass arrests of women. Between 1932 and 1937, the FBI reported that the number of arrests of women increased by 75 percent; the number of arrested men rose by only 40 percent in these same years. Ultimately, the crisis of police legitimacy translated into a crisis for poor people, and especially for poor women on city streets.[53]

Morals arrests fueled Depression-era police drives. Among the individual crime categories, most women nationwide were charged with larceny, which accounted for 16 percent of all women's arrests in 1935. However, when multiple morals offenses are combined, including disorderly conduct, vagrancy, and prostitution, these morals misdemeanors accounted for over a third of all women's arrests. Across all categories of petty and sexual offenses—vagrancy, disorderly conduct, prostitution, and "other sex offenses"—the proportion of women arrested was consistently higher than the proportion of men. In 1935, for example, 15 percent of women arrested were charged with vagrancy and disorderly conduct; only 11 percent of men arrested were charged with these status offenses. Prostitution, of course, remained exclusively a woman's crime: 11 percent of women arrested were charged with that offense, compared with less than 1 percent of men. While a larger proportion of arrested men had a previous record, women were more likely to be arrested for the first time, indicating that a substantial portion of the female adult population was being newly thrust into the criminal system. And 65 percent of arrested women were under the age of thirty, as compared with just over half of the men, indicating a definite police interest in the behaviors of young women.[54]

The campaign to drive up arrest rates was further accelerated as urban departments offered payments to vice officers in exchange for arrests that held up in the courts. In 1933 New York Police Department commissioner James S. Bolan introduced a "new system of paying bonuses to policemen" when their prostitution arrests resulted in convictions. While the bonuses were doled out in an effort to incentivize officers to make "clean" arrests, this policy merely shifted the payoff structure from one between officer and vice operator to one between officer and department.[55]

Whether departmental encouragement came from material incentives or political pressures to restore police legitimacy, throughout the Depression, police ramped up their arrest activity targeting women. As a result, poor women were at high risk to have regular contact with the police in cities across the country. According to Box-Car Bertha, a semifictional composite of poor, transient white women who engaged in commercial sex during the Depression, "In my world somebody was always getting arrested."[56]

This new crime-fighting police regime intensified, but did not materially change, the racially haphazard nature of arrests that police made during Prohibition. FBI arrest statistics illustrated both the violent neglect and the aggressive policing that Black women continued to experience. Throughout the 1930s nationwide, the proportion of white prostitution arrests rose as Black arrests fell. And between 1935 and 1939, the rates of white arrests on prostitution charges outpaced Black arrests. Black women were subject to fluctuating police practices in the Depression. At the city level, the scale and intensity of Black women's disproportionate policing lurched up and down from one year to the next. For example, between 1935 and 1936 in Los Angeles, the percentage of Black women arrested on prostitution-related misdemeanors dropped from 46 percent of all women arrested to 10 percent. These statistics suggest that, while Black women were deeply exposed to the violence of sexual policing, during this period, there was no clear racial program of morals enforcement in place, even amid the brewing storm of arrest-heavy police practices. In Chicago and New York, police were already deploying strategies to systematically target Black women, and soon enough, police leaders nationwide would adopt these practices to politically profit from sexual policing.[57]

· · · · · ·

Erratic rates of arrest of Black women for morals offenses reflected the transitional nature of urban policing as the racial and sexual landscape of U.S. cities shifted across the early twentieth century. The interrelated developments of Black migration, vice relocation, and hardening racial segregation were converging in cities like Chicago and New York on a larger scale than other cities nationwide. Little wonder, then, that Black women in Chicago and New York were policed in such overwhelming disproportions. These cities anticipated the post–World War II future of urban morals enforcement and forecast the ways in which reformist legal institutions of policing and surveillance would be transformed from tools to reclaim poor and immigrant white women into structures to target and criminalize Black women.[58]

There was a moment during the turbulent years of the 1930s when it was not clear whether police would emerge unscathed from the scandals of Prohibition. What might have been the end of policing as urban residents knew it proved to be a pivotal moment for U.S. police departments. FBI director J. Edgar Hoover looked back on the 1930s as "the Renaissance of law enforcement," and historian Dorothy Moses Schulz characterizes the decade as "the dividing line between early and modern law enforcement." Between Prohibition and World War II, the public face of American policing substantially changed from a brutal, incompetent, and lawless political liability to a weaponized and professional crime-fighting regime. During wartime, sexual policing shuttled local police departments nationwide through this transformation.[59]

2 Bad Girls and the Good War
The Nationalization of Sexual Policing in World War II

In 1941 twenty-two white women were taken from a San Francisco jail and packed into a courtroom to await the judge's verdict. They had been arrested the night before on vagrancy charges after a police "cleanup" of downtown bars. Just a few years earlier, a roundup of the city's poorest residents would have been a familiar scene in Depression-era courtrooms as police flexed their "crime-fighting" muscle. But during wartime, these defendants represented something more sinister than the "moral hazard" of poor or working-class white women: they were traitors to the home and the home front. The presiding judge, Theresa Meikle, leaned into her female authority to vent her disapproval of the defendants, some of whom "were married and with children," as the *Los Angeles Times* reported. "A woman is far better off at home than leaning up against some bar," Meikle lectured, faulting the women especially for intruding on "a man's haven." "I don't know what's happening to American women, going into bars the way they do."[1]

The spectacle in Meikle's courtroom brought to life what one criminologist called the "public hysteria" of the American home front. During World War II, authorities as diverse as federal and military officials, local law enforcement authorities, religious leaders, academics, and reporters grew increasingly alarmed that white women were betraying their domestic duties and encroaching on men's "havens." Long considered the domestic guardians of the Victorian moral order, when white women took advantage of the expansion of public life during wartime, they promptly found themselves singled out as agents of crime, disease, and social decay, targeted in police raids like the one that hauled the women before Meikle. In this episode, as in so many others during World War II, law enforcement served a central role in the preservation of a white male supremacist moral order rooted in white women's domesticity.[2]

Over the course of this tightly compressed half decade, more than fifteen million civilians moved—with half crossing state lines—to get new jobs, to be near enlisted loved ones, or simply to pursue what one sociologist called "individual participation in the common adventure" of total war. White women in particular were aggressively recruited to participate in campaigns for defense preparedness and morale boosting. "Suddenly [we] were of tremendous importance," Dellie Hahne, who worked as a nurse's aide during the war, recalled in an oral history. "It was hammered at us through the newspapers and magazines and on the radio." They were enlisted to provide military support services to servicemen, to work in defense industries, and in Hahne's words, "to dance with the soldiers" at the USO.[3]

After years of going without in the Depression, women seized on the opportunities born out of wartime tumult—but these changes came with a cost. As white women wrested new lives from their unprecedented spatial and social mobility, popular anxiety over the gradual relaxation of sexual norms boiled over. At the same time that white women were recruited to wartime work, they were punished by law enforcement authorities for stepping beyond the confines of the home. Wartime exigencies demanded the escalation of two competing dynamics—the mobilization and taming of women's bodies—that delivered fresh possibilities but also laid the burden of social anxieties about the rattled moral order on white women's shoulders.[4]

These dynamics were racialized from the start. Federal, military, and local law enforcement authorities were decidedly less anxious about Black women's public lives than they were about white women's. Indeed, Black women's work sustained the reigning moral order constituted by dependent white womanhood with valorized ties to domesticity and laboring Black womanhood with accordingly dishonored ties to motherhood and home. "The Black woman has worked all of her life and she really was the first one to go out to work and know how to make ends meet, because it was forced on her," Fanny Christina Hill, who worked at North American Aircraft in Los Angeles during the war, said in an oral history. Within the Black community, too, a distinct strain of male leadership insisted that women continue to work during the war. Captain H. A. Robinson, a Black U.S. Army chaplain, worried that "too many young women would rather live on the 'fortune of soldiers' than to accept jobs at any price," implying that when Black "women of leisure" abandoned their economic duties, they became susceptible to moral downfall. The fears surrounding women's labor and sexual morality in wartime were bound up in racially inflected meanings of womanhood.[5]

Federal officials took up the responsibility of stanching white women's new freedoms, which, in many ways, their own wartime policies had unleashed. In March 1941 the federal Social Protection Division (SPD) was established—a sprawling program to police and detain women that involved representatives from the army, the navy, and numerous public agencies and private social hygiene organizations. Organized under the Federal Security Agency, the SPD was charged with the responsibility of safeguarding the nation's moral order. Law enforcement was the centerpiece of the SPD's wartime program, best illustrated by the appointment of Eliot Ness, formerly a Prohibition-era FBI agent, as director of the SPD. Armed with an agenda putatively directed at the control of venereal disease through the repression of prostitution, the SPD advanced a national police program that instructed that "clandestine prostitutes and promiscuous persons need constant vigilance from patrol cars and foot patrolmen." Every police officer during wartime was now expected to act as "a vice squad member." An array of federal carrots and sticks compelled police departments to devote tremendous energy to an intensive morals campaign, which SPD authorities spun as a patriotic contribution to the war effort. Still reeling from Depression-era morals enforcement scandals, many beleaguered police welcomed this opportunity to revamp their reputation through the mass arrest of women. Between 1940 and 1944, national arrest rates of women soared, with women accounting for 17 percent of all arrests in 1944—a figure that wouldn't be matched again until 1985. Nearly 40 percent of these arrests were for morals offenses, including vagrancy, disorderly conduct, and prostitution.[6]

This national program of policing was built on earlier preoccupations with white female purity. Unprecedented numbers of white women were cast under wartime suspicion: poor or working-class women of European descent who were marked as racially different just a decade or two before were increasingly folded into the category of whiteness; and middle-class women who might have avoided an officer's scrutiny previously were now rhetorically (if not materially) targeted as deviant threats. White women's socialization with servicemen was hyperpoliced on city streets, while law enforcement authorities neglected Black women in segregated neighborhoods. Even as Black women continued to confront erratic and disproportionate policing, their rates of arrest actually slowed, particularly during the early years of the war. Indeed, some federal officials expressed ambivalence over pushing for a national law enforcement agenda that would interrupt white men's sexual access to Black women.

As federal authorities crafted their social protection program and police forces deployed these policies on the ground, the sexual policing of women during World War II became a vehicle to enforce a reigning moral order—a vehicle, in other words, to preserve both the color line and gender inequality. Discretionary wartime morals enforcement was driven by an agenda to restore the sexual purity of white womanhood, to reinforce the degradation of Black womanhood, and to affirm white male sexual prerogative. "Social protection" meant protecting the white moral order amid the upheaval of wartime demands.[7]

The consolidation of police power served to contain the very transformations in women's sexual and economic lives that World War II accelerated. But this wartime project continually exposed its own failures. Eradicating venereal disease may have been the ostensible goal for the massive morals roundups, but rates of sexually transmitted infections remained high in neglected and underresourced Black communities. Police action also failed to reverse white women's rising workforce participation and sexual liberalization. Indeed, even in these years of upheaval, white women's sexual practices were gradually becoming normalized—social protection and law enforcement authorities struggled to identify with certainty the moment when women's sexual practices became women's sexual criminality. After World War II, much as wartime success had served to bolster the authority and reputation of law enforcement, police practices would continue to be marked by the failure to achieve their decades-old goal: the reclamation of chaste, domestic white womanhood.

"I Can't Give You the Exact Words of It":
Changing White Sexual Mores and Meanings

The moral panic surrounding women during World War II was in some ways driven by responses to real transformations in sexuality that had been in process throughout the urbanizing twentieth century. Wartime forces of mass migration and urban employment accelerated changes already under way to women's mobility, wage-earning capacity, and sexual practices. Historian Amanda Littauer argues that women across the class and racial spectrum were engaging in sex outside marriage at "unusually high rates." At the same time, despite the undisputable presence of men in these encounters, women alone were singled out as the "problematic sexual agents." "Our girls as a rule have one answer to a proposition, and it isn't 'no,'" probation officer Mary Edna McChristie sighed in 1944.[8]

White working women played a decisive role in the wartime moral panic over sexual practices. Their increasing paid employment was seen as a key driver in the revision of the American moral code. "There has been a distinct shift of moral standards since the last World War," criminologist Sheldon Glueck declared at a 1941 Social Protection Division meeting, suggesting a few possible causes, including "literature," "greater locomotion," and "greater freedom of women in industry." Racist hierarchies structured the popular meaning of working women. Black women had been historically subjected to the social role of workers, and white authorities accordingly devalued their motherhood and commitments to their own homes. White women, conversely, were assigned the role of mothers, and their ties to their homes were popularly glorified. The growing presence of white women in the paid labor force was a particular affront to husbands, male workers, and white observers—they regarded it as a dangerous perversion of a prevailing social order that rested on the domestic motherhood of white women and the labor of Black women.[9]

White women's earning power was by no means equal to civilian men's, but their wages rose enough during wartime to spark fears that white women could no longer be tamed by economic dependence on men. Authorities believed that women's relative economic autonomy would inevitably lead to sexual autonomy—which, given the extremely broad definitions of morals laws, meant sexual criminality. According to one police chief, the "promiscuous girl . . . who has become unbalanced by wartime wages and freedom" posed "a much more difficult problem than the out and out professional prostitute." Some critics charged that women, unaccustomed to earning a living wage, were likely to be irresponsible with their money—in other words, that promiscuous spending would necessarily lead to promiscuous behavior. The Los Angeles County health officer believed that civilian workers were at risk for acquiring and spreading sexually transmitted infections because many of the workers were "women who have never before received the bonanza wages of expanding industrialization." FBI director J. Edgar Hoover testified in a 1943 hearing for Department of Justice appropriations that white women "are going to work in factories, they are getting large salaries, making them feel free and independent. That feeling leads them into these crimes that they are committing." He agreed with a congressman's reproachful assessment that this was why "[we] need . . . a return to the old-fashioned method of life so far as the home and the church are concerned." Hoover's law enforcement authority made his subtext clear: if white women living in an "independent economic state" strayed from the home and church, they would walk directly into police jurisdiction.[10]

Authorities were especially alarmed by the prospect of a new generation of sexually active white women hailing from the middle class. The media latched onto the narrative of "patriotutes" struck with "khaki fever." They usually used such terms to describe young white women who were animated by misguided patriotism, wanderlust, and the wages to fund their adventures. In fact, those white women who defied traditional sexual norms were more complex than this sensationalized portrait suggested. One bartender explained to federal investigators in a 1940 survey of "prostitution conditions" in a town east of Los Angeles that the women he served were "not 100% whores," but rather they were "widows, chippies, married women . . . that sort of thing." "They work," he said, and "fill dates as a side line to grab off a few shackles." Throughout the 1940s, authorities grappled with the fear that the sexually deviant white women they had presumed to be poor were in fact populating the nation's respectable class.[11]

Middle-class white women and those making decent wartime wages were central to authorities' argument for surveilling women in wartime, but it was in fact the poor women scraping by in lower-paying service jobs who became the prime targets of police action. Women working as waitresses, hostesses, and food handlers in taverns, lunch counters, and grills aroused the suspicions of federal officials and local police. Waitressing, especially, was a sexualized job. Servers were typically paid only in meals and tips, so women preferred to work later hours when tips were better, which generally meant they served crowds of men. The SPD circulated anecdotes of servicemen tipping their waitresses only "if they say yes," making explicit a presumed connection between service work and sex work.[12]

Women received the bulk of the blame for taking these jobs, with little criticism for either the leisure spots refusing to pay them a living wage or the soldiers trying to proposition them. Many observers dismissed the notion that women in the service industry worked out of economic need; rather, they worked "to make the acquaintance of men easily and quickly," as one psychiatrist who studied "promiscuous patients" argued. "Certainly not all waitresses are prostitutes," social worker Mazie Rappaport, who worked primarily with white women, allowed. But she argued, "Just as certainly most prostitutes and promiscuous girls have had some experience as waitresses." The jobs that remained available to poor white women, then, exposed them to police action.[13]

In the eyes of social scientists and law enforcement authorities, white women's sexual behavior held dangerous implications for the future of the white family. "The greater sexual laxity of the generation in their teens and twenties during the war may eventually lead to modifications in the definitions of sexual conduct," sociologist Francis Merrill warned in *Social Problems on the Home Front*. This was a particular concern to Sanford Bates, former director of the federal Bureau of Prisons, who articulated the racist dimension of authorities' anxiety when he worried aloud that moral revisioning might lead whites to resemble "colored families where a totally different kind of culture prevails than what has been the rule." The erosion of sexual mores in American culture by society's erstwhile "good girls" forced a reckoning at the highest levels of national authority. In order to shore up the prescriptive authority of, and regain social control over, the white family, wartime officials frantically sought to understand—and to contain—white women's "greater sexual laxity."[14]

As white women's apparent sexual practices scrambled the racial compass of sexual propriety, bewildered officials at all levels of authority—federal, state, and local—puzzled over how to define white female sexuality during wartime. Pausing to consider the social and moral distance Americans had traveled since World War I, officials admitted that they now had to contend with "the problem of a liberal code of behavior in much greater proportion than you had [before]," according to Ernest Groves, a sociologist committed to the "conservation of marriage and the family," at a 1941 SPD meeting. Social protection authorities spent hundreds of hours in meetings, conferences, and lectures debating the exact turning point when white women's sexual (and sexualized) behavior became sexual criminality. Sexually profiled white women were still judged with a conflation of "promiscuity" and "prostitution" that carried over from the Progressive era. One exasperated doctor at a social protection conference argued, "As far as I am concerned, I would like to spread the word 'prostitute' to over twenty or fifty million people."[15]

During this period of pervasive sexual ambiguity, women confounded the hierarchies of race and class that social scientists and law enforcement officials relied on for moral clarity. Authorities recognized that their deliberate plans to contain white women's sexuality hinged on what were variously called "inadequate" and "arbitrary" definitions of sexual immorality. "We know that the line between what makes some of these girls delinquent and others non-delinquent wears pretty thin at times, sometimes nothing more than the accidental circumstance of becoming known to the court," Fred Kearney, an SPD field supervisor, conceded at a 1942 social protection conference. And at the local level, when police leaders aimed at the moving target of women's sexuality amid the social transformations of wartime, they struggled to draw and police clear lines of morality.[16]

Early one Sunday morning in March 1945, local police raided the apartment of Emily, a white woman, in Taunton, Massachusetts, the site of Camp Myles Standish, a major point of military embarkation for the New England seaboard. The previous night, Emily had gone out with some friends, including her roommate Media—an out-of-work waitress whose race goes unmarked but whose name suggests Portuguese descent—and an army lieutenant. The group drank, danced, and listened to the "colored orchestra" at the nearby Indian Room. After the nightclub closed, the friends were eating hot dogs and sipping coffee in Media's car when she and Emily noticed that police officers "kept staring at" Media. When Media asked "why they were looking at the car," the police turned around without a response and walked away. The group returned to Emily and Media's apartment. Shortly thereafter, police raided their home, where the women were observed drinking with a military captain and a white civilian man.[17]

While the military officer was dismissed, all women present were arrested and charged with being idle and disorderly (along with the white civilian man, who had challenged the policemen's authority to conduct the raid). The women hired lawyers and brought their case to trial. In court, Police Captain James Boyd testified that he found Media sitting on the officer's lap: "She pulled her dress down when I entered the room," he noted. Media's lawyer, arguing that "most girls wear pretty short skirts now," pressed Boyd to justify her arrest. "I am not finding any fault with her sitting on his lap," the police officer admitted. "That is all right." Then what specifically, the lawyer asked, does "idle and disorderly" mean? "I don't know that I can give you the exact words of it," Boyd said. The police captain added that he "didn't have to see" any actual immoralities take place; he appraised the apartment and was "satisfied" that something sexually criminal had happened.[18]

One of Boyd's rank-and-file police officers was not so sure. Media testified that she began crying during the raid and that she had asked one of the policemen why she was being arrested since she "wasn't doing anything wrong." The officer replied, "I don't know what to do . . . after all it is Captain Boyd that is doing the raiding." The Taunton police advanced a raid on Media and Emily according to a hazy rubric of sexual suspicion containing uncertain elements of race, gender, and class: Media was unemployed and yet she or Emily was able to afford a lawyer to represent them. Media's ethnicity went unmarked throughout the court proceedings, suggesting that broader swaths of women of European descent were now included in a category of whiteness that would have been denied them just twenty years before—and yet it was Media who initially caught the attention of the police. Wartime fluctuations of who and what constituted a moral threat and how to contain this threat made sexual policing illegible even to the officers imposing the crisis of arrest on the women.[19]

Federal and local law enforcement authorities had well-worn legal arrows in their quiver to deal with sexually profiled women. Prostitution-related misdemeanors, such as disorderly conduct, vagrancy, lewdness, and prostitution, remained, for the duration of these wartime years, broad enough in many jurisdictions to encompass any woman suspected of "[offering] her body for money or other consideration." But authorities increasingly doubted whether these laws were appropriate to rein in a rising generation of morally ambiguous women.[20]

Women like Emily and Media appeared to be beyond their control. "The old-time prostitution . . . is sinking into second place. The new type is . . . the young woman in every field of life, who is determined to have one fling or better," according to John Stokes, director of the Institute for the Control of Syphilis at the University of Pennsylvania. "Such relations are outside the legal control framework entirely." This, of course, was not true—morals misdemeanors could be enforced against women "in every field of life"—but many authorities believed that the growing incidence of sexual activity among economically self-sufficient white women was a new problem that demanded a different "framework." Federal authorities were compelled to develop a new logic to justify the deployment of the control techniques targeting the "new type" of white women. The World War I playbook provided a readymade framework that federal authorities could use.[21]

"Epidemic of Promiscuity": White Women and the Nationalization of Morals Policing

During World War I, state and military officials had identified venereal disease as the greatest domestic threat to national security. Women who engaged in nonmarital sex were considered the chief carriers of sexually transmitted infections, and they therefore became public enemy number one. By zeroing in on "promiscuous" women as vectors of disease, authorities were able to justify a massive crackdown on women in public spaces. Authorities during World War II propped up this aging belief that any women who had sex with a man who was not her husband was a public health danger. Dr. George Dunham, lieutenant colonel in the U.S. Army Medical Corps, wrote in 1940 that "[the] prostitute—professional, clandestine, or amateur—may be considered to be invariably the source of infection." The problem of venereal disease, then, was clarified during wartime as a problem of women's morality—and because authorities demonstrated very little concern about rates of infection among Black people, this was specifically a problem of white women's morality.[22]

For all the continuities between the two wars, however, social and political differences in the 1940s meant that the policing of women invariably differed from its previous iteration. First, the gradual easing of white sexual norms, and the growing popular tolerance of white men's sexual license—not to mention the improvements in disease treatment—meant that federal and military authorities now had to contend with an "epidemic of promiscuity" in far greater proportion than previously, according to SPD officials. Second, in order to respond to this "epidemic," SPD officials took advantage of broad central government powers in wartime to secure voluntary cooperation from local police departments to implement a federal law enforcement agenda—the first attempt to nationalize morals policing since the coercive and widely disparaged federal effort during Prohibition.[23]

The disease carrier federal authorities most urgently wanted to contain was the white woman, regardless of her class or occupation. Indeed, middle-class women inspired a substantial share of the panic. One police chief at a 1942 social protection conference argued, "The 'tavern chippy,' in her many varieties . . . is the most dangerous of all as a source of venereal infection. Often these girls are from good families. . . . They present the most nearly insoluble phase of the whole problem." The efforts to clamp down on the sexuality of white women "from good families" fueled the SPD's venereal disease control program and enabled the mass conscription of local police to the federal project of sexual surveillance and arrest. In the federal anti-venereal disease campaign that the SPD waged, the implicit meanings of "protection" were articulated: the protection of white servicemen's sexual prerogative and the white moral order (see figure 2.1).[24]

Wartime policies upheld a sexual double standard. Even as federal and army officials bemoaned the relaxation of sexual norms among women, they were compelled to update their policies to match the increasingly open climate for the sexual license of white men, and especially white men in uniform. Male restraint—the cornerstone of World War I social protection measures—took a backseat during World War II to the celebration of masculinity and validation of the white male "sex drive." In a significant

FIGURE 2.1 World War II poster, ca. 1940. Federal authorities obsessed over the sexual practices of "the better class of girls" during wartime. White women were imagined not only as the primary source of sexually transmitted infections but also as a grave threat to the white social order more generally. Courtesy of the Social Welfare History Archives, University of Minnesota Libraries.

departure from World War I policy, army officials made condoms and prophylaxis widely available for men. Nearly fifty million condoms were sold or freely distributed each month during wartime. Lieutenant Colonel Dunham of the U.S. Army Medical Corps urged that servicemen should be free "to visit and seek recreation in civilian communities"—to do otherwise would "seriously impair morale"—but women must be prevented from visiting sites "where they would have the opportunity to meet soldiers."

Clearly, federal and army authorities were reluctant to regulate men's sexual practices. Women bore the full weight of sexual regulation.[25]

To a much greater degree than in World War I, federal authorities put local law enforcement in charge. "The job of actually cleaning up these 'venereal disease swamps' belongs to the police department," Janet Burgoon, a regional supervisor in the SPD said at a 1942 conference. And SPD director Eliot Ness agreed that "vagrant women, delinquent girls, prostitutes who solicit in taverns and on the streets, must be apprehended." The federal SPD policy provided a clear illustration of the triumph of aggressive, crime-fighting policing forged in the Depression. Ness approvingly quoted FBI inspector L. R. Pennington, who argued, "It does not appear that a 'sob sister' or psychological approach will capably handle the situation. It is only by vigorous and continuous enforcement of the law that you can hope to succeed."[26]

In order to implement this crime-fighting policy, World War II venereal control policies expanded the Progressive-era antiprostitution project of muscular police repression. As in World War I, members of the staunchly repressionist American Social Hygiene Association—which defined prostitution as "the giving or receiving of the body for indiscriminate sexual intercourse" both "with" and "without" hire—maneuvered their decades-old agenda onto the national wartime platform and presented repression as the only choice for modern policy makers. In May 1940, before war was officially declared in the United States, the Eight-Point Agreement—the federal repressionist principles that local police and health authorities were expected to uphold during wartime—was set forth between the War and Navy Departments, the Federal Security Agency, and state health departments. The Eight-Point Agreement included mandatory reporting for the "sexual contacts" of infected servicemen, "forcible isolation" for "recalcitrant infected persons," and vigorous law enforcement participation in the "repression of commercialized and clandestine prostitution."[27]

Despite the broad federal commitment to the police-led repression of "promiscuity" and prostitution, it was not a popular strategy. An SPD report cited a Gallup poll indicating that "less than half the people favor repression" and concluding, "Much remains to be done." In a military town east of Los Angeles, one investigator noted with approval that "[an] active police department, encouraged and stimulated by a right minded citizenry have managed to keep . . . the problem reduced to a minimum," but unfortunately "[many] persons . . . regard the present 'set up' as a mistake" because, as one local businessman informed the investigator, "soldiers need women" and "business men need business." Locals resented the reformist "long hairs" trying to make "this town a holier than that place."[28]

Even at the highest levels of authority, wartime officials had to persuade members of their social protection team to come around to police-driven repression. Criminologists like Sheldon Glueck harbored lingering doubts about the efficacy of repression and preferred the regulation strategy of the old red-light districts: "In the first place you prevent prostitution; in the next place you allow boys to obtain contraceptives at army stations. Therefore where will they get their sexual gratification? Are you proposing that they shall invade the nonprofessional classes for this sort of thing?" he asked. "I am just as much concerned about the spread of illegitimate sex and disease among the better class of girls in the community as I am concerned with the fighting efficiency of our forces." Authorities in both the prostitution regulation and repression camps shared the same guiding motivations—the social protection of white men's sexual prerogative and the moral protection of an idealized, middle-class white womanhood—but they disagreed over the best use of police power to achieve this goal.[29]

The debate between repression and regulation was about more than just differing moral strategies. Repression was, for federal authorities, a vehicle to organize police departments and standardize morals enforcement practices nationwide. The failure of Prohibition still lingered in many policy makers' memories, and when, in 1942, a national law was floated to make prostitution a federal offense, it was rapidly shot down in meetings as inviting yet another "debacle." Local police departments were slow to fall in line with the repression campaign, and SPD authorities lobbied hard to win voluntary and, they hoped, long-term cooperation from them. The swift replacement of the short-lived SPD head, American Social Hygiene Association officer Bascom Johnson—who had been deeply involved with the repression efforts during World War I—with Ness, a former FBI man, clearly indicated the new importance of police to the national wartime program of mass sexual surveillance and control. "Every police department in America . . . has the same policy pertaining to murder, robbery," Ness explained at a 1942 meeting. "On the other hand, we find a difference of policy on what has been construed to be the moral aspects of law enforcement." Ness was determined to win consistent local police cooperation in the realm of morals policing. Authorities mustered the full threat of federal power—and the promise of federal largesse—in order to establish prostitution repression as the cornerstone of federal wartime policy and, in the process, to standardize an aggressive morals enforcement program nationwide.[30]

To entice local police into participating in the repression campaign, the SPD under Ness courted and flattered police chiefs, creating several "national police advisory committees" devoted to different angles of law enforcement and tapping police chiefs to serve on these federal committees. In this way, local police departments would feel that they were contributing to federal policy making, rather than relinquishing local control. "I think police chiefs are sick and tired of having experts from Washington come and tell them how to run their business," Ness told a table full of police chiefs at a 1942 National Police Advisory Committee for Social Protection. He sought to win the endorsement of these "fellows" so that police leaders in communities across the country could feel confident that federal guidelines were supported by "men dealing with the local problem and it will mean a great deal more than if it is some 'hot shot' from Washington." Police chiefs and city administrators who fell in line with the repressionist law enforcement program were rewarded with federal contracts and policy-making influence.[31]

Behind the flattery lay a legislative threat. The May Act, passed in 1941 and in effect for the duration of the war, made "lewdness, assignation, [and] prostitution" federal offenses in broadly defined military and naval zones. It gave the FBI full authority to move into a noncompliant area and assume local law enforcement control. As an additional stick, invocation of the May Act could also mean that military officials would declare targeted zones out-of-bounds for servicemen on leave. "Unless community sources of infection, prostitutes and promiscuous women, are cleaned up, we'll declare Blankville 'off limits,'" one federal public service announcement warned. "That's not good for your town or for your citizens."[32]

It was widely acknowledged that the May Act was a last resort, and it was only invoked twice—both times in the South—throughout its life-span. "It is not necessary to have many prosecutions under [this act]," Arthur McCormack, representing the Conference of State and Territorial Health Authorities of the United States, testified at a preliminary congressional hearing before the vote on the May Act. "But having the authority you are able to persuade a great many people to do things that you could not do if you did not have the authority that is conferred by this legislation." In propping up the enforcement powers of the May Act and publicizing the repression campaign, federal authorities provided the propaganda, enticements, and threats to back up local police nationwide as they voluntarily carried out the federal repression regime of mass arrests and detention. Charles Taft, assistant director of the Office of Defense Health and Welfare

Services, explained to an assembly of police chiefs from around the country that behind the May Act lay a strategy to guarantee that "[if] we can help you build up a public opinion that supports a sound program . . . we can count on the police department to do the job."[33]

The federal campaign to nationalize a repressive program of morals policing roped in all police officers, not just those detailed to vice. One manual produced by the National Advisory Police Committee in collaboration with the SPD, *Techniques of Law Enforcement against Prostitution*, instructed police departments to operate "on the basis of 'every officer a vice squad member.'" While some prewar police officers may have seen morals policing as a debasing, unrewarding task and preferred to delegate it to other men with this specific assignment, in the repressive wartime climate, all officers were ordered to adhere to "general police duties[, which] most certainly include observation and arrest of morals violators." The elevation of morals policing as a patriotic wartime effort certainly helped to muffle rank-and-file police resistance.[34]

Law enforcement chiefs across the country welcomed this repression mandate to burnish their tainted reputations and expand their policing power. At a time when the war was draining manpower from local forces, the anti-venereal disease repression campaign delivered an easy and patriotic route to produce record-breaking arrest statistics and reinforce their urban authority. "The prevention of venereal disease through repression of prostitution is a patriotic duty due the armed forces," Michael Morrissey, president of the International Association of Chiefs of Police and SPD representative, declared in a 1944 *New York Times* article on the "police war" against the "pick-up girl."[35]

Police officers publicized and celebrated the mass arrests of women as their contribution to the war effort. Nationwide, between 1940 and 1944, there was a 95 percent increase in arrests of women on morals charges. While prostitution arrests rose only 17.6 percent, across all categories of sexualized misdemeanors, the figures spiked: disorderly conduct charges increased 183.8 percent; vagrancy, 121.1 percent; and "other sex offenses," 134.6 percent. In 1943 the deputy chief of the Los Angeles Police Department announced that his department had made nearly eight thousand morals arrests the previous year, adding, "This is only one way in which the Police Department is cooperating with the Military Authorities." Edward Sullivan, the police chief in Newport, Rhode Island—whose force, despite being depleted by 23 percent, had in one year managed to take

349 women in custody—testified to an investigating congressional committee, "We are very proud of our [arrest] record."[36]

These arrest policies translated into racially specific police practices targeting white women on city streets. Police routinely surveilled them in downtown districts and, especially if they were observed in the company of servicemen, officers would promptly pick them up for questioning or arrest. The Boston Council of Social Agencies reported that "the composite picture of a Boston pick-up" surveilled by police was white and unmarried. Nationwide, whites accounted for over two-thirds of prostitution arrests throughout the war—racial proportions that would never be matched again in the twentieth century. In Los Angeles white women accounted for 68 percent of "sexual offense" arrests in 1943; a decade earlier, they had accounted for 49 percent. Just a little farther south, SPD investigators found that in San Diego, 90 percent of women arrested in 1943 were white.[37]

In the name of protecting soldiers' health, police forces received the tacit support of congressmen and federal authorities to deploy their discretion as broadly as necessary to apprehend women. In 1943 Clifford Peterson, the San Diego police chief, testified before a congressional committee investigating congested wartime areas. "We have adopted a vigorous attitude toward the V.D. problem," Peterson declared. "Frankly if we have any reason of suspecting a girl of being a streetwalker or prostitute we arrest her." Hoping to discover the limits of California law, Massachusetts representative George Bates asked, "How are you going to arrest a girl if she has a job in the daytime in a war production industry here and she is just doing a little street walking as a side issue? Is your law broad enough to take care of this?" Peterson conceded that the courts had challenged his department's application of California's vagrancy laws. "You are working under a subterfuge instead of the law—stretching the law just a little," Oregon representative James Mott suggested. "We are using every means to cover this situation," Peterson replied. He was not reprimanded by investigating congressmen for this "subterfuge."[38]

The federal repression campaign empowered police to engage in rampant violations of women's civil liberties, including, as outlined in a 1945 SPD memo, "the practice of making arrests on suspicion of venereal disease," "[making] arrests for vagrancy . . . where there was a suspicion of promiscuity and venereal disease," "the use of police as contact tracers," and "the deputation of law enforcement officers as health officers." Contact reports obtained from servicemen were usually vague—for example, a "blonde named Maisie"—but police officers frequently used this confidential health information to justify women's blanket arrests. In 1942 a Boston policeman arrested twenty-four-year-old Dorothy—a white waitress separated from her husband in the Coast Guard—on an idle and disorderly charge. The officer testified that he had seen Dorothy drinking in Scollay Square, Boston's predominantly white entertainment district, and an investigating probation officer confirmed that "a service man [with a sexually transmitted infection] said that [a] girl named Dorothy, answering [defendant's] description, was responsible for his condition." Though Dorothy's medical test came back negative, she was still sentenced to probation for a year. In the 1945 memo, an SPD consultant admitted, "The staff of the Social Protection Committee is familiar with these problems." But while some federal authorities disavowed these practices, they did little to stop them.[39]

Second only to being found downtown with servicemen, white women were most likely arrested if they were seen with "colored" men or in racially segregated neighborhoods. Though mass policing during wartime was spun as a protective public health intervention, it remained a mechanism to enforce racial segregation. In 1944, after observing the apartment building of Jeanette, a white woman, in the South End, one of Boston's Black neighborhoods, a squad of four police officers "rapped on [her] door" and "demanded the door be opened." Jeanette let them in and police immediately eyed "some male attire on the bed which was later identified as belonging to" her "colored" codefendant, Amos. Though Jeanette and Amos both "denied having intercourse," they were convicted of fornication and placed on probation for two years.[40]

Women in wartime who sought to lead autonomous lives free of supervision triggered sexual profiling by police. Wartime housing shortages were especially acute for single women and women with children across the color line. Landlords preferred to rent rooms to men: renting to women was undesirable because, as one landlord explained, "we need some house or building to . . . take care of women in supervised quarters where check could be kept on their movements and where we could help them to either stay decently or go before some deplorable fate befell them." Those women who did not want or were refused admission to "supervised quarters" were pushed onto streets and into tenements, rooming houses, hotels, and bars, which heightened their exposure to local authorities. Single rooms often had no kitchens and women had to go out for food. Additionally, women in these temporary rooms felt socially isolated spending their leisure time in a blank, anonymous space. "I go crazy staring at the four walls of that hotel room," one woman flagged as "promiscuous" explained to a psychiatric social worker. "I get so lonesome that I go out to bars just to see people and have someone to talk to." The psychiatrist reported with disapproval that "some patients preferred to live alone and did not wish to make arrangements in residence clubs or with private families because of the possibility of supervision of their behavior." Police also routinely patrolled urban housing to surveil women living alone. "Scarcely a night goes by that we don't make two or three arrests," one building manager in Portland, Maine, reported to journalist Agnes Meyer.[41]

Police departments used the repressive campaign during wartime to present a more professional, patriotic face of local law enforcement and to shore up their support among white audiences. Charles Hahn, the executive secretary of the National Sheriffs Association, listed the victories police had achieved during wartime, including making the "streetwalker, because of good police patrol . . . almost extinct," and concluded in 1945 that "police work has ascended several rungs in the ladder leading to its public acceptance as a profession." Police leadership also recognized that after the demands of wartime policing ebbed, they would have a readymade apparatus in place to maintain high levels of aggressive morals policing. When a 1945 article in the *Nation* speculated that the police "may sink back into their pre-war indulgence," Hahn responded, "Police chiefs today are virtually begging for a continuation of strong community support which would guarantee continued repression." A regional investigator for the SPD reported from Los Angeles in 1945 that "the city administration and the police department are cooperative and carry on [an active campaign directed against promiscuous activities], on their own motion, because they believe a repression program not only reduces venereal disease, but also lowers the crime rate in the community." Through the nationalization of the repressive federal campaign, urban police forces found the authority and public validation to conduct mass arrests on morals charges, which, Hahn declared, "make for a new era in police work."[42]

"The Continual Fight for Decency": Domestic Policing in Black Neighborhoods

The federal repression program of tough morals enforcement ostensibly heralded a "new era in police work." But white repression depended on the "old" era of police work—specifically, the perpetuation of the police regime of violent neglect that segregated vice to Black neighborhoods. The federal wartime police project of controlling sexually transmitted infections by targeting sexually profiled white women did not disrupt—indeed, it complemented—the widespread law enforcement practice of what wartime authorities called "tolerance" in Black neighborhoods. This policy exploited the vulnerability of residents who were confined to communities marked as immoral and lawless, at once permitting police negligence and legitimizing police abuse in Black neighborhoods. "Repression" in wartime, then, masked the ongoing twentieth-century urban practice of containing, and sporadically interrupting, vice in Black neighborhoods. Within Black neighborhoods marked as sexually deviant, Black women were rendered as both sexually available to white men and sexually criminal by law enforcement authorities from the federal to the local level. These racist and sexist logics that drove law enforcement practices meant that Black women were subject to distinct forms of policing, shadowed by the persistent threat of police harassment and violence on city streets, and particularly vulnerable to police violation of their homes.[43]

Even as the SPD touted its program of total repression, police practices in Black neighborhoods exposed a different reality. It was well known among federal authorities that a "failure of law enforcement officials to practice a single standard of law enforcement" prevailed, especially in the enforcement of "laws against prostitution and allied activities in Negro communities," according to a report produced by the SPD-sponsored National Venereal Disease Committee. Reports, surveys, and statistics from across the country streamed into SPD offices attesting to community and police indifference to the sexual practices of Black women, drawing a marked contrast to the intensity with which white women were surveilled and policed. An SPD study of a military town in Tennessee found a general attitude prevailed that "the community would be less concerned about the problem of prostitution among colored girls than among white girls as this would be assumed to be a natural pattern for colored girls." One social worker explained that in a military installation in Louisiana, it was assumed that "'easy' standards [were] common to colored people." From Alabama, an SPD representative reported that "Negro prostitution, although it existed, was largely unrecognized by the authorities." In Arizona, another SPD report indicated that there was a "general feeling that ordinary standards can't be applied to 'Jigtown,'" where "Mexicans & Negroes live."[44]

These beliefs were certainly not unique to military towns in the South. In Boston, the Massachusetts Society for Social Hygiene reported, "Although several bars and cafes [in the South End, a predominantly Black neighborhood] are notorious as meeting places of servicemen and girls, and are thus foci of infection[,] . . . conditions have been allowed to continue without abatement." And at a social protection meeting in Newark in November 1944, it was discussed that "promiscuous prostitution is flourishing" in predominantly Black neighborhoods, but "the police are not doing enough to clean up the situation." The officers' main priority was, rather, "to maintain a separation of the races" within those neighborhoods.[45]

In this moment, when the highest priority was the enforcement of traditional white morality through the regulation of white women's sexual practices, the racial disparities in policing were glaring. The half decade during wartime was punctuated by years when national arrest rates of white women for morals offenses increased as Black women's rates dropped. Between 1938 and 1941, for example, the FBI reported that white arrests for prostitution increased by 41 percent, while Black arrests rose by only 33 percent. In Los Angeles the percentage of Black women arrested on sexual offense charges fell from 33 percent to 19 percent between 1941 and 1943; the percentage of white women, however, rose from 53 percent to 68 percent during these years. Juvenile delinquency rates mirrored these trends, revealing the law enforcement emphasis on policing the sexuality of youthful white women: the Children's Bureau reported that "delinquency increased twice as fast among white girls as Black girls" in wartime, and journalist Agnes Meyer reported that while "Negro delinquency has dropped, white delinquency increased." These statistics do not indicate an easing up of police action against Black women—their arrest rates remained disproportionate to population figures—but rather the alignment of police priorities with federal authorities' wartime obsession with the containment of white women.[46]

Even so, health department officials and SPD authorities did pay belated attention to rates of infection among Black people. Because of the stark disparities in educational and health resources, predominantly Black communities experienced higher rates of infection, a reality that authorities met with relative equanimity compared with their panicked reaction to rates of disease among whites—rates that actually decreased throughout the war thanks to whites' greater access to prophylactic stations and health care. "All too often the largest and best facilities are established in areas where they are least needed and/or where they are least accessible to the people in greatest need," an SPD representative said in a 1944 speech. "The Negro constituency has been overlooked." If anti-venereal disease campaigns were indeed focused on the eradication of infection, federal officials would have aimed to deliver equal preventive and medical care to Black neighborhoods at best—or, at worst, attempted to match the coercive policing and carceral quarantine orders of women in white neighborhoods. But neither policy was consistently practiced in Black neighborhoods. While by the late years of the war, the SPD made overtures to police departments to make "a drive against commercialized prostitution in the Negro area," these campaigns were a partial and inconsistent addendum to the concerted efforts targeting white women specifically and in service to white public health more broadly.[47]

Federal authorities "searched diligently" to understand why police-driven venereal disease repression efforts "were usually less effective in Negro neighborhoods than in white neighborhoods," as Ness lectured at a "Negro Conference." Regional supervisors reported a variety of reasons for local indifference to Black people's health and sexual practices, citing cultural and moral "deficiencies" in Black neighborhoods, such as a "careless or fatalistic attitude on the part of the Negro . . . and a willingness to 'take a chance' of becoming infected" and "a defeatist attitude towards promiscuity amongst the negroes." Occasionally, these appraisals featured a recognition of socioeconomic deprivation, including "a definite lack of recreation facilities for the Negro industrial worker, civilian, and particularly for the Negro girl."[48]

However, in a private, top-level meeting on venereal disease in 1942, a different reason emerged. Concerned about the recreational opportunities for white servicemen, military and federal officials betrayed ambivalence over instituting a program of total repression in communities of color where "the girls are very pretty and normal inhibitions are loosened when the boys get down there," according to Charles Taft, assistant director of the Office of Defense Health and Welfare Services. His colleague Geoffrey May (no relation to the sponsor of the May Act) agreed, "The customs are so different . . . and their family relationships are so different, that it makes it very difficult to utilize the same types of controls." While Taft and May's speculations came up in a debate over police operations in Puerto Rico, Lieutenant Colonel Thomas Turner offered, "It is very similar to the negro problem here."[49]

The color line was nested inside the gendered double standard, propelling the discriminatory enforcement of the repression campaign. As Charles Johnson wrote in his 1943 book, *Patterns of Negro Segregation,* "The interracial sex mores prohibit relations between Negro men and white women and tend to condone relations between white men and Negro women." This was especially true during World War II when federal and military officials frankly stated their goals to protect white men's sexual "urges" and to police the sexual morality of "the better class of girls." Baked into these two aims was the tacit approval of funneling white men toward economically strapped Black neighborhoods for sex. In a 1942 "Negro Study" commissioned by the SPD, Black sociologist John Ragland observed that "white johns continued to go into the [vice] district after the houses had been closed and were catered to by Negro housewives who said they needed the money to aid in the support of their children." White men, and especially white servicemen, were rarely reined in by military and police authorities in Black neighborhoods.[50]

Because of rampant segregation and segregationist policing, Black women did not have easy access to the downtown districts where white women were typically singled out for police surveillance and discipline. Barred from housing, hotels, and public entertainment in most city centers, Black women's movement was generally restricted to bars, nightclubs, and rooming houses or apartments shared with family and friends in segregated neighborhoods. In one SPD report on "venereal disease exposure," researchers concluded that Black people were more likely to socialize in a private home, as opposed to a tavern, brothel, street, or hotel. "It should not be overlooked that this practice is closely related to the fact that relatively few places are available to colored people for any purpose," the authors wrote.[51]

Under these conditions of segregated life, in neighborhoods marked as lawless and sexually deviant, the home—an otherwise sacred font of white morality—was consistently violated by police. Black women were especially vulnerable to sudden police invasions in their homes. Emma, a twenty-four-year-old "tall, slim colored girl" who, according to an investigating probation officer, talked "with a slight stutter" and did "day work for Jewish families" in Boston, was perennially subject to police raids in her home throughout wartime. She had left Georgia in 1934 and moved to Boston to join her aunt and uncle who had "partly arranged" her marriage to a man more than twice her age. After four years, Emma had given birth to their daughter, and her husband—who, as one friend reported, "treated her shamefully; did not even supply milk for her child"—had left her, having become "interested in another woman." Emma's daughter was "adjudged neglected" by the Division of Child Guardianship and the state consequently seized custody. Shortly after losing her daughter, Emma was plagued with headaches that were so bad "she could 'hardly keep from screaming.'" Emma traced these headaches to "a beating she received last summer . . . when she was hit on the head by a man who jumped out of a doorway. Said she was lying in an alley from 1 A.M. to 4 A.M." before she was taken to the hospital, where she remained unconscious until the following day. By 1939 Emma had no family she could depend on in Boston. Her uncle had turned on her, denying that he had ever facilitated her inauspicious marriage, blaming Emma for her own misfortunes—claiming, for example, "she was drunk when she was assaulted last Summer"—and stating that "she is a street walker [and] he does not see how she escapes getting arrested."[52]

Emma most certainly did not "escape" arrest. Between 1939 and 1945, she was arrested eight times on a variety of morals offenses, including fornication, idle and disorderly, and drunkenness, not counting the instances when police picked her up on "suspicion" and subsequently released her. For Emma, being in the company of a white serviceman could simultaneously arouse the suspicions of police and potentially shield her from arrest: one time, policemen followed Emma and "an Army sergeant" as they walked to her building; the officers "went in" and broke up the pair, letting Emma off with a warning that "they were watching her." At least four times, however, Emma was apprehended after police invaded her apartment. In June 1941, Officer Michael O'Brien testified that he saw Emma and her Black codefendant, Benjamen, "standing on the corner" of a South End intersection talking to a white man. Later, O'Brien followed Emma and Benjamen as they walked toward their home and, while the pair was still chatting outside their apartment, broke in and "sat behind the sofa for ten minutes" awaiting their return. When Emma and Benjamen entered the apartment with a racially unmarked man, the policeman "then came from behind the sofa" and arrested Emma and Benjamen. O'Brien augmented his "evidence" with ostensibly damning testimony that "the previous Saturday night he observed this house and arrested a white woman from the premises" on a morals charge. Emma was found guilty of being idle and disorderly and sentenced to three months in jail.[53]

This was the wartime police regime in Black communities, where Black women like Emma lived under the threat of male violence and police invasions alike. Ostensibly "rehabilitative" white authorities, such as probation officers, who were charged with investigating and remedying the conditions that triggered women's arrests, dismissed Emma's apparent signs of trauma from abuse at the hands of her husband and the man who attacked her on the street. White or racially unmarked men moved—with rare exceptions—freely through Black communities, powered by a presumption of sexual access to the women who lived there. These men compounded Emma's exposure to police, who delivered arbitrary and invasive punishments. And just as the state disparaged Emma's motherhood by seizing her child, law enforcement authorities violated the privacy of her home. While white women were policed on the street to punish them for their alleged betrayals of family and home, law enforcement actions denied the sanctity of both for Black women.

The weight of police involvement in Emma's life, however, should not be seen as a sign that police were consistently involved within Black communities. When residents needed police, they were slow to—or simply did not—respond to neighborhood calls. The failure of federal and local authorities to carry out a single standard of law enforcement in Black neighborhoods during wartime stoked the amplifying demands from Black residents for safe and consistent police protection. "One of the most frequent complaints we hear from Negro leaders is that relating to inadequate and inefficient policing in Negro sections," an SPD representative said at a venereal disease conference. In 1941 a woman living in Boston's South End wrote in a letter to the governor of Massachusetts that she "could not stand the continual fight for decency" in her neighborhood. She protested that when she and her neighbors called the police and asked them to stop people from using the street as a "public toilet" or dumping "old fish" in vacant lots, the officers simply said, "What do you expect in this neighborhood?" In Los Angeles, Berle Maxson, the secretary-treasurer of the Watts Chamber of Commerce, wrote a letter to the Police Commission in 1943 requesting "better police protection." The Police Commission rejected the request as excessive.[54]

If residents' calls for better police protection were heard, they risked delivering more police predation instead. When police officers did act in Black neighborhoods—typically around local elections or in response to a politically motivated "cleanup" campaign—their performance remained as brutal and lawless as in prewartime years. In 1940, in advance of a mayoral election, Los Angeles police leadership sought to distract from public outcries over revelations of officer graft and bribery by staging a "Central avenue blitzkrieg" in the city's Black neighborhood, turning the customary payoffs for vice protection into a trap to arrest over 350 residents. "Negro citizens are being beaten and slugged by Mayor Bowron's Cossak Police department," the editors of the *Los Angeles Sentinel*, one of the city's Black newspapers, fumed, adding that residents "are sick and tired of the old gambling, prostitution hooey that has been flaunted . . . by the mayor." Following the "frequent beating, mistreatment and false arrests, of law abiding men and women" in Boston, one resident, Maurice Smith, informed the governor in 1941, "Tempers up this way are growing tighter than the wetted gut in a rain-soaked tennis racket. . . . [That] stage has been reached where anything can happen and probably will unless something is done to keep these police officers within the Law."[55]

During a meeting of the National Advisory Police Committee, a major in the air force stated that "the increasing Negro problem" was "dynamite." Federal authorities name-checked pervasive racial inequities, but they chiefly blamed police neglect on the apathy of "Negro leadership." In a clear signal of the rising demands of Black people for racial justice during World War II, federal officials began to twist residents' calls for safe, dignified, and lawful police protection as the cause of police neglect of Black neighborhoods. At the Negro Conference, Ness claimed that "racial tension" and "super-sensitiveness" led to "the interpretation of much police action as racial persecution directed toward prostitution repression in these areas," which discouraged police intervention. At the same conference, Raymond Clapp, an associate director in the SPD, argued that "the tendency of many Negroes to charge the police with unfair discrimination when they do attempt to strengthen enforcement in Negro neighborhoods" was a "deterrent to police action." Clapp suggested that "Negro leaders can help correct lax enforcement by voicing the desire of their group for the repression of vice and crime," which, of course, many were actively doing. Outraged residents' wartime challenges to negligent and brutal policing reflected the surge in civil rights activism during these years, and demands for changes in police practices—and sexual policing practices in particular—would animate postwar mobilization in Black neighborhoods.[56]

• • • • • •

The sexual policing of women in World War II represented the fullest—and final—expression of early twentieth-century morals law enforcement practices: the sexual policing of white women through police-led repression campaigns in downtown districts; and the erratic, brutal, and invasive policing of Black women in racially segregated neighborhoods that were officially tolerated zones of vice. In ways explicit and implicit, federal wartime authorities crafted the policy architecture to make this racialized pattern of law enforcement both possible and patriotic. And as police officers translated this policy into everyday practices of racial discretion, they preserved the color line and gender inequality that, together, constituted the prevailing moral order.

In 1943 policewoman Rhoda Milliken delivered a rare critique of the federal repressionist police program. "Too often both local law-enforcement and health controls degenerate into a persecution of individual women," she wrote. "[The repression campaign] is interpreted as authorization to ride ruthlessly over human rights and needs, leaving in the wake a scrap heap as costly as it is disfiguring to the community." World War II was indeed a crisis for the unprecedented numbers of women across the racial spectrum who were arrested and most likely convicted and jailed: in 1943, 82 percent of people charged with sex offenses nationwide were found guilty.[57]

But the crisis for policed women during wartime proved to be a boon for both federal and local law enforcement authorities. In the SPD, federal authorities hit on a winning formula to gain greater influence over local police departments through enticements and threats. This laid the groundwork for a federal-local relationship that, while contested, would nonetheless yield fruitful cooperation from local forces in federal crime crusades across the twentieth century. And police departments emerged in the immediate postwar period as "professional" stewards of urban social order. Among white audiences, police contributions to the war efforts through the repressive venereal disease control program effectively cleansed local forces of any lingering stains of scandal from the Depression era. Morals law enforcement targeting women during World War II may have been "costly" and "disfiguring to the community," but it boosted the accumulation and consolidation of state power.

Even so, the repression campaign did not resolve the original problem that propelled social protection authorities: how to contain white women amid the irrepressible sexual and economic transformations of the twentieth century. As women's workforce participation and sexual liberalization became gradually normalized, law enforcement authorities—rejuvenated by their wartime morals drives—would remove white women from their agenda for public order and focus their attention, instead, on efforts to contain Black people. Black residents would not let this development happen without a fight.

3 **Los Angeles: Land of the White Hunter**
Legal Liberalism, Police Professionalism, and Black Protest
....

Late one night in October 1961, Los Angeles police officers V. C. Dossey and C. H. Watson charged Betty, a white woman, with disorderly conduct. The officers were patrolling a predominantly Black neighborhood in South Los Angeles—an area that was, according to police, "plagued by females" engaging in suspect sexual practices. From their radio car, Dossey and Watson observed Betty "cruis[ing] in a manner designed to attract" the attention of men. They stopped to question her, but she became "hostile" and refused to identify herself. A search of Betty's belongings turned up more apparent evidence of her sexual criminality, including a "contraceptive kit." Later, when officers interrogated her at the police station, she delivered in "the most vulgar and profane language . . . her opinion of 'blue coats.'" Dossey and Watson figured they had everything on Betty they needed to make a legitimate morals arrest.[1]

But in a surprising twist, the charges against Betty were dismissed by the city attorney's office. A deputy for the city prosecutor advised the police department "to be very restrictive and conservative" in their enforcement of this morals misdemeanor—in other words, that officers should lean on the side of nonenforcement, because the city prosecutor was newly "reluctant" to pursue these cases. Before World War II, the incriminating combination of a white woman in a Black neighborhood, carrying items associated with nonreproductive sex, and daring to disrespect police officers, would have very likely been sufficient to yield a conviction. Now, in a rare admission of error, the chastened Los Angeles Police Department (LAPD) leadership admitted that "it would have been wiser to have released" Betty without pressing charges.[2]

Betty's case is emblematic of an important turning point in the twentieth-century history of sexual policing: the deepening racial inequity of morals enforcement. As white women's presumed nonmarital straight sexual practices were gradually decriminalized, Black women were increasingly targeted for allegedly engaging in the same.

In 1964, three years after Betty's arrest, Los Angeles county supervisor Kenneth Hahn declared "an all-out war against narcotics and open prostitution" in his predominantly Black district in South Los Angeles. Coordinating with the sheriff and district attorney, Hahn orchestrated "accelerated enforcement activities" in the neighborhood. A weekend vice raid kicked off the campaign, with over one hundred "suspects" rounded up and led onto waiting buses. Though these two episodes transpired in different jurisdictions of city and county, the city prosecutor's reluctance to prosecute a white woman in 1961 and the coordinated mass morals arrests of Black women just a few years later illuminate the racial divergence of sexual policing in the midcentury United States.[3]

Los Angeles reveals two critical dimensions of the postwar racial history of morals law enforcement. First, it showcases how midcentury processes of sexual liberalization in social science and legal reform influenced law enforcement authorities' "reluctance" to pursue white women like Betty, while preserving police officers' discretionary power in morals law enforcement to target Black women. By the end of 1961, liberal legal reforms in California effectively decriminalized nonmarital straight sex. But morals law reform did not proceed in a race-neutral vacuum. Rather, it took shape within the postwar context of rapidly and decisively segregating urban neighborhoods and the aggressive police mobilization to contain the growing Black population—as a result, white women were increasingly shielded from citywide morals enforcement even as Black women were relentlessly policed. Second, Black rebellions against police gained momentum in Los Angeles during these years, in part touched off by this racial inequity of morals enforcement. In segregated Los Angeles, it is no coincidence that mounting police repression and Black protest collided during a period of ascendant sexual liberalism. The racial inequity in morals policing—exacerbated by liberal morals law reform—was a powerful, if underappreciated, factor in the many clashes between police and Black residents that culminated in the 1965 uprising in the Black neighborhood of Watts.[4]

Unequal police practices were a long-standing problem in Los Angeles's Black neighborhoods, but as California morals laws relaxed between the mid-1950s and the early 1960s, the racial inequity of morals law enforcement deepened. Police arrest statistics in Los Angeles confirm the widening racial disparity in midcentury morals enforcement: between 1954 and 1963, the number of white women arrested for prostitution-related offenses decreased by 20 percent, while the number of Black women increased by

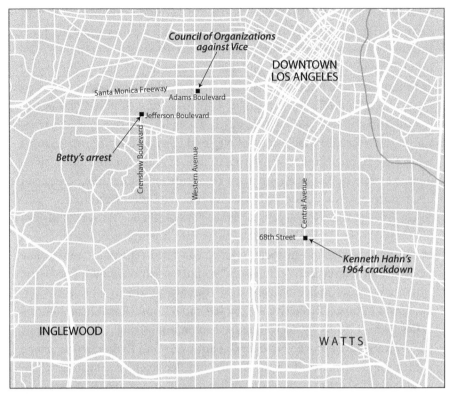

MAP 3.1 South Los Angeles, ca. 1960.

roughly the same amount. Police leaders lashed out at the putative constraints imposed by liberal court rulings, but through their racially coded appeals to police "professionalism," officers retained broad discretionary power in Black neighborhoods to conduct vice raids, crackdowns, and mass arrests for morals offenses.[5]

To Black residents of Los Angeles, morals enforcement in Black neighborhoods was a flagrant example of police discrimination. Many residents were particularly outraged that a nightly caravan of "white hunters" drove into Black neighborhoods and accosted Black women with impunity, and Black women continued to be harassed by police—even as white women were conspicuously freed from police action. By the mid-1960s multiple and competing forms of Black protest, ranging from demands for tougher morals policing to violent battles with police attempting to arrest Black women on morals charges, arose in Los Angeles to challenge the racial inequity in morals enforcement.[6]

Redefining Sexual Criminality, Deepening Racial Divisions

An onslaught of postwar statistics delivered inescapable evidence that white American sex was increasingly happening outside the legal sanction of marriage. Alfred Kinsey's *Sexual Behavior in the Human Female*, published in 1953 to a storm of publicity (no doubt primed by his 1948 best seller on the "human male"), forced readers to peer behind the Victorian veil that obscured white women's everyday sexual habits. In dispassionate scientific language—a foil to the media accounts that sensationalized his work—Kinsey detailed the frequency, variation, and partners in Americans' sexual careers, ultimately exposing the myth of extramarital chastity that governed legal norms. "Kinsey demonstrated that much of Americans' sexual activity took place outside of marriage," historian Miriam Reumann argues, "and that the majority of the nation's citizens had violated accepted moral standards as well as state and federal laws in their pursuit of sexual pleasure."[7]

The midcentury brought with it a dawning awareness that morals laws across the country created a broad class of "law abiding law breakers," according to the authors of the 1950 edition of *Social Disorganization*, a social science textbook. In this period of acute contradictions—when more white women were engaging in nonmarital sex but domestic white womanhood was prized with a renewed vengeance—the gap between sexual practices and sexual laws was magnified and held up to broad critique. Reproductive rights attorney Harriet Pilpel argued in 1952 that American morals laws "are honored more in the breach," and popular author Christopher Gerould had more colorful language for the moral legal code: "American sex laws are a vast garbage heap of discarded attitudes and worn-out prejudices, piled up and preserved over centuries in the statute books." As the country's changing sexual mores became an undisputed fact of twentieth-century life, a gathering force of postwar social scientists, lawyers, and popular critics challenged the wasteful and misguided deployment of morals misdemeanors like disorderly conduct and vagrancy.[8]

At the heart of these postwar challenges was an effort to redraw the line that separated a "law abiding law breaker" from a criminal. Reformers' newfound attention to the question of which women were "overcriminalized" did not imply that there was no place for criminalization—concepts of female deviance certainly had not disappeared. The door remained open for some women to be deemed appropriately criminalized, or perhaps even undercriminalized. But what behavior counted as deviant, and among whom, and what kind of deviance registered as a criminal problem, was undergoing a significant recalculation.

Social scientific explanations, suffused with a mélange of environmental, biological, and pathological factors, guided definitions of women's criminality onto familiar racist tracks. Women's sexuality was reappraised within distinct environments—the "home" for white women and the "slum" for Black women—leading to a redefinition of white women's nonmarital sexuality as a private, individual "sickness." According to the popular social science and social hygiene literature of the period, such deviance required psychoanalytic treatment rather than legal intervention. Black women's nonmarital sexuality, however, was reaffirmed—by way of a glancing sociological recognition of structural urban deprivation—as a public, community-wide criminal tendency requiring stiff morals enforcement. So it was that when social scientists, lawyers, and judges pushed for legal reforms to narrow the gap between sexual practices and sexual laws, they ultimately, if indirectly, deepened the divide between white sexual legality and Black sexual criminality.

As liberal critics mounted their case for an updated moral code, they continued to prize heterosexual marriage as the source of "mature" and "normal" sexual pleasure. Indeed, a key tenet of sexual liberalism held that mutually satisfying sex was a necessary cornerstone of fulfilling marriages; and although growing numbers of midcentury liberal reformers were tentatively warming to the possibility of noncriminal sexual relations outside marriage, wedlock remained the unequivocal site of the most "well-adjusted" sex. Kinsey, along with his colleagues and readers who applauded a frank airing of pervasive sexual practices, believed that greater education and transparency in matters of sex would promote healthier relations between the sexes and, therefore, healthier marriages. The criminalization of straight sex, and its attendant moral stigma and shame, frustrated these efforts to forge strong marital bonds through sexual openness. "Our antisexual cultural attitudes, which are so tragically inculcated in our statutory laws and our everyday customs . . . sabotage the sexual happiness of millions of our married populace," wrote Robert Veit Sherwin, a divorce lawyer and co-founder, in 1957, of the Society for the Scientific Study of Sexuality. What most exercised these critics was sex laws' affront to otherwise respectable people and these laws' injurious effect on middle-class marital stability.[9]

By framing their critique of sex laws as a threat to marital happiness, social scientists and legal scholars demonstrated the limits of sexual liberalism as a remedy to the racial, gender, and class inequities built into morals law enforcement. "As sexual liberalism took hold among the white middle class, it raised new issues for the maintenance of sexual order," historians John D'Emilio and Estelle Freedman argue. "In particular, how could the legitimation of heterosexual eroticism remain within 'responsible' limits?" The emphasis on marital sexual fulfillment did not have to automatically imply the strengthening of gendered or raced stratifications within the sexual order. However, in a midcentury culture fixated on the cleaving of suburbanizing white patriarchal nuclear families and Black families in hypersegregating cities allegedly fraught with "social disorganization," sexual liberalism became a vehicle for widening the racial discrepancy between sexual practices and sexual criminalization. "As Black urban communities grew, the Black family and Black sexual mores appeared as a convenient counterpoint, identifying the line between what was permissible and what was not," D'Emilio and Freedman conclude.[10]

Throughout the postwar period, social scientists and researchers were influenced by two major population shifts that changed the racial meaning and experience of American cities. During World War II and continuing throughout the midcentury, millions of southern Black refugees fled to cities in the North and West. This tremendous movement converged with the rapid proliferation of racially restricted, federally subsidized suburbs as white male breadwinners and their families were drawn to cheap mortgages for homes outside the cities. By 1965 Black people were more urbanized than whites, with nearly three-quarters of the total Black population living in American cities. This development was especially prominent in Los Angeles, where, despite the city's racial diversity, Black people were hypervisible as the city's major demographic of color. In 1960 Black residents outnumbered "Spanish-surname" residents in the city by more than seventy-four thousand, and because they experienced more acute forms of housing exclusion than any nonwhite group in Los Angeles, the majority of Black Los Angelenos were concentrated in just nine neighborhoods in South Los Angeles (an area made up of thirty neighborhoods).[11]

Racist hierarchies of sexual morality—of white purity and Black deviance—had been mapped onto spatial segregation for decades. But midcentury social science played an important role in establishing Black people, and the neighborhoods to which they were confined, as the "counterpoint" to white normality. Environmental criminology, an influential school of thought that held that people's socioeconomic conditions produced their behaviors, was almost reflexively applied to Black people, perpetuating a long twentieth-century sociological project that bound Blackness with criminality. Although "environmental" explanations for Black criminality drew on sociological and structural factors to explain Black people's supposed deviance, this midcentury school of thought focused exclusively on Black behaviors and forms of crime most visible in Black neighborhoods and ignored or downplayed the preponderance of white deviance and criminality. The authors of *Social Disorganization* claimed that "the deteriorated social areas in which the Negro is forced to live are conducive neither to high standards of conduct nor to law-abiding behavior."[12]

Black sexuality was understood as a public and community-wide disorder, intimately connected to the "ghetto" or the "slum" to which Black people were confined. As a result, environmental social science provided a direct route from the systemic degradation of Black neighborhoods to the inherent sexual criminality of Blackness. Contrary to widely publicized evidence that sexual norms were loosening across all social strata, a 1949 California Special Crime Commission report insisted that "the more illicit sexual and immoral codes are often perpetuated and practiced" in the "slums" where Black people lived.[13]

Postwar social science ratcheted up the association between Blackness and immorality while unraveling the relationship between white womanhood and sexual criminality. Another influential school of thought circulating during this period—the psychiatric worldview—argued that white women who engaged in nonmarital sexuality were not criminals but rather individuals who were "maladjusted" to their otherwise healthy domestic environment. White women who deviated from prevailing codes of sexual morality were not criminals in need of punishment; instead, they were "neurotics" suffering from a "pathology of sex" who required "treatment" so they could be reabsorbed back into their "normal" surroundings. White women, then, became increasingly seen as individual psychological subjects whose nonmarital sexual practices, while not necessarily morally acceptable, were also not appropriately considered criminal. (Of course, poor white women remained the most likely of the declining numbers of white women to be arrested on morals laws—but at every stage of the criminal process, from sentencing to probation or parole, they were also more likely to be considered eligible for rehabilitative "treatment.") The legal retreat from regulating nonmarital straight sex was closely related to this reappraisal of white sexuality within the private, individualized, and suburban domestic sphere.[14]

The important distinction to note is that while both sexually profiled Black and white women in this period were cast as prone to deviance—

Black women because of their environment, and white women because of personal maladjustments—Black women's sexuality was more likely to remain criminalized. White women's sexual "abnormality," social scientists, psychiatrists, and criminologists argued, should be understood as a psychological, rather than criminal, condition. As nonmarital heterosexual sex became the practiced norm among women, a question remained for legal reformers to sort out: To what extent was nonmarital straight sex criminal behavior? Racist interpretations of social science would help determine which women would be considered pathological offenders requiring psychiatric treatment and which women would remain sexual criminals requiring state intervention.

Criminalizing the Environment:
The Racial Limits of Morals Law Reform

Reformist liberals may have been committed to relaxing the laws that regulated nonmarital straight sex and decriminalizing white women's sexual pathology, but few were keen on the prospect of relinquishing moral legal control altogether. "The criminal law should be based upon the moral law," New York City judge John Murtagh and reporter Sara Harris affirmed in *Cast the First Stone*, their popular 1957 account of prostitution; but they added, "It does not follow, however, that all moral offenses should be designated as crimes."[15]

In compromises taking place in the courts, conference rooms, and state legislatures across the nation, legal reformers resolved the tension between easing criminal sanctions on sex and preserving police discretion to enforce morals law in the race-neutral language of criminalizing "public morality"— a move that deepened the legal justification that Black women in their neighborhoods were likely sexual criminals, even as white women were, to an unprecedented extent, released from criminal judgments (though they remained subject to pathological diagnosis). Operating from the circulating social scientific presumptions of white normality and Black deviance, when legal reformers turned to the penal code and sustained the criminalization of the public "flouting" of moral codes, they helped to create the conditions for white women to unequally benefit from the gradual legal permissions of sexual liberalization.

The midcentury tensions and outcomes in moral laws reform were best illustrated in the American Legal Institute's multiyear project to produce the Model Penal Code (MPC), which was finally released in 1962. While the

MPC was merely a suggested framework that states eager to modernize their penal code could borrow, it reflected and advanced the reformist legal thought circulating during this period. The MPC was the culmination of what Louis Schwartz, an MPC coreporter and University of Pennsylvania law professor, called "a new pitch in intensity" over the debate around "legal moralism," or the appropriate role of the state in the enforcement of morals. Many MPC reporters were "uneasy about [the attempt] to regulate private sexual behavior." They agreed that the threat of legal punishment was ineffective to deter crimes against morality—including "alcoholism, narcotic addiction, prostitution, and deviant sexual activity"—arguing instead that "therapy is necessary and may be effective" for this category of crime. However, a vocal faction held fast to the "outright regulation of morality." So the reporters reached a compromise: while the MPC proposed that "promiscuous noncommercial sexuality" be decriminalized, it affirmed the repression of "open flouting of prevailing moral standards as a sort of nuisance in public thoroughfares and parks."[16]

By agreeing to leave the enforcement of "prevailing moral standards" up to police discretion, MPC reporters left Black women vulnerable to continued sexual criminalization. MPC drafters well knew that, especially in the realm of morals enforcement, "prosecutions for sexual derelictions are arbitrarily selected" and that morals offenses "facilitate . . . police discriminations more often than general compliance with legal norms." Indeed, many legal and criminological critics of the existing moral penal code recognized that because of class, racial, and gender hierarchies, the discrepancy between law and prevailing practice fell hardest on poor and nonwhite women. "Young girls and women, especially those in the lower economic and social groups, often pay a serious price for sex experience outside the bounds of matrimony . . . [and] are punished severely for conduct that is widely prevalent among all levels of society," the authors noted in *Social Disorganization*. Police officers played a central role in determining whether a presumed sexual offender was arrestable, and race, in turn, played a central role in informing the officer's judgment. "Apparently the Negro woman in our culture does not rate the same consideration accorded white women," the authors of the California report *Girls and Young Women in Conflict with the Law* wrote in 1958.[17]

By upholding the power of law enforcement to police public morality, MPC reporters effectively, if unintentionally, ratified officers' suspicion of Black women in their own neighborhoods. One consequence of empowering police to adjudicate public morals was the strengthening of the officer's "totalitarian tendencies by 'criminalizing' the environment," as criminologist Jerome Skolnick argued. "If the policeman's job is to observe deviations from 'normality,' a more rigid definition of normality will make him more watchful and suspicious." Morals laws "incline the police to a more rigid conception of order which heightens both the perception and presence" of crime in the environment in which Black people were segregated. Because the very presence of Black women in the city was read, by white police and whites more generally, as a "deviation" from public morality, when states updated their laws in the spirit of the MPC, the context in which they were enforced meant that Black women would likely be excluded from the legal permissions of sexual liberalism.[18]

The midcentury flurry of legal analysis and reform proposals produced real changes to morals laws. In the final weeks of 1961, the California State Supreme Court struck down Los Angeles's capacious municipal morals ordinances. Carol Lane—a white woman variously described by the press as a "Hollywood model," a dancer, and other suggestive monikers—was at the center of the challenge case. She had been arrested by Los Angeles police in her home in a white neighborhood and charged with "resorting" to engage in illicit sex. The "resorting" law under challenge empowered police to arrest any person found in any physical place, public or private, "for the purpose of having sexual intercourse with a person to whom he or she is not married, or for the purpose of performing or participating in any lewd act with any such person." Municipal judge Kathleen Parker convicted Lane after hearing police testimony that an officer had "watched through a window as men on two different occasions visited Miss Lane in the bedroom of her apartment." Lane appealed her case up to the California Supreme Court, which decided in her favor.[19]

In the ruling, the justices reasoned, first, that police had not supplied any proof that Lane had accepted money "or other consideration" in her rendezvous. Next, the majority argued that, while laws against commercial sex were abundantly developed in California's state penal code, "neither simple fornication or adultery alone nor living in a state of cohabitation and fornication" was a crime in the state. The Los Angeles ordinance, which effectively criminalized nonmarital straight sex, conflicted with a higher legal power and was, on those grounds, struck down. This single ruling also felled a host of Los Angeles morals ordinances that deployed similarly overbroad language. The court's argument that nonmarital sexual practices—which, significantly, took place indoors in this case—were not and could not be made a criminal offense in the state of California reflected the liberalizing conceptions of women's sexual privacy that were being developed during this period. The fact that the early beneficiaries of this new privacy were white women reveals the racial limits of privacy as a substantial right.[20]

Because *In re Lane* hinged on the conflict between municipal and state legal authority, the Supreme Court justices did not specifically take on the issue of police power. However, police discretion was a crucial mechanism in the enforcement of the interchangeable and broad suite of public order offenses, such as disorderly conduct and vagrancy, which provided an additional weapon for law enforcement to police the presumed sexual behavior of women. Determining the limits of this police discretion drove efforts to reform vagrancy laws in the early 1960s. The network of vagrancy law reformers who sought to rein in police excesses was distinct from the social scientists and lawyers taking aim at sex laws, but their work overlapped in the enforcement of vagrancy laws against women. While targeted women were only one group in a larger universe of challengers taking aim at vagrancy laws through the midcentury—including civil rights and antiwar activists, beatniks (and later hippies), and poor Black men—each group's argument contributed to an escalating debate over the scope of police power.[21]

When California legislators set out to reform the state's vagrancy law in 1961, they faced a tricky, and perhaps impossible, challenge: to strike a balance between, on the one hand, protecting the discretionary power of police to enforce public order and, on the other hand, curbing the police tendency to use this discretion to target racially and economically marginalized people. How could a vagrancy law stop police officers from arresting people based on "looks, not acts," while still preserving police officers' power to arrest "suspicious" people? Along with trying to balance these cross-purposes, legislators knew as well that a previous legislative attempt to overhaul the state's vagrancy law had been vetoed by the governor. Not surprisingly, the eventual reform law delivered mixed results. A "loitering" provision authorized an arrest "if the surrounding circumstances . . . [indicate] to a reasonable man that the public safety demands" identification of the suspicious target. The emphasis on the environmental definition of a lawful target of police discretion provided a race-neutral avenue to make the continued criminalization of Black neighborhoods lawful and legitimate. The reformed vagrancy law that Governor Pat Brown signed into law in 1961 showcased the liberal potential of the courts and legislatures in this period—and the often racist, illiberal results that remained an open possibility.[22]

These legal reforms, in political and practical intent, were designed to modulate police officers' discretionary power. But police leaders and rank-and-file officers saw legal liberalism as a grave assault on their autonomy. Going on the offensive, they demanded unfettered power and public obedience through a rubric of midcentury police reform known as "professionalism."

Badge Heavy: Race, Gender, and Police Professionalism

Midcentury police officers routinely demonstrated their allegiance to a white supremacist social order rooted in racial segregation and heteropatriarchal morality. Police were both "emotionally and politically" invested in enforcing that social order, as criminologist Jerome Skolnick wrote in his 1966 study of police departments. This, of course, could be generally said of officers across the twentieth century. However, in the postwar period, the officer's commitment to this social order was freshly challenged on multiple fronts. Police felt hemmed in, on one side, by the courts' increasing support for sexual liberalism and civil liberties; and, on the other, by multiplying activist demands for racial equity and police accountability. In these years of mobilizing activisms, police leaders felt pushed on the defensive, and they borrowed the language of civil rights liberalism to declare themselves "the maligned minority," according to one 1963 California report on "police-minority group relations."[23]

The strict enforcement of social hierarchies was both a personal affinity among officers and a politically useful tool for police departments to attract white support. Despite the pervasive sense of police resentment, the LAPD actually enjoyed enthusiastic white support for officers' enforcement of the racist and sexist status quo. In Los Angeles, where twentieth-century urban development was driven by white, Protestant, and Republican interests, the decline of white urban majorities amid the accelerating movement of Black migrants to the city unleashed powerful white demands to protect whiteness by containing Blackness. Given this context, it is reasonable to take literally LAPD chief William Parker's statement in his opening address as chief in 1950 that "Los Angeles is the white spot of the great cities of America today. It is to the advantage of the community that we keep it that way."[24]

As social scientists cycled through midcentury urban police departments in fieldwork across the country, they invariably commented on endemic racism, where a "negative attitude toward Negroes was a norm" and "if a policeman did not subscribe to it . . . he would be somewhat resented by his fellows." As sociologist William Westley found in his investigation of one midwestern department in the 1950s, police officers considered people in the "slums"—and, Westley noted, "for the police, the Negro epitomizes the slum dweller"—as "inherently criminal both culturally and biologically." Policemen claimed that Black people were "lacking in morality, ready to commit a crime." In his work, Westley demonstrated how the police presumption of Black immorality and criminality translated into a presumption of the sexual criminality of Black womanhood: "The nigger women are all whores," one officer told Westley. "They just love crime, they're naturally criminals." Under these conditions, Black people, and Black women specifically, were profoundly vulnerable to police violence. But this rampant racism and sexism was not merely an issue of personal police prejudice. Rather, it was built into the logic and structure of police power. The definitional gendered anti-Blackness of police forces provided a critical pathway for officers to assert broad discretionary authority over rapidly transforming postwar cities.[25]

Police leaders throughout the country presented their officers as the friends and protectors of what one midcentury magazine article on law enforcement called the "Vital Four": man, wife, child, and home. In postwar America, magazines, movies, novels, and all manner of circulating white culture—backed up by discriminatory housing, employment, and public accommodation laws—indicated that the "Vital Four" was a whites-only preserve. A public relations fantasy of postwar policemen, like Sergeant Joe Friday, the television hero of *Dragnet* (which Parker consulted on), presented a force of "ordinary, [white] middle-class Americans, who had no discernible accent, lived in residential suburbs, and . . . relaxed in backyard swimming pools," historian Robert Fogelson writes. Loosened residential restrictions for city workers and boosted wages, combined with artificially low federal mortgage rates in the suburbs, helped to lift rank-and-file officers into a class of "upwardly mobile paraprofessionals," more closely resembling the white middle-class population whose approval they sought. Whether or not the vision of a police patriarch heading up a stable family with a home and a swimming pool matched the rank-and-file officer's material reality, the policeman's racial and class allegiances were clarified in the suburban aspirations of the professional officer. As

Herman Goldstein, a midcentury criminologist who worked with the Chicago Police Department, observed, a white officer would likely view a "Negro march in favor of open housing" as a threat to not only public order but also "the values of the very people upon whom he depends for support in his day-to-day work." One LAPD officer recalled that Black residents in their neighborhoods during this period were "as foreign to most of us as an enclave of Martians." In both aspiration and action, officers demonstrated a rigid commitment to racial segregation and patriarchal sexual morality—what William Turner, a retired FBI agent, called a "turn-back-the-clock ideology" in his popular account of American police.[26]

Police leaders saw the liberal reforms of morals laws, and of criminal laws more generally, as a move to restrict their discretionary authority over public order. California reforms like the *In re Lane* ruling and the revised vagrancy law were tributaries in a powerful force of legal liberalism coursing through American courts across the midcentury. Perhaps most representative of the liberal turn, the Warren Court (1953–1969) heard and validated proliferating arguments for the existence of individual rights to due process and the constitutional obligation of the police to honor these rights. Rulings like *Miranda, Mallory,* and *Escobedo,* which strengthened the rights of the accused in criminal cases, united police leaders and rank-and-file officers alike in a political mobilization nationwide to reframe legal liberalism as an assault on social order and, more important as an attack on the embattled defenders of social order—the police. Law enforcement authorities decried the courts' "civil-rights binge," and Parker lamented that American police work had been "tragically weakened" by a "judicial takeover," which he called a "revolt against legally-constituted authority." He issued a clear rejection of police as civic servants accountable to the law, the courts, and the public they ostensibly served, and fought, instead, to win supreme authority over the cities they policed.[27]

Parker, the LAPD's leader from 1950 until his death in 1966, was at once a creature of and a defining force in the midcentury law enforcement mobilization. He crystallized an influential strain of politics that defined "law" as total police autonomy and "order" as racial segregation and patriarchal moral traditionalism. Parker appealed to white audiences by arguing that his force alone was fighting "to protect the moral reputation of the community." In doing so, he was delivering a promise that he would defend the city's white interests from any, or all, of the agents of racial, sexual, and individual liberalism that he saw circling his men and challenging their authority: the courts, the urban "jungles" that housed a "horde of migratory perpetrators," and the "so-called freedoms in matters of morals leading to . . . our ultimate decline and fall."[28]

LAPD officers under Parker's leadership profitably stoked rising white fears of racial and sexual disorder and the growing revolt against liberalism in order to justify the retrograde authority of their department. An LAPD lieutenant charged that a Black neighborhood in South Los Angeles was "one of the blotches on the picture of Los Angeles as a moral, upright community," a situation that threatened the "morale and morals" of his officers. At a meeting on prostitution in Black neighborhoods, Parker said that "the presence of such lawless elements, despite extreme measures of law enforcement, is frightening." Smearing *In re Lane* as a "Bill of Rights for Prostitutes," he warned that the decriminalization of "promiscuous sexual conduct" would "lead to the demoralization of the force." The "demoralization" of police, in his logic, led directly to "anarchy" and "the destruction of our civilization." "Our way of life cannot survive if we so relax and broaden our laws that almost any individual's standard will conform with them," Parker declared in a keynote speech delivered to the International Association of Chiefs of Police in 1952. In his opposition to the relaxation of morals laws, Parker sounded two notes that were crucial for the nationwide political mobilization of police: the necessity of police authority to secure a decaying moral order and the (sometimes implicit, sometimes explicit) racism and sexism foundational to that moral order.[29]

On a local television program in 1965, Parker delivered perhaps the most explicit claim for police protection of white families against a mythic rising tide of Black criminality: "It's estimated that by 1970, 45 percent of the metropolitan areas of Los Angeles will be Negro," he warned. "If you want any protection for your home and family . . . you're going to have to get in and support a strong police department. If you don't do that, come 1970, God help you." Consolidating the police department's base around white supremacy was a conscious strategy on Parker's part: "From an ethnological point-of-view, Negro, Mexican, and Anglo-Saxon are unscientific breakdowns; they are a fiction," he declared in a 1955 speech. "From a police point-of-view, they are a useful fiction and should be used as long as they remain useful." For the frequently overlapping white audiences who were hostile to both sexual and racial liberalism, Parker was "the white community's savior, their symbol of security," according to Otis Chandler, publisher of the *Los Angeles Times*.[30]

"Professionalism," the watchword of postwar police, was the framework in which police couched their claims to fully autonomous, aggressive police action. Efforts to professionalize municipal police forces through better training and less political cronyism had been under way since the Progressive era. Postwar professionalism, which the LAPD famously pioneered, reflected a historically specific set of police priorities and reforms that—like the "crime-fighting school" of the post-Prohibition era—were generated from internal police leadership. As scholar Edward Escobar writes, two fundamental tenets underlay postwar police professionalism: police autonomy and a "war-on-crime orientation." On its face, police professionalism suggested a neutral improvement of standards, technology, and training in police departments. However, in the context of challenges to police authority— from the courts, from Black residents, and from a diverse assembly of legal and social critics—and in the context of police umbrage in the face of these attacks, police professionalism became a coded appeal to white audiences for strong police authority to enforce a racist and sexist social order with methods the police alone deemed appropriate.[31]

Police professionalism recast policemen as skilled workers enforcing their own expert interpretation of the law, rather than public servants governed by the rule of law. When police leadership presented their rank and file as "professionals," just like lawyers, engineers, or accountants, this posture was freighted with a demand for the right to set the standards by which their performance was evaluated and the freedom to set the terms in which they performed their work. As a "specialist" in crime, a police officer's discretion—rather than criminal due process—became the truest and most legitimate expression of law enforcement. While the criminal system was ostensibly based on the presumption of an individual's innocence until proven guilty, "the policeman believes . . . he has the *ability to distinguish between guilt and innocence*" and he "tends to maintain a presumption of guilt," criminologist Skolnick wrote. "The policeman feels that most trials are a waste of taxpayers' money since, as one law enforcement spokesman put it, 'We do not charge innocent [people].'" By affirming their "professional" skills to accurately detect criminals, then, midcentury police officers laid a claim to operate according to their own rules and standards.[32]

Police claims to professionalism did not just manifest in occupational orientation and attitude, but also in material police practices. Arrests were a key measure of "professionalized" police forces. Parker established what historian Martin Schiesl calls a "very arrest-conscious department," and LAPD officers were held to "performance standards," which meant that midcentury police officers effectively had arrest quotas they were expected to fulfill. In the data-driven imperatives of professional police departments, police administrators judged the "efficiency" of a division by calculating "cleared cases," which were merely the numbers of interrogations and arrests. Cleared cases did not measure crimes solved, convictions obtained, or even charges ultimately filed against a suspect; nor did they distinguish between crimes reported by citizen complainants and police complainants, the primary instigators of morals charges. For example, a police officer could report that he apprehended a Black woman on sexual suspicion, and regardless of whether he filed a charge against her, or whether her charge held up in court, this arrest would count as a "cleared" morals case, effectively juking the crime rate in Black neighborhoods. "It is very easy to clear cases with mass round-ups and tissue-thin arrests," one investigator affiliated with the Southern California chapter of the American Civil Liberties Union (ACLU) noted.[33]

The professional imperative to make arrests enforced prevailing racist and sexist hierarchies and justified unequal police practices in Black neighborhoods. In the early 1960s, the citywide average for cleared cases was approximately one-third; however, in divisions with the heaviest concentration of Black residents, the percentage was over one-half. In other words, as the ACLU-affiliated investigator noted, "the police make more arrests in the ghetto on a percentage basis." This "arrest-conscious" strategy at once created and fulfilled the white prophecy of Black criminality and police "efficiency." Through clearance rates, police leaders could present a portrait of professional officers diligently attacking the "crime problem" in Black neighborhoods—a vision sustained in practice by officers' illegal rousts, arbitrary interrogations, and evasion of due process principles. These arrest statistics were also useful in deflecting challenges to police authority: Parker dismissed "criticism of the police by certain minority groups" as a ruse to "distract attention from the high incidence of criminal activity within those groups."[34]

Significantly, police officers also believed that in order to fulfill their duties, they needed to be "badge heavy" in Black neighborhoods. Criminologist James Q. Wilson wrote in 1968 that "the patrolman believes *with considerable justification* that teenagers, Negroes, and lower-income persons commit a disproportionate share of all reported crimes" and that police officers would consider themselves "derelict in their duty if they did not treat such persons with suspicion, routinely question them on the street, and detain them for longer questioning if a crime has occurred in the area." This racist worldview often meant that violent and aggressive police practices in Black neighborhoods were justified as an occupational norm. Police officers interpreted their degraded vision of Blackness as a mandate—indeed, as a professional requirement—to "put the fear of God into" Black people in order to win compliance. As one officer told Westley, "In the white districts you got to treat people psychologically but in the central district [the "slum area mostly populated by Negroes"] you have to use a rougher voice and show more authority because they don't understand."[35]

Because officers believed their work required the unstinting obedience of Black residents, they were acutely sensitive to everyday gestures of disrespect, including "affronts" such as requesting police identification or a reason for interrogation or arrest. In the absence of voluntary submission, the tenets of professionalization—autonomy and a "war on crime" orientation—authorized officers to seize it by force. One police officer in Westley's study argued that "the use of force is called for when the policeman is treated in a derogatory fashion": "You don't have to have some colored woman spit at you and take it," he explained by way of example. The presence of an audience—where officers were in danger of "losing face"—was also a powerful inducement to police brutality in tense encounters where officers believed they needed to assert their power when challenged on city streets, especially in Black neighborhoods. Rather than simply deploying brutality, as officers might have done before World War II, they now had the framework of professionalism in which to expect and demand "respect" from their targets.[36]

A paradox emerged: as the status of police departments across the nation steadily rose among white audiences, with the premier "professional" force in Los Angeles leading the charge, police officers themselves felt persecuted, bitter, and disrespected by the communities they were charged with patrolling. After interviewing police officers across the country, journalist Paul Jacobs reported that there was "a sense of crisis in the police world, a feeling that . . . they are surrounded by enemies at a time when they are the last bulwark of civilization." In the context of legal liberalism and civil rights activism, police officers felt great umbrage at the very moment their star was rising as providers of "professional" service.[37]

Morals law enforcement played a peculiar dual role in the professionalization of police. Officers both detested the work of morals policing and depended on these laws to sustain a public image of aggressive "full enforcement" in targeted neighborhoods. On one hand, as a 1955 study, "The Negro and the Police in Los Angeles," noted, the requirement to "enforce unpopular laws" aggravated officers' occupational resentment. The demand for police "efficiency" in prostitution enforcement created "a type of 'professional' police practice in which the concern for legality is minimal," Skolnick wrote. Given this thankless task, it was not surprising, he continued, "to find police demanding working conditions from the courts to lighten their burden" and demonstrating hostility toward "due process principles in their attempt to enforce legal morality." However, as legal scholar Wayne LaFave argued in a 1962 article, if police were determined to win submission to their authority from targeted populations and maintain a public image of aggressive enforcement, morals misdemeanors provided a sure route to achieve both objectives.[38]

Black women were extremely vulnerable to the umbrage of "professional" police forces. Consider the case of Treyola Terry. In September 1961 Terry, a public school teacher, was shopping for a stroller for her son in South Los Angeles when she noticed two white men "leer" at her from their car. The men, plainclothes officers A. L. Lamoreaux and J. L. Williams, apprehended Terry because she was observed in an area "frequented by prostitutes" wearing "tight-fitting" trousers and high-heeled shoes. Without first stopping for an interrogation, the plainclothes men "rushed up to" Terry, flashed a badge quickly before putting it away, and said, "We are police officers, come with us." Terrified, Terry did not believe they were police—she later said they looked like "thugs"—and she thought she was being abducted. As Terry struggled to get away from the men, she grasped onto the antenna of a nearby parked car, screaming and pleading for help. The fight attracted a crowd of thirty bystanders. One woman yelled, "Help that girl!" As an audience gathered, the officers "twisted both of [Terry's] arms behind her back," cuffed her, and choked her as they pushed her into the back of their car.[39]

Terry's experience was not particularly unusual in the longer history of morals enforcement in Los Angeles, or urban policing generally. However, what distinguished this case was the operation of "professionalism" in the LAPD's defense of itself in the complaint process that ensued. The demands of police professionalism could spur officers to escalate their violence. But it also provided a shield to protect officers from accountability for the violence they committed. To deflect the amplifying challenges to police action during this period—including both organized protest and the swift assembly of on-the-ground bystanders—postwar police departments introduced internal investigative departments to check officers' conduct. Internal discipline divisions were more a victory for, than a concession from, police departments. Parker's Internal Affairs Division was a move to avoid citizen police review boards—maligned by national police leadership as a Communist front—that activists began to demand (and, in Philadelphia, successfully created). Many victims of police brutality mistrusted the internal investigations of police departments, and with good cause. In 1956 Marie Wade, a Black woman, was given a choice of jail time or paying a fine after she was found guilty of filing a "false report" with the LAPD's Internal Affairs Committee that a motorcycle officer "had beaten her about the head with his flashlight." Nevertheless, these internal checks bolstered the image of a disciplined, professional police force, and police leaders regularly cited the availability of such channels of complaint in order to quell public protest.[40]

Terry opted to avail herself of these channels to make her complaint. At the same time, however, she also hired a lawyer and brought her story to the local chapter of the National Association for the Advancement of Colored People (NAACP), which likely took on her case because, as one sympathetic police commissioner observed, Terry "is a very nice-appearing woman with a very cultured look and smile and certainly her speech and voice reflect considerable training." These combined pressures pushed the LAPD to produce a lengthy investigative report. In a distinct midcentury touch that showcases the obsession with white middle-class optics that characterized Parker's "professional" department, one point of contention between Terry and the LAPD revolved around the state of the officers' appearance: while Terry charged that the men who apprehended her were "shabbily attired, not wearing neckties," the police investigation claimed "that the officers were neatly dressed, wearing white shirts and ties." Ultimately the report concluded that the officers "conducted themselves properly." The report added that because Terry "unfortunately became so highly emotional [she] caused the incident under consideration." Either to indicate the diligence the police undertook in their internal investigation or to highlight the extraordinary waste of time this process represented, Parker noted at the close of the report that "this investigation consumed" over 130 man-hours. Parker submitted his report to the Board of Police Commissioners (BOPC)—the appointed five-person body serving as the final arbiter of internal LAPD discipline—which rubber-stamped its approval.[41]

Days after the BOPC signed off on the report, the Los Angeles NAACP turned over Terry's case, along with nine others—six of which had already been investigated by the LAPD—to the Black *Los Angeles Herald-Dispatch*. The story ran under the headline, "Trend Shows Police Brutality Abuses and Terrorizing Directed to Afro-American Women." Los Angeles police leadership were apoplectic. The BOPC sent a fuming letter to Roy Wilkins, executive director of the national NAACP, chastising the local chapter for circulating "a libelous and provocative report . . . impeditive of the progress towards improved race relations." In multiple inflamed responses, LAPD officials emphasized the department's professionalism and "exemplary level of discipline" to delegitimize the NAACP's charges. One LAPD internal investigator, quoted in the *Los Angeles Times*, argued, "If the NAACP has complaints, there are lots of places it can take them," including the BOPC.[42]

Through professionalism, police laid their claim to unquestioned autonomy and authority. In this way, the ongoing violence of police operations in Black neighborhoods was deemed "professional" and justified as "effective." LAPD officers were both empowered to practice and shielded from accountability for the "abuse and terror directed to Afro-American women." As journalist Paul Jacobs wrote of the LAPD, "A primary source of the department's inadequacy [to deal with racial tensions] is precisely the set of qualities of which it is so proud." However, as the showdown between Treyola Terry, organized activists, and police leadership suggests, Black residents were mobilizing to fight the "professional" tactics of American police.[43]

Black Protest and the Racial Politics of Morals Enforcement

As Black people came to constitute a larger percentage of the American urban population, a new generation of Black residents experienced an enduring twentieth-century dynamic: the simultaneous violent neglect and aggressive policing of their neighborhoods. This dynamic, as in earlier decades, was especially visible in the discretionary enforcement of morals laws. The "Negro districts" to which Black people were confined by vigilant police—the frontline enforcers of racial segregation—served as the city's vice playgrounds for slumming white men, or so-called white hunters. But even as police permitted vice activities in Black neighborhoods at their discretion, they also disproportionately targeted Black people for morals arrests (gambling for men and sex offenses for women in these years). "Much of the commercialized vice is foisted upon the colored community by virtue of the larger community's willingness to permit such activities to flourish there," one police manual noted in 1947. Los Angeles police played a crucial role in buttressing the white myth of Black immorality and criminality, especially through the enduring practice of funneling vice to the city's segregated Black neighborhoods. This created a vicious tautology: police restricted vice to Black neighborhoods because of prevailing racist beliefs about the deviance of Blackness; and because vice was pushed into Black neighborhoods, these were believed to be the primary sites of lawbreaking.[44]

For Black residents, the racial discrimination in morals enforcement was an especially combustible issue because it was made possible by, and reflected, a meshwork of urban oppression: residential segregation, racist myths of Black criminality and hypersexuality, and the unequal delivery of state goods, including police predation rather than protection. Unequal police practices were not new to Black neighborhoods, but as California morals laws relaxed during this period of legal liberalism, the racial inequality of morals law enforcement was exacerbated and a new generation of residents rose up to fight back.

The decriminalization of white women presumed to be engaging in nonmarital straight sex was a visible legal trend in the years surrounding the *In re Lane* ruling. White women in Los Angeles were granted an unprecedented measure of sexual freedom from the law. Arrest statistics after the *In re Lane* ruling and the vagrancy statute revision are especially illustrative of this shift: between 1961 and 1962, white women's arrests dropped by 12 percent, while Black women's arrests rose 18 percent. One Hollywood sheriff explained to a *Los Angeles Times* reporter that "today's liberal judicial interpretations" shielded white women from legal punishment. To Black residents, the conspicuous removal of white women from police officers' list of sexually profiled women threw the racial disparities in morals enforcement into sharp relief. "An investigation of any neighborhood, regardless of its racial complexion, will disclose prostitution in some form," a Black community leader and short-lived member of the Police Commission protested. "To point out the [Black] district as a vice area because colored people live there, without naming other sections where similar conditions exist, seems biased to me and designed to discredit Negroes."[45]

Another result of the racial disparities in morals enforcement was especially infuriating to Black residents: white men enjoyed license to come to Black neighborhoods to solicit Black women simply "because they happen to be walking in their own neighborhood," a writer for the *Los Angeles Sentinel*, a Black newspaper, fumed. A chorus of Black journalists and residents protested that "invading hordes of Caucasian motorists" trolled Black city streets nightly to "boldly accost women of all ages [and] stations of life." They zeroed in on the hypocrisy of white men, "well clad, driving expensive automobiles" in Black neighborhoods, "cruising for dates" during a period of stark urban racial segregation—a time when, as one LAPD officer recalled, "Black people could not venture" into the white districts of the city "without a strongly documented purpose." The spatial affront of Black residential exclusion, racially segregated vice, and cruising white hunters was a problem for Black people living in cities across the country. In an article on a Black neighborhood dubbed "the land of the white hunter" by the newspaper, a resident was quoted linking restrictive housing with vice segregation: "What we do resent . . . is the white man who drives here under the cover of darkness to solicit women, who if they moved next door to him would see him sell his house the next day." To Black residents, police officers were not so different from white hunters: both presumed that any Black woman they saw walking in her neighborhood—like Treyola Terry, the schoolteacher—was engaged in commercial sex (see figure 3.1).[46]

During the early 1960s, many women brought to local chapters of the NAACP and the ACLU their experiences of being arrested on morals charges simply because they were on city streets. One such woman was Roxie Williams, who was arrested after she sought police protection from white men who solicited her and loitered outside her home. Williams, a working mother, stated that she was sitting in her parked car outside her home when two white men approached her. "One of the men put his head into the car and said, 'What about it, baby?'" Frightened, she "jumped out of the car," ran into her house, and called the police. When officers arrived twenty minutes later, the white men were still stalking outside her home. Williams pointed them out to the police. "The police officers ignored me and talked in a friendly manner with the Caucasians," she reported. When Williams tried to tell the police officers that the white men had accosted her, Officer Schwiezer responded, "If you don't shut up, I'll kick your ass." Then, "without warning," he placed Williams under arrest for a morals misdemeanor and ordered her into the back of the squad car. As the officer got ready to take Williams to the station for booking, he tepidly cautioned the white men, "You guys get out of here and don't be caught down here anymore." Williams pressed her case to trial and was ultimately found not guilty, but she wished she "had had the money to hire an attorney" to sue for false arrest. The police, Williams testified, were going to have to "change their attitude," because "the younger generation is not going to tolerate what we took." The vulnerability of Black women to unchecked police action

FIGURE 3.1 The conspicuous deepening of the racial inequity in sexual policing outraged Black residents. Police and white hunters alike presumed that any Black woman they saw walking in her neighborhood was engaged in commercial sex. Courtesy of Russ Marshall, 1965.

highlighted to a new generation the exposure of all Black residents to arbitrary arrest and violence.[47]

In previous decades, Black people protested with appeals to their respectability and through good-faith requests to police leaders for dignity and equity in morals enforcement. This strain of activism did not disappear in the midcentury. Particularly during these years of such pitched political intensity, when critics of the police were smeared as criminals themselves, Black protesters were careful to frame their critiques in a way to preempt white rejoinders of Black criminality and licentiousness. When residents dared to publicly take on the delicate matter of "Black prostitution" in a political culture in which the myth of Black hypersexuality prevailed, many were compelled in their negotiations with white authorities to pledge their commitment to middle-class sexual morality—and, through this respectability, to justify safe and dignified policing in their neighborhood.[48]

On the more conservative end of the spectrum of Black protest politics, Black Los Angeles businessmen and professionals joined respectability politics with a successful bid for tougher morals law penalties targeting Black women. In 1960 the Council of Organizations against Vice (COAV) was formed, headed up by real estate broker Cecil B. Murrell. Members allied with police officers and mobilized for aggressive police action against Black women suspected of engaging in prostitution—sacrificing, in effect, the poorest members of their community in an effort to win better police protection for themselves and their class, and to preserve their own patriarchal authority within the Black community. Unlike activists in the NAACP, ACLU, and many other mainstream organizations at the time, COAV members had "no complaint about police enforcement" in their neighborhood, as one insurance executive stated at a meeting. COAV worked with police leaders and city council members to push through amendments to the municipal ordinances for sex offenses, increasing the fines and lengthening jail sentences for convicted women. While sentencing was technically beyond the scope of police authority, these amendments were intended to help the police "make it tough on prostitutes," according to Laynard Holloman, a COAV member. COAV members won their amendments, but it was a short-lived victory: six months later, *In re Lane* struck down the local ordinances, punitive amendments and all.[49]

While COAV's efforts were ultimately voided, the members' collaboration with city councilmen and police leadership to bolster the sexual criminalization of Black women exposed the outer limits of cooperation with law enforcement that Black residents were willing to tolerate in this period.

Indeed, COAV members met resistance within the Black neighborhoods they sought to "clean up." Amid the intensifying pitch of the civil rights movement, Black people expanded the repertoire of tactics they employed to protest vice in their neighborhood while affirming the dignity, respect, and due process to which all residents were entitled. Many Black residents rejected COAV's narrow version of respectability politics, which pitted "decent" women against "harlots" in a dubious pursuit of more police and more arrests in Black neighborhoods. Black residents—both individually and through affiliations with multiple organizations, including the active chapter of the Los Angeles NAACP—argued that the "poor, unorganized, social outcast" Black woman was not the enemy of Black residents: her treatment at the hands of brutal policemen was bound up with the treatment of all Black women and, indeed, all Black people. The *Sentinel* editorial board argued that police officers targeted poor Black women instead of white hunters because the Black women, and members of the Black community in general, were "easier to slap around"—and, as an extra bonus, the LAPD could also "run up big arrest statistics that way" to further justify the criminalization of Blackness.[50]

An important shift was taking place. In the early 1960s the enduring register of respectability protest clashed with an emboldened brand of resistance as residents directly challenged both the social license of white hunters and the political license of discriminatory police. Early signs of public fracture in the Black politics of morals enforcement emerged at an open meeting organized by COAV in December 1960. A packed auditorium had listened to a lineup of authorities speak: a judge, a prosecutor, a police officer, and a state assemblyman. But when attendees discovered that they would not be allowed to ask the speakers questions, the "meeting was tossed into an uproar": "Either we talk or we go home," one woman demanded before she headed over to join the countermeeting assembling in the foyer. The controversy over the "gag rule"—and the impatience to directly address the officials present—indexed both the audience's rejection of COAV's efforts to run a gagged meeting with state authorities and without resident input, and their rising frustration at the evasions and inaction of law enforcement. Some residents were especially incensed at COAV's cooperative relationship with law enforcement authorities to win greater punishment for Black women. COAV "is taking a rather shortsighted view in thinking that stiffer fines and sentences are the answer" to vice in Black neighborhoods, the *Sentinel* editors wrote after the meeting. Thomas Neusom, a lawyer affiliated with the Los Angeles chapter of the NAACP and chairman of the law enforcement section of the United Civil Rights Committee, challenged COAV members to consider "the danger of unrestricted police activity in any community."[51]

Neusom's warnings about "unrestricted" police activity in the wake of Black calls for tough policing were well founded. Two months after COAV was formed, police responded with "night raids" that exclusively targeted Black women. In one night, over twenty women were arrested. These raids were part of a citywide trend: law enforcement authorities responded to Black frustration over the racial inequity in morals enforcement with vice crackdowns on Black people in their neighborhoods. As the COAV episode illustrates, Black residents could most effectively exert influence over police practices when they demanded more police action against Black people. However, as the racial disparity of sexual policing hardened in the early 1960s, protesters amped up their critiques against police. They began delivering public indictments of the fundamental practice of morals enforcement itself.[52]

Some Black activists challenged the legality and basic purpose of police vice raids. In a letter to the Los Angeles sheriff, the Police Malpractice Committee of the Los Angeles chapter of the Congress of Racial Equality issued a measured warning to law enforcement on the eve of a "promised crackdown on vice," insisting that "people must be treated with full regard to their rights as citizens, and their possible guilt shall be established through the due processes of law—and not in the streets of Los Angeles." And at a rally in 1964, protesters "packed the Southern Baptist Church" to address local vice conditions. As the *Los Angeles People's World* reported, the crowd "was not appeased" by the crackdown that was taking place in their neighborhood. People demanded to know "why the conditions had been allowed to exist" in the first place, and while general outrage was directed at the presence of vice, many speakers vented their anger that "basic economic and social problems . . . are being evaded" by city authorities.[53]

As Black uprisings began spreading across the nation's urban map, observers worried that the police-sanctioned racial inequity in morals policing was likely kindling for furious conflagrations in Black neighborhoods. The *Los Angeles Times*, the voice of white, business-aligned residents, warily turned its gaze to the "highly volatile situation" in Black neighborhoods: "Because of the inter-racial nature of this vice problem, an explosive situation could be developing," one journalist reported. "Los Angeles is one of the few major cities in the nation that have kept race violence from spilling onto the streets. But there are bitter people in the [predominantly Black]

West Adams district today." In 1964 Mrs. John Richardson—a white property owner who inherited a duplex her parents had purchased in South Los Angeles in 1934 "while the area was a white neighborhood"—wrote a concerned letter to Kenneth Hahn, her county supervisor. Watching the rapidly deteriorating "reputation" of the neighborhood, Richardson sounded a note of alarm, not only because of her increasing property taxes but also because of the looming threat she saw of a "bad race riot" if vice conditions persisted apace.[54]

In 1964 Hahn was up for reelection. Particularly in election years, authorities dreaded public uproar over vice. During these years, the anxiety about losing the confidence of white property owners like Richardson was compounded by these rising fears of a "bad race riot." Hahn convened law enforcement representatives from the district attorney's and the county sheriff's offices to discuss the Black neighborhood in which Richardson owned property along Central Avenue, sitting roughly halfway between COAV's hub of operations west of downtown and Watts farther south. At this meeting, the undersheriff informed the authorities that "we have intelligence reports" indicating that "school people, mothers, and other citizens in the area" were planning "public demonstrations" to protest the presence of vice and the way it was policed (or not) in their neighborhood. The undersheriff "pointed out the undesirability to all concerned of such demonstrations." When Hahn flexed his considerable muscle from the county board of supervisors to try to preempt these protests, he drew from a well-worn playbook among local authorities, calling for more vice raids and more arrests in Black neighborhoods. By exploiting the political currency of police vice raids targeting Black residents, Hahn was at once reinscribing the presumed criminality of Black people and purporting to improve conditions in Black neighborhoods. He hoped the raids would appeal to political constituencies that might otherwise be opposed: residents, both Black and white, who were glad to see authorities at last taking action after decades of police neglect; and white voters who agreed that the criminalization of Blackness was a necessary feature of well-ordered urban governance and applauded tougher policing of Black people.[55]

In April 1964 Hahn declared his "all-out war against narcotics and open prostitution" with mass roundups of Black residents. But warning signs indicated that the heightened tension between Black people and police might shape residents' reaction to this round of crackdowns. One confrontation between sheriff's officers and Black people in the months leading up to Hahn's "all-out war" indicated that some Black people were increasingly willing to physically assert their denial of the legitimacy and value of morals policing.[56]

One night in September 1963, plainclothes sergeant John Barwicki lingered on the corner of Central Avenue and Sixty-Seventh Street, where he baited two women—Gloria, an unemployed waitress, and another unknown woman ("Suspect #3")—to offer him sex for money. "After grasping both suspects by the arms," Barwicki walked them toward his unmarked car. At this point, "approximately 20 unidentified male Negroes . . . began crowding around blocking the sidewalk," according to the sheriff's report. Barwicki was trying to push through the gathering audience when James, an unemployed Black cook, called out, "That blue-eyed white man is mistreating those women. Make him turn those women loose." As James and other men in the group pushed and distracted Barwicki, both women "wrenched free" and ran down the street. James held Barwicki back as the officer tried to go after the women. When Barwicki managed to pull out his gun, James gave chase. Backup swiftly arrived, and Barwicki was joined by Deputy Kenneth Jones; together the officers cornered James inside a nearby hotel: "Necessary force was used to restrain him." While the officers were beating James, another nearby deputy caught up to Gloria, cuffed her, and charged her with disorderly conduct. Suspect #3, however, got away. The sheriff's department later recorded—in highly mediated language—that James, dazed and battered after the ordeal, said, "I knew you were a sheriff and I knew that the girls were prostitutes, but I didn't want to see you arrest them. I thought those other guys would help me, but it didn't work out that way." By late 1963, bold residents started to push back when police arrested Black women off the street—an index of frustration that was coming to a boil.[57]

The weekend that Hahn launched his vice raid in April 1964 coincided with a series of violent confrontations between police and Black people. At least three clashes erupted in instances in which vice was otherwise absent. Yet "all three incidents," the *Los Angeles Times* observed, "occurred in the same area where shortly after midnight deputy sheriffs conducted vice raids that resulted in 110 arrests." In each confrontation, as police moved in to handcuff men, "a crowd closed in," as the *Los Angeles Sentinel* reported, and people disrupted an arrest by throwing rocks and bricks or obstructed the arrest by chasing the officers, tripping them, or trying to "wrestle the handcuffed prisoner from the officers." When the school-community coordinator at a local high school delivered his response to the weekend battles at a "somber" city hall press conference the following Monday, the racial inequity of morals enforcement was the first grievance he listed. The *Los Angeles Sentinel* reported that he spoke the "consensus of the community": "The climate of today is an explosive one. The [community] knows that vice, prostitution and gambling are participated in by other communities which are overlooked by the police. [So] they respond explosively when the vice squad raids Central Los Angeles."[58]

For decades, Black residents' serious grievances of police disrespect, harassment, abuse, and murder were regularly dismissed, denied, ignored, or belittled, or the residents were treated to even more doses of the hostile, racist policing that outraged people in the first place. The August 1965 uprising in the Watts neighborhood did not involve morals enforcement. Rather, it was ignited by routine stops for alleged traffic infractions (in this case, by the California Highway Patrol), yet another source of police harassment and Black frustration. However, the many confrontations between police and Black people that punctuated the months leading up to the Watts uprising demonstrate that the sexual policing of Black women was a major and underappreciated factor in the violence. The racially unequal enforcement of morals laws was a substantial motor of police power and Black anger.[59]

· · · · · ·

In the aftermath of the Watts uprising, Los Angeles politicians and law enforcement authorities reaffirmed their investment in the aggressive morals policing that had in part triggered the Black rebellion in the first place. Significantly, these officials pointed to *In re Lane* and liberalizing morals laws as a key source of racial disorder. In the fall of 1965, just weeks after Watts, Los Angeles county supervisor Warren Dorn floated a proposal to place a "decency amendment" on the statewide ballot that would "restore local determination over laws on crimes which were taken away in 1961 by the California Supreme Court." Los Angeles district attorney Evelle Younger endorsed the Dorn amendment, and then, by fusing relaxing morals laws and white fears of Black crime, he made his case for mass morals policing in Black neighborhoods: the "recent riots have . . . supplied [the] proof," he argued, that Los Angeles needed "a return to the law as it was prior to the Carol Lane decision." By linking the Watts uprising with a demand for tougher morals laws, the district attorney's call for stricter morals enforcement was not intended as an effort to recriminalize white women's nonmarital sexual practices. It was, rather, an effort to double down on the criminalization of "frightening" residents in Black neighborhoods, and specifically the sexual criminalization Black women.[60]

Dorn eventually withdrew support for his own "decency amendment," citing his willingness to work with the state assembly to restore local police authority. His detractors claimed that the amendment was an opportunistic stunt to win political notoriety and higher political office. But regardless of intent, the proposal to nullify *In re Lane* and the enthusiastic endorsement it received from Los Angeles law enforcement authorities indicated the powerful traction of white myths of Black sexual criminality, and signaled that morals policing would continue to be central to white crime politics targeting Black neighborhoods. Indeed, when Ronald Reagan gave his first gubernatorial message to the state legislature in 1967, he outlined a six-step agenda in launching his war on crime. Returning "lawmaking authority over vice to cities and counties" was the first item on his list.[61]

The social construction of women's moral crime underwent a profound change in these years. White women's nonmarital straight sexual practices were still considered immature, abnormal, or unhealthy—but in a marked contrast to the first half of the twentieth century, they were not necessarily considered criminal, and state intervention was a diminishing police priority. While Black women's presumed sexual practices were formerly treated to erratic and ambivalent (though nevertheless violent and disproportionate) police action, their sexual practices increasingly supplanted white women's as the presumed major threat to urban social order. As white women began to gain greater legal freedom and sexual privacy by the mid-1960s, Black women were subject to intensifying policing.

The freshly recalibrated racial logics of sexual policing consolidated around the notion that mass morals misdemeanor arrests in Black neighborhoods were an important way to contain Black violence specifically, and Black people generally. This narrative provided a key political justification for law enforcement authorities to win expanded discretionary police powers in the face of liberal due process restraints. Throughout the late 1960s and 1970s, the law enforcement lessons of mid-1960s Los Angeles proved to be foundational for the criminological theory of "broken windows" policing. This highly discretionary and racist police practice of targeting low-level, behavioral misdemeanors as a technique to prevent larger-order crimes and exert control over marginalized communities would contribute tremendous intellectual energy to the wars on crime and drugs in the early 1980s. The sexual policing of Black women would become a crucial testing site for this law enforcement project, as it had been in mid-century Los Angeles.

4 Boston: The Place Is Gone!
Policing Black Women to Redevelop Downtown

In February 1975 Kevin White, Boston's young, ambitious mayor, took a tour of the Combat Zone. Just one block from the arboreal serenity of the Boston Common, the Combat Zone was a pulsing, neon-lit, five-acre stretch of bars and nude dancing clubs, crammed with peep shows, pornographic bookstores, and movies theaters beaming X-rated CinemaScope films on giant screens. The mayor and his entourage cruised down shrieking Washington Street alongside titillated businessmen, suburban would-be swingers, and moonstruck local teens. White dancers in elaborate, feathered costumes idled outside, shivering as the sweat from their last act dried in the icy Atlantic air. The Naked i Cabaret's signature sign flashed above their heads: neon legs arrayed in a semicircle like a lotus blossom, frenetically splitting open and closing up, the slit of an eye peering out from the center of the legs. Washington Street spilled into LaGrange Street, a rusty, pockmarked alley, the nightly home to a crush of commercial sex and drunken brawls. The sexual entertainment on offer in the Combat Zone posed both a problem and a possibility for Boston authorities.[1]

The city had only itself to blame for the Combat Zone, the unintended byproduct of an enormous urban renewal project in the mid-1960s. After midcentury city planners razed the honky-tonks and burlesque theaters in "good old Scollay Square" to make way for the brutalist Government Center complex that crowned Washington Street, new and—thanks to a series of equivocal Supreme Court obscenity rulings—more sexually explicit entertainment genres sprang up a few blocks to the south on lower Washington and rapidly proliferated.[2]

Sexual entertainment districts like the Combat Zone compounded a growing list of problems that plagued the entire aging Northeast urban corridor: dwindling tax revenues, inflating expenditures, deteriorating infrastructure, worsening Black poverty, and brewing white resentment. Newspapers issued dire prognoses of Boston: it was "a sick city" and "dying on the vine." By allegedly degrading the city's reputation, and worse yet, prime downtown property values, the Combat Zone delivered the final

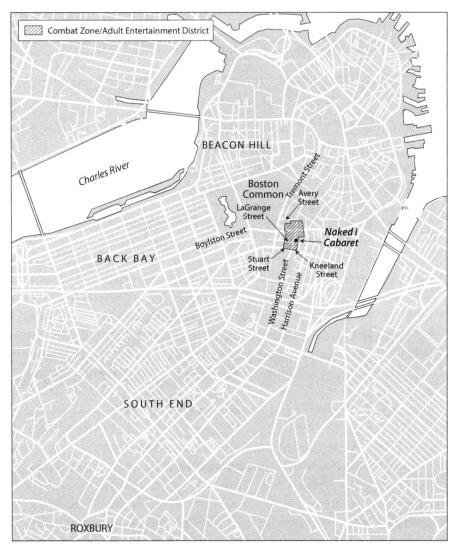

MAP 4.1 Downtown Boston, ca. 1975.

insult to Boston's injuries in the 1970s. Whatever bright optimism had buoyed the "New Boston" urban planning initiatives at midcentury had curdled in the austerity that characterized the new decade.[3]

Mayor Kevin White faced mounting civic pressure to reckon with the "economic and moral decline" in the Combat Zone. At the turn of the 1970s, he and his city managers had to confront their troublesome downtown district without the public funding or political will to push through the huge "bulldozer" urban renewal projects of the early 1960s. But they also recognized that the city's "RED areas," or restaurant, entertainment, and drinking areas (in which the Combat Zone was squarely located), were a badly needed "shot in the arm of Boston's economy," as one journalist for the *Back Bay Ledger-Beacon Hill Times* wrote in 1972, and were crucial to "the drive to persuade suburbanites to spend more money in the city."[4]

White sought a cheaper approach to stem the rising tide of sexual commerce while at the same time nurturing a "safe, profitable, and vibrant" entertainment district, which, as a *Boston Globe* journalist observed, "a convention city demands." In 1974 the Boston Redevelopment Authority (BRA), the city's planning agency, threaded this tricky political needle by rezoning this downtown area specifically for adult entertainment—officially renaming it the Adult Entertainment District (AED)—and forbidding such business everywhere else. Planners spruced up the AED by installing fresh signage and planting trees, and the BRA pledged $2 million in additional redevelopment funds for more changes to come. In establishing the AED, the aims of city hall and the BRA had been clear from the start: to contain urban sexual commerce and attract consumer spending dollars and investment capital.[5]

To both supporters and detractors, the AED seemed to be a permissive liberal solution that bucked the city's notoriously puritanical tradition. City authorities and planners framed the district in turns—sometimes by the same boosters—as a cosmopolitan tolerance of modern sexual entertainment and a necessary first step in halting the growth of the same. However, authorities set hard limits on what they were willing to tolerate in the AED experiment: Black women would not be welcome as the Combat Zone was renovated from urban blight to profitable nightspot.

One telling downtown encounter during White's conspicuously "incognito" tour of the Combat Zone—now the freshly minted AED—in 1975 illustrated the centrality of race to the AED project. The mayor's excursion was an election-year junket to show Boston voters that the AED experiment was working. At the Two O'Clock Lounge, White, accompanied by several city hall aides and a reporter, watched "a statuesque blond woman in a feather shawl . . . strutting to brassy soul music." After visiting a few more bars, the mayor appraised his visit to the AED. "You know, my idea of a city has room for these places," he said. "I don't condone everything that goes on here, but if they don't disturb the theaters or residential areas, what harm are they doing?" One snag, however, interrupted the entourage's night out. While the men were walking to another bar, White was approached by "a young, black woman in yellow knickers and feathered hat."

Throughout the evening, white dancers inside the bars had joined the mayor's group, chatting and hustling for drinks—violations of the city's liquor license—and the mayor had not complained. In fact, he had even remarked, "These girls seem like good people." But outside, as the women changed from blond to Black, the mayor's live-and-let-live demeanor soured. "At least it's not like that [here] . . . the way it is in New York," White grumbled to his city manager. "Mayor, it's worse," his manager replied. Blackness threw the limits of the sexual liberalism embedded in the AED project into sharp relief: city officials were warming to the possibilities of white adult entertainment, but the urban experiment consistently rested on principles of racial segregation and racist policing.[6]

Coding the revamped Combat Zone as "safe" and appealing to visitors from the suburbs, city planners implicitly suggested that a successful adult entertainment district was intended to be zoned for whiteness. Indeed, one crucial impetus for redeveloping the downtown district was the increasing visibility of Black women in it. As Black economic isolation, discriminatory practices citywide, and the changing spatial dynamics of interracial sexual commerce drew increasing numbers of Black women onto Combat Zone streets, the presence of Black women in formerly white downtown spaces ignited a powerful narrative linking race, sex, and violence. Black women became oversignified with sexual deviance and violent criminality amid the urban crisis. White residents and business owners worried that Black women would derail redevelopment projects designed to return white capital to the economically ailing city. Their mounting panic translated into stepped-up demands for tough policing—often issued from the same liberal supporters of the AED.

Boston Police Department (BPD) leaders argued that they had a role to play in urban politicians' plans for economic recovery, which depended on the white perception of a crime-free downtown. BPD manager William Bratton, who headed up an experimental program in the mid-1970s targeting street crime in downtown neighborhoods "threatened with decay and destruction," argued that "with crime declining, development could begin." In a city riven by racist violence and animated by renewed challenges to police discretion, officers identified morals policing as their pathway to power. Through the sexual policing of Black women, the separate goals of political officials and law enforcement authorities—to redevelop downtown Boston and to secure urban authority, respectively—united.[7]

But the BPD in the mid-1970s was not led by a proud reactionary like the Los Angeles Police Department's Chief William Parker. Indeed, this turning point in Boston's policing tactics unfolded during a moment of concerted liberal reform. Even as the BPD advanced the first substantial wave of racial inclusion for officers of color, these reforms did not disrupt the consolidation of police authority. On the contrary, reform helped the BPD diversify its repertoire and agents of urban repression and spatial banishment.[8]

The white panic over Black women's presence in the historically white downtown sparked a realignment of urban capital and local police that delivered Boston—and cities like it nationwide—to the modern era of gentrification; violent, if racially inclusive, policing; and Black criminalization and spatial banishment. The city's bid to win private capital depended on the deployment of state force targeting sexually profiled Black women to make the city an attractive investment and, ultimately, to implement a new urban economic order organized around private investment capital, white home ownership, and downtown commercial entertainment. Boston's history restores the importance of racist and sexist segregation to early gentrification efforts within a political context of sexual and racial liberalism and police reform. White economic security, personal safety, and, to a certain extent, sexual freedom were realized through the constriction of Black women's mobility on city streets.[9]

Making Downtown White

The population shifts that had so alarmed white Los Angelenos, and which Parker had so profitably exploited—whites seizing on cheap federal mortgages in the racially restricted suburbs and Black people locked into cities—were especially pronounced in Boston. After World War II, white homeowners and businesses fled the deteriorating postindustrial hubs of the Northeast, taking their tax dollars and investment capital with them. By the mid-1970s, federal and state governments matched this trend of urban disinvestment and began to withdraw financial support for the struggling cities. As city leaders navigated the urban crisis of the 1970s, then, they were determined to reverse the postwar financial drain by bringing white economic investment, consumer dollars, and residents back from the suburbs.[10]

Between 1960 and 1970, as Boston's overall population shrank, the Black population grew by over 65 percent—a rate of increase that was greater than that in other northern cities like New York and Detroit during this period. While Black people still made up a smaller percentage of Boston's residents than in these other large cities, "their visibility and concentration did increase greatly" on account of their "dramatic" population growth during the 1960s, according to a city-commissioned report. Even as Black people claimed a larger share of the city's population, they remained confined to, at most, four neighborhoods: Roxbury, the South End, Dorchester, and Mattapan. Black Bostonians' experience of intensifying residential segregation mapped onto a post–civil rights pattern nationwide. "Segregation" hardly described living conditions in American cities during this period. The Ford Foundation called it "urban apartheid."[11]

Black city residents in Boston, like their Northeast corridor counterparts generally, were also weathering a worsening economic storm. Boston suffered from the same combination of industrial abandonment, factory automation, and suburbanization of business that had undermined urban vitality across the Northeast and Midwest since the 1950s. Across the nation's urban landscape, the result was a hobbled city core and the economic displacement of tens of thousands of workers who lived there. "The presence of the non-landowning Black [has been made] superfluous in many urban areas," a Black lawyer testified at congressional hearings on unemployment and crime in 1977. "And now, when there are so many of us in the cities, we find that the policies of the Federal government deem the cities superfluous."[12]

Despite the improving lot for a few, Black peoples' incomes had fallen relative to whites'. A National Urban League report found that across the 1970s, Black people had "lost ground." Black unemployment had risen, and more Black people were living in poverty by 1980 than they were in 1970. These conditions fell hardest on Black women, who, compared with white men, white women, and Black men, were the most likely to be underemployed or unemployed. As the pay gap between men and women continued to widen, Black women most often found work in what Columbia University economist Eli Ginzberg called "deadend" jobs paying starvation wages with no shift stability and no benefits. Without affordable childcare, women with children had an especially difficult time finding work that could accommodate their schedules and welfare payments were, as Ginzberg reported, "not high enough to live on." For these reasons, substantial percentages of women who headed their families lived below the poverty line: 20 percent of total women and 33 percent of "minority women," according to the federal Women's Bureau.[13]

The problem of urban poverty was reframed as a problem of urban criminality, and specifically a problem of urban Black criminality. "Black people are fast becoming the symbol of the high crime rate in America,"

Paul Parks, a Model City administrator for Boston, wrote. By the 1970s, social welfare programs were folded into law enforcement programs through the federal Law Enforcement Assistance Administration (LEAA)—"the one money source [for cities] in Washington that has not dried up," according to Parks. Since at least the midcentury, "criminality" had been used as the codeword for, and definition of, urban Blackness. As Black criminologists and neighborhood leaders protested, "street crime" was simply a euphemism for "Black crime." Indeed, the crime statistics that were heavily trafficked throughout the decade came from the FBI Uniform Crime Reports, which had no metrics for measuring fraud, finance crime, or the destructive, large-scale criminal operations typically perpetrated by white men. Rather, the FBI fed white political fear by showcasing the numbers of arrests for small-scale property offenses and offenses against public order, which overrepresented Black people. "Selective enforcement . . . is very much the backbone of" the Uniform Crime Reports and definitions of criminality in general, said Roger Lamb, a Department of Justice community relations director, at a National Urban League symposium in 1977.[14]

The urban crisis, then, was characterized by twinned panics that cities would fall to poor Black people and also, not unrelatedly, to criminals. In 1969 Senator Edward Kennedy warned that if Boston "becomes a city filled with crime, if it becomes a city lived in only by the very rich and the very poor, if . . . it gradually becomes an all-Black city rather than an integrated city, then our problems will overcome us." That same year, when the BRA chief said, "We must make cities again into good places to live for people," he was not referring to making cities more hospitable to increasingly impoverished Black people. Rather, he urged city managers to "bring middle income people back."[15]

Even as politicians and official wrung their hands over the Blackness of Boston, at the turn of the 1970s there were signs of a white residential comeback in Boston. The *Boston Globe* reported in 1977 that it had become "trendy-chic" for "young couples, who, a few years back, would have chosen suburbia," to buy up homes in the historically diverse, though predominantly Black, South End neighborhood. To city leaders, the fragile promise of a "renaissance to intown living" demanded a hardline approach to crime. They reasoned, first, that street crime threatened to halt the urban migration of young professionals; and second, that only tough policing would stop street crime.[16]

Urban white liberal homeowners led the way in pressuring city officials to adopt hardline crime policies. Colin and Joan Diver, young white professionals who had moved their family to the South End in the hope of joining a multiracial community, were, by the mid-1970s, so frustrated with street-level muggings and commercial sex that they mobilized for draconian measures like "preventive detention," stiffer bail restrictions, and ramped-up morals arrests. "A few years earlier," J. Anthony Lukas wrote of the Divers in his account of Boston's busing wars, "Colin couldn't have imagined himself taking that position," but by 1975 he was decrying "the utter and widespread lawlessness which is destroying our community."[17]

The punitive turn among Boston's white liberals was part of a nationwide reversal. In her 1973 book on prostitution in New York, journalist Gail Sheehy claimed that cities had outgrown the "civil libertarians of the Sixties" and were now fighting "a battle against crime of the rankest kind. If it is lost," she warned, "the legitimate businesses, tourists, frightened residents and probably the last of the middle class will flee our urban centers." To protect the tax base in American cities, Sheehy argued for stringent anti–street crime policies that prioritized middle-class urban welfare over individual rights.[18]

Many of the same urban white liberals stoking punitive crime politics in Boston were in fact proponents of the AED: affluent white homeowners in neighborhoods adjacent to the Combat Zone like Beacon Hill and the Back Bay worried about Combat Zone spillover. The decision to create an adult entertainment district in the famously puritanical city was, to be sure, not a foregone conclusion. As elite civic pressure groups collaborated with the BRA to address the Combat Zone, the city pushed for wholesale clearance proposals in the spirit of the controversial urban renewal projects of the early 1960s. These plans were perennially bogged down in debates and delays throughout the cash-strapped early 1970s. Just as important, there wasn't much political will to bring out the bulldozers: Bostonians had learned their lesson from the Government Center redevelopment project that had produced the Combat Zone itself. Because of Boston's compact scale, planners and their supporters feared that if the city razed the Combat Zone, commercial sexual entertainment would reappear in nearby respectable neighborhoods. As Joan Wood, director of the League of Women Voters, wrote in a letter to the Zoning Commission registering the league's endorsement of the AED plan, "these amendments would lead to the containment of adult entertainment and adult bookstores where they presently exist downtown and would prevent the spread of such uses elsewhere where they could very easily create blighting influences." The dominant logic of the AED, then, was not necessarily sexual liberalism but sexual containment.[19]

The plan to rezone the Combat Zone as an adult entertainment district and forbid such businesses elsewhere dovetailed nicely with the city's dual-pronged goal for economic turnaround: retaining affluent white residents while attracting suburbanites and tourists with money to spend. The BRA and its allies sought to fortify the rising property values in white and whitening neighborhoods like the South End through the creation of a "fenced in and civilized" Combat Zone. And the AED would, in turn, entice tourists, suburbanites, and adventuresome locals with "part carnival, part titillation, [and] a little mystery thrown in," according to one BRA task force member. "Couples from the suburbs might come here for a night out," said Debra Beckerman, the public relations consultant for a consortium of Combat Zone nightclub owners. "A little risqué, perhaps, but a place where they'd feel safe."[20]

The pitch for a "safe" and crime-free AED was implicitly racist. In the early 1970s, when BRA planners initiated the project to transform the Combat Zone into a suburbanite-friendly district, activists in Roxbury understood that the turning of these urban gears posed a direct threat to Black residents: "The old combat zone is being renovated into a new plaza, and whites are moving into the South End," Tim Germany, a community patrol organizer in Roxbury, said in the *Bay State Banner,* Boston's Black newspaper. "They're making downtown white and they're gonna rip-off Black folk." The project to make downtown white came to fall most heavily on Black women, who—as White discovered on his own tour of the Combat Zone—were a rising presence in the zone. Indeed, many observers identified Black women as specific agents of urban violence and economic decline there.[21]

"Marauding Gangs of Teenage Black Women"

In Boston, as in cities nationwide, so-called white hunters, or white men soliciting Black women for commercial sex, had cruised Black neighborhoods with only minimal police interference for decades. Black Bostonians, like their Los Angeles counterparts, struggled mightily against this routine invasion of white men. In 1969 Ted Parrish, a prominent housing activist, attempted to make a citizen's arrest on a white hunter in the South End. Police sided with the captured white man and charged Parrish with armed robbery. But Parrish appealed his case and prevailed when the superior court dismissed his charges. After Parrish was vindicated by the court, nervous city councilors lined up to support his efforts to resist white hunters. The councilors wanted to avoid a repeat of Boston's Black uprising in 1967, which was triggered after a Black women–led sit-in at a Roxbury welfare office was violently shut down by police. The city council easily passed a local white hunter ordinance that criminalized men who solicited women. The law received scant media attention and was rarely, if ever, enforced.[22]

But by 1969, Boston's white hunter ordinance was largely moot because white men were not coming into Black neighborhoods in the same numbers as before. After the 1967 uprising and during this period of rising Black power, white hunters—never a welcome presence in Black neighborhoods—became subject to increasingly overt expressions of hostility from local residents like Parrish. By the early 1970s, the geography of Boston's interracial sexual commerce changed. According to two researchers in 1971, "White customers are afraid to go into ghetto areas." In Phillip Vitti's memoir of his years as a white undercover Boston police officer in the 1960s, he wrote that the "Ghetto Riots," as he put it, "spell[ed] the end to white solicited street-level prostitution in Black neighborhoods."[23]

When white hunters abandoned their traditional haunts in Boston, Black women began venturing into the downtown commercial entertainment district that by custom had been dominated by white people. As Black women transgressed old racial boundaries to follow white men—the most affluent and frequent solicitors of commercial sex—the Combat Zone was increasingly declared by white observers to have entered a period of decline. One evening in the mid-1960s, a Combat Zone regular was on the sidewalk chatting with Vitti, the undercover officer, when a Black woman walked past them. "Look . . . the stovepipes are moving in," the regular exclaimed. "The place is gone!" A similar dynamic was playing out in cities nationwide: following the 1964 Black rebellion against police in Harlem, Black women moved to Times Square. "Most civic leaders and today's reformers date the deterioration of Times Square to when Black prostitutes and ghetto street youth discovered the Forty-second Street stop on the A train," street-based church workers reported from New York.[24]

Black women had little choice about their visibility on city streets. Though the AED was characterized by a high concentration of bars and nightclubs where encounters might be less exposed to police action, Black women were barred from entering most establishments. "Many bar owners, hotel keepers, and landlords do not allow Black prostitutes to use their premises; thus Black women are forced onto the streets and into blatant solicitation where the risk of arrest is highest," radio producer Gail Pellett reported in a 1975 program on prostitution in Boston. One woman on Pellett's show suggested that the Combat Zone was actually *re-segregated* as more Black women moved into the area throughout the late 1960s and early 1970s: "I was the last . . . Black woman to get barred out of the bars that are functioning now wide open. . . . They got all the Black girls out of . . . the Two O'Clock"—the first stop on the mayor's AED tour—"all of the bars," she said, except two. Lauri Lewin, a white woman who worked as a dancer in the Combat Zone, recalled in her memoir that her club's bouncer "still regretted that Blacks could come into the Zone at all, and he sabotaged their freedom of movement." The white owners and managers of Combat Zone nightspots believed that the presence of Black women made the venue appear dangerous, and this phenomenon was not unique to Boston. One prostitution-hotel owner in New York City explained in 1973 how he kept a "clean" house: "I keep all the colored out." Federal laws banning racial discrimination in public accommodations did not protect Black women from the racist priorities of adult entertainment profiteers.[25]

Throughout this period, Black women testified to the discrimination that pushed them out onto the streets and into police officers' line of vision—even as white women continued to work relatively unhindered in the bars. "The Black girl has a much harder time on everything. She'll get kicked out of the hotel much faster than a white girl," a woman who went by Barbara explained in an interview. "A white girl, if she's got any kind of class about her, can work anywhere. . . . If you're Black, they kick you out faster."[26]

By the 1970s, the inequality between white and Black women—in terms of street-level experience, exposure to arrest, and physical safety—had deepened. A leader of the Prostitutes Union of Massachusetts (PUMA), a service and advocacy organization that was formed in 1976, was fully aware of the protections her whiteness afforded her: "The cards are pretty much stacked in my favor because I'm indoors and I'm white," she said at a PUMA meeting. The racial stratification in downtown adult entertainment districts during the 1970s underscored a national trend that had been building since the midcentury: white women moved through urban space with relatively less friction even as Black women throughout the city grew more vulnerable to intensifying legal punishment (see figure 4.1).[27]

Still, visibility on downtown streets alone was not enough to fully account for the targeting of Black women. White women certainly worked outside as well, and even though, as Preston Williams, a Black police

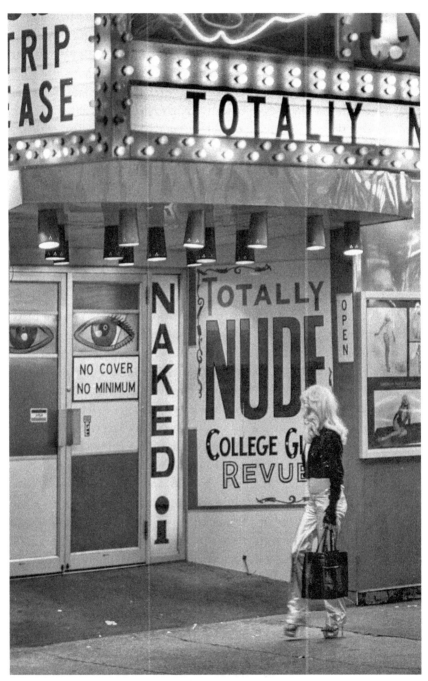

FIGURE 4.1 In the Combat Zone, "for any Black or white woman, it was rough outside." But white women moved through urban space with relatively less friction even as Black women grew more vulnerable to intensifying policing. Courtesy of Spencer Grant, 1974.

officer in Boston, recalled, "for any Black or white woman, it was rough outside," there was no question that white officers "liked the white girls and were a little easier with them." If police apprehended a Black woman, they were likely to be "nasty," Williams said. In 1973, when law enforcement officials in Boston faced charges of racial discrimination in sexual policing, the assistant district attorney insisted that "white prostitutes normally plied their trade in bars, cafes and hotels and are harder to detect than black prostitutes who work the streets." However, police accounts from this period indicate that white women were not "harder to detect" but, rather, less policed than Black women. Detective John Murphy testified in court that he only spent "about five to ten minutes inside [entertainment] establishments" in the Combat Zone. Instead, he spent "most of the time patrolling the street and most of the arrests are made on the street." The arrested women, he said, "were predominantly black." Ousted from downtown bars and clubs, Black women were driven outside, where police focused their efforts.[28]

In this post–civil rights period, individual officers rarely explicitly named the racial motivations behind discretionary sexual policing. But a definite, if occasionally tacit, racist logic that Black women were presumed to be the greater urban problem sustained police practices. Black women were banished from nightspots for the same reason that they were closely policed on the streets: the presence of Black women downtown was tightly associated with violence and crime. This narrative was made plausible for reasons delivered in both race-neutral and race-specific terms. First, it was widely held among law enforcement officials that sex workers caused ancillary street crime. "[Prostitutes] attract all the vermin—the muggers and robbers," the captain of the New York City morals division said, adding the outrageous claim that "if it weren't for the street girls, the crime rate would hardly exist." In Boston, a superior court judge argued in his ruling denying the appeal of a Black woman convicted on common nightwalking charges that "[criminal activities] accompany the operations of the prostitute" and that street crime was a "sordid fact" in "the life of the prostitute." As many prostitutes' rights activists noted, if women on the street did in fact "attract" muggers, it was because they were thought to carry large amounts of cash, had no legal recourse to report the crime to the police, and were therefore prime targets for robbery. They were, in other words, victims, rather than inciters, of street crime.[29]

The belief that commercial sex produced street criminality bled into a second narrative: that sex workers were themselves violent criminals.

Sometimes these claims were delivered in ostensibly colorblind language: one journalist wrote that a "violent new breed of prostitutes" was emerging. Police officers agreed that "the hooker on the street these days is no longer just a prostitute," as a Boston vice squad chief claimed: "She's a mugger, a pickpocket, a robber, and worse." But local accounts from white Boston residents and business owners provide evidence that they imagined this "violent new breed" of women as Black, providing a distinct iteration of a longer history of associating Black womanhood with sex and violence. For example, a Combat Zone nightclub owner recalled that "the street scene around here was a horror" because of the "marauding gangs of teenage Black women." And in 1975 a *Boston Globe* reader wrote to the editor complaining that "an evening stroll" was so often interrupted by "a half dozen hookers in search of your wallet": "What has happened to this city?" the writer asked. "Are we afraid to act because these ladies and thugs belong to one or another minority group?"[30]

Despite the colorblind language in which the narrative of prostitution and violent criminality was occasionally delivered, Black women's downtown experiences with law enforcement in the mid-1970s provided a telling indication of which women were presumed to present the greatest threat of urban violence and deterioration. Nancy Marin, a Boston Municipal Court probation officer, testified in 1973 that two-thirds of the women she worked with who stood trial for prostitution-related charges were Black. In the *Boston Globe*, a police sergeant in the city's vice squad estimated that 80 percent of the women arrested for prostitution in 1974 were Black. One feminist lawyer explained the basic formula for a prostitution arrest in Boston: "People are picked up because they are Black, and women, and in a certain area," by which she meant downtown. The presumption that Black women caused urban decay and criminality drove highly discretionary police practices.[31]

This prevailing logic was most visibly manifested in the court practice of issuing "floaters." Floaters were rulings handed down from Boston Municipal Court judges to an arrested woman in which the court would suspend her sentence if she, as one probation clerk in the court explained, "goes back to wherever she came from." While floaters were an ongoing, if only sporadic, court practice across the twentieth century in Boston, this ruling became more common in the late 1960s and throughout the 1970s.[32]

Black women were the majority of, if not the exclusive, recipients of this disposition. "We don't consider this banishment, which is not . . . lawful," the probation clerk said, defending floaters, "but if a girl offers to leave town the Judge will suspend the sentence on her." Of course, in practice the "offer" to leave was more often a court order. And when the judge issued the order to leave town—in full view of the police complainant who originally arrested the defendant—the judge marked the woman as criminal simply because of her physical existence in the city. For example, Judge Francis X. Morrissey gave Omelia, a Black woman charged with being an idle and disorderly person, two weeks to leave Boston. "If picked up after that," he warned, she would be sent to prison. Morrissey emphasized that Omelia did not "have to be doing anything physically wrong" to be apprehended by police; rather, if she was "present in Boston after two weeks" and seen by police, she would be sent to prison. Police officers and municipal judges alike also regularly offered to give Black women a break if they agreed "not [to] set foot in the Combat Zone again"—a coercive arrangement that amounted to a neighborhood-level floater. Floaters were egregious examples of the extraordinary power that Boston police wielded over Black women in service to redeveloping city streets.[33]

Such brazen deployment of police discretion prompted activists to challenge the racist and sexist violence inherent to sexual policing. Throughout the 1970s, sex workers and their allies across the country exposed the enduring connection between sexual policing and police brutality. Their testimony was amplified nationwide through what was called at the time the prostitutes' rights movement. Gloria Lockett, a Black activist in California who later became a leader in COYOTE (Call Off Your Old Tired Ethics), wrote that before the police put arrested women in the patrol car, "they would take our purses, dump them on the ground, and make us pick the things out of the gutter. . . . One time the [patrol] car was so crowded [with arrested women], one officer made me sit on his lap, handcuffed." Women who were spared arrest, however, were still exposed to police abuse: "The police would take the hands of the women who were not going to jail, and they would burn them on the hood of the [car] engine."[34]

These encounters between women and the police were charged with the threat of sexual violence. Police routinely raped sex workers. "They take you in the paddy wagon and say, 'If you blow me, I'll let you go,'" Lesley Weeks, a white PUMA activist, told the *Harvard Crimson*. In Boston, police sexual violence had a cruel racist twist: After sexually assaulting women in exchange for nonenforcement of the law, white police officers would release white women to "secluded spots downtown." Black women would be taken to all-white South Boston, the raging heart of the antibusing campaign, and pull them out of the car, "honking the horn of their patrol car to draw the terrified women to the attention of local thugs," a practice reported by the *Boston Globe*, a local feminist newspaper, and confirmed by former BPD officers Preston Williams and Valimore Williams. The unique vulnerability of Black women to morals arrests created a pernicious cycle of violence: the presumption of Black women's sexual criminality empowered police officers to target them on the street with impunity; these degrading and harmful police practices in turn justified systematic violence against Black women.[35]

During the 1970s, Black activists increasingly named and challenged this cycle of violence. "It's always open season on Black women," the leaders of Black Women for Wages for Housework charged. "The terrorism that is practiced by the Man and by individual men against prostitute women is a terror we all know, a terror in the Black community that always falls first and heaviest on Black women." Whether Black women were actively engaging in commercial sex or not, they confronted the same meshwork of state and nonstate terror: respectability could not protect them against the violence generated by discretionary police power.[36]

In this pitched political climate of opposition to police power, even law enforcement authorities began to reflect on their own violent practices. A 1969 documentary about the Kansas City Police Department called *Law and Order* captured a scene in which a white police officer choked a Black woman until she nearly lost consciousness in the course of arresting her for prostitution. As a Black police officer turned federal authority watched *Law and Order* in an LEAA office conference room, he struggled with what he saw: "I found myself reacting defensively. . . . Yet I know officers who would have done exactly the same thing." And in a federally funded 1977 study, criminologist Herman Goldstein argued, "Programs such as the wholesale harassment of street prostitutes and other petty offenders through illegal arrest . . . have often taken place with the full knowledge of the prosecutor and judges who review such cases. None of the checks built into the criminal justice system seems to curtail these illegal practices where they have been known to exist." As sex workers and their allies testified to the violence produced by sexual policing, they forced a substantial challenge to morals enforcement onto local and national agendas.[37]

Police Confront Victimless Crimes

One inescapable political demand stalked debates about the AED and public exposés of police violence: decriminalization, or the repeal of so-called victimless crimes. Challenges to the enforcement of victimless crimes—typically marijuana use, gambling, abortion (until 1973), homosexuality, and prostitution—were the next generation of the liberal and civil libertarian attacks on "legal moralism" of the mid-1960s. By the early 1970s, a new wave of challengers led the vanguard of the campaign: sex workers, allied feminists, gay and trans activists, and radical clergy. Sex workers breathed new life into the enduring argument that morals enforcement was a major source of police extortion and abuse of power. As city, state, and federal crime commissions assembled at the turn of the 1970s to reckon with the Black uprisings in the waning years of the 1960s, activists amply documented and reprised the perennial fact that morals policing bred law enforcement corruption and brutality.[38]

Bostonians, reckoning with their own scandal-ridden police department, were particularly receptive to calls for the decriminalization of prostitution laws. In 1975 the department was named in a federally funded report as "one of the worst police departments in the nation." Officers racked up brutality charges, and an average of six hundred resident calls for help went unanswered daily. In response, a diverse and bipartisan array of Massachusetts politicians proposed legislation to decriminalize prostitution, and the prostitutes' rights organization PUMA gained citywide allies and national publicity for its decriminalization activism. Even Francis Sargent, the former Republican governor of Massachusetts, argued that police departments should "give lower priority to chasing streetwalkers": "In September, 1976, Boston police arrested 1900 prostitutes," he wrote in a *Boston Globe* editorial. "Do you feel any safer?"[39]

Optimistic supporters of decriminalization believed that the AED could provide a pathway to liberalized morals laws. State congressman Barney Frank—who represented residents in neighboring Back Bay and Beacon Hill and regularly proposed legislation to legalize prostitution because he believed the effort to "wipe out commercial sex" was a "waste of time"—supported the AED in the hope that contained commercial sex could eventually lead to legalized commercial sex. And internal BRA memos indicated that some city planners agreed that the "logical next step [of the AED] would be to legitimize prostitution within the district." But despite the chatter of BRA memos, the BRA maintained its public stance that the AED was not designed to take away police power. Indeed, BRA officials argued that containing the city's adult commerce "will make the area easier to police." They were not wrong: when police were pressured to produce arrests in the AED, officers simply parked wagons on either end of the heavily trafficked

LaGrange Street and apprehended the trapped women (many of them Roxbury residents, according to news reports).[40]

The rising calls for the depolicing of commercial sex aggravated rifts among police leaders and rank-and-file officers. Robert diGrazia, the newly installed BPD commissioner who had been imported by Mayor White from Saint Louis in 1972 to clean up the corrupt department, infuriated officers when he signaled his tacit (but not public) support for downgrading prostitution enforcement as a department priority. The outspoken reformist, California-born, ethnic Italian diGrazia—who was often seen sporting a cheeky lapel pin shaped like a pig—was an inflammatory figure the day he assumed his post with a mandate to reform the hyperlocal and Irish-dominated BPD rank and file. As Superintendent John Doyle recalled, "The attitude of Commissioner diGrazia was that 'victimless crimes' were not our chief priority," adding, "I don't subscribe to that." Privately, diGrazia confirmed that he believed "that prostitution was not something we should really spend a lot of time on," especially when his strained forces were already overextended policing the violent white resistance to school desegregation.[41]

DiGrazia was not necessarily representative of police chiefs nationwide: his contemporary, the Los Angeles Police Department's chief Ed Davis, disparaged "victimless crimes" as a "propaganda term" and wielded his considerable national influence to force consideration of decriminalization off the table at a meeting of the National Advisory Commission on Criminal Justice Standards and Goals in 1973. Instead, Davis favored fighting crime with "some old-fashioned Bible-thumping morality." But neither was diGrazia an outlier: for a brief year in self-consciously cosmopolitan San Francisco, the police chief, Charles Gain, experimented with a policy of "easy-going tolerance toward street prostitution."[42]

In Boston, the nonenforcement of prostitution laws was a nonstarter for white rank-and-file officers. With political support from politicians like Barney Frank and Kevin White, the AED smacked of liberal permissiveness and provoked the resentment of many Boston law enforcement authorities. Vice officers, especially, who saw the AED as an attack on the value and integrity of their work, "despised the Combat Zone and the BRA for having legitimized it," according to one researcher. But while many rank-and-file officers may have shared an ideological affinity with Chief Davis three thousand miles to the west, for many officers, their defense of prostitution laws came from economic considerations.[43]

The majority-white BPD rank-and-file had a material investment in the perpetuation of morals laws. While police officers typically denied the existence of arrest quotas, payment structures within the BPD incentivized officers to make as many petty arrests as they could. Frank DeSario, a vice squad officer in Boston, recalled that police received one day off "for any misdemeanor arrest": "in a very short time," DeSario wrote, he accumulated nearly a month off for arrests they made "either in the Combat Zone or in Roxbury." As the Boston police union grew in strength throughout the late 1960s and 1970s, patrolmen won generous overtime payments for all court appearances, and as a result, one federal report found that "some police officers became . . . more zealous in making arrests as a method of supplementing their income." In this way, despite police protests, the AED was uniquely profitable for them. As one Boston newspaper editorialized, "The vice squad could go out of business if it didn't have to keep going into the Combat Zone to arrest some of the lady-type hustlers." At this low point of BPD legitimacy, the AED both challenged police authority and promised material rewards.[44]

Despite the veneer of sexual liberalism that overlaid the AED concept—and the political opportunity it provided for advocates of depolicing—without any changes in the penal code, the Combat Zone continued to offer police a lucrative source of arrests and authority. Seen in this light, we can understand why a police leader would come around to the idea of an adult entertainment district. And the narrative that linked Black women, sexual deviance, and violent criminality became a useful one for many police officers as they reconciled the challenge and promise of the AED. In 1973 Deputy Superintendent Joseph Saia came out in early support of the AED concept: "If we are going to be a convention city we should have a [good entertainment] section such as this where conventioneers could drink and bring their wives to see the floor shows . . . without fear of being mugged or robbed." Saia's invocation of Combat Zone crime provided an important addendum to his support. Just a few months after he publicly endorsed the AED, he led a Combat Zone crackdown that netted a total of 250 arrests. He explained that this crackdown was necessary because "prostitution had led to other crimes, particularly robberies and assaults." The "permissiveness" of the AED, then, did not meaningfully constrain police authority. Rather, the attendant racialization of sexual deviance and violent crime that underwrote the AED affirmed the legitimacy of BPD morals enforcement. In much the same way, when diGrazia set his sights on diversity and inclusion reforms in the BPD, white rank-and-file officers howled—but this seeming affront to white police in fact only served to bolster their power.[45]

Racial Inclusion and Racial Targeting: The Tactical Patrol Force and the Vice Squad

When diGrazia took over the BPD in 1972, he arrived with a reform mandate to root out the corruption and brutality endemic to vice policing. And he certainly embraced his role as the flamboyant and outspoken police reformer. "Practically speaking, we have two standards of justice: One for the 'haves' and another for the 'have nots,'" diGrazia testified at a congressional hearing. "Unfortunately, because of past selection procedures and . . . 'machismo' values in the police-field, we have had difficulty in turning around the attitude" that made this double standard in law enforcement possible. As the *New York Times* observed, diGrazia frequently contended that "this is basically a racist society." However progressive his reform rhetoric, he nevertheless reckoned with a set of political limitations—not to mention an investment in the power of his department—that was characteristic of liberal big-city police leadership nationwide in the 1970s. DiGrazia had to push through BPD reforms that drew from the period's contradictory preoccupations with the preservation of civil liberties on the one hand and white social order on the other hand—while fending off relentless challenges from his hidebound majority-white rank and file.[46]

It was widely agreed that contemporary policing demanded an update of traditional "night-stick techniques." Police brutality had historically aggravated the relationship between officers and Black residents. And in the realm of morals enforcement, reform-minded authorities were beginning to recognize that "arresting streetwalkers in ghetto neighborhoods has been a source of police/community friction," according to one LEAA report. Many Black residents believed that sexual policing was a distraction from the more pressing need for respectful and responsive police protection. For example, in 1970 Roxbury activists, frustrated with inaction from Boston police, formed their own community patrol to combat burglaries in the neighborhood, which disproportionately victimized Black residents. Tim Germany, a patrol leader, gave an illustration of community priorities, explaining, "We aren't going to get into the prostitution or drugs or numbers scene." And Black politicians in Boston joined the effort to strike down prostitution laws. Doris Bunte and Mel King, neighborhood activists turned state representatives from Roxbury and the South End, respectively, cosigned legislative proposals to decriminalize prostitution—legislation that was considerably to the left of Barney Frank's perennial bill for legalization.[47]

Reformist police authorities like diGrazia understood that sexual policing, along with the policing of other low-level misdemeanors, was a liability in police relationships with Black residents, and a barrier to overhauling retrograde departments. However, a pervasive white fear of urban crime made tough-on-crime policies necessary even for liberal politicians. Urban police chiefs, then, confronted countervailing pressures: to improve their "community relations" with Black residents while cracking down hard on "street crime." Never comfortably aligned even in the abstract, in practice, these two objectives proved to be mutually exclusive—especially when they unfolded in the hostile relationship between Black residents and the police officers they viewed as "an occupying force within the community," according to a federal Congressional Black Caucus report in 1972. Urban police chiefs, therefore, had to wrestle with the problem of how aggressive police tactics targeting Black residents could be framed as a reparative effort at "community relations."[48]

DiGrazia's appointment would seem to be, at first, a victory for Black residents. But while he was remarkably liberal even for his time, he was nonetheless a police chief committed to the "professional" police principle of departmental autonomy, and he resisted activist overtures for a meaningful partnership with Black community leaders. In 1972, for example, when a fresh surge of Black political mobilization sent five Black representatives to the State House (including King and Bunte, who proposed prostitution decriminalization legislation), the newly formed Massachusetts Black Caucus held a series of citywide meetings with 1,500 residents to discuss "both police violence and police protection." The caucus received a community mandate to take its proposals—dealing with the analysis of crime statistics, police training and monitoring, and community patrols—to diGrazia. He stonewalled the Black politicians. Whatever solutions the BPD offered to the "community crisis" would necessarily come from within the force, rather than through external civilian review, oversight, or even input.[49]

The internal reforms that diGrazia developed also had to be muscled past the rising militancy of white rank-and-file Boston police officers, who, in their opposition to the "liberal outsider" chief, built what would become "one of this country's most aggressive police unions," according to a federal report. But there was one sector of the BPD where the divided interests of reformer diGrazia converged with the desires of his rank-and-file members: the Tactical Patrol Force (TPF).⁵⁰

Throughout the 1970s, police departments in cities nationwide poured resources—much of them provided by the federal LEAA—into building up elite paramilitary anticrime police squads, which targeted street crime through both overt displays of high-tech weaponry and equipment and covert maneuvers and decoy tactics. Police chiefs of all political stripes threw their support behind these anticrime units. In Boston the premier anticrime unit was the TPF. Like many of its counterparts nationwide, the TPF was created in late 1962 to target "high crime incidence areas of the city," with the greatest concentration of police action in Black neighborhoods. By 1974 the TPF's everyday function was clarified to be a "selective enforcement group concentrating on the reduction of street crimes," primarily downtown and in Black neighborhoods. When diGrazia added a "150-man, citywide, anti-crime unit" to the TPF, it was one of the rare issues on which he and his rank and file agreed.⁵¹

The TPF was styled as a highly specialized cadre of men trained in urban combat and dispatched to extinguish major urban violence, but in fact street crime and small-scale morals misdemeanors were the bread-and-butter work of this elite squad. A legal committee investigating LEAA-funded projects like the TPF found that "new technology and tactics" that were "appropriate for military operations" were instead aimed at "nonserious crimes," such as disorderly conduct, vagrancy, and sex offenses, and "frequently [resulted] in increased harassment of the nonserious offender." In Boston, TPF officers regularly busied themselves with arrests for petty offenses and worked decoy details where they entrapped women they suspected of engaging in prostitution. One white TPF officer recalled that he and his partner often "made some good grabs" for handbag snatches, fights, and prostitution downtown. These practices were on display in other cities. In Miami, for example, an elite anticrime unit called Operation Impact was formed to devote the "total mobilization of police resources" to street crime, and especially "the suppression of street vice." Prostitution arrests under Operation Impact increased 73 percent.⁵²

The TPF provided great newspaper copy for the BPD on the successful exploits of the special officers, whose military veteran status was often invoked in TPF profiles. But these anticrime units frequently drew protests of racist "crude and brutish behavior," according to one white criminologist. Indeed, the 1967 report of the National Advisory Commission on Civil Disorders, popularly known as the Kerner Commission, concluded that the deployment of tactical squads nationwide was a significant "source of friction" contributing to the hostility many Black residents felt toward the police. In Boston, Black residents marched against the TPF and protested that the squad's practices amounted to an "armed siege" of their community.[53]

The TPF exemplified the BPD's dilemma of how to implement tough policing while improving Black community relations. During this period, one way the BPD leadership resolved the problem was through racially inclusive hiring and assignments. This measure purported to include, while simultaneously targeting, Black residents. Under pressure from Black community leaders after the Roxbury uprising in 1967, the department began a concerted recruitment drive for Black police officers. This affirmative hiring continued through the 1970s, when local representatives from the National Association for the Advancement of Colored People and other community organizations won a five-year equal employment consent decree. Black hiring was a liberal solution that placed token individuals on the force—in 1972, for example, the BPD was still 98 percent white—while leaving undisturbed the logic of crime and policing that riveted the department's energies on Black people. Black power activists, especially, scorned this ameliorative measure, and to more moderate Black leaders, inclusive hiring was, at best, an incomplete victory. Valimore Williams, a Black police recruit from the class of 1968, reflected in an oral history that the policy was merely a way for the department "to skip around the issues [while] still holding on to the old racist attitudes."[54]

Black officers in Boston, especially in the late 1960s and early 1970s, did not typically get assigned to elite squads like the TPF. One notable exception was the Soul Patrol, the BPD's short-lived anticrime unit fully led and manned by Black officers. The Soul Patrol lasted roughly two months in 1971 before the white-dominated police union forced the unit to "integrate." (It is worth noting that commercial sex was "not the priority" for the Soul Patrol, according to member Preston Williams.) Instead, Black police officers were sent to Black neighborhoods to walk a highly visible, public-facing beat, where the department hoped that the presence of Black officers would mute residents' protests and perhaps inspire good-faith cooperation. But after the Massachusetts Association of Afro-American Police (formed in 1968) pressured the BPD to desegregate its paramilitary squads, ten Black officers, including Valimore Williams, were assigned to the TPF.[55]

As Black officers pressed for inclusion in these elite assignments, white police brass nationwide started to agree with them. Among police leaders,

Black officers were considered desirable personnel for these anticrime units because it was assumed that Black officers would be more knowledgeable of presumptively Black street crime. As a result, when Black officers were brought onto prestige squads like the TPF, they were generally assigned to focus on street crime and morals enforcement rather than homicide. The commander of one of Detroit's anticrime units testified at congressional hearings on street crime in 1973 that "Black officers are a high priority item for many . . . functions within the police department, including vice [and] narcotics," both allegedly majority-Black crimes that police departments responded to by heavy saturation in Black neighborhoods. Morals enforcement, then, provided a helpful way to resolve the tension between Black hiring and the deployment of anticrime squads to pursue majority-Black police targets. Assigning Black officers to morals enforcement lent an air of credibility—and, importantly, Black validation—to a police project that was increasingly disparaged in this period as a corrupt waste of resources that disproportionately targeted and harmed Black residents.[56]

DiGrazia also took steps to integrate another discredited police unit: the vice squad. This was a reformist move to shake up prevailing practices of corruption and brutality while assigning Black officers to a squad that disproportionately targeted Black residents. But Black officers were dramatically outnumbered on the squad—diGrazia increased the racial composition of the twenty-officer squad from one to three Black men—and they were seen as interlopers by the white rank and file. White BPD vice officers vigilantly watched Black officers, waiting to pounce at their first misstep and laying traps to sabotage their careers. After diGrazia personally interviewed Preston Williams and assigned him to the vice squad, a white woman in the Combat Zone propositioned Williams multiple times; he repeatedly refused, and later learned that she had been dispatched by white officers to set him up.[57]

As a relatively large and politically conscious wave of Black recruits joined the force after 1968, they distinguished themselves from their "arrest at all costs" and weapons-ready white counterparts. The early wave of Black officers had a stated political commitment to "helping people in [my] community," as Preston Williams said, and they considered their form of morals policing in the 1970s distinct from white policing. But the token Black police officers on the vice squad could not change the fundamental dynamics of power and violence that structured Black women's encounters with police. On the occasions when women who had been abused by white officers turned to Preston and Valimore Williams for help, both officers said they could only give the unsatisfying answer that the women had to make a complaint against the police department. One time, Preston Williams nearly came to blows with a white officer who was brutal with Black women, charging that "you don't do that to them white girls." Valimore Williams recalled taking a more procedural route, threatening to report white officers to the department's internal Special Investigation Unit if the abuse continued. But, as became clear in the course of two weeks in November 1976, it was precisely this professional internal discipline mechanism that galvanized the department's autonomy and empowered the BPD to perpetuate its most egregious practices of collusion and abuse in the course of morals enforcement.[58]

As a strong current of reform coursed through the BPD during the mid-1970s, the combustive politics of race, police public relations, and morals enforcement came to a head in the AED. Indeed, while some hopeful observers believed that the AED was a step to unwinding discretionary police power, it actually became the prime factor in traditional Boston officers' vanquishing reformist incursions and the triumphant reclamation of their power through the sexual policing of women on downtown streets with broad and unfettered discretion.

"Robber Whores" and the Restoration of Police Power

After four years of butting heads with his own department (and increasingly with city hall), diGrazia resigned from the BPD in November 1976. The deployment of Black personnel to elite anti-street crime units like the TPF and the vice squad had not been diGrazia's only strategy to rein in corrupt practices in the BPD. As one of his many reform projects when he assumed his post, diGrazia had created the Special Investigation Unit (SIU), an internal department watchdog, and immediately tasked SIU investigators with documenting police practices in District 1, the downtown police district, which included the Combat Zone. When diGrazia resigned, he leaked to the Boston newspapers an explosive 572-page SIU report covering nearly three years that found "deeply entrenched" corruption and "obvious gross incompetence" in the District 1 command staff and on down the ranks.[59]

SIU investigators gathered widespread evidence of police collusion with Combat Zone business owners. The report found routine nonenforcement of "illegal sexual activities" in order to "[enhance] the business prospects of bars, hotels and other adult entertainment facilities." But police officers also engaged in aggressive morals arrest drives—"which were really insignificant when compared with the total problem of illegal sexual activity"—that directly targeted women "on busy streets." As the SIU report noted, women in the Combat Zone were frequently used as canaries in the mine to alert the payoff men of District 1's officers that police action was forthcoming: "Multiple arrests of prostitutes . . . had the effect of warning the entire district that 'the heat was on.'" Two officers—the so-called Golden Boys who "could do no wrong" with their superiors—were singled out in SIU revelations that the men had raped women in exchange for nonenforcement of prostitution laws, along with several other confirmed officers who perpetrated violence against sex workers. This brutality was possible because command staff "were fully aware of the above activities and took no disciplinary action against offending officers, thereby giving tacit approval to such practices." Finally, the SIU report charged that District 1 officers "staged 'spectacular' [morals] raids" that were typically "cover-up tactics" in response to political or media pressure. When scandals in the Combat Zone escalated two weeks after diGrazia leaked the SIU report, the BPD would return to this favored tactic.[60]

Late on the evening of November 15, Andrew Puopolo and six other members of the Harvard football team headed to the Naked i in the Combat Zone after the annual Harvard-Yale game celebration at the Harvard Club. As the white football players left the nightclub in their suits and ties, they were approached by two Black women, Cassandra McIntyre and Naomi Axel—universally identified as "prostitutes" in the news coverage—who followed the men to their parked van. One woman got in the van—it is unclear whether she was invited in—and after McIntyre and Axel left, the team's defensive tackle found his wallet missing. The Harvard men chased after the women, first on foot and then in their van. When one of the players spotted Axel from the van, the men rushed out. At that moment, a group of Black men confronted the football players and "began scuffling with [them]." In the fight, Puopolo was fatally stabbed. According to the popular media account, Puopolo was "an outstanding young man" who had been murdered by "robber whores" and "tough guys with knives" in a "cruel and senseless tragedy . . . because that same criminal element had inundated the Combat Zone."[61]

Conspicuously absent from the media coverage was why a group of Black men ran up to the football players in the first place. Black BPD officers Preston Williams and Valimore Williams both knew McIntyre. She was not a "prostitute," the officers said; she was a pickpocket. Sixteen-year-old McIntyre was a "little skinny thing" who could run fast and had friends nearby in the Combat Zone—including one man, she testified in court, she had known "all [her] life"—who could help her in case she got into trouble. "She'd call the guys," Preston Williams explained, and say, "Get this guy off me!" McIntyre's story exposes an element of the Puopolo story that was sidelined in the media coverage: she believed she was in physical danger when she called for help and her friends ran to her defense. This retelling presents a credible account of vengeful white football players taking justice into their own hands by attacking a young Black woman. But McIntyre's—and even individual police officers'—narrative was subsumed by dominant logics that fused Blackness, sexual deviance, and violent criminality. Axel's and McIntyre's inherent value and their struggle for bodily integrity were erased in the popular narrative that "a bright Harvard athlete's life [was] snuffed out by a group of Black Combat Zone–types of no value to society," as one critical *Boston Globe* columnist wrote years after the incident. Axel and McIntyre, as Black women in the Combat Zone, were seen as an urban problem appropriately managed through private and state force.[62]

Despite the apparent operation of racism in the public narratives of the Puopolo murder, it took many years for an explicit discussion of the racial dimensions of the case to surface. The "myth-power of the killing," as one *Boston Globe* columnist wrote, was strong. Belated media attention was paid when the Black men were tried for Puopolo's murder—and retried, after the defense successfully argued that the first trial was laden with racial prejudice. Years later at a rally in 1979 protesting the local Ku Klux Klan, one of the defendants' mothers spoke out against the "racist media campaign" that had targeted her son. In the eye of the storm in 1976, however, the women who worked on Combat Zone streets provided an immediately clear-eyed assessment of the situation. Lois, a racially unmarked woman, told a reporter that "there are no racial problems among the vast majority of the women who work in the zone"—suggesting that white outsiders looking for a thrill, like the Harvard football players, brought the racial hostility and violence to the confrontation. And, Lois added correctly, "if it had been anyone else that was stabbed the whole incident would have been overlooked by the media and the police." Indeed, a serial killer had murdered at least three women in the Combat Zone the year before. And throughout the 1970s, many other women who were last seen in the area had disappeared: white women occasionally received an incomplete investigation and a few newspaper inches, and Black women warranted even less attention.[63]

While no women were arrested in the case of Puopolo's stabbing, the police held court in the streets of the Combat Zone. Joseph Jordan, a former commander of the vice squad, had been appointed as BPD commissioner in October to replace the outgoing diGrazia. He assumed his new post on diGrazia's effective resignation date, November 15—the same day of the Puopolo stabbing. Referring to the Combat Zone, Jordan declared that he would "give the streets back to the people." Local reporters applauded him. Jordan "promised a strenuous effort against street prostitution and he is delivering," a *Boston Herald* columnist wrote. "The shit just hit the fan," according to a PUMA leader. "There were wholesale arrests. . . . It was just outrageous. And the harassment continued" for years. In the immediate aftermath of the stabbing, police parked their wagons in the Combat Zone and rounded up women they found in the street. By December, Jordan had struck an agreement with county prosecutors to redouble his force: he deployed a special anticrime squad from the district attorney's major violators unit, which had been established earlier in the year "to deal with racial violence," as the *New York Times* reported.[64]

An alliance of feminist, lesbian, and sex workers' rights critics charged that the BPD's crackdown was a convenient—and violent—distraction from the SIU report. At a press conference, PUMA member Janet Parlin called the mass arrests "a grandstand play by police officials to counteract" the report's corruption findings. Amy Hoffman, an editor for the *Gay Community News*, wrote in a feminist newspaper that the "crackdown on prostitutes has been used to draw the media away from publicizing this report." Local leaders of the National Organization for Women delivered a sharply worded assessment of morals enforcement on behalf of the women targeted in the crackdown: "We believe that prostitutes are, on the one hand, brutalized without legal recourse, and, on the other, the subject of flagrantly selective law enforcement." Moreover, activists underscored that the police abuse of women was an essential feature of the BPD's aggressive efforts to redirect public outrage toward women and away from the police.[65]

But the protests were drowned out as the public image of Boston police officers enjoyed a complete overhaul in a little over two weeks. Whether the AED was understood as a site of sexual liberalism or sexual containment, and whether the experiment was deemed a success or—in the aftermath of the Puopolo stabbing—a failure, sexual policing served as a consistently important strategy for police to demonstrate their usefulness to the city by keeping downtown "safe." In this way, the sexual policing of Black women was a necessary corollary to the city's project of returning white capital to the city.

Success through Failure

For the BPD and city hall, perhaps the most fortunate outcome after the Puopolo stabbing was the discrediting of the AED concept. Urban authorities and audiences accepted that the experiment was a "failure," as Jordan charged, because of the "robber whores" and the "hoodlum element" in the Combat Zone. The triumph of the myth of violent Black sexual criminality after the Puopolo stabbing provided a crucial and convenient narrative that achieved two ends. First, it delivered popular authorization to the BPD to aggressively enforce morals laws. And second, the massive, post-Puopolo crackdown in the Combat Zone legitimized the broader and more persistent removal of sex workers from downtown city streets in order to prime the area for what remained the long-term goal of the BRA and city hall: downtown development.[66]

Within weeks of the Puopolo stabbing, city planners unveiled a "long-range plan" to isolate and shrink the Combat Zone in order to make real estate in the district appealing to investors. Morals enforcement played a central role in this development scheme: "The police crackdowns, which have depressed land values within the zone, combined with rising property values outside the zone, have made the zone acreage attractive to developers," the *Boston Globe* reported. Throughout the 1980s, developers bought up parcels of the Combat Zone to build luxury hotels, condominiums, and shopping complexes to create what one critic called "just another Yuppie enclave." The city extended "tax breaks and other incentives . . . to businesses that open near the Zone," according to the *Los Angeles Times*. As a result, one real estate agent told the *Times*, "property is exploding down here." State force was a crucial "incentive" that the city promised to lure capital. Police were consistently on hand to smooth the path for incoming capital: journalists noted the "heavy police presence" in the Combat Zone.[67]

The spaces and people that the city welcomed downtown were as indicative of the priorities ordering urban governance as the spaces and people that were excluded. For example, the offices of the Department of Public Welfare were transferred away from their convenient, accessible location in the Combat Zone and replaced with retail. And in 1984—ten years after the AED was officially formed—a planned shelter for runaway youth was scrapped after a representative of an investment firm, which was developing a $130 million complex in the Combat Zone, demanded that the mayor and the BRA review the situation "to see that this project is not in conflict with what was promised us." A developer who planned to build condominiums was found to buy the shelter property, and Mayor White's successor, Raymond Flynn, showed his gratitude to the new buyer by directing the police "to crack down on prostitution and other activities" in the area. That same year, as executives from Swissair Associated Companies weighed a prospective move to downtown Boston, they had "tough questions" for Flynn about his plans for the Combat Zone: the *Boston Globe* reported that "as an added incentive to lure [Swissair], he pledged to 'clean up' the Combat Zone." As these examples show, the mobility of white capital and bodies was facilitated by the repression and displacement of the city's poorest and most vulnerable people. Black women in the Combat Zone remained key police targets in order to bolster the confidence of investors and prepare the city to absorb an influx of private capital.[68]

· · · · · ·

The new economic order in Boston was forged in crisis. It was not the Puopolo stabbing, nor even the urban crisis of the 1970s, but rather the everyday crisis of arrest and forced removal to which Black women were disproportionately and systematically subjected. The AED experiment and subsequent downtown redevelopment provide a clear example of the racism and sexism that underwrote the restructuring of urban law enforcement and governance in Boston. Even in the earlier iteration of this project—the zoning of the AED—short-lived overtures to sexual liberalism were conditional on the sexual policing and spatial banishment of Black women. The transition to private investment and white homeownership and consumption was achieved through a brutal whitening of downtown space. As early as 1980, researchers for a BRA-sponsored report on the Combat Zone found that downtown was "increasingly becoming off-limits to people who are not affluent [and] are not white." State force and private wealth—the material forces behind gentrification—were both enabled by and enriched through the repression and displacement of Black women in city space.[69]

Police reform ultimately legitimized and authorized unfettered discretionary policing. Reforms like racially inclusive hiring, which unfolded alongside efforts to perpetuate aggressive police tactics like the buildup of the TPF, sustained both the prevailing logics of Black criminality and the necessity of discretionary sexual policing to secure urban welfare. The BPD ultimately reclaimed its authority through the simultaneous practice of hiring and targeting Black residents—dual practices that left Black women, especially those observed downtown, vulnerable to police action. We will next see these forces converge in Atlanta, a liberal, Black-led city, where Black women were central to firming the realignment of interests among police, downtown business elites, and urban managers. Black women's bodies became a laboratory for urban managers to test new legal and political strategies to cast a wider net of police surveillance and arrest in order to target people deemed a threat to urban wealth.[70]

5 Atlanta: From the Prostitution Problem to the Sanitized Zone
Broken Windows Policing and Gentrification

Throughout the summer of 1976, Dan Sweat, the white president of Central Atlanta Progress (CAP), a consortium of downtown business elites, blasted Reginald Eaves, the Black Atlanta police commissioner. Sweat published editorials and cycled through meetings with the likes of the Rotary Club, the Atlanta Chamber of Commerce, and the Atlanta Convention and Visitors Bureau, hammering home his message: "We cannot afford to become an 'easy' city for prostitution." Peachtree Street, the city's downtown spine, was blighted with vacant buildings and run-down shops. Firms were leaving, Sweat argued, "because of the increasing blackness" of downtown, and the people who remained were bad for business. Even as he ticked off his list of major offenders—muggers, pickpockets, panhandlers, street vendors—Sweat reserved a major share of outrage for one particular group: "As more and more of the prostitutes who solicit on the sidewalks are observed to be black, the assumption arises that Atlanta is 'easy' on black prostitutes, creating more serious overtones for the problem." Sweat's ultimatum was clear—if Atlanta's first Black city hall, and in particular its first Black police commissioner, couldn't save downtown Atlanta from Black criminals, he and the investors, corporate executives, and developers he represented would. "I am fully convinced that the fate of the city . . . is decided in the board room, not the Council chamber," Sweat declared to a roomful of Rotarians.[1]

Two years later, Sweat won the first of many victories in his "board room" takeover of Atlanta police. CAP entered into a financial partnership with the city of Atlanta to fund a police demonstration project, the anti–street crime Mobile Action Unit. This experimental unit delivered a "supersaturation of officers" downtown, including a dozen horse-mounted patrols and eighty-four officers.[2]

Throughout the 1970s, investment capital bypassed Atlanta's central business district—historically white but increasingly Black—and concentrated in the "golden crescent" of the white northern suburbs just outside the city. Writing about Atlanta in the 1970s, one political scientist explained, "The harsh fact is that some investors are skittish about investing in a predominantly black community." Downtown boosters sought to increase white investment by hitching their wagon to the rising star of convention and tourism business. But they were dismayed to receive letters from valued "corporate customers" who complained, as one member of the chamber of commerce in Bethlehem, Pennsylvania, wrote in 1978, that her "delightful" visit to the "very progressive" city was marred by "the number of very obvious prostitutes in and around the convention area."[3]

Atlanta's politicians, law enforcement authorities, and business leaders wrestled with the same issue of multiplying pornography establishments that delivered Boston's urban authorities to the solution (however temporary) of the Adult Entertainment District: how to return capital, conventions, and white people to a downtown district associated with "Black prostitutes" and street crime. As in Boston, the growing Blackness of Atlanta's historically white central business district and the perception of downtown as a site of sexual criminality were mutually reinforcing—and both in turn allegedly threatened the city's economic prospects. Sweat argued that "the growth of pornography is seriously retarding our economic growth." He had a vision for the urban redevelopment of the downtown corridor along Peachtree Street—what he called an "economic reclamation"—that would "force the sex and porno palaces out." CAP's goals, then, were typical of the dominant concerns preoccupying urban authorities in major cities throughout the 1970s as they searched for capital to replace steadily declining public funds and tax revenue.[4]

In the mid-1970s, urban authorities in Atlanta also toyed with the idea of a downtown adult entertainment district. Supporters felt it was a viable containment strategy, invoking Atlanta's storied history of white madams like Abbie Howard (the real-life inspiration for *Gone with the Wind*'s Belle Watling) and the city's segregated sex district, which was shut down during the nationwide wave of Progressive-era repression. In 1976 Eaves—the first Black person to command the Atlanta Department of Public Safety and Sweat's perennial target—specifically named the Boston experiment when he urged Atlanta residents to explore the possibility of "special zones where prostitution is allowed." Eaves saw prostitution enforcement as distinct—and indeed, a distraction—from "more severe or violent offenses such as robberies, rapes, homicides or burglaries." Despite CAP's hardline campaign, it, too, had considered the merits of "zoning methods to isolate adult entertainment." In 1975 CAP conducted a study of adult entertainment

Atlanta   139

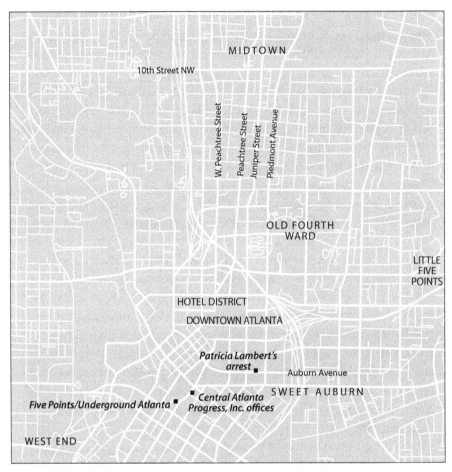

MAP 5.1 Midtown and downtown Atlanta, ca. 1985.

districts, focusing in particular on Boston, and found that the Adult Entertainment District proved to be a "wise and effective method of dealing with the problem" of urban adult entertainment.[5]

Eaves's public support of prostitution legalization and CAP's own consideration of an adult entertainment district indicate that the role of the police in Atlanta's economic revitalization was still under construction. And yet within just two years, CAP leadership dismissed their previous findings and coordinated with city politicians and police leaders to develop a law enforcement agenda that aggressively targeted morals misdemeanors downtown and oversaw its enactment. By 1978, strategies to reduce or de-escalate morals policing would be discarded as a misguided artifact of the

1970s in favor of heavy police enforcement of low-level misdemeanors to establish a "sanitized zone" downtown.[6]

The distinct racial and urban context of Atlanta—specifically, the new Black political leadership and highly mobilized businessmen committed to shaping municipal governance according to their own designs—laid the groundwork for a model of downtown policing that would anticipate urban trends nationwide. Ultimately, Atlanta's urban authorities and business leaders rejected the overtures to sexual liberalism in the Boston experiment and instead devised new law enforcement strategies to repress, rather than contain, sexually profiled women—and later an expanded list of "derelicts"—who were thought to bring economic and social deterioration. As city authorities and downtown boosters alike doubled down on an urban economy dependent on convention and tourism dollars, CAP steered ostensibly liberal Atlanta toward a model of tough governance that would become known, by the early 1980s, as broken windows policing.[7]

Police and "the Prostitution Problem" in Maynard Jackson's Atlanta

Throughout Maynard Jackson's 1973 campaign for mayor of Atlanta, and immediately upon his election as the first Black big-city mayor in the South, he had to reckon with the related political issues of downtown business, crime, and law enforcement. White Atlantans feared that a Black mayor would "manipulate policies to avenge white racism," as historian Maurice J. Hobson writes. The city's business elite braced themselves for the tectonic shifts in the racial dynamics of Atlanta's politics.[8]

In his first term, Jackson seized on his election mandate to meaningfully expand the participation and inclusion of all Black Atlantans beyond the Black middle-class powerbrokers who had historically exerted a measure of influence on the city's civil rights agenda. The mayoral overhaul of the city charter restructured political districts and "signaled the end of centuries of white political domination" in Atlanta, according to political scientist Mack Jones. Members of CAP, in particular, were alarmed that the increased access of Black residents to urban politics would disrupt the traditionally cozy relationship between city hall and downtown business. "From the perspective of the business community," one white observer wrote, "black political empowerment represented a potential danger," particularly if the Black electoral majority "mobilized around resentment against the white elite." For decades, mayors had been "responsive and accommodating to business interests." Now, Jackson was insisting that business be responsive and accommodating to his priorities of racial justice.[9]

Sensing the changing political landscape, the CAP board of directors moved to install a "new and more politically sophisticated" executive director, Sweat, a public servant who had logged time in the city's antipoverty program, two city hall administrations, and the Atlanta Regional Commission, the city's urban planning arm. "Political sophistication" for the CAP board must have meant a stomach for playing hardball: Sweat immediately went on the offensive, and his relationship with the new mayor was "fraught with considerable friction." Shortly after Jackson's election, CAP orchestrated a collective letter from businessmen to the mayor warning that "crime, the white flight to the suburbs, poor schools, a perception of the Mayor as 'antiwhite,' increasing 'blackness' of the city, congestion and other problems were seriously imperiling center-city prospects." As this list indicates, material concerns were mixed in with racist umbrage. Sweat acknowledged that businessmen were "doubly galled" by their downgraded status with the city's powerbrokers because "they haven't gotten used to the idea of a black Mayor in the first place and are ready to jump on anything he does." In 1974 the president of CAP put Jackson on notice that "businesses may move from the downtown area due to concern over a fear of crime, racial and employment problems, and various other matters." The message to the mayor was to cooperate with white Atlanta elites, or face accelerated capital flight from downtown.[10]

One particular point of aggravation for CAP was the way that city hall limited its traditional access to, and political influence over, police leaders. Eaves's appointment as commissioner of the Department of Public Safety was steeped in racial conflict. Jackson's first goal as mayor had been to dismiss John Inman, the white police chief and longtime culprit of Black charges of discrimination and abuse. But Inman fought his termination in court and won. In response, Jackson appointed his former Morehouse College classmate, Eaves, to head the newly created Department of Public Safety, responsible for both the fire and police departments. This "superchief" position was designed to supersede the authority of the police chief. The politics of Eaves's appointment, as well as his immediate shake-ups in the police department—for example, the demotion of more than fifty white sergeants—enraged Atlanta's white elites. As Sweat explained to a reporter, before Jackson's election and subsequent appointment of Eaves, "the old style was that a white businessman could pick up the phone and talk directly with the police chief. They didn't have that kind of access with Eaves, and many of them were frustrated by this."[11]

Throughout Jackson's first term, CAP and its frequent collaborator, the Atlanta Convention and Visitors Bureau (ACVB), responded to their sense of exclusion from law enforcement authority by pumping reports of unchecked downtown prostitution into the media. Sweat denounced "prostitution, bathhouses, massage parlors and other forms of 'visual pollution in Atlanta,'" while ACVB president Bennett F. Tuck declared that "we've got to solve the problem of open prostitution and those visual eyesores on Peachtree Street," which were "most emphatically a deterrent in our efforts to make Atlanta the nation's number one convention city and vacation destination." In 1976 a three-part series on "adult entertainment" ran in the *Atlanta Constitution* featuring Sweat. Reflecting the concerns of downtown elites, the reporters framed the issue as a failure of "almost completely ineffective" law enforcement and reform proposals that "deal only with containing the problem, not eliminating it."[12]

CAP's sustained public outrage over downtown commercial sex posed a unique political problem for Jackson: this smear campaign threatened to associate his race-conscious administration and police leadership with white visions of emboldened sexual criminals. Jackson and Eaves acted quickly to distance themselves from any taint of urban vice and to register their staunch disapproval of such activities. In a personal anecdote served up to the *Constitution*, after Jackson was solicited by three women on Peachtree Street as his chauffeured limousine idled in rush-hour traffic, he reportedly called Eaves and demanded that the police "clean it up!" But in 1976 the administration was reluctant to undertake the labor- and cost-intensive campaign of morals enforcement necessary to repress adult entertainment.[13]

Jackson and Eaves offered two reasons: rights and resources. The mayor, a practicing lawyer before he pursued political office, explained in a formal statement to reporters that "the city does not wish to violate anyone's constitutional rights nor to devote scarce police resources to the harassment of [adult entertainment] establishments to the exclusion of work on more serious crimes." The issue of rights was connected to the issue of resources—Jackson and Eaves were working under the constraints of a hiring freeze on the Atlanta Police Department while a 1973 discrimination lawsuit filed against the police department by the Afro-American Patrolmen's League was under way. But their critics condemned the mayor's "compulsive devotion to the letter of the law when it comes to constitutional rights" and implied that the rights-oriented administration was unfit to enforce laws in Atlanta. Downtown businessmen charged Jackson with going "overboard to avoid stepping on anyone's constitutional toes."[14]

As the downtown elite campaign against vice heated up, Jackson leaned on the city's prosecutorial authority. He appointed Mary Welcome, the liberal daughter of a Maryland legislator and a surgeon, as Atlanta's first Black chief prosecutor. In her brief tenure with the city, Welcome won the nickname "Wild Mary" for launching a rigorous "war on local vice." "I am a very strict advocate of the law," she explained. "I don't care what the law is, whether I agree or disagree with it. I will enforce it." However, Welcome did offer several justifications for "forcefully" prosecuting morals laws, including a defense of "the people who have businesses downtown who are exposed to it."[15]

A series of scandals and tragedies forced Jackson to abandon his efforts to manage law enforcement on his terms and to pivot, instead, toward a more business-friendly police agenda in downtown Atlanta. Since his initial appointment, Eaves had faced revolt among the white police officers under his command who fought what they saw as a Black takeover of their department. Eaves was hounded by Atlanta's white-dominated police union—and "scolded" by a federal judge—for "hiring more black policemen than white," according to the *Baltimore Afro-American*. White fears of inverted racial hierarchies and Black revenge for long-standing police abuse ultimately set the course for Eaves's downfall: just weeks before the mayoral election in 1977, when Jackson was running for a second term, widely publicized allegations surfaced that Eaves permitted Black police officers to review their promotion exams in advance. "The white business establishment was particularly disturbed by the scandal," the *New York Times* reported. Sweat charged that the Eaves affair harmed the city's reputation for "clean government" and scared off investors, worsening the city's real estate losses and banking mismanagement amid the mid-1970s recession. After a prolonged investigation into promotion practices under Eaves, a freshly reelected Jackson relieved the commissioner of his post.[16]

Throughout the summer of Jackson's tumultuous reelection campaign, CAP had seized on the white perception of a downtown crime crisis—an alleged disaster for business—to push through the organization's law enforcement agenda. Convention boosters, business executives, and hotel managers traded fuming letters with Sweat about "the prostitute problem in the downtown hotels, the panhandlers, the watch salesmen and the muggings." In June 1977 Sweat organized a Crime Task Force composed of "business and convention interests." The task force argued that perceptions of crime downtown "can lead to the deterioration of a healthy business climate" and recommended the increased visibility of police downtown.[17]

Though Jackson prevailed in the election, he emerged vulnerable on crime politics. When the Crime Task Force released its report in December, Jackson endorsed its recommendations and entered into a public-private partnership with CAP to create a Mobile Action Unit targeting street crime downtown. The city and CAP each committed $300,000 per year for a three-year police demonstration project downtown. Atlanta provided fifteen officers for a new Downtown Foot Patrol, six new officers for a horse-mounted patrol, eighty-four reassigned officers, training programs for private security, and technical support staff. In return, CAP provided downtown space for a new police precinct "in the heart of Atlanta's hotel district," support for the certification of private security guards, and computers. The goal of this demonstration project was to target "the non-violent variety [of crime] that predominates in downtown," according to a newsletter for the ACVB, another funding partner for the Mobile Action Unit.[18]

If law enforcement policy was a major sticking point between CAP and Jackson during his first term, it also proved to be a key arena in which city hall and downtown business elites smoothed their "fraught" relationship in Jackson's second term. The Crime Task Force reported after the first year of the demonstration project that "the increased visibility of police in the downtown is one of the primary reasons for better relations between the police bureau, businessmen, and the media." As evidence of the project's success, the task force noted that "several major corporate building projects have been announced." The demonstration project also ushered in material changes in police practices citywide: after one year of assigning more police officers to downtown street-level enforcement, the Atlanta Police Department exported the project to "two crime plagued public housing projects." The Mobile Action Unit experiment was the first step in a corporate redirection of police priorities and practices in Atlanta.[19]

In 1979 two separate fatal shootings of white people downtown enflamed white perceptions of a violent, dangerous downtown and ratcheted up CAP's leverage. That June, Marc Tetalman, a doctor visiting Atlanta for the national meeting of the Society for Nuclear Medicine, was murdered downtown during an attempted robbery; four months later, Patricia Barry, an administrative assistant for a downtown law firm, was walking back to work after her birthday lunch when she was slain by a Black man with a mental illness who then turned the gun on himself. These tragedies triggered an outsize crime panic that distorted the actual experience of violence in the city. During the same summer, between Tetalman's and Barry's killings, Black working-class residents were enduring the terror and trauma of the Atlanta child murders, which lasted for years and ultimately claimed the lives of at least thirty poor and working-class Black youth and young adults.[20]

Downtown business elites recognized that there was a great racial disparity in the violence that Black and white Atlanta residents faced. Indeed, CAP found in its research that downtown was the site of only 6 percent of the "major crimes" in the metropolitan area. But CAP was concerned that "many Atlantans and visitors alike, regardless of facts, felt their public safety was not always assured." Tetalman's murder, connected as it was to coveted convention business, was an especially alarming threat to Atlanta's economic aspirations. Throughout Jackson's second term, as he confronted (and disappointed) working-class Black residents fighting for better protection for their children, the mayor also made increasing accommodations to downtown elites to signal that their public safety and economic security were a city priority. Black activists in People United for Freedom argued that Jackson's agenda betrayed those most likely to experience violence—namely, "Black and poor communities." "When politicians talk about a 'crime wave' they are mainly concerned about crime that threatens the profits of the big corporations downtown," they charged.[21]

Anticipating Broken Windows

The CAP-led Crime Task Force honed its agenda in 1977. But its target (perceptions of crime) and proposed solution (more police for low-level misdemeanors) presciently anticipated the broken windows theory of policing that George Kelling and James Q. Wilson would introduce to popular audiences in their enormously influential 1982 article in the *Atlantic*. Kelling and Wilson wrote in their article that urban "disorder" increased the likelihood of violent crime. Definitions of urban disorder, they conceded, were "inherently ambiguous." Objects of disorder (such as "untamed weeds" or even the titular "broken windows") were discussed interchangeably with humans, including "panhandlers, drunks, addicts, rowdy teenagers, prostitutes, loiterers, the mentally disturbed." Kelling and Wilson maintained that these "disreputable or obstreperous or unpredictable people" were "not violent people, nor, necessarily, criminals," but nonetheless, they allegedly produced the urban conditions in which violent crime flourished. This formulation readily collapsed so-called disorderly people into criminals themselves. In order to reclaim the streets from these latent carriers of urban violence, as the broken windows theory went, police officers must be empowered to perform aggressive "order-maintenance" policing, which would reverse the otherwise inevitable slide from disorder to criminality. Kelling and Wilson delivered a gripping narrative of urban deterioration caused not by material deprivation but by behaviors that offended middle-class sensibilities. The broken windows theory, then, offered a powerful justification to forcefully police behavioral and aesthetic effrontery in order to prevent violent crime and spur the economic and social revitalization of cities.[22]

Broken windows was not only a criminological theory of policing. It was also a revisionist history of policing in the United States. Kelling and Wilson recalled with nostalgia an imagined period before World War II when police helped families "reclaim authority over the streets" from suspicious people: "young toughs," "prostitutes," and "petty thieves." Rights, they wrote approvingly, "were something enjoyed by decent folk" who, not coincidentally, "could afford a lawyer." This revised history exposed the criminologists' political hostilities to the postwar construction of legal protections for individual rights—or what they referred to as "legal restrictions" on police—and their sympathies for the unrestrained police authority that broken windows policing required. Kelling and Wilson singled out for particular scorn the court rulings and decriminalization campaigns of the 1970s that sought to establish checks on discretionary urban law enforcement and made "depolicing" a viable and attractive police reform. In this account, cities were unpleasant, uncomfortable, and sometimes even frightening places to live not because of the entangled, deeply racist histories of industrial and political abandonment—namely urban deindustrialization and slashed social supports—but rather because police were forced to abide by civil liberties protections.[23]

Broken windows policing offered a full-throated defense of broad police discretion. Kelling and Wilson urged readers to turn away from a concern for the protection of individual rights and toward the protection of the rights of "decent folk." As a result, they elevated the "perception of disorder" and "fear of being bothered by disorderly people" from subjective personal opinions to legally actionable police priorities. Officers should be empowered to take "informal or extralegal steps" to enforce ad hoc community standards of order, the criminologists wrote, even if their actions "probably would not withstand a legal challenge." Kelling and Wilson conceded that there was no way to ensure that police officers, armed with the wide latitude to enforce "inherently ambiguous" standards of order, would not become "agents of neighborhood bigotry." All they could do was "hope that by their selection, training, and supervision, the police will be inculcated with a clear sense of the outer limit of their discretionary authority." While Kelling and Wilson admitted that broken windows policing had not been proven to reduce crime rates, they argued that the program would successfully redistribute fear, minimizing the fear of "respectable" people and, implicitly, amplifying the fear of poor and marginalized urban residents. This, they argued, was a necessary law enforcement shift that would have a positive impact on the economic and social health of the city.[24]

Broken windows policing, then, was characterized by five elements: an aesthetic regime that prioritized middle-class perceptions of crime over the actual incidence of crime; the conflation of so-called disorderly people with criminals; aggressive discretionary police enforcement of low-level misdemeanors to clear people deemed disorderly off city streets; a rejection of due process liberalism in favor of the rights of middle-class and elite residents, most likely property owners; and finally, the highly publicized inclusion of community groups aligned with these goals to legitimize the program. Each of these five elements would surface in the implementation of broken windows policing in liberal, Black-led Atlanta.

Sexually profiled women remained a central and unifying symbol of precisely the sort of destructive "disorder" that broken windows policing was designed to address. To be sure, "promiscuous and scantily clad prostitutes," as Kelling wrote, were just one group in a larger galaxy of disorder. The controlling narrative that linked Black womanhood, violent sexual criminality, and urban decline was one tributary in a racist logic that located the source (rather than the outcome) of urban failures in the poorest and most vulnerable residents. But sexually profiled women were held up as an important justification for strict and unequivocal misdemeanor policing that facilitated the expansion of broken windows policing to include a broad range of "disorderly" people. "Public drunkenness, street prostitution, and pornographic displays can destroy a community more quickly than any team of professional burglars," Kelling and Wilson wrote in the *Atlantic*. Across the 1970s, as politicians, businessmen, and police tested new law enforcement strategies in direct response to sexually profiled women, they landed on the same conclusion as Kelling and Wilson.[25]

In 1977 the members of CAP's Crime Task Force did not explain why they considered increased police presence necessary to confront urban disorder. However, within a few short years, the broken windows theory would supply the analysis to link "perceptions of crime"—the white desire for the elimination of "distasteful worrisome encounters"—with increased law enforcement. "Serious street crime flourishes in areas in which disorderly behavior goes unchecked," Kelling and Wilson argued. This bit of "folk wisdom"—which the criminologists argued was "a correct generalization"—validated the unexamined assumptions of downtown business interests. Guided by its members' "folk wisdom," CAP experimented with increased misdemeanor policing, which would soon become axiomatic among urban officials and law enforcement authorities. CAP's early work offers one explanation for the stunning success of broken windows policing in 1982: Kelling and Wilson ratified the impulses of downtown business elites with criminological authority.[26]

Legalizing Broken Windows Policing

"Folk wisdom" would not be enough to push through Atlanta business elites' agenda of mass misdemeanor policing. Throughout the 1970s, Atlanta remained in the national spotlight as home to the nation's highest homicide rates. But CAP members and their business allies insisted on devoting strapped city resources to clearing out sexually profiled women, "derelicts," and Black male "harassers" who made white, middle-class visitors to downtown uncomfortable. Within an urban climate of the serial killing of Black youth, a rationale needed to be developed to justify stepped-up police focus on low-level misdemeanors. CAP's public justifications and legal agenda for aggressive prostitution enforcement helped to establish the legislation that would authorize the otherwise unconstitutional practice of broken windows policing.[27]

The issue of prostitution enforcement was especially useful for this purpose because, as a low-level offense that authorities identified as a cause of larger-order crimes, commercial sex served as the bridge that gave police the power to go after other forms of street disorder more generally. In Atlanta, as in cities elsewhere, commercial sex was linked to violent criminality to justify aggressive misdemeanor enforcement. The general manager of the Marriott downtown angrily claimed, with no supporting evidence, that "90% of the violent crime problem we have here at the Marriott is related to the prostitution problem." CAP advanced this logic in a 1979 report it spearheaded on crime in Atlanta. While "prostitution cannot be placed in the same category" as violent crimes, the authors argued that commercial sex should remain a "continuous concern," because "robberies[,] assaults, and

Atlanta   149

other crimes also result from this type of activity." The authors added that "from a public relations perspective, perceived or actual prostitution" could have a negative impact on downtown business.[28]

Commercial sex was a major pressure point for downtown business interests throughout the late 1970s. A few out-of-town executives withdrew their convention business from Atlanta because they were "totally aghast how low the morals had sunk to in downtown Atlanta" or because a sales representative had been "accosted during the evenings by prostitutes [and] he and his family just did not feel comfortable." CAP allies diligently forwarded this correspondence to city council members and the mayor's office. Frustrated, Sweat suggested "a summit meeting with Mayor Jackson" and the commissioner of public safety. An editorial in the *Atlanta Constitution* sustained these efforts, arguing that Jackson had allowed an "aura of permissiveness" to develop in the city that hindered the practice of "no-nonsense law enforcement." This pressure delivered results. In a 1979 meeting, Jackson declared to hundreds of city officials and businessmen that "hookers' effect on the economy and urban development of the 'fragile' Midtown community cannot be lightly dismissed."[29]

There were also signs of CAP's influence on police leadership. Lee Brown, the Black public safety commissioner appointed to replace Eaves, rejected the earlier claims issued from his post that scarce police resources should be used to target more serious crimes. When Brown released the Anticrime Action Plan at the end of 1979, he acknowledged that previous police leaders had prioritized violent crimes. Instead, Brown issued an agenda to address "the overall crime problem . . . across the full spectrum" of offenses. Prostitution earned its own prong in his eleven-point plan, which targeted the elimination of "street hookers": "Prostitution is not a 'victimless crime,'" the report stated. "Its presence does not just impact upon a city's image or moral reputation. Inexorably connected with street Prostitution is Robbery, Mugging, Aggravated Assault, and at times, Homicide."[30]

Atlanta's urban authorities were warming to the prescription of rigorous mass misdemeanor policing to ostensibly prevent serious violent crime. But despite the support of city hall and the police department, the challenge of legalizing status policing—the practice of policing people based on subjective perceptions of disorder—remained. In 1972 the Supreme Court struck down vagrancy laws in *Papachristou v. Jacksonville* as unconstitutionally vague. In the wake of this ruling, competing legal experiments were tested throughout the 1970s and 1980s to, on the one hand, hasten the demise of vague morals laws or, on the other, restore the discretionary power of police to target suspected agents of urban disorder. Atlanta, with ample pressure from CAP, pursued the latter strategy. However, civil libertarian and feminist lawyers pushed hard for the former, seeking to build on the momentum of *Papachristou* to overturn status laws that remained on the books, especially loitering laws.[31]

In 1973 the American Civil Liberties Union received funding from the Playboy Foundation to create the Sexual Privacy Project; with the support of Ruth Bader Ginsburg, then–general counsel for the ACLU and founder of the Women's Rights Project, attorney Marilyn Haft pursued the decriminalization of prostitution-related misdemeanors. Local lawyers took up this work too, appealing women's prostitution-related convictions in cities nationwide—in some cases all the way up to state supreme courts, as in New York (1976), Massachusetts (1977), and Georgia (1978). Arguments for decriminalization involved matters of gender discrimination, due process violations, and freedom of speech rights. But at its core, this work was an effort to redefine the legal scope of police discretion that powered morals law enforcement.[32]

As lawyers fought to overturn the prostitution-related laws on the books, urban and state lawmakers responded to the loss of vagrancy laws with an updated class of morals laws—loitering with intent laws, such as "loitering with intent to commit prostitution." These laws did not merely criminalize neutral gestures such as hailing a car or standing on the street, which would now be constitutionally endangered, but rather criminalized these neutral gestures as proof of *intent* to commit a crime. Intent laws sought to empower police to target a wide range of so-called disorderly behaviors—a legal workaround that, in practice, bore a striking resemblance to unconstitutional status policing. Despite the lengthy roster of urban residents who were targeted by loitering laws, prostitution-related offenses were, as historian Anna Lvovsky writes, the most "commonly litigated" loitering violations after *Papachristou*. Women's sexuality was the field on which prosecutors tested the power of police to act as street-level judges of people's criminality.[33]

The foundational test case on the post-*Papachristou* legal terrain was *People v. Smith* in New York. In October 1976 Toni Smith challenged her conviction on a new law criminalizing loitering with intent to commit prostitution, which the New York legislature had passed to allow the police to remove women from downtown Manhattan in advance of the July 1976 Democratic National Convention. In Smith's lower court trial, a police officer testified that he had seen Smith standing on a city street "near several other known prostitutes" outside a hotel that he claimed "catered to prostitutes and their clients" and talking to three men walking by—in one case she allegedly "touched [a man's] arm"—before entering the hotel with one. When Smith and the man reemerged about five minutes later, the officer "had a conversation with the man" and then arrested her. Smith challenged the validity of the police officer's discretion, protesting that she could have been asking for directions or "talking about the baseball score," and argued that this statute gave police "virtually unfettered discretion . . . and thereby encourages arbitrary and discriminatory enforcement."[34]

The district attorney's team, however, countered that the unique experience and training of police provided an important brake on the officer's discretion. This expertise enabled "trained policemen . . . [to] distinguish a Times Square hooker from a female political worker." The lower court agreed with Smith, but in a decision that would be echoed in subsequent cases throughout the 1980s, the higher court reversed the ruling by affirming the "superior insight into criminal activity" that police brought to the streets. "Particulars obvious to and discernible by any trained law enforcement officer [made it] a simple task" for police to determine the innocence or criminality of "casual street encounters."[35]

People v. Smith signaled that courts were increasingly reconceiving police discretion not as an example of unconstitutional police overreach but rather as a compelling indicator of police qualifications to appropriately enforce these laws. Morals enforcement was redefined as a neutral application of police expertise. As a corollary, judges affirmed that sexual criminality was an objectively knowable fact of life on the streets that police officers were uniquely trained to identify and relay to the court. The reliance on police testimony in prostitution-related cases was surely not new—in the early twentieth century, police officers had prosecuted cases against women in some courts, and across the decades, judges typically believed the testimony of police over women—but by the late twentieth century, police observations were increasingly enshrined in court rulings as a specific form of professional, expert knowledge. For example, as one municipal court judge presiding over prostitution trials explained, "Police officers very seldom exaggerate or lie." A police officer's testimony was "more accurate" than the defendant's because "he is trained and has no self-interest." Decades of police practices had refuted this judicial faith in police neutrality. Nevertheless, as this first wave of loitering with intent laws was tested in courts, the presumption of special police expertise authorized the expansion of discretionary police power that would make broken windows policing possible.[36]

The nationwide legal battles over status policing came to Atlanta in 1978 with *Lambert v. City of Atlanta*. That summer, the Supreme Court of Georgia heard a challenge to the city's 1974 municipal ordinance prohibiting "loitering in a public place for the purpose of soliciting for prostitution or sodomy." The Atlanta loitering ordinance under dispute gave police officers broad discretion to arrest women who "manifested" public indications of enticement or solicitation. These manifestations included a host of innocuous physical gestures. According to the law, a legitimate suspect "repeatedly beckons to, stops or attempts to stop, or engages passers-by in conversation, or repeatedly stops or attempts to stop motor vehicle operators by hailing, waving of arms or any bodily gesture." The law also stated that police could arrest a person who "is a known prostitute, pimp, or sodomist," effectively criminalizing anyone who had previously come to police attention or been arrested in the past—regardless of what they were doing at the time of arrest, even for merely walking in public.[37]

In 1977 Patricia Lambert was arrested on this charge twice in downtown Atlanta. Officer J. P. Ansa testified in municipal court that he arrested Lambert because "we observed this female waving to vehicles and engaging in conversation with several males" before walking into a nearby hotel. Perhaps most damning, Ansa claimed that Lambert was also seen going into bars "with white males"—a marker of whiteness that indicated Lambert was Black. Finally, Ansa argued that the "female is a known prostitute to myself" even though she did not appear to have any record before her 1977 arrests.[38]

Lambert's lawyer, Glenn Zell—presumably working pro bono, since Lambert declared her poverty during court proceedings—perennially served as defense for many prostitution- and adult entertainment–related cases in Atlanta. He vigorously objected to Ansa's ostensible evidence and his "unbridled discretion" more broadly. "It's absolutely legal [to talk to people and walk in and out of places] and if she's guilty, then everybody in this courtroom is guilty of walking out of a bar, walking out of a hotel, because I've done it a hundred times," he argued in the lower court trial. Zell concluded that the "vague, overbroad" Atlanta municipal loitering law "leaves in the hands of an arresting officer unfettered discretion to determine whether an offense has been committed." Lambert's right to exist on city streets "is left entirely to the pleasure of the police; thus inviting arbitrary and selective enforcement."[39]

Zell took specific aim at the judicial presumption of police expertise that had been developed in *People v. Smith*. Ansa testified that Lambert was arrestable because he observed her enter a hotel with different men—but here Ansa's surveillance ended. In Zell's cross-examination, he asked, "You don't know what they did when they went out of your sight? You have no way of knowing?" Ansa admitted this was true. Moreover, Ansa had not overheard any of Lambert's conversations with the men. The officer had charged Lambert based purely on her physical presence in the city and her socialization with white men. The loitering law, Zell argued, was "facially unconstitutional because it effectively licenses the policeman on the beat to create his own subjective standard, on an ad hoc basis, as to what may or may not constitute" sexual criminality.[40]

Zell was responding to judicial trends when he challenged the deficiencies in police expertise. However, Atlanta prosecutors—led by the Jackson-appointed solicitor Mary Welcome—were more concerned with defending the economic need for the city's loitering law than defending the expertise of police officers enforcing it. "Atlanta is a fast growing urban city that has become a favorite among convention goers . . . well known for its several professional sport teams and its active night entertainment spots. These conditions offer great attraction to persons who linger on our streets for the purpose of soliciting, inducing or inticing [sic] others to commit acts of prostitution or sodomy," Welcome's office wrote in its response to Lambert's appeal. "Some sections of our City are covered with hundreds of street walkers." Local authorities argued that state-level laws against prostitution and sodomy, which required greater evidence to convict, were useless to solve this alleged problem. The county solicitor general noted in an amicus brief in support of the city's case that Atlanta's ordinances were important tools for local law enforcement because "the burden of proof is less and punishment is less, so guilty pleas are more frequent and thus a policeman's work is over quicker." Prosecutors warned that overturning Atlanta's loitering law "would cause harm to citizens of our City," dismissing the harm of accelerated policing and convictions on targeted women, their families, and communities that Lambert fought against in her appeal.[41]

The Georgia Supreme Court's verdict was mixed: Lambert won her case, but her constitutional challenges to loitering laws were defeated. She ran up against *People v. Smith*, which the justices cited as they unanimously dismissed the constitutionality argument in her appeal. (Indeed, Atlanta prosecutors had argued that the loitering law was constitutional because it contained an element of intent and therefore conformed to the ruling in *People v. Smith*.) However, the justices did ultimately reverse Lambert's conviction and strike down the ordinance. They did this on the same grounds that the California Supreme Court voided California morals ordinances in 1961 in the *In re Lane* case, discussed in chapter 3: because the city laws preempted the higher power of the state criminal code.[42]

This ruling left authorities with only the state's prostitution law—which required that police observe evidence of a "proposition" in order to make a lawful arrest. When police protested *Lambert*, they read directly from the CAP script. Joe Amos, the deputy director of the Atlanta Police Bureau, told *Atlanta Constitution* reporters, "We've gotten letters from citizens from out of town who said . . . they were appalled at the number of streetwalkers." Amos was particularly galled that "there's no more fear in [women's] minds." The chief of the vice squad argued that since the loitering ordinance was struck down, prostitution "has been responsible for robberies and some larcenies."[43]

CAP members seized on the opportunity of this legal loss, shifting their antiprostitution campaign into high gear. With the Atlanta Chamber of Commerce and other allied organizations, they threw themselves into a lobbying program to win "legislative actions . . . creating new laws prohibiting solicitous behavior [which] is injurious to the welfare, safety, and quality of life in our city." Jackson and other urban officials immediately called for new legislation to augment the state prostitution law. Prodded by Atlanta legislators, the Georgia General Assembly passed a law that allowed cities and counties to enact their own loitering ordinances. Three months after the *Lambert v. City of Atlanta* ruling, this new law was rushed to the governor for his signature.[44]

Atlanta's city council swiftly voted to reinstate its ordinance. With the freshly granted power for cities to pass their own loitering laws, CAP pursued an increasingly sophisticated legal strategy for "fighting the prostitutes," as Sweat wrote in a 1984 memo. The Atlanta City Council steadily passed new legislation to affix mandatory penalties to the loitering law in order to discourage "leniency" both from police on the streets and in the courts.[45]

Both nationally and locally, these resurrected loitering laws helped to lay the groundwork for legalizing broken windows policing more broadly. Subsequent versions of loitering with intent laws would target alleged homelessness, gang membership, and drug dealing. In some cities, prostitution-loitering laws served as the specific template for new drug laws: for example, in Saint Petersburg, Florida, a prostitution-loitering law was expanded in

1989 to target drug-loitering. (The law was later struck down as unconstitutional by the Florida Supreme Court.) In Atlanta, too, observers recognized that the city's prostitution-loitering law could become a pathway to expanding the scope of discretionary police power to criminalize "derelicts." The grand jury empaneled in 1980 anticipated that "the crime of loitering may be another useful tool for law enforcement and will help reduce the incidence of persons simply 'hanging around' in suspicious situations."[46]

Armed with these new legal tools, Sweat worked at the turn of the decade to broaden the purview of downtown enforcement targets, organizing "strategy sessions" with downtown businessmen and civic groups "to get winos, derelicts, panhandlers, and watch and ring salesmen off the streets." CAP also began circulating harassment forms for people to share their experiences with "unsavory characters" downtown, which CAP then forwarded to police. While CAP's project was assiduously colorblind, these harassment forms reflected the unmistakably racist hostility that drove their law enforcement agenda and gave white residents an opportunity to clarify their police priorities. As one man wrote in a letter to Jackson, "I am becoming a bigot because these blacks (downtown) roam the streets at will." The harassment form helped to diversify CAP's repertoire of white middle-class outrage, tapping into the South's deep legacies of the protection of white womanhood. The vast majority of these forms were submitted by white women—or on behalf of white women by their male bosses in downtown offices—reporting unpleasant encounters with poor Black men who asked for a quarter, "loitered" outside, "fanny pinch[ed]," or called the women names like "white racist bitch." Sweat fumed to a commanding police officer that "the derelicts . . . are getting much bolder," and demanded in a memo to the police chief "more police surveillance and patrols" and "strict enforcement" of morals ordinances from the police.[47]

Bowing to CAP's pressure—and still in damage control after the Tetalman and Barry murders—the mayor rolled out a twenty-one-point anticrime plan, which built on the permissions of the reinstated loitering law: in addition to enforcing new legislation that criminalized the consumption of alcoholic beverages in downtown Atlanta, the plan included reassigning or adding 189 officers to street duty (a hiring spree made possible after the Atlanta Police Department discrimination lawsuit was settled), accepting federal Law Enforcement Assistance Administration funding for various programs, and instituting a Court Watch program to "determine the severity of penalties to criminals." To keep the heat on city hall to implement the twenty-one-point crime plan, CAP assembled yet another task force, this one called the Public Safety Task Force. Task force members—CAP's usual allies, representatives from downtown law firms, businesses, and hotels—argued that police visibility "has decreased drastically" and there was "little or no follow up by the specialized squads" that had been created by the mayoral plan. In August 1981, just before mayoral elections, the task force recommended that police "harass and arrest disorderly people" and "take a harder stand on drunks and derelicts that wonder [sic] around our city." One lawyer, who had submitted a harassment form on his secretary's behalf, asked a question that surely resonated with the Public Safety Task Force members: "When is this City going to stop giving lip service to cleaning up the mess in downtown Atlanta?"[48]

Mobilizing Residents for Broken Windows Policing

Owing to the city charter that Jackson had overhauled in his first term, he could not run for a third consecutive term in the fall of 1981 (he would, however, run and win a third term eight years later). Andrew Young, Jackson's preferred successor, launched a campaign to take his place. In an effort to end Jackson's influence for good, Sweat declared that "the patience of downtown businessmen with City Hall's policing policies had 'worn out,'" and business elites threw their support behind a white liberal state legislator, Sidney Marcus, dubbed the "great white hope." Their hopes were in vain, and Young won easily in a runoff.[49]

Despite (or perhaps because of) the downtown businessmen's obvious distaste for the Black mayor, Young immediately set about courting them. At a luncheon for the business elite two weeks after his election, Young explained, "It's obvious I didn't need your help to get elected, but I can't run the city without you." Sweat, for one, was very impressed with Young. "Andy Young's style is much easier for a white person to deal with," he said. "He doesn't come down so heavy-handed and so much isn't made into a racial issue." Young was approvingly described by white Atlantans as "civilized" and "a friend and a man with a head for business."[50]

White business elites responded to Young's overtures by demanding aggressive police action for misdemeanors on behalf of economic profitability. The members of the CAP-led Public Safety Task Force delivered a message to Young that they expected him and his judicial and enforcement appointees to take a "hard line against crime." During Young's tenure as mayor (1982–1990), CAP's campaign to frame downtown "derelicts" as a problem requiring police action became the defining logic of urban officials.

Indeed, the Comprehensive Development Plan prepared by city officials in 1986 listed an ongoing effort to "intensify crime deterrence efforts by increasing police effectiveness and visibility" as a key strategy for economic development. With Young at the helm of city hall, CAP and its allies were able to test the outer limits of their hardline agenda.[51]

Young also presided over widening economic inequality that mirrored broader national trends. Relative to other cities, Atlanta was fiscally healthy and, owing in part to CAP's zealous efforts, the economy "continued its energetic expansion," as the city's Department of Community Development reported in 1986. But these gains were distributed upward and failed to reach increasingly impoverished residents. Deepening wealth disparities were both interracial and intraracial, particularly in Atlanta, the "mecca of the Black middle class." White and Black middle-class residents continued to decamp to the suburbs, and by 1985, the city's population was 68 percent Black, up from 51 percent in 1970. The authors of a 1988 report on the city's economic status found that Atlanta was "Blacker and poorer than most [U.S. cities], but yet it resides in the midst of one of the fastest growing, most dynamic regional economies in the country." Throughout the 1980s, Atlanta had the second-highest poverty rate in the nation. By 1984, federal urban funding that was once earmarked to address this need dropped dramatically, from $49 million to $9 million. Federal subsidies for housing support in Atlanta were cut by 74 percent, contributing to the nationwide emergency of homelessness. The trebled crises of crack cocaine addiction, the AIDS epidemic, and the mental health deinstitutionalization movement, all unfolding alongside severely diminished or nonexistent treatment supports, exacerbated these rising rates of homelessness and poverty.[52]

While the political and legal justifications to support broken windows policing were often delivered in race- and gender-neutral language, popular media stamped a face on the presumed problem. Especially as crack cocaine addiction ravaged cities nationwide, poor Black women were singled out as the literal reproducers of what was, in fact, the state's structural failures. Newspapers fixated on the high rates of addiction among "young, child-bearing women" who were virtually always coded or illustrated as Black. "It is more than a drug, this crack," one journalist wrote. "It is women hiking their skirts in dim hallways for $5. It is babies left in garbage cans and surrendered to the arms of strangers. It is filthy hovels where the rodents practice better personal hygiene than the human occupants." In 1989 the *New York Times* reported, "By making wide inroads among women, crack has undermined a last vestige of family structure in inner-city neighborhoods."[53]

Black neighborhoods were presented as wastelands bereft of humanity—rather than sites of organized state and capital abandonment—a portrait that demonized Black women and the next generation of Black children as terrifying monsters. The *Atlanta Journal-Constitution* ran a column by Jeff Dickerson that asked readers to "consider the sad tale of Little Sally: Every day her Momma told her she was a loser. . . . So guess what: She grew up to be a loser. Not just a loser; a prostitute." Dickerson insisted that degraded Black motherhood—rather than material, everyday experiences of violence and exploitation—created a dangerous generation of women with poor self-esteem. Sally's turn to sexual criminality was directly connected to crack and the violence in "little 'Beiruts' in D.C., Atlanta, everywhere." "Sally is black America," Dickerson wrote. The "carnage these self-disrespecting people reap is spreading—possibly to you."[54]

Law enforcement dominated this media discourse: one study found that 66 percent of all quotes in *New York Times* coverage of crack cocaine came directly from police officers. As a result, the national narrative was packed with rhetorical alarm bells, arrest statistics, and law enforcement solutions. The onslaught of police-driven media accounts like these had a palpable effect on public opinion: in 1986, 3 percent of Americans reported "drug abuse" as the country's most urgent problem; by 1989, that number had spiked to 64 percent.[55]

As the media plastered the culture with images of degraded Black womanhood and authorities whipped up public support for antidrug policing, the war on drugs became a war on Black women. By 1990, the percentage of all women arrested in Atlanta who tested positive for any drugs (71 percent) was higher than that of men (62 percent). An astonishing 94 percent of women arrested on prostitution charges tested positive for drugs—more than the 90 percent of women arrested for drug possession. Police (ably assisted by social scientists) fed the media a steady diet of stories of drug-addicted sex workers. While it was certainly true that some women lived at the nexus of drug addiction and sex work, these statistics suggest that police were more likely to arrest the poorest and most vulnerable women, whom they suspected of engaging in sex work *and* drug use—a discretionary strategy, perhaps, to rack up additional charges or fish for a charge that would stick best in court.[56]

In this fertile political climate for law enforcement, Atlanta business elites and the city's public safety commissioner, Lee Brown, developed a new prong in their law enforcement agenda: a plan to recruit city residents in the fight for broken windows policing. This agenda item was called "community policing," and it was lifted directly from the broken windows playbook. "Police-community relations" programs had taken root in the 1940s in response to Black protests against police brutality. After the uprisings of the 1960s, community policing programs were tested to temper the inflammatory hostilities between police and Black residents. These initiatives could run the gamut from police-led athletic leagues with urban youth to assignments for officers of color to liaise with resident groups. But one characteristic that united these police-community programs was the participating departments' refusal to allow meaningful citizen oversight of, and police accountability to, their work.[57]

Given the capacious definition of police-community programs—and the strict limits on their community control—even broken windows policing could be defined as a community policing program. Kelling and Wilson opened their *Atlantic* article with an admiring description of a pilot program that increased foot patrols in Newark, where white police officers "defined and enforced [rules] in collaboration with the 'regulars' on the street." With these informal rules in place, "noisy teenagers were told to keep quiet" and "if a stranger loitered" or "bothered people waiting at bus stops," the police would interrogate and arrest them. Locals reported offenders of the informal rules to the police and "also ridiculed the violator." This experiment, and the broken windows theory that Kelling and Wilson developed from it, promised to repair relationships with Black residents while maintaining a monopoly on police control in Black neighborhoods. But more important, it offered a pathway for broken windows to gain public legitimacy through the cover of community collaboration.[58]

Brown, who would go on to build his law enforcement career on community policing in Houston and New York, first allied with Atlanta's business elites to implement this project. In 1982 the Department of Public Safety entered into the Police/Community Action Agreement with the Atlanta Business Coalition, whose members included CAP and the Atlanta Chamber of Commerce. This partnership, which was federally funded by the Law Enforcement Assistance Administration, formalized the commitment of the Department of Public Safety to "[increase] visibility and operations in the Central City and firm enforcement of laws which enhance the security of residents and visitors" in downtown Atlanta. In practice, the agreement stipulated that the city would establish permanent and increased patrols downtown; "operate a derelict van," which relocated individuals from downtown to an "appropriate facility"; and "deploy Operation Clean-Up," the codename for a police crackdown targeting sexually profiled women, men soliciting for sex (both straight and queer), and youthful "curfew violators." This "community partnership" model was later expanded to include residents citywide: the Department of Public Safety rolled out the Partnership against Crime program, which by 1985 had sixty-one community group affiliates. One year later, the Atlanta Department of Community Development argued that "increasing citizen awareness and involvement" in crime would have a beneficial impact on the city's economic health.[59]

Community partnerships like these converged with a nationwide trend of resident organizations across the color line fighting urban crime on their own terms. Police both discouraged and embraced these community initiatives. For example, since at least the 1960s, poor and working-class Black residents had been organizing volunteer patrols to compensate for the failures of police departments to provide adequate protection in their neighborhoods. During the Atlanta child murders, angry and frightened public housing residents organized the Bat Patrol, securing their neighborhood with baseball bats and firearms because they believed the police could not protect them. Jackson's administration and police leadership battled these volunteers and made requests (laced with threats of arrest) that the patrollers leave their protective work to the police. However, when Atlanta residents demanded stronger alliances with police and stricter law enforcement—rather than asserting the futility of the police and mobilizing for their own self-protection—they received a much warmer response from the city.[60]

Throughout the 1980s, middle-class urban residents garnered media attention for their organized demands of strict prostitution law enforcement. Atlanta residents who lived in downtown's Midtown neighborhood complained that prostitution threatened their property values, exposed their children to "this filth," and (without any evidence or even personal anecdotes to support this claim) brought "attendant problems of drugs, burglary, vandalism." "The people in the neighborhood were just tired of sharing their neighborhood," one woman explained to a *Constitution* reporter, articulating the sense of possessive reclamation that drove the residents' mobilization. "Basically all we're concerned about is that the police have the power to deal with the prostitutes." One Black resident, a real estate agent, offered his distinct concern that his wife "can't get out of the car . . . without getting propositioned or verbally accosted." Critics monitored these community developments closely: one white sex worker who attended the Midtown neighborhood meetings believed that residents were primarily concerned with "gentrification," or "planting a few trees and getting rid of the hookers, the poor people, the shelters for the homeless, the drug treatment centers."[61]

In 1981 predominantly white homeowners in Midtown and neighboring areas created the Neighborhood Planning Unit Prostitution Task Force, which consisted of city council members, a city planner, and various business and neighborhood associations. One member, who characterized the women she observed in her neighborhood as a "herd," claimed that her furious neighbors were on the verge of violent action: "They're going to start shooting people." Residents organized a "take-back-our-streets rally" in Midtown, and the president of two downtown business associations advocated for a "citizens march to protest against both prostitutes and property owners who rent to them." Mayor Young assured the members of the Prostitution Task Force that "we are arresting people," and he promised to press for crackdowns to "send a signal" that sexually profiled women would not be tolerated in the city. A lieutenant in the police bureau credited the "public outcry" with "helping us to do our jobs better" through tougher enforcement policies and expanded manpower.[62]

This partnership between residents and urban authorities culminated with the establishment of the Mayor's Task Force on Prostitution (MTFOP) in Atlanta, which released its final report in 1986. The MTFOP's work reflected a commitment to urban redevelopment sustained by aggressive morals enforcement, though it was delivered in the language of liberalism. While municipal task forces in other cities during these same years were unabashedly punitive, Atlanta's task force signaled the city's ostensible cosmopolitan sexual liberalism. Alongside city council members, judges, and police leaders, Dolores French, the white president of Hooking Is Real Employment, was appointed to the group (though not without controversy: Midtown residents rallied again, protesting her participation, while sex workers and their allies assembled for a counterrally and won the greater share of public attention at the action; see figure 5.1). The MTFOP claimed no objections to "private consensual adult sex" and members did not prioritize "prostitutes operating privately out of public view"—in other words, predominantly white sex workers were not a major concern.[63]

This sexual liberalism comfortably accommodated the MTFOP's adherence to a core tenet of broken windows policing: that "street prostitution and associated street activities (e.g., pimping, public sex, drug dealing,

FIGURE 5.1 Atlanta protest and counterprotest, 1985. Nationwide, residents in gentrifying neighborhoods demanded tough sexual policing. In Atlanta, sex workers and their allies organized a counterprotest that won the greater share of attention—but it was the middle-class residents who got Mayor Andrew Young's support. John Spink/*Atlanta Journal-Constitution* via AP.

mugging, robbery, etc.) pose the greatest threat to public safety." Street prostitution, frequently associated with Black women, was the primary concern because it allegedly "impede[s] the general upgrading of these areas." And because street prostitution was identified as the "greatest threat" to both public safety and economic development, the task force recommended diverting enforcement resources from women who primarily worked indoors (like French) and instead "targeting the city's limited resources to control street prostitution" and engaging in "more police 'sweep' operations . . . with an eye towards the arrest of all persons found to be in violation of the law." As the Atlanta MTFOP demonstrates, liberal policies and postures were perfectly compatible with aggressive, broken windows–style policing, which would disproportionately harm Black women.[64]

The executive committee of CAP generally supported the MTFOP report. But they were sufficiently discontented with the report's hands-off approach to indoor sex work that they passed a special resolution urging "even more strongly than the Task Force report" for stronger prostitution sanctions and stressed that CAP "in no way endorses . . . decriminalization of prostitution or any related crimes."[65]

While white residents were the core members of the citizen mobilization, a growing number of Black people agreed that aggressive misdemeanor policing was necessary to create a safer Atlanta for Black residents. Throughout the late 1980s and early 1990s, a Black lawyer, Larry Thompson, who had served as U.S. attorney general for the northern district of Georgia and would later become deputy attorney general under George W. Bush, wrote multiple reports for the conservative Heritage Foundation that were circulated in Atlanta's white and Black press. Thompson argued that "many Blacks do not see strong law enforcement efforts as a threat to individual civil liberties" but rather they are "correctly viewed as essential to preserving the rights of personal security and safety for the vast majority of Black citizens who are law-abiding." To this end, Thompson urged Black readers to "support tough (and sometimes expensive) measures that target street crime, especially in neighborhoods that are vulnerable to burglaries, robberies, muggings, drug dealings, and prostitution." Black city council member Marvin Arrington, who became council president in 1980 and harbored mayoral ambitions, insisted "that law and order is no longer a racist code phrase for use by whites only." This elite conservative messaging resonated for some Black residents across the economic spectrum, because as their neighborhoods were devastated by the structural failures of the 1980s, tough-on-crime policing endured as one tactic where Black residents saw traction in their demands. After a crackdown at a public housing site, the resident manager, Eunice Palmer, wrote a letter of gratitude to the police chief "for the outstanding services rendered. . . . I thank God for this blessing of being able to walk through the complex without seeing young men and women standing on the sides of the buildings selling drugs or selling their bodies for drugs."[66]

One crucial political innovation of broken windows policing was the strategy to consolidate the discretionary authority of police through a race-conscious bid to rescue Black neighborhoods. "Illegal loutish behavior," Kelling wrote, "most tragically . . . affected those with the least resources to deal with it: the poor, minorities, elderly, and other inner-city residents." Black neighborhoods were indeed seized by the interlocking crises of poverty, homelessness, drug addiction, and the AIDS epidemic throughout the 1980s. Kelling and Wilson's argument allowed broken windows advocates to make a claim that strongly resonated in a conservative political moment of rising impatience with civil rights and civil liberties activisms: that aggressive policing programs that diminished people's individual rights were in fact the morally and politically correct choice for observers concerned about the welfare of urban Black residents. Critics of expanded police powers were dismissed as elite, paternalistic, and naive defenders of individual rights who did not have to suffer the consequences of living in impoverished neighborhoods. "Far from being terrorized by anti-loitering laws, curfews and building searches," two legal scholars from the University of Chicago argued, "many inner-city residents *support* these measures as potent weapons against the crime that drastically diminishes their economic and social prospects." Black supporters of expanded police powers ranged from conservative elites to besieged residents with few other viable political options available to them beyond demanding more police.[67]

The Safeguard Zone

In 1986 CAP began exploratory planning for its most ambitious project to date, the Central Area Study (CAS), which was charged with producing a comprehensive set of urban policy recommendations. The CAS was formed in partnership with real estate developers, corporate executives, and representatives from the Bureau of Police Services, the U.S. Department of Justice, the Office of Economic Development, and Mayor Young's office. This study was notable because it was CAP's second such venture: the first CAS report, released in 1971, focused on urban transportation and infrastructure. The dramatic shift in CAP's priorities, from urban planning to urban policing, reflected the broader logics that shaped urban governance nationwide. Moreover, the organizational structure of the CAS II exposed the power hierarchy embedded within this public-private partnership: CAP contributed the lion's share of the $1.7 million to fund the study, set the agenda for CAS II task forces, and, as one historian writes, "monopolized leadership at every level of decision making."[68]

The CAS II report represented the culmination of CAP's nearly decade-long crusade for the muscular enforcement of morals laws and for closer collaboration between police, business elites, politicians, and politically aligned citizens. Arguing that "Atlanta's Midtown area is plagued by street prostitution and accompanying drinking, drug use and fighting," CAS II members made elaborate recommendations for short-term and long-term crime control, statistics gathering, public relations, increased reliance on private security guards, better coordination with courts and corrections to discourage "leniency," "expanded incarceration capacity," and the continued expansion of the Partnership against Crime program. CAS II working group members suggested that the Bureau of Police Services "aggressively implement the recommendations of the Mayor's Task Force on Prostitution" and "provide increased training . . . regarding the new anti-loitering ordinance, and refresher training in all ordinances that address street crimes."[69]

But these older priorities were repackaged with a robust defense of broken windows policing as the most viable policy solution to crime. CAS II members devoted some attention to searching for root causes of heavily racialized crime. They identified the behavioral response to a lack of economic opportunity as the prime culprit. A "'culture of crime' flourishes in many poor minority neighborhoods today," they argued, because poor Black residents were so thoroughly locked out of the dominant urban economy. As a result, "the traditional values which preserve social order aren't relevant within these populations." CAS II members brushed aside the question of "a restructuring of the social order" as beyond the scope of the study, and their priority of police intervention was clear: "Government-sponsored social support, such as many of the programs of the 60's, has been judged a failure." While some welfare programs still might offer lessons for future policy makers, CAS II members urged that any such proposals be weighed against the new gold standard of crime control—"law enforcement and our burgeoning correctional system"—and compete for "public acceptance of the direct link between conditions of inequality and crime."[70]

CAP's most controversial proposal to realign social policy with law enforcement initiatives issued from CAS II working groups. In September 1986 the police effectiveness subcommittee of the CAS II project hashed out the details of a "'sanitized' zone that must be established along the Peachtree Corridor that would be absolutely free of crime." The "sanitized zone"—or as CAS II working members carefully rebranded it for public consumption, the "Safeguard Zone"—called for a consolidated downtown police unit "with sufficient police personnel to saturate the Zone twenty-four hours a day, supported by mounted, scooter, vehicular patrols, and utilizing state-of-the-art fixed and mobile communications equipment"; a "creative pay/incentive program for police"; and a "major publicity campaign to accompany implementation of the recommendations." In a strategy paper that was circulated for all CAS II participants, drafters argued that the Safeguard Zone would serve as "an effective public statement that lawlessness will not be tolerated, backed up by the police action to establish its validity." Drawing on the broken windows–inspired language of "quality of life" initiatives that were taking hold in cities like New York and Los Angeles, CAS II members argued that in the Safeguard Zone, police officers should "effectively enforce 'quality of life crime' ordinances and provide significant control of the movement of street persons, transients, hangers-on, loiterers and the street vendors," or what the CAS II Public Safety Task Force called "Human Urban Blight."[71]

The Safeguard Zone proposal explicitly set out to criminalize the poor. This work consolidated CAP's long record of strategically targeting specific groups, such as sexually profiled women and Black male "harassers," to force open the scope and purpose of police power on downtown streets. The justification for policing the studiously race-neutral population of "street persons" depended on middle-class perceptions—and these perceptions in turn transformed a wide range of poor people into criminals. Some Atlanta politicians embraced the Safeguard Zone, and CAP's broader criminalization agenda, including Ira Jackson, a Black city council member: "You're going to have to get tough on loitering and on any kind of crime that occurs in [the Central Area] because if you don't, you'll be defeating your purpose."[72]

But the Safeguard Zone did not have unanimous support among the CAS II members or city residents. Critics who worked on the CAS II Public Safety Task Force immediately charged that the Safeguard Zone was a tactic to displace and criminalize homeless people—an affront to constitutional protections and basic human decency. Task force members Rev. Joanna Adams, a white woman, and Black criminologist Julius Debro argued that it was not a crime to be homeless and that "more services"—instead of more police—"must be provided" for people experiencing homelessness. When news broke of the zone proposal, church-based housing advocates and homeless activists immediately organized high-profile protests. "We're talking about arresting people simply being on Peachtree Street if they don't look white middle class," one critic told the *Atlanta Journal-Constitution*. Another charged that "much of the safeguard zone has racist overtones." Owing to these actions focusing on CAP's demonization of the homeless—strategically timed to coincide with Christmas—the Safeguard Zone met with popular derision.[73]

Pushed on the defensive, CAP's policy architects emphasized that the "Safeguard Zone is NOT designed to be a vagrant-free zone but rather an area of good security, one [in] which lawlessness will not be tolerated." Sweat shifted attention away from the rights of poor and marginalized

Atlantans and toward what he called "the rights of taxpaying citizens [who] must also be protected from harassment by unruly street preachers and street persons." And the architect of the Safeguard Zone, Bob Schmitz—a veteran military careerist and "public safety specialist" who had been recruited to report directly to Sweat on the CAS II project—reminded the task force members "that we must also consider the concerns of . . . afraid citizens, those with a bad perception of the Central Area."[74]

Despite CAP's efforts to reframe the debate about the Safeguard Zone as a question of the rights of "taxpaying" and "afraid" citizens, the protests of people experiencing homelessness and their allies successfully thwarted the implementation of the proposal's original design. When sexually profiled women were at the center of law enforcement initiatives, CAP had reliably gained traction. Its work faltered when the organization tried to expand its net to ensnare poor people as a blanket group. But these stumbles only slowed the juggernaut of CAP-led police policy that delivered the city to the brink of the Safeguard Zone. Days after Young took a public stand against the Safeguard Zone, he recanted because he did not want to disrupt the opening of Underground Atlanta, an entertainment development downtown, nor invite any further protests or undesirable media attention during the 1988 Democratic National Convention in Atlanta. (This embarrassing flip-flop prompted the mayor to engage in a publicity stunt in which he pretended to be a homeless man for a day.)[75]

In February 1987 the members of the CAS II Public Safety Task Force completed their revised report. While the language was softened—people experiencing homelessness were specifically characterized as "more likely to be victims than perpetrators of crime"—the recommendations for a consolidated and renamed Central Police Zone remained intact. Sweat and other task force members had "secured approval of the concept" from zone commanders of the Bureau of Police Services. And after briefing the city hall manager (and future mayor of Atlanta) Shirley Franklin, CAS II leaders reported that "there were no objections expressed about the Central Police Zone at that time." That summer, Young and the Atlanta City Council president "announced a $50 million bond initiative to fund a crime package implementing the recommendations of the CAS II report." A week before Young rolled out the bond initiative, the mayor ordered "aggressive, non-violent enforcement" of public order laws downtown "at the instigation of the same business leaders" who had demanded the Central Police Zone, according to the *Atlanta Journal-Constitution*.[76]

CAP did not win the Safeguard Zone or the bond initiative—which failed to win popular voter support—but opponents would be forced to reckon with the CAS II recommendations for years to come. When voters returned Maynard Jackson to city hall for a third and final term in 1989, his transition team floated another Safeguard Zone proposal—this time called a "Hospitality Zone." Jackson's team explicitly framed the proposed consolidated police district as a measure to create a protected space for middle-class visitors, who, as many critics pointed out, typically violated the same public order laws like loitering and public drunkenness that police enforced against poor and Black people. Given the blowback from the first effort, Sweat acknowledged that Jackson's proposal "ain't going through."[77]

Even so, there were some law enforcement victories during this time. In 1988 city council members approved a budget package that earmarked over $2.5 million in funding for more police officers and the construction of new headquarters. The arc of Jackson's career reflected the profound reorientation of criminal policy in cities nationwide: in his earliest work, the mayor and his police chief argued for individual rights and the value of redirecting morals enforcement resources in order to focus on violent crimes. Yet by the start of his third term, Jackson was willing to test out the limits of aggressive misdemeanor enforcement policies.[78]

CAP leaders had sculpted the political environment in which Jackson operated. Their proposals for police-heavy policies, however contested, established the parameters of the politically possible in the city. And despite their appeals to Black politicians, the CAS II report made it clear that middle-class whiteness was their desired endgame for the police saturation and mass misdemeanor enforcement downtown: the report's illustrations were portraits of an imagined Atlanta dubbed "the shared vision," and they featured exclusively white pedestrians strolling down pristine commercial streets, attending the theater, or supervising children in front of their well-manicured townhomes that sat in the shadow of high-rise condominium buildings. This "shared vision" was, in fact, the reclamation of urban space by middle-class whites, violently enforced through misdemeanor policing (see figure 5.2).[79]

Though Kelling and Wilson inspired a generation of policy makers and city residents to demand aggressive police practices, CAP had been wending its way toward this same vision of "sanitized" urban whiteness years before broken windows policing was first introduced. Under Sweat's guidance, CAP first landed on its influential police program through publicizing and

THE SHARED VISION

FIGURE 5.2 "The Shared Vision" presented in the 1987 Central Area Study II, a project funded and directed by Central Atlanta Progress, illustrated the white middle-class reclamation of urban space, violently enforced through misdemeanor policing. Courtesy of the Atlanta History Center.

targeting the "problem" of sexually profiled Black women. As Atlanta's history demonstrates, the intensified targeting of Black women for morals misdemeanors exposes the overlapping and mutually reinforcing logic of criminalizing the poor that propelled the crime policy experiments of the 1970s into the broken windows consensus of the 1980s.

・・・・・・

Perhaps what is most surprising about the broken windows theory is the speed with which it was accepted as a social truth, and the consensus that rapidly formed around more policing as the solution to the failures of cities to nourish and sustain all residents. To be sure, the racialization of crime—and the specific postwar reconfiguration of Blackness as a significant threat to urban viability—had been under construction since the era of emancipation. And young Black men were certainly singled out by police, white residents, and, later, Kelling and Wilson themselves as a significant source of urban violence and criminality. But this preoccupation, which is replicated by historians, obscures not only the distinct ways Black women were targeted, criminalized, and harmed by broken windows policing but also the ways in which the sexual criminalization of Black women enabled the implementation of such policing. At key junctures, urban authorities marshaled the specter of "Black prostitutes" to win political and legal victories. Rhetorically, prostitution was a recurring theme, first in CAP's programs and later in Kelling and Wilson's work, and it unified the highly publicized police-citizen antiprostitution alliances that sprang up in cities across the nation during the 1980s. Legally, prostitution was the testing ground for a new class of misdemeanors and punitive mechanisms that empowered police to engage in the otherwise unconstitutional practice of status policing.

The evolution of CAP in Atlanta demonstrates that material work had to be undertaken, both within CAP's ranks and citywide, to overturn the enduring logic that disorder was not a crime. CAP's successful efforts in the late 1970s indicated that urban powerbrokers were hungry for logics and laws to authorize and deploy punitive criminal measures as the solutions to urban poverty. By the Reagan era, the logic of the broken windows theory helped to naturalize the criminality of disorder. Presenting broken windows policing as "a positive and wholesome strategy to 'defend' communities," scholar Bernard Harcourt writes, "tapped into a longstanding project of social order and helped to normalize the idea that surveillance, interrogation, and punishment of the disorderly is 'natural, necessary, preordained.'"[80]

Nationwide, misdemeanor morals arrests soared throughout the 1980s. Between 1980 and 1989, arrests for all offenses rose by nearly a third, but women were arrested at a much faster rate than men: women's arrests increased by 48 percent, while men's arrests increased by only 24 percent. During these same years, women's arrests rose faster than men's in nearly every morals offense category: a 23 percent increase for prostitution (compared with 12.5 percent for men), a 69 percent increase for sex offenses (40 percent for men), and a 46 percent increase for disorderly conduct (8 percent for men). Where local statistics exist, this spike was reflected at the city and state levels too. For example, in 1976, there were six thousand prostitution-related cases in the New York criminal system; by 1986, there were sixteen thousand cases. In Los Angeles, prostitution-related arrests nearly doubled between 1974 and 1984, and the sheriff's department county arrests nearly quintupled in these same years. In Florida, between 1976 and 1986, the total arrests of adult women for prostitution-related offenses increased by 165 percent. Atlanta statistics are spotty during these years, but a snapshot of arrests between January and August 1983 provides a clear racial portrait of enforcement: 137 white women (and 16 white men) were charged with prostitution-related offenses, compared with 247 Black women (and 47 Black men). Racist and sexist morals enforcement was especially prominent in disorderly conduct arrests: 97 white women (and 15 white men), compared with 531 Black women (and 67 Black men).[81]

While the proportion of Black people arrested for morals misdemeanors nationwide was outrageous, it was actually not as stark as it was in the late 1960s and 1970s. The proportion of white people arrested for public order misdemeanors rose throughout the long 1980s: from 35 percent in 1974, to 44 percent in 1980, and finally to 61 percent in 1991. One researcher in Florida noted the "decline in proportional [racial] disparity" in arrests of Black and white women throughout the 1980s. The shifting racial proportions of people arrested, combined with the increased volume of misdemeanor arrests, do not suggest that police priorities changed to decelerate the targeting of Black women. Rather, they suggest that as police patrolled the streets with greater powers to arrest sexually profiled women, white women—particularly those who worked in the shrinking but still definitely live downtown commercial sex districts—were increasingly caught up in police sweeps that remained nonetheless hostile to, and in fact driven by, law enforcement campaigns against Black women on city streets.[82]

The expansion of police power in the realm of morals enforcement meant an expansion of the field on which police historically engaged in corruption and brutality. In 1986, an *Atlanta Journal-Constitution* columnist ran an interview with a racially unmarked sex worker named Sweetpea. She detailed the unique forms of abuse that sex workers were vulnerable to, and the ways that police officers exploited this vulnerability. What most outraged Sweetpea was that "cops will go to bed with a prostitute and then arrest her. I don't think that is right." Another reporter interviewed Amy ("young, black, and beautiful"), who offered the same appraisal of Atlanta police: "The cops here are bad." Throughout the 1980s, reports surfaced in Atlanta and nationwide of police raping sexually profiled women, or extorting women for sex or money in exchange for not arresting them. Sex workers and their allies named and challenged the ways that sexual policing uniquely created a meshwork of state and nonstate violence against women, forcing open a political debate about the gender-specific harms of broken windows policing.[83]

Broken windows policing came to life in the wake of the civil rights, Black power, and women's liberation movements—a historical reality that compelled police leaders, politicians, and white property owners to spin their calls for the mass clearance of "disorderly" people from city streets as politically palatable. Supporters of broken windows characterized these new policing practices as delivering long-overdue racial justice to severely distressed Black neighborhoods. But how could the mass arrest and spatial banishment of sexually profiled women possibly be spun as a form of protection for women—or even as feminist? A rising mobilization to end violence against women provoked intense debates among feminists and triggered major feminist protests against, and collaborations with, the broken windows regime. One central question that divided feminists was whether police were the problem—or the *answer* to the problem—of violence against women.

6 Taking Back the Night
Feminist Activisms in the Age of Broken Windows Policing

Throughout 1979, Andrea Dworkin traveled across North America delivering "The Night and Danger," which she called her "Take Back the Night speech." Dworkin was a leader in the movement of marches called Take Back the Night (TBTN), in which feminists protested violence against women by reclaiming city streets in the dark hours—when, as Dworkin declared, "men become more dangerous" and women are treated as "prey, targeted to be beaten or murdered or sexually violated." In her speech, Dworkin advanced a worldview in which male domination was women's universal condition. Biological sex—what she called "male sexuality, drunk on its contempt for all life, but especially for women's lives"—was the source of men's domination over women. Race, along with many other categories of difference, played a minor role in the scope and severity of women's vulnerability to violence. Though Dworkin did allow that Black women "are singularly and intensely punished by law and social mores," she argued that they "are used as all women are used." She similarly conflated all manifestations of male violence, both civilian and state powered. "The policemen of the night—rapists and other prowling men—have the right to enforce the laws of the night: to stalk the female and to punish her," Dworkin said. State power was irrelevant to the total domination of individual male predators. This analysis would animate the activism of a predominantly white cohort of feminists known as dominance feminists, who devoted their energies to fight the violence of individual men against a largely undifferentiated population of women.[1]

Dworkin and dominance feminists, however, did not hold a monopoly on what it meant to "take back the night"—and from whom. In cities nationwide, multiracial groups of antiviolence feminists organized decidedly different versions of TBTN marches. Activists affiliated with the Black feminist Combahee River Collective, sex workers' rights organizations, and the international anticapitalist Wages for Housework (WfH) network countered dominance feminists by naming the particularly powerful capacity of the state to produce and compound male violence against women; and by centering the experiences and struggles of women acutely and disproportionately vulnerable to violence: poor Black women.[2]

Starting in the late 1970s, serial murders in dozens of cities—including San Diego; Los Angeles; Oakland; Seattle; Portland, Oregon; Vancouver; Detroit; Pittsburgh; Rochester; Boston; Newark; Washington, D.C.; and Pensacola—terrorized Black women. When law enforcement authorities belatedly addressed these killings, the victims' social status was routinely marked according to the police logics of sexual criminality: they were described as "prostitutes" or, when no police record could be found, "street women." Black feminists and their allies mobilized to publicize and condemn these murders and the conditions that had made them possible. In Los Angeles, Margaret Prescod, an outraged WfH-affiliated organizer, formed a Los Angeles alliance called Black Coalition Fighting Back Serial Murders, protesting that "the serial murders, the problems with the investigation and the low-profile media coverage of these murders are all examples of women's lives not counting, and Black prostitute women counting least of all, therefore exposing the double burden of racism and sexism."[3]

In July 1986, Black Coalition Fighting Back members and WfH activists launched a multicity TBTN action with coordinated vigils, pickets, and die-ins protesting police neglect in the face of the serial murders of poor Black women in South Los Angeles. Prescod charged that police demonstrated a lethal indifference to Black women, and especially Black sex workers and sexually profiled Black women deemed worthless and disposable: in contrast, the recent serial murders of white women in Los Angeles had sparked public hysteria and immediate police attention. But at this TBTN action, Prescod and her allies did not only challenge police neglect—they went a step further by connecting police neglect with police violence in neighborhoods of color. Members of the Black Coalition Fighting Back demanded that the Department of Justice devote resources to the serial murder case and also "investigate reports of alleged police harassment, intimidation, and illegality against Black and poor immigrant communities locally." As a WfH activist later wrote, the July 1986 action was "different from other TBTN groups nationally because their focus was not only the violence of individual men against individual women, but also the violence of the State against women generally, and in particular against women of color."[4]

Antiviolence feminists like Prescod broke the mainstream silence on the nationwide crisis of serial murders of Black women in two distinct ways. First, they exposed and challenged the state's powerful role as a generator of violence against women, especially through the selective, racist enforcement of prostitution laws (and, ultimately, through the very existence of prostitution laws that enabled this discriminatory enforcement). And second, they argued that the discretionary police power to harass, arrest, and abuse women left Black women profoundly vulnerable to nonstate harm.[5]

As broken windows police programs took off, these antiviolence activists exposed the linkages between policies of aggressive misdemeanor arrests and the serial murders of women. Members of the WfH-affiliated U.S. Prostitutes Collective (U.S. PROS) argued that because broken windows policing was geared toward clearing "disorderly" people off city streets, these police practices directly contributed to the murder of sex workers and sexually profiled women. "Raids against prostitute women are a go-ahead to violent men," they said in a statement. "After all they too are removing 'bad women' from the streets." At a Los Angeles press conference and vigil in support of the Black Coalition Fighting Back, U.S. PROS put it more bluntly: "The police hunt down hookers, so the message is that anyone can hunt down hookers." In this specific iteration of TBTN actions, feminists took aim at the state, and specifically prostitution laws and their discriminatory police enforcement, as a powerful multiplier of Black women's vulnerability to violence and an important barrier to their economic and physical autonomy.[6]

Operating from different ideological analyses of gender oppression and the state, dominance and antiviolence feminists pursued very different activist agendas. The divergent politics driving the distinct TBTN actions reflected a deeper political cleaving among feminists throughout the 1980s, often referred to as the "sex wars." Debates over pornography—whether it was a form of sexual expression warped by racist and patriarchal institutions, or whether it was, as dominance feminists maintained, a form of violence that both incited male oppression and proved men's domination over women—served as a flashpoint for the rancorous polarization of feminists during these years. This theater of the sex wars is well documented. Competing activist agendas around prostitution laws in the 1980s, however, are less chronicled, and they demand reappraisal. Stripped of the debates about free speech and censorship that subsumed the pornography debates, the prostitution debates foregrounded urgent feminist issues: the role of the state in simultaneously producing the protection of some women and the predation of others; the racist and sexist state practices that materially shaped the density and velocity of oppressions women experience across axes of race, class, and sexuality; and finally, the desired terms of engagement with the state—if any—to win safety for all women.[7]

Picking Up the Pieces: Black Women Fighting Back

Over the weekend of January 27, 1979, two friends, Christine Renee Ricketts and Andrea Lorraine Foye, went to downtown Boston, danced at "Combat Zone discos," and relaxed at a juice bar. It was the last weekend the young Black women were seen alive. When Ricketts's mother reported her daughter missing to the police, the officers waited to file a report, telling the mother instead "that the girl had probably gone off with a pimp." Two weeks later, the women's bodies were found stashed in a duffel bag and left on a side street in the Black neighborhood of Roxbury. Within a week, two more Black women were murdered; by March, six Black women had been murdered—one woman for every week that had passed since the death of Ricketts and Foye.[8]

Black residents were terrorized by the exponentially growing murders of Black women. The Boston Police Department and local reporters poured salt on the community's wounds, through both their racist presumption of the women's sexual criminality and their corresponding reluctance to respond with anything matching the urgency Black residents felt. In April 1,500 people came together at a memorial rally and vigil to grieve the loss of the six murdered women. When Sara Small, a victim's aunt, delivered her address, she asked, "Who is killing us?" As author Jaime Grant later wrote in a feminist newspaper, *Sojourner*, Small's question resonated on multiple levels: to Black residents at the memorial, the "us" was, broadly, Black people; to the white women present, the "us" was heard as "women." But to the Black feminists standing in the crowd, the "us" that Small invoked was Black women, "whose vulnerability was multidimensional in a city infamous for racial violence and where sexist violence was commonplace." Small's question was multivalent, but no speaker at the memorial rally addressed the specific vulnerabilities of Black women to violence. One month after the rally, the number of murdered Black women would double to twelve.[9]

In Boston, Los Angeles, and other cities directly affected by the serial murders of Black women, antiviolence feminists incorporated this specific crisis of violence into their campaigns. As these predominantly Black but multiracial activists negotiated distinct political perspectives in their coalitional work, they confronted two historically rooted dilemmas that shaped their organizing priorities and demands: first, debates over whether to make demands on the police or dismiss such work as futile; and second, how to navigate the fraught terrain of Black sexuality and the enduring myth of hypersexuality. Antiviolence feminists worked on parallel, and sometimes competing, agendas to fight for women's dignity and safety, but they agreed that—as Black feminists were among the first to articulate—racism and sexism compounded Black women's vulnerability to male violence.

Barbara Smith, a Boston resident and founding member of the Black feminist Combahee River Collective, remembered leaving the April rally "absolutely steaming." The roster of mostly male speakers had declared that "we need to protect our women; women need to stay inside the house," Smith recalled. "Nothing about sexual politics or sexual violence. . . . Well, why was it all women being murdered, if the only reason they were being murdered was because of race?" The rally offered no racial analysis of violence against women, or gendered analysis of violence against Black people. Without this analysis, the strategies for Black women's safety offered at the rally were impractical, deeply paternalistic, and isolating, freighted with the false logic that women could only be safe indoors and with male protection.[10]

Black feminists in Boston responded by building a race- and gender-specific analysis of serial murders and violence against women. After the rally in 1979, Smith went home and immediately typed up a draft of what would become a pamphlet, *Six Black Women: Why Did They Die?*, and read it over the phone to members of the Combahee River Collective. As more women were murdered, tens of thousands of bilingual copies of the pamphlet would be distributed: "In the face of police indifference and media lies and despite our grief and anger, we have begun to organize ourselves in order to figure out ways to protect ourselves and our sisters, to make the streets safe for women. . . . Our sisters died *because* they were women just as sure as they died because they were Black. . . . Both our race and sex lead to violence against us" (see figure 6.1).[11]

In addition to the specific analysis of racist and sexist violence, Smith and the members of the Combahee River Collective delivered language to make affirmative demands for "our rights as human beings to be free of physical abuse, free of fear." Alongside statistics of violence against women and a poem by Ntozake Shange, the pamphlet printed a list of strategies for mutual and self-protection, such as "Travel in pairs or groups," "Learn some

FIGURE 6.1 "Rest in peace, sister! Know that we will not rest." Barbara Smith, cofounder of the Combahee River Collective, with megaphone at an April 1979 protest. Black feminists recognized that racism and sexism compounded Black women's vulnerability to male violence: "Why was it all women being murdered, if the only reason they were being murdered was because of race?" Photo by Ellen Shub, courtesy of the Estate of Ellen Shub.

simple self-defense like how to get out of a hold or how to use available objects as weapons," and "Get to know your neighbors on your street. Keep an eye out for each other." The enormous demand for the pamphlet signaled the strong desire for this community-based knowledge. "Many women greeted the pamphlet with a sigh of relief," one observer commented.[12]

The Combahee River Collective's work galvanized the creation of several local coalitions to provide vulnerable women with strategies for community building and individual self-defense. As community-wide mobilization ramped up throughout 1979, feminists in a TBTN Coalition planned a massive march and rally. The unique vulnerability of sexually profiled women and sex workers was not a central analytical point for the TBTN Coalition. Members of the coalition—including the Combahee River Collective, Black residents, white feminists of various political stripes, and

Taking Back the Night   179

members of the Prostitutes Union of Massachusetts—certainly recognized the power of police to both multiply and ignore Black women's exposure to violence. "We have discussed, and continue to discuss, the presence of the criminal justice system and its relation to violence against women," one coalition position statement read, noting that "the criminal justice system itself is a perpetual abuser of poor and Third World men and women alike." And they were well aware that police narratives of sexual criminality produced even more violence against, and neglect of, Black women. However, as TBTN Coalition members sought to balance their distinct perspectives and priorities, they strained to reach consensus on the desired response to the interrelated issues of sexual criminalization, state violence, and violence against women. "There are those of us who want to work to make the present system more accountable," the coalition position statement read. But "there are others of us who have worked with victims . . . prisons . . . and with the police in various contexts, who feel that there is a certain dead end in working with a system that continually acts in a racist & sexist manner and continually channels only poor people through its doors." The TBTN Coalition struggled to reconcile competing goals: Work to change a racist and sexist regime or build alternatives to that regime?[13]

At the TBTN march and rally in August 1979, an estimated five thousand people marched. In a TBTN Coalition statement read at the rally, the organizers charged that "the legal system which we have been taught to rely on for our safety and justice betrays us constantly." While the rally organizers sought to build popular awareness of dangers—both state specific and nonstate—that women faced in Boston, "none of the community organizations involved in the crisis spent much time or faith on the Boston police or the criminal justice system," according to *Sojourner* writer Grant. "Clearly the state cannot be relied upon to provide women's safety," coalition members told the rally protesters in 1979. "We must do that ourselves."[14]

But other feminists in the city were literally putting the state on trial. In a July 1979 action held one month before the TBTN march, a different coalition of feminists staged a "Women's Court" outside the state house in Boston. They charged Massachusetts governor Edward King and his "accomplices"—officials at the federal, state, and municipal levels, including legislators, judges, and police—with "rape, conspiracy to rape and perpetuate violence against women, and uphold men's power over women in order to uphold their own power over everyone." Trial cosponsors included some members of the TBTN Coalition—such as the Prostitutes

FIGURE 6.2 Public street trial, July 1979. Featuring Margaret Prescod, of the New York Prostitutes' Union, and Tita Weirnamont as the defendant, Massachusetts governor Edward King. "Charges: Rape, conspiracy to rape and perpetuate violence against women, and uphold men's power over women in order to uphold their own power over everyone." Image from *Gay Community News*, courtesy of Northeastern University Libraries, Archives and Special Collections Department.

Union of Massachusetts—as well as the Boston Area Rape Crisis Center and a slate of groups aligned with the anticapitalist WfH network, including the Rape Action Project, Black Women for Wages for Housework USA, and Wages Due Lesbians (see figure 6.2).[15]

The witnesses called to the stand argued that state-sanctioned poverty locked women in risky situations—and sexual criminalization turned the deadbolt. King perpetrated violence against women by pushing for welfare and social service cutbacks and restrictions on abortion rights, by enforcing prostitution-related misdemeanors, and by assuming "a do-nothing attitude towards the recent outbreaks of murders and rapes of Boston-area women." The governor was found guilty, and one of his legislative aides was presented with a petition with four court orders: to criminalize marital rape; provide financial compensation for victims of rape to cover all associated medical, legal, emergency housing, and abortion costs; repeal prostitution-related misdemeanors; and fund "financial independence" for every woman "in order to avoid situations where she is in danger of violence." "In an atmosphere of thirteen unsolved murders of Black women in Boston," cosponsoring members of Black Women for Wages for Housework wrote in a press release, "the treatment that comes directly from economic and legal institutions (the Welfare system, the health care system, the laws and the prisons) is tantamount to a second rape which allows for, facilitates, and enforces all rape."[16]

At the street trial, the sexual criminalization of women was woven through the court's argument, presented as a crucial link connecting the social and political structures that entrapped women in poverty and produced conditions that exposed them to violence. Women who represented sex workers' rights organizations or identified as "ex-prostitutes" were among the witnesses testifying in the Women's Court. Prescod—who by 1986 would become a leading force in the Black Coalition Fighting Back Serial Murders in Los Angeles—traveled to Boston to speak out at the street trial on behalf of the New York Prostitutes' Union. She later joined the delegation that was invited into the executive office of the state house to present the women's verdict and demands.[17]

In 1979 both Boston coalitions in the Women's Court and the TBTN Coalition agreed that the state was a hostile actor in women's lives, and both sought to empower women with strategies for collective action and defense. But what distinguished the Women's Court action from the TBTN rally was the street trial organizers' efforts to center the experiences of women directly affected by prostitution laws, in addition to their demand for the repeal of prostitution-related misdemeanors. Drawing from the voices and vulnerabilities of sex workers and sexually profiled women, only the Women's Court coalition explicitly held the state accountable for the violence that women confronted in their everyday lives. The street trial and the TBTN march reflected two distinct strategies to respond to a crucial feminist dilemma: how (or whether) to engage with a violent state, and on what terms. This organizing work raised a second, and related, dilemma: how to defend and protect sex workers and sexually profiled women while avoiding the social and political injury of the whore stigma, to which Black women were uniquely vulnerable.

The dilemma of how and on what terms to engage with the state was especially charged in the arena of prostitution laws, delivering distinct challenges for Black women organizing in their self-defense. The deep legacies of segregated vice districts, and the attendant narrative that Black people were naturally accustomed to or tolerant of prostitution, haunted Black sexual politics. Racist myths of Black hypersexuality—and the pervasive police logic that poor Black women were sexually deviant and an unwanted street presence—powerfully shaped the possibilities for Black activist discourse, contributing to silences, evasions, and tactical speak-outs among activists grappling with the violence produced by prostitution law enforcement. Some Black residents carefully guarded their respectability and sought to distance themselves from any association with sex workers. Despite activists' appeals for the dignity of all Black residents, Black women suspected of engaging in commercial sex remained beyond the limits of many political agendas. This was especially true throughout the 1980s as Black women were represented as the public face of the intertwined crises of crack cocaine addiction and poverty, and as Black tough-on-crime politics were amplified in the media.[18]

Gloria Lockett directly confronted the erasures and evasions woven into the Black community's fraught negotiations with sexuality. She got her start organizing in the early 1980s with the San Francisco–based organization COYOTE (Call Off Your Old Tired Ethics), the organization famous for launching the sex workers' rights movement. In 1985 Lockett founded the California Prostitutes' Education Project, which provided direct health services to at-risk Black women in Oakland and San Francisco. "The Black community is very downing, very opinionated. However, I think that it's easier to accept a Black prostitute than it is to accept a lesbian or gay person in the Black community," she said. "I think that's because prostitution is about money, and people understand that. . . . But still it's very difficult." Lockett saw her activism, in part, as a way to make the community "downing" visible and to "let Black women know . . . that it's all right to have a past. We all have closets," she said, expanding queer imagery to include straight and straight-presenting women whose presumed sexual deviance nevertheless exposed them to social stigma and state punishment. Throughout the 1980s, a number of Black women were setting out to do the difficult work of, as Lockett said, being "a voice for people who were working the streets and getting arrested—which meant mostly Black people." This was multifacing work, directed in part at white activists so that they understood that "Black women's issues were different from white women's issues." But Lockett and other activists like her also delivered their message for Black people "to let my people know that prostitution was not an all-white issue," and for Black women especially, so they could cultivate an affirmative relationship with their lived experiences.[19]

Lockett also worked hard to raise the visibility of the serial murders of Black women and their relationship to sexual policing. In 1985 she was invited to testify at hearings before the New York State Bar Association on prostitution laws. Lockett pointedly—and repeatedly—urged the members to reckon with the serial murders of women, which they considered beyond the scope of their investigation. "The prohibition of prostitution contributes to this violence by spreading the view that prostitutes are bad women and thus are legitimate targets for abuse," she testified. "When the primary role of police is to entrap them into soliciting an act of prostitution and then arrest them, their role of enforcers of the law against rape and other violence is undermined. As a result, the police tend to view violence against prostitutes less rigorously than other violence. And prostitutes are reluctant to go to the police for help when they are assaulted." While Lockett was critical of both prostitution laws and their mode of enforcement, she framed her argument within a larger affirmation of Black women's lives: "We have a problem with human dignity here," she said. "Lack of dignity promotes violence."[20]

The same year that Lockett testified, Prescod moved from New York to Los Angeles, bringing her analysis and activism to another city besieged by the serial murders of Black women. As Prescod built the Black Coalition Fighting Back Serial Murders, she and the coalition members, like Lockett, resisted the prostitution stigma by critiquing the stigma itself, rather than the women who were burdened by it. These activists insisted on a politics of dignity and humanity: anticipating global campaigns demanding human rights for sex workers, they urged community members and police to recognize the value of all Black women's lives. "There is no hierarchy of human life," the Black Coalition Fight Back members wrote in a statement to the Los Angeles Police Commission in 1989. "We demand there be no double standard in police policies when it comes to prostitutes or alleged prostitutes." Throughout the 1980s, as multiracial coalitions of antiviolence feminists surged in cities nationwide, activists like Prescod and Lockett dared to focus on, and assert the inherent value of, the lives of sex workers and sexually profiled women.[21]

As Reagan-era policies—which simultaneously slashed welfare supports while lavishing funds on broken windows policing—gained momentum across the 1980s, Prescod delivered a feminist critique. In 1987 the Los Angeles City Council unanimously approved a "Band-Aid" measure to spend over $4 million on three months of overtime for Los Angeles Police Department officers. LAPD chief Daryl Gates said that his officers, many of whom were slated to be deployed to the predominantly Black and Latinx neighborhoods of South Los Angeles, would concentrate on "street crime," including gang activity, drug selling, and commercial sex. These overtime payments promised to strain a city budget that was already facing shortfalls and that was, according to the *Los Angeles Times*, "expected to be the most stringent in years" with "the most drastic cuts in services" since the 1978 passage of property-tax restrictions with Proposition 13. Mayor Tom Bradley—a former police officer himself, and the first (and only) Black mayor of Los Angeles—did not block the funding increase. But he did not enthusiastically embrace the "shortsighted" measure either: "Every cent we pay for police overtime in the next few months will come from next year's bare-bones budget," he argued. This measure provided a stark example of the shifting economic priorities in the Reagan era: the redirection of funding away from welfare policies and toward carceral policies, including heavy police concentration in communities of color.[22]

Prescod argued that by enriching law enforcement at the expense of social programs, "Reaganomics is forcing more women into prostitution." Instead of spending money on the "wasteful futility" of policing, she demanded funding for scholarships, healthcare, housing, and "other social services where women and children are hardest hit." In her protest of the budget increase for police overtime, Prescod defined broken windows policing, to which sexually profiled women were especially vulnerable, as an urgent issue for all poor women. She connected the overtime funding—and the expensive law enforcement policies that directly diminished welfare supports—to the unique and disproportionate racial and gendered harm they produced. "The first to suffer from such cuts are the poorest in our communities—women and children. Therefore, the police lining their pockets results in even more poverty and further criminalization of a community with few options to survive," members of the Black Coalition Fighting Back wrote in a statement. "Drugs and prostitution are then used as an excuse for saturation policing. Once again women pick up the pieces."[23]

This pathbreaking genealogy of activists protesting the serial murders of Black women provided an analytical toolkit and a strategic roadmap for the future. Barbara Smith, Gloria Lockett, Margaret Prescod, and the members of the organizations they helped to build forged alliances on the haunted terrain of Black sexuality and mobilized groups with overlapping and divergent political commitments—Black and anticapitalist feminists, churchgoing Black women, middle-class white feminists, and sex workers—on behalf of stigmatized and criminalized Black women. In their fight to dismantle a state-sponsored complex of gender-based violence, these coalitions struggled with formidable tasks: to overturn powerful racist myths of hypersexuality and patriarchal logics of individual safety. During these same years, however, dominance feminists were able to tap into a constellation of ready-made narratives of police protection and individual male villains.

Dominance Feminism and Its Convergence with Broken Windows Policing

Dominance feminists argued that the origin of universal domination over women was male sexuality—and prostitution and pornography were the ultimate manifestations of men's deployment of sex to oppress women. By locating the founding injury of male domination in sex, they advanced a naturalized vision of male oppression within a biological (and therefore, they argued, self-evident) gender binary in which the infinite circumstances, differences, and contexts in women's lives were not analytically salient. "For every real difference between women, prostitution exists to erase our diversity," Evelina Giobbe, founder of the dominance feminist–aligned organization Women Hurt in Systems of Prostitution Engaged in Revolt (WHISPER), wrote, "while reducing all of us to meat to be bought, sold, traded, used, discarded, degraded, ridiculed, humiliated, maimed, tortured, and all too often, murdered for sex." These sorts of broad claims rested on an unquestioned biological binary that downplayed sociopolitical differences of race and class—differences that, as Vednita Nelson pointed out, significantly shaped women's material conditions, social relationships, and experiences with police.[24]

Nelson, the advocacy director of WHISPER, was one of the few Black women working with dominance feminists. In 1992 she gave a speech at a University of Michigan Law School symposium, "Prostitution: From Academia to Activism." With legal scholar Catharine MacKinnon on the faculty, Michigan Law was an epicenter of dominance feminism. In Nelson's speech, "Prostitution: Where Racism and Sexism Intersect," she protested the Black community's preoccupation with violence against Black men and their silence on the horrifying reality of violence against Black women. But she also delivered a critique of her dominance feminist allies and urged the white women present to "make a concerted effort to end racism, beginning with an examination of their own racism, and . . . take active stands against racial injustice in society." As Nelson closed her talk, she demanded to know, "How can mainstream feminists claim to care about Black women and racism when they fail to speak out against . . . the police who target [our daughters and sisters] for arrest and imprisonment, while their abusers, the johns that prey on our community go free?"[25]

For Nelson, law enforcement authorities were certainly not the only driver of what she called "white-supremacist" and "male-supremacist" power. But she understood that police were a crucial force in alienating Black women "from most social institutions except those that perpetuate the cycle of poverty and despair." A combination of state punishment and neglect compounded the cascading processes of economic isolation, social marginalization, and criminal system intervention in the lives of poor Black women.[26]

The dominance feminists in attendance at the 1992 Michigan Law symposium certainly shared Nelson's concern. But as legal scholars like MacKinnon moved "from academia to activism," it was clear that, despite the hierarchies of difference they invoked in scholarly writings, their work would repeatedly prioritize the universality of women's oppression—which, inadvertently or not, produced a feminist politics that privileged whiteness. Through their work, they demonstrated faith that the state, the courts, and the police could be taught a feminist lesson that would make all women safer. But as Nelson's speech showed, there was little reason to expect that this logic of protection would be extended to Black women, who were much more familiar with the state's capacity for punishment and neglect. With whiteness masquerading as universality—and with only glancing attention to how race and class shaped women's relationship to the state—dominance feminist legal scholars' solutions remained invested in the protective value of state structures. This contributed to their failure to answer Nelson's call to "fight racist and sexist oppression."[27]

Black feminist legal scholars have closely engaged with the influential work of dominance feminist law. In her study of dominance feminism, Kimberlé Crenshaw—who developed the concept of "intersectionality"—writes that "it may be the case that MacKinnon's theories privilege interventions that simply do not move the needle much for women of color. However, advancing this argument would require a kind of reasoning that moves from the general critique to the specific illustrations, i.e. what are the particular ways that the theory misdirects the practice." This section builds on Crenshaw's argument by grounding dominance feminists' material work in the specific illustration of prostitution laws.[28]

Dominance feminists argued that activists were wrong to identify "'the state' rather than male supremacy in its entirety, as the source of our oppression," as law professor Kathleen Lahey argued at a 1987 conference cosponsored by WHISPER and held at New York University Law School. To be sure, law enforcement was not the singular or originating site of women's oppression. In the universe of social meaning-making and political power, the law was just one of many impositions. But it was an extremely powerful one. According to the broken windows logic, sexually profiled women posed a threat to—indeed, "victimized"—the communities in which they lived, and for this reason, they needed to be policed and removed from city streets. By targeting only certain women, police officers created a specific social meaning of Black women, inscribing their status as deviant, dangerous, and harmful criminals. This social meaning, in turn, heightened Black women's vulnerability to state and interpersonal male violence. These same police practices also triggered state processes erecting barriers of access to basic goods that women in already precarious living situations required for stable and autonomous lives, such as cash, healthcare, housing, and childcare.[29]

Feminists like Prescod identified the state, and especially the police, as a powerful multiplier of women's oppression. But for dominance feminists, law enforcement was just a footnote to male supremacy. MacKinnon argued at the Michigan Law symposium that criminal law only upheld—and did not meaningfully shape, differentiate, or compound—the natural state of gender-based exploitation. "Getting the criminal law off [women's] backs may keep the state from reinforcing their subordinate status but it does nothing to change that status," she said.[30]

Dominance feminists did not deny the power of law enforcement, or the law itself. Clearly, with law schools providing so much institutional support and legal scholars bringing tremendous intellectual energy to dominance feminism, the law was important to these activists. In occasional asides, dominance feminists argued that prostitution laws primarily enforced against women should be repealed. However, they were loath to advocate for decriminalization or ally themselves with feminists who did. Decriminalization was considered a misguided tactic that played directly into men's hands by legitimizing the state sanction of "sexual slavery," which was, regardless, compulsory in a male-dominated society. So while dominance feminists agreed that prostitution laws unfairly punished women, they pursued other legal remedies, leaving criminal laws, and the police power these laws authorized, intact.[31]

Instead, dominance feminists organized their activism around the inherent harm produced by prostitution itself and the individual men involved. It was at this precise juncture that dominance feminism converged with the logic of the broken windows theory, producing a politics that—while originating from a very different political orientation—arrived at an agenda that harmonized with the expansion of law enforcement authority. In a 1988 report on prostitution submitted to the Gender Bias Study Commission of the Supreme Court of Florida, dominance feminist-aligned historian Philippa Levine delivered a broken windows narrative, by way of gender-based analysis, to justify the maintenance of prostitution laws: "The prominence of prostitution in working-class and poor neighborhoods simply adds to the burden already endured by those who live in poverty," she wrote. "They, too, have a right to live in safe, clean, and harmonious neighborhoods and to walk their streets unmolested."[32]

Levine's colleague at Florida State University, Margaret Baldwin, a dominance feminist law professor, conjured a vision of the harmful disorder in women's lives. Presuming that women engaged in commercial sex were abject and socially isolated, Baldwin argued in a law review article that the personal relationships of family, friends, and motherhood "are only memories or dreams for women and girls in prostitution." In place of these social connections, "prostituted women share their lives" with a roster of men who bore a conspicuous resemblance to George Kelling and James Q. Wilson's "undesirable" people: "johns, dealers, liquor store clerks . . . drifters, alcoholics, and loners." In much the same vein as Kelling and Wilson, Baldwin and her feminist cohort placed their faith in the salubrious power of criminalization to ward against the looming harms of "drifters, alcoholics, and loners."[33]

Baldwin demonstrated a tendency to prefer, and even welcome, criminal system intervention. In the dreary and disorderly environment she painted in her law review article, she suggested that the "coercive relationships prostituted women have with [agents of the state]," including police and corrections officers—the women's "constant companions"—have "more to offer prostituted women than anyone or anything else on the immediate horizon." Baldwin even issued a defense of criminalization: "arrest and incarceration can play an important role in the repertoire of prostituted women's survival strategies," with jails functioning as shelters and providing "temporary respite from violence, hunger, and the prostitution itself," and criminalization itself sending a validating "message" to women that "prostitution will harm her, or that the violation and despair she feels is real."[34]

Baldwin was well aware of, and cited, reports and lawsuits documenting the violence that attended the enforcement of prostitution laws. And dominance feminists recognized that law enforcement was a distinctly racist practice that unequally targeted Black women for surveillance, harassment, and abuse. In Levine's Gender Bias Study Commission prostitution report, she noted that police "constantly referred to any suspected prostitute woman as 'bitch'" and participated in "a process of brutalization, of dehumanization." But these concerns were submerged in the larger work of overcoming the domination of individual male nonstate actors. Despite her research findings of state violence, Levine strongly recommended leaving criminal prostitution laws intact, arguing that "the maintenance of criminality [of prostitution] was a more appropriate, and in the long run, a more humane response." In her view, "the chief end [of criminalization] is protective rather than punitive and . . . it is the status, lives, and peace of mind of *all* women—not just those definitionally engaged in prostitution—that we aim to protect." By insisting on a focus on "all" women, dominance feminists betrayed a lack of concern for sex workers and sexually profiled women specifically, a great faith in the protective value of criminalization, and a zero-sum logic that improving the status and state treatment of sex workers would worsen conditions for women who don't sell sex (or were not profiled as such). As a result, their strategies left the most vulnerable women exposed to the continued harassment, degradation, and violence of police intervention.[35]

In their lawmaking work, dominance feminists sustained a vision of both the police and the courts as neutral protectors of women—a stance that was strikingly at odds with their analysis of total male domination. At the 1992 Michigan Law conference, MacKinnon introduced the idea of civil law remedies to equip women harmed by commercial sex to sue men for damages. She had first developed this tactic with Dworkin a decade earlier, when they codrafted municipal ordinances in Minneapolis and Indianapolis that allowed women to sue the producers and distributors of sexually explicit material. (While both ordinances passed, they were subsequently vetoed by the mayor and struck down by an appeals court, respectively.) The antipornography civil ordinances were one battle in the so-called sex wars, which sparked extreme polarization among predominantly white feminists. Just a few years later, however, dominance feminists won the much quieter passage of state legislation that gave women involved with prostitution a civil remedy for legal action in Florida and Minnesota—laws that remain on the books and inspired the passage of similar laws in dozens of states.[36]

MacKinnon and her allies framed the legal remedies as "civil rights" legislation, but in practice these laws were closer to tort law: an injured plaintiff (in this case, a "prostituted woman," in the dominance feminist parlance) had standing to sue a responsible party (her "pimp") in court for monetary damages. MacKinnon drew her rationale for women's legal standing from the Thirteenth Amendment, and she argued for the use of the constitutional protections against chattel slavery as a legal tool for women ensnared in "sexual slavery" to sue for violations of their civil rights. In this way, MacKinnon, along with many other dominance feminists, revived and revised the Progressive-era preoccupation with "white slavery," the early twentieth-century reform movement against the sexual exploitation of primarily white and European-born women. Dominance feminist Kathleen Barry, who specifically placed her work in this moral reform tradition in her 1979 book *Female Sexual Slavery*, bluntly explained to reporters that "[prostitution] is like Black slavery in the nineteenth century." However, in this updated version of the white slavery (now "sexual slavery") narrative, dominance feminists made the Victorian analogy literal. "For Black women in the United States, the relation between prostitution and slavery is less one of analogy than of continuity with their sexual use under slavery," MacKinnon argued. She was certainly right to connect the legacies of white male sexual predation endemic to enslavement with contemporary sexual violence against Black women. But in a characteristic move among dominance feminists that undermined their racial analysis, they made the slavery analogy literally and universally true across all axes of oppression: Dorchen Leidholdt, a white lawyer and founding member of the Coalition against Trafficking in Women, denounced "the chattel status of our bodies" at the National Conference on Women and the Law in 1985.[37]

MacKinnon's proposed "civil rights" legislation was intended to be used "to sue pimps for sexual slavery." Despite the shapeshifting capacity of state authorities to devise and deploy evolving tools of arrest and banishment against marginalized populations—for which sexually profiled women were an important test case—dominance feminists found the most dangerous power in the individual "pimp." These civil law proposals paradoxically assumed that women who ostensibly lived in fear of, and economic dependence on, their pimps would muster the emotional and financial resources to antagonize their pimps through civil legal action. Moreover, these civil law proposals did not indict larger state-sanctioned structures in the reproduction of interpersonal and state violence against women. At the heart of this practical, change-making arm of dominance feminism was a commitment to individual remedies that upheld the legitimacy and power of the state.[38]

The first such civil law that allowed women to sue pimps passed in Florida. It was the direct outgrowth of Baldwin and Levine's advocacy work for the Gender Bias Study Commission of the Supreme Court of Florida. The final 1990 report of the commission reflected the influence of dominance feminism. While the commissioners did find fault with the state's enforcement of prostitution laws—concluding that laws are discriminatorily enforced and the state failed to offer adequate "treatment and rehabilitation"—they focused much more attention on the victimization of women by individual pimps. Two central and contradictory themes emerged in the report. First, based on the testimony and research of dominance feminists, the report authors wrote, "Adult prostitutes are 'grown-up juvenile prostitutes.' . . . The legal fiction that they are self-determining adults because of their age is counterproductive in eliminating prostitution." Second, despite this infantilization of women who remained, nonetheless, criminals, the commissioners also recommended the enactment of civil remedies for women "against their pimps." It was not clear how women infantilized, criminalized, and stripped of agency could become "self-determining adults" in their pursuit of civil cases against individual men. Incoherent as the underlying logic was, the law passed in 1993.[39]

However, the first—and, within the first ten years after the law's passage, the only—reported case testing the viability of the Florida law shattered the dominance feminist logic. The two plaintiffs in the 1997 lawsuit, Kimberly Balas and Teresa Shumate, sought to transform the legal tool targeting pimps into the dominance feminists' political bête noire: a workers' mechanism to win redress from exploitative bosses in the sex industry. Balas and Shumate brought a suit against Marjorie Ruzzo, a co-owner and operator of a "leisure spa," who "collected about fifty to sixty percent of each employees' earning from performing sexual acts." Ruzzo, the plaintiffs charged, "exploited" the workers, requiring them to pay "substantial sums of money to attend 'metaphysical workshops' . . . designed to . . . foster dependency and loyalty" to the boss, and she threatened to have the women arrested if they did not submit to body cavity searches to ensure that they had not hidden additional wages.[40]

This test case illustrated the vast chasm between dominance feminists' theories and women's lived experiences and needs. The plaintiffs did not understand their relationships exclusively in the language of male dominance; rather, the women conceived of their oppression as unfair labor conditions. Moreover, as this case shows, not everyone who oppressed women were men. Balas and Shumate's suit also exposed the power of criminalization—in this case, Ruzzo's threat to call the police—to be used as a stick to silence women or wrest their compliance. Finally, this case indicated which women were more likely to have the economic and social capital to test their legal standing in court: oral arguments, for example, indicated that "at least one of the employees has a college degree and gave up a well-paying, legitimate job in order to engage in this profession for the greater reward."[41]

The case also exposed the courts' refusal to adopt the dominance feminists' worldview by treating all women engaged in commercial sex as victims. Indeed, the evidence of the plaintiffs' pursuit of greater wages through commercial sex was used against the women in court to prove that they were not "coerced" and therefore had no claim to better treatment—because, as one judge put it, the civil remedy was not meant to be a "general prostitute's relief act." The ruling exposed the sexism of the court, which undermined the civil remedy itself. And the reflection of the plaintiffs' social location indicated that, despite the dominance feminists' insistence on the universality of male domination, civil remedies would be more likely pursued by women with a greater measure of material and social resources—which in turn would make them illegible as "victims" to the courts.[42]

The dominance feminist push for civil remedies was underpinned by a remarkable faith in the law to evenly and neutrally offer redress to women. These campaigns for civil action legislation betrayed an adherence to liberal conceptions of women's equal possession of individual rights—a vision seemingly at odds with dominance feminism's deep skepticism of any escape from male power, and especially within the historically white and male supremacist arena of the state. All women equipped with civil remedies to sue their pimps were presumed to enjoy a fair and equal hearing in the courts.

What was especially surprising about this presumption of court neutrality was that throughout the 1980s and into the 1990s, individual rights in criminal law—and specifically, the individual rights of sexually profiled women—were under assault, especially as status laws were resurrected under the guise of loitering with intent laws, as discussed in chapter 5. At no point did the dominance feminists who mobilized on behalf of this legislation speak to the power of criminalization to abrogate a sexually profiled woman's standing in court. Dominance feminists defended individual suits as usefully accommodating of different women's experiences and claims: "The civil rights proposal does not depend on the claimant's membership in any specific protected class, or on having any particular status," law professor Beverly Balos, who helped draft the legislation for Minnesota's civil remedies, wrote approvingly. However, this logic failed to consider the very different relationships women had with the courts and their unequal access to the time and money necessary to pursue redress. Ultimately, these civil remedies exposed a misguided belief in the power of individual civil suits to meaningfully reorder towering and complex systems of oppression. As historians and scholars of civil law have argued, civil remedies may have offered individual reparations to some plaintiffs, but they left intact and unchallenged the deeper and more powerful operation of criminal law to define humans as criminal threats to society.[43]

Beyond civil remedies, dominance feminists also lobbied hard for strict criminal enforcement against "men who traffic in women's bodies for their pleasure and profit," according to Giobbe, the founder of WHISPER. Because the dominance feminists of WHISPER believed that the abolition of prostitution laws "socially and legally sanctions the buying and selling of human beings for sexual use and abuse," they were ambivalent about decriminalization. They preferred instead to press for the criminalization of individual men through arrest campaigns like "reverse stings" and so-called john schools. However, by sidelining the sexual criminalization of women in favor of lobbying for the heightened criminalization of individual men, dominance feminists ultimately sustained the power of law enforcement authorities, leaving women vulnerable to intensified police action.[44]

On a purely rhetorical level, the ease with which state officials appropriated dominance feminist language to buttress the power of law enforcement was on display in a 1992 WHISPER newsletter. This special-edition newsletter reported on a 1991 delegation of white dominance feminists from the United States representing WHISPER and the Coalition against Trafficking in Women, including Giobbe, Kathleen Barry, and Dorchen Leidholdt, who traveled to Geneva to address the United Nations Working Group on Contemporary Forms of Slavery. The WHISPER Action Group—a coalition of legal scholars, law students, and WHISPER activists that, in collaboration with law enforcement authorities and with funding from the Minnesota Department of Corrections, was instrumental in the passage of Minnesota's civil remedy for women in commercial sex—submitted a statement to this working group. WHISPER published the statement in its special newsletter. Arguing against the outright abolition of prostitution laws, the WHISPER Action Group members wrote, "A more compassionate and effective approach would be *to remove criminal sanctions* against women used in prostitution and to create public policies which hold those who economically benefit . . . or purchase sexual compliance . . . accountable to the criminal justice system." The editors of that same special newsletter uncritically printed a letter of support from the mayor of Saint Paul, who borrowed the action group's language but made some telling revisions: instead of decriminalization for women, he wrote, "a more humane approach would be *to establish criminal sanctions* that divert prostitutes into programs designed to help them escape sexual exploitation and to create public policies which hold" individual men accountable.[45]

Rhetorical alliances aside, the dominance feminist agenda of targeting men materially contributed to the intensified criminalization of sexually profiled women in the age of broken windows. One example of this pattern can be seen in spatial exclusion orders, or legal banishment programs developed to target alleged prostitution, drug sales, gang membership, and homelessness. Beginning in the late 1970s, some cities began experimenting with "restricted areas"—scaled-up and institutionalized versions of the "floaters" discussed in chapter 4. Known variously as "map area restrictions," "prostitution-free zones," and "Stay Out of Areas with Prostitution" (SOAP) orders, these spatial exclusion orders affirmed the right of police officers to identify and banish sexually profiled women from designated urban areas, typically downtown or mixed-use areas with rebounding property values that city stakeholders had a vested interest in recapitalizing. Spatial exclusion orders took many forms. In some cities, police officers had the authority to impose spatial restrictions on women in lieu of arrest, before they had been convicted of a crime. However, exclusion orders were more often appended as a condition of probation. While they would not gain traction until the mid-1990s, as with the loitering with intent laws, some city and state authorities worked to expand the early antiprostitution banishment measures to a broader regime aimed at the removal of the broken windows theory's most wanted.[46]

Exclusion orders dramatically institutionalized into municipal—and, in at least one case, statewide—practice the gross imbalance of power between police and marginalized women on city streets. One Portland, Oregon, police officer embraced such orders in the mid-1990s as a "great tool": "I'm the big hammer; I get them off the street. They feel it's *their* street so they can do what they want. I'm not hands on—I don't talk to them. Even if they didn't do anything, I just get them off *my* street." Exclusion orders, then, empowered the officer to wordlessly establish territorial control over the city and banish women on sight "even if they didn't do anything." This power was sustained by the broken windows logic that violently removing humans from city streets was a necessary process to revitalize the city.[47]

As spatial exclusion orders gained popularity in cities nationwide, they were often rolled out in conjunction with dominance feminist initiatives that targeted men who solicited women. For example, the 1995 spatial exclusion order in Wichita, Kansas, was implemented alongside a bundle of reforms that included a revised ordinance to allow for the arrest of men. But these orders were typically applied to women more than men. After persistent challenges, the 1993 "Prostitution Free Zone" policy in Portland, Oregon, was eventually terminated in 2007 after challengers successfully argued that, in addition to its being expensive and racist in its enforcement, more women than men were saddled with exclusion orders.[48]

A 1997 antiprostitution pilot program in Saint Petersburg, Florida, led by police officer Sandra Minor illustrates the compatibility of dominance feminism with aggressive, mass misdemeanor policing. First, Minor's team established the broken windows theory guiding their experimental project and explained why prostitution was targeted: "Prostitution negatively impacts the area it's located in . . . [the area] can experience negative economic impact including but not limited to a decrease of property value and patronage." Then, in a dominance feminist–inspired spirit, the police team argued that the "victims" of prostitution included "the prostitutes themselves," and they initiated several dominance feminist–endorsed mechanisms of state power, including mandatory participation in a "treatment program" for the women and the targeted arrest of "johns." However, the Saint Petersburg police team also lobbied hard, and successfully, for a broadened municipal prostitution ordinance to "assist the patrol officers" in making arrests of women. Perhaps most egregiously, the language in this new ordinance criminalized a woman who asked or searched for information that would identify a man as a police officer. Finally, the Saint Petersburg pilot program also won spatial exclusion orders attached to women's (but not men's) conditions of probation. Such orders—which remain a favored tool to "end demand" for prostitution by present-day dominance feminists—illustrate how dominance feminist narratives and agendas could sustain aggressive broken windows policing practices that primarily harmed women.[49]

Because the broken windows theory focused on policing behaviors, it easily accommodated feminist-inflected logics of women's protection. Wesley Skogan, an early popularizer of broken windows policing, argued that it would target disorderly behavior "such as catcalling, sexual harassment, drinking, and prostitution." Here, he rhetorically conflated sexual harassment and prostitution as equivalent disorders that state intervention would remedy. The compatibility of broken windows and dominance feminism was reciprocal. By emphasizing the degradation of prostitution but downplaying the prevalence of state violence in prostitution law enforcement, dominance feminism, in turn, delivered a legitimizing veneer of political correctness to the broken windows regime.[50]

Broken windows policing was pitched as a strategy to take back the streets from what one New York City criminal justice coordinator described as the "utter and complete seizure of public turf by the boldest and most visible anti-social and criminal elements." However, police leaders and politicians could not just bluntly agitate for the mass clearance of poor women from city streets that they desired—they had to appeal to mainstream feminism. Law enforcement authorities readily incorporated dominance feminist arguments that prostitution harmed women. The protectionist rhetoric of dominance feminism propped up police, offering a powerful justification for the consolidation and perpetuation of police authority over poor and Black sexually profiled women. By adopting the logic of "protecting" women from degradation by individual male villains through the enforcement of prostitution laws, police officers were empowered to see their aggressive enforcement practices—which had previously been challenged as wasteful, abusive, and constitutionally deficient—as humane, valuable, and even feminist. In this way, punitive policies of arrest and banishment were spun as protections for women.[51]

Law enforcement authorities repeatedly invoked the degradation of women in prostitution as a justification for punishing policies and practices. At the 1985 New York State Bar Association Commission hearings to review prostitution laws, Linda Fairstein, an assistant district attorney for New York County and chief of the Sex Crimes Unit, argued that prostitution—in addition to "almost inevitably" producing violent crime—was also "a very un-feminist activity." "There is a terrible degradation of the human being . . . who is the prostitute and terrible vulnerability of the prostitute throughout the process." In this spirit, Fairstein issued her support for a proposed mandatory jail sentence law for women convicted twice of prostitution-related offenses. At the rank-and-file level, some police officers may have previously considered prostitution enforcement as degrading and "of trivial importance." But a 1991 study of a large urban police department found that vice officers were "re-evaluating upwardly the worth of their vice enforcement practices." They increasingly believed that by enforcing prostitution laws against women, they "lessen the probability that vulnerable young women will be lured into illegal and humanly-debasing activities." The policies and rhetoric that dominance feminists deployed to challenge male domination exposed their blind spots to state power—and ultimately their loyalty to state power—which led to these harmonies with law enforcement.[52]

Activists affiliated with WfH consistently responded to this dominance feminist position with scathing critiques. "The split in the women's movement on the issue of women working as prostitutes has always led to so-called feminists strengthening the hand of the police against everyone," Nina Lopez-Jones, a member of the WfH-aligned English Collective of Prostitutes, wrote. "And since Black people are the first to suffer at the hands of the police, ignoring, or even soft-pedaling, the role of police illegality in any of our lives, assists and supports every racist effort to segregate and muffle Black self-defense and protest." In 1983 the English Collective of Prostitutes, Black Women for Wages for Housework, and Women Against Rape circulated a statement protesting an impending—and ultimately canceled—action by "anti-porn groups": "By refusing to come out on the side of women in the sex industry, they have in effect taken sides against us," the activists wrote. "Is the women's movement going to fight for more power for women, *including women in the sex industry,* or more power for the police?" As Lopez-Jones observed, the consolidation of police power in the 1980s was yet one more iteration in "a long tradition of using the protection of [white] women as a pretext for racist and repressive legislation and activities." With devastating precision, these activists articulated the failures of dominance feminism to meaningfully protect all women nearly forty years ago—and yet the dominance feminist logic continues to play an outsize role in contemporary politics.[53]

・・・・・・

The competing work of these activists was not a sideshow in the feminist sex wars, nor in the larger conservative political restoration that was being instantiated during the same years. Indeed, by excavating their state-specific engagements with law enforcement during the ascendance of broken windows policing, we can see that these activists established the terms of engagement both with and against the state that would reverberate into the twenty-first century. As predominantly Black women in the United States mobilized in defense of all Black women's lives against police violence, dominance feminists appealed to the state, demanding protection from individual men and thereby strengthening law enforcement authorities' claims to discretionary power. While both groups of feminists were tapping into complex historical legacies of marginalized people's demands on police—for protection *by* police and protection *from* police—their activism in the long 1980s is especially illuminating because it confronted, and shaped the course of, the "blue revolution": the consolidation of police power through street-level enforcement practices, departmental policies, and court rulings.[54]

Where feminists analytically locate harm has grave—even lethal— consequences for the strategies they take up. For dominance feminists, the source of harm in commercial sex was not located in interactive and compounding processes of economic isolation, state failure, social marginalization, and police action (or neglect) across intersecting axes of oppression. Rather, they argued that commercial sex itself, the male domination that it expressed—and even the women who engaged in it—produced the most urgent social harms. "Those who are prostituted and those who seek their services are 'problem' groups, problems both for themselves and for society," dominance feminist historian Levine concluded. Just as Kelling and Wilson took aim at "victimless crimes" as a condescending liberal excuse to relinquish social responsibility for disorder, dominance feminists found in such crimes—specifically prostitution and pornography—a patriarchal scheme to legitimize the victimization of women and perpetuate the sexual subjugation of women. Decriminalization, as Levine argued, represented an "abandonment of proper governmental authority," and like broken windows proponents, dominance feminists lobbied for active intervention by the police and the courts to remedy social harms. As the concept of harm allegedly produced by "disorderly" people in broken windows theory mingled with the concept of harm produced by individual men advanced in dominance feminism, these powerful narratives converged to substantially narrow the scope and possibilities of political debate over prostitution laws and their highly discretionary, discriminatory enforcement by police.[55]

The critical, animating tension among feminists was their analysis: whether activists developed intersectional, structural interrogations of the relationship between state and nonstate violence or proceeded from an analysis of universal patriarchy and the totalizing harm of individual nonstate men had a material impact on their political tactics. Civil laws that enabled women to sue their pimps may not have "move[d] the needle much for women of color," as Crenshaw speculated. But spatial banishment laws and the feminist inflection of broken windows policing materially contributed to women's vulnerability to a powerful matrix of violence. Activists today must continue to dismantle the police logic of individual harm and punishment that dominance feminists helped to boost.[56]

Dominance feminist work was also considerably easier than the antiviolence feminist work discussed here. By focusing on the harm of individual nonstate men, dominance feminists had a set of political scripts to draw from, as well as ready allies in law enforcement who were seeking to justify the broad expansion of police powers. Black and multiracial groups of antiviolence feminists, on the other hand, had a complex agenda and powerful targets. They not only had to contend with deeply rooted stigmas of sex and race and prevailing myths of Black women's sexual criminality. These feminists also had to decide whether it was better to make reparative demands on a violent state or build up community capacity for mutual protection—for activists working with scarce resources, this was, and remains, a key tactical dilemma.

The legacies of the Black women organizing for community and self-defense in the wake of the serial murders of Black women are palpable in the contemporary feminist-of-color mobilizations against violence, such as Women With A Vision, INCITE! and the Say Her Name campaign. In the activist genealogies traced here, Black women throughout the 1980s were driven by a commitment to confront police power through a refusal to erase the most vulnerable women from activist agendas and an affirmation that, as the Black Coalition Fighting Back argued, "there is no hierarchy of human life." Crucially, these activists created an analytical framework for understanding how state violence has a multiplicative effect on nonstate violence and how both are intimately connected and mutually compounding. The lessons of this history are ongoing and urgent. There is inherent danger in feminist demands on the state that do not challenge the discretion and prerogatives of the criminal legal system but rather sustain and contribute to the consolidation of its power.[57]

Epilogue
These Streets Belong to All of Us

· ·

These streets [don't] belong to the police. They belong to all of us because we pay our tax dollars so we should be able to walk freely.
—Interview with African American trans woman, September 21, 2007, quoted in Alliance for a Safe and Diverse DC, *Move Along: Policing Sex Work in Washington, D.C.*

We must reckon with the fact that in twenty-first-century cities, law enforcement authorities and politicians have engineered a situation in which the perception of urban "safety" is built on profound violence: the arrest, abuse, and banishment of women—poor, trans, undocumented, Latina, Asian, Indigenous, and Black. The women who have been surveilled, harassed, entrapped, arrested, and assaulted by police may not be as visible as the male casualties of police power. But in our overpoliced and gentrified cities, we bear daily witness to the outcomes of the harm done to them. Luxury condos, outrageous rents, trendy shops and restaurants—and a powerful army of richly funded police to protect this property wealth—are at once the stark proof and perverse erasures of state violence against women.[1]

Efforts to banish sexually profiled women from cities continue into the twenty-first century. In February 2013 Atlanta police chief George Turner and mayor Kasim Reed pushed for the passage of an antiprostitution banishment law in the city's Midtown. Anyone convicted of a prostitution-related offense would be banished from downtown Atlanta—regardless of whether they lived there or not—and subject to immediate arrest if police saw them downtown again. After a second conviction, they would be banished from the entire city. Men who solicited for sex were ostensibly targeted too, but according to a local television news report, Turner's overriding goal was to "kick prostitutes out of the city of Atlanta." Reed racked up support from business and condominium owners in the Midtown Ponce Security Alliance. A reporter for the *Atlanta Journal-Constitution* wrote that "the Broken Windows theory has been the group's North Star." The economic motivation of the banishment law was clear: this was part of the mayor's efforts to gentrify Midtown and "promote downtown living."[2]

Atlanta's banishment law was yet another battle in the decades-long war to consolidate police power and urban wealth through the relentlessly violent removal of sexually profiled women from city streets. As of 2012, at least eighty-three cities had adopted banishment measures—also known as "prostitution-free zones" or "Stay Out of Areas of Prostitution" (SOAP) orders—including Seattle, Oakland, Miami, and Washington, D.C. Pressure from police-aligned feminists pushed law enforcement to spin these laws as strategies to go after male buyers of sex and "end demand" for commercial sex. But battles like the one in Atlanta underscored the real objective for city authorities who embraced banishment. For police departments, banishment orders were a vehement expression of officers' total power on the streets—a "great tool," as a police officer in Portland, Oregon, said, that helps him to get women "off [*his*] street" even if "they didn't do anything." And for politicians, this police power was put to economic use. Manny Diaz, a former mayor of Miami, proudly credited the city's "mapping" banishment program—which he claimed "rid the area of prostitutes"— with ushering in a "transformation" of Biscayne Boulevard, now studded with "Miami's trendiest restaurants and shops."[3]

This issue does not only directly affect sex workers, sexually profiled women, and their loved ones. Like loitering with intent laws, antiprostitution banishment programs have provided the template for urban authorities to target a longer list of vulnerable city residents. Since the mid-1970s, when systematic banishment programs were rolled out in citywide (and, in the case of Illinois, statewide) experiments, politicians and law enforcement authorities monitored the progress of these programs closely to calculate how they could test the bounds of constitutionality for similar programs targeting people profiled as drug sellers, gang members, or homeless. In Seattle, for example, SOAP orders provided the model for Stay Out of Drug Area (SODA) orders. Sexual policing widens the urban carceral net: it is tightly knitted into sprawling structures of urban law, economy, and government.[4]

· · · · · ·

Broken windows policing is a program that crowns officers as the arbiters and defenders of urban safety and order, as the ultimate solution to what scholar Clare Sears calls "problem bodies." But the broken windows program needs laws to sustain it, and morals misdemeanors generate that power. Kate Mogulescu, who runs the Criminal Defense and Advocacy Clinic at Brooklyn Law School, which represents people charged with prostitution-related misdemeanors and survivors of human trafficking, says, "There is no other law that I can think of that gives the police that much power and discretion." Prostitution-related misdemeanors enable the kind of law enforcement discretion that a 1971 report, *Struggle for Justice*, found "awesome in scope and by its nature uncontrollable." Within this context, people who lack access to legal resources or political influence can only "hope that by [police] selection, training, and supervision, the police will be inculcated with a clear sense of the outer limit of their discretionary authority," as George Kelling and James Q. Wilson, the architects of broken windows policing, wrote in their 1982 article. The mandate to enforce public order laws provides officers with a vast cover to operate beyond the scrutiny of the public.[5]

With this breathtaking authority and discretionary power, sexual policing is structured as an inevitable and unaccountable breeding ground of state-sponsored violence and abuse. New York investigations have found daily police harassment—with officers approaching sexually profiled women and asking, "You're not dead yet?" One woman reported that "the police are nasty, sarcastic, degrading." It is common for police to intimidate women and threaten them with jail if they refuse to act as informants. Women are denied the freedom to go shopping, wait for a bus, get their hair done, visit friends, or generally live their lives. Police officers harass them simply because of their presence on city streets. "They want you to be homebound," one woman said. In one report, 27 percent of women surveyed experienced police violence. The women were terrified of "[getting] a creepy cop" or a "psycho cop"; "sometimes they become very abusive with power." One woman said her greatest fear when getting arrested is "not coming home at all." Sexually profiled women, especially those with prior arrest records, do not have the resources or political clout to demand accountability—attempts to lodge complaints of police abuse with internal department watchdogs typically go nowhere—and police are free to exploit that vulnerability.[6]

Sexual abuse is the second most prevalent form of police violence—and this is likely an undercounting. Rape and the extortion of sex in exchange for the withholding of arrest are built-in features of sexual policing. Most common are the officers who ask women, "You wanna get arrested or you wanna give up some head?" A Black woman interviewed in 2007 said, "I had one cop who was like, 'Well, if you do this sexual favor for me, then I won't take you to jail.' And I was like, 'Take me to jail, 'cause I am not for free.'" A Washington, D.C., study found that nearly one in five sexually profiled people was "asked to provide sexual favors or services to police officers." In addition to sexual extortion, police, both off-duty and in uniform, are frequently women's paying customers.[7]

Police sexual violence is a legally sanctioned tactic of morals enforcement. Undercover entrapment encourages police to engage in sexual acts with women to gain "evidence"—a practice that, for women, is experienced as sexual assault. It wasn't until 2017 that Michigan banned police officers from engaging in penetrative sex with sexually profiled women. But these legal niceties cannot shield poor and marginalized women from the gross imbalance of power that is written into the law. In thirty-five states, armed police are protected from sexual assault charges by claiming that their sexual encounters with women are "consensual." Sexual "contact" by police officers in the enforcement of morals laws remains legal in nearly all states; when lawmakers in Alaska tried to ban police sexual contact, the Anchorage Police Department quashed the bill. Women have reported being stalked, intimidated, and forced to perform anal, vaginal, and oral sex by undercover police before being arrested. One woman was so terrified after an undercover officer banged on her door, demanding anal sex and refusing her repeated requests for him to leave while her baby cried in the background, that when she finally relented—pleading with him not to "be rough"—and the backup squad raided her apartment, she urinated on herself. Notable exceptions of officers called to account—like Daniel Holtzclaw, the Oklahoma City officer who serially raped Black women with drug and prostitution records; or Henry Hollins, the New Orleans officer who kidnapped and raped a woman "with his gun and Taser at arm's length"—hide the untold instances of officers who were not held accountable. Indeed, in most cases, these violent actions are considered the legitimate performance of officers' duties. "The undercover can have a nice, cold beer and watch a girl take her clothes off—and he's getting paid for it," said retired sergeant Stephen Antiuk. These practices legitimize broader forms of police sexual violence against marginalized women: the African American Policy Forum reports that Black women are at the highest risk of any demographic group to experience police sexual violence.[8]

When sex workers and sexually profiled women do report nonstate sexual assault to police, "most [officers] treated reports of rape by prostitutes as false reports," according to a federally funded 2010 study, which found that "in one city it was common practice [for police] to claim that prostitutes claimed rape only to get the free gynecological examination required by the city." As a result, women who dare to report rape to police are in danger of being arrested for both prostitution *and* filing a false report, as happened to one Black woman outside Charlotte, North Carolina, in 2020. Proposed solutions like layering on laws that give sexually profiled women immunity to report other crimes—introduced in Vermont in 2020 and again in 2021—have no impact on discretionary police power. Similarly, the ongoing police-aligned feminist projects to shift police attitudes on gender-based violence only buttress discretionary police power by placing public trust in police training rather than demanding public oversight. Women's testimonies and scattered glimpses behind the veil of police power expose the routine fact of violence that is woven into sexual policing—all of it authorized in the name of urban safety and, grotesquely, protection for women.[9]

Trans women of color are profoundly vulnerable to state neglect and police violence. In the 2015 U.S. Transgender Survey, more than half of the respondents reported some form of violence or abuse by police, with Indigenous trans women most likely to experience police violence. As Andrea Ritchie writes, searches, frisks, and pat-downs are daily sources of humiliation as officers seek "[to assign] a gender, to punish and humiliate trans people, to satisfy their curiosity, or for sexual gratification."[10]

Morals laws justify these practices as legitimate police work. In New York the loitering-prostitution law was widely regarded as a "walking while trans" law. Police arrested women based on their clothing and appearance. At least one officer admitted under deposition that he would "look for 'Adam's apples' when considering whether to detain" a sexually profiled woman. Another New York Police Department officer explained that "when you put pressure on cops to come up with [arrest] numbers . . . it's the black, it's the Hispanic, it's the LGBT community. We go for the most vulnerable." As lawyer Mogulescu says, "You cannot be a trans woman of color standing on the street without risking arrest." The stakes of these misdemeanor arrests were made brutally clear in 2019, when Layleen Polanco, a trans woman awaiting trial at the Rikers Island jail because she could not afford the $500 bail, was found dead in her cell. After over four decades on the books, New York's loitering law was finally repealed in February 2021 thanks to the tireless organizing of predominantly Black and Latinx queer and trans activists and their allies. But countless other morals misdemeanors remain in effect nationwide. "There's notions that we're not supposed to exist," said Bamby Salcedo, founder of the Trans Latina Coalition. "The police have also internalized all of that and perpetrate that [violence]. So because we have to survive in some type of way, because we're not supposed to exist in this world, we're criminalized simply because of who we are."[11]

Systematic police targeting compounds trans women's vulnerability to nonstate violence. In a chilling parallel to the serial murders of Black women across the 1970s and 1980s, there is an epidemic of violence against trans women of color. In 2020 the Human Rights Campaign documented the murders of forty-four transgender people—the highest number since the organization started tracking this data in 2013. As a Latina trans woman said in an interview, "The police are never there when you need them the most. Especially if you are a transgender girl or gay [or] LGBT."[12]

Seen from the perspective of sex workers and sexually profiled women, "law and order" is lawless, violent, and chaotic. Women's experiences with sexual policing expose the lie that police provide safety and protective services. On the contrary, police create violence and danger. Prostitution-related laws make punishment, not protection, the job of police. Public order enforcement gives police the mandate—and the excuse—to harass, arrest, and assault sexually profiled women simply for being on city streets. Women may occasionally report helpful and positive encounters with individual officers, but decency is up to the officer's own discretion—and while violence is written into the legal repertoire of police tools to secure urban order, decency is not. As one anonymous Washington, D.C., resident said, "I feel less safe with the police than without them."[13]

· · · · · ·

When the banishment law was proposed in Atlanta, organizers in the Solutions Not Punishment Collaborative swiftly and successfully mobilized to shut it down. They were not alone. Throughout the early twenty-first century, sex workers, formerly incarcerated people, trans and nonbinary people, and their allies have won victories against banishment laws in Washington, D.C., and Portland, Oregon. But banishment laws are only one weapon in police departments' arsenals. Activists continue to fight the police practice of using condoms and other tools of personal protection as evidence against sexually profiled women. And little has changed since 1987, when an interviewed woman said, "There are so many laws they can use on you. It's completely sickening to me."[14]

Since the first wave of demands to abolish prostitution-related laws in the 1970s, decriminalization has gained momentum in the twenty-first century. In 2015 Amnesty International joined at least ten other international organizations in recommending decriminalization "based on evidence and the real-life experience of sex workers themselves that criminalization makes them less safe." In addition to the work in New York, sex workers and their allies have successfully pushed for the introduction of legislation to fully repeal prostitution-related laws in Vermont, Oregon, and Washington, D.C. City councils in Seattle, Washington, and Burlington, Vermont, have repealed municipal prostitution-loitering and prostitution laws, respectively, but police there can still deploy the state-level laws.[15]

Inheritors of the dominance feminist legacy—now called carceral feminists—staunchly oppose decriminalization proposals. They consider pimps and the "sex industry" itself to be the greatest source of harm to women and maintain strong support for the involvement of police to criminalize the buyers and profiteers of commercial sex (though of course in many instances these same men have been proven to be law enforcement themselves). Already in the United States, laws designed to target the men who profit off commercial sex have criminalized as "pimps" women who live together, give each other rides, share information, or pool money. Sexual policing has historically produced more gender-based violence, with poor women and women of color extremely vulnerable to this harm. There is no evidence to suggest that gender-reversing the police targets has changed or reduced this pattern. The carceral feminist position betrays a deep faith in the protective capacity of the police, which a century of law enforcement history has shown to be gravely mistaken, especially for impoverished women—and indeed all people—of color. Carceral feminists, like their Progressive-era predecessors, ultimately aim for the total abolition of commercial sex on behalf of women's salvation. Progressive moral reformers only succeeded in the degradation and segregation of Black neighborhoods, the escalation of state and nonstate violence against targeted women, and the expansion of police power. Today's carceral moral reformers will fare no better in the historical record if their proposals succeed.[16]

For over a century, reformers, social scientists, activists, and even some law enforcement authorities have argued that sexual policing is patently unreformable and the morals laws that sustain sexual policing must be repealed. The decriminalization of prostitution-related misdemeanors is a necessary first step to reduce police harm and violence against women. However, as Robyn Few, the founder of the Sex Workers Outreach Project-USA, reminds us, decriminalization is "not the solution itself." The modern history of sexual policing has abundantly demonstrated that police and their urban allies will vigilantly guard their discretionary power, devising new laws that maintain law enforcement's stranglehold on street-level power. Carceral feminists, to say nothing of police unions and other police-allied constituencies, will actively defend law enforcement in this fight. Decriminalization, then, must be accompanied by a broader mobilization for people power—not police power. The time to demand accountability is over; the search for police accountability contains an implicit expectation that departments will act in good faith with the public. But law enforcement authorities have consistently proved themselves unwilling to meaningfully and transparently engage citizens concerned about the systematic abuse of police power. And sexual violence is baked into the practice of morals enforcement itself. The rare cases in which officers are indicted or convicted do not change the legal structures in which such corruption and brutality flourished in the first place—if anything, these exceptional displays of "justice" only serve to reassure outraged citizens that clean, benevolent power has (once again) been restored.[17]

The harms of sexual policing reverberate beyond the directly targeted women and their families and communities. Though it has taken distinct forms across the last century, sexual policing is, at its core, a site of legal control and a factory for producing ideas about normative gender behaviors. In this way, the criminalization of prostitution means the criminalization of all people who identify as a woman. Whether discretionary racialized sexual policing renders women unfree or only provisionally free—whether the punishing boundaries of lawful womanhood are daily barriers or simply invisible—morals enforcement exists to structure the limits of social, economic, and political possibility. The movement to abolish sexual policing pushes beyond merely the repeal of morals laws and demands the decriminalization of gendered life. Decriminalization is about resisting state and nonstate violence against the most vulnerable sexually profiled women *and* about rejecting gender-based policing because it is foundational to exploitation, subjugation, and unfreedom in this country. Centering sexual policing in abolitionist demands serves to underscore the profound police violence and victimization inherent to ostensibly protective law enforcement. Under the cover of providing a public safety service, police legitimize their violence and claim expanding authority over city residents—even those who don't realize their behaviors are subject to, or enforced through, broad, brutal discretionary state power.[18]

Police power can be dramatically reduced, first and foremost by draining it of its lifeblood: discretionary morals laws. Police must be fully denied their discretionary power to enforce public morals. This would in turn deny officers their authority to enforce a predatory and exploitative vision of public order. Instead, as Margaret Prescod argued decades ago, the enormous sums of money that are currently dedicated to stings, crackdowns, and street clearance arrest drives should be redirected to social supports, housing, education, and healthcare funds—with a firm and impenetrable barrier in place that separates police from the distribution of care and resources. The surest way to revitalize cities for all is by prioritizing the health and welfare of those who daily confront and navigate state violence as they work to support themselves and their families: poor women. Fully inclusive and livable cities are vastly less expensive, both economically and morally, than those that simply dispatch police to solve urban problems with a gun and a cage.[19]

Police power is not a naturally occurring phenomenon. It is human-made and political, and that reality makes it fragile. Modern police departments rose to power through morals enforcement. Denying their authority over women's bodies is a crucial next step in unmaking police power.

Acknowledgments

On my mother's last lucid day, I told her I had been accepted to the PhD program in history at Brown University. I've since marked my milestones as a historian against the years I've spent without her. It gives me great pleasure to thank the many people who have sustained this work, and me, in her absence.

Megan Marshall ignited my love for women's history and encouraged me early and often. She first suggested I consider applying to PhD programs, and we have since celebrated wins and mourned losses together. How fortunate I am that Megan is now a beloved friend.

My mentors' faith in this book kept me going, especially when I could not muster the faith myself. I am deeply grateful for the privilege to learn from Robert Self, Tricia Rose, and Amanda Littauer. Robert taught me how to be both generous and unflinching in the storm of the past (and the present). Tricia taught me to center my commitments and stay focused on the urgency of women's experiences. Amanda taught me how to become a mentor: she was exceptionally kind when I first accosted her at a National Women's Studies Association conference; and she graciously took on my project, providing essential critiques for the book and career guidance.

Archivists are heroes, saving us from the dystopia of historical amnesia, if only we listen and care. I want to especially thank the archivists who fought to rescue doomed or sealed files, suggested records I would never have known to request, and gave me tours of the stacks: Libby Bouvier at the Massachusetts Supreme Judicial Court Archives, Marta Crilly at the Boston City Archives, Jessica Herrick at the California State Archives, Haley Maynard at the College Park National Archives, Kelly Wooten at the Sallie Bingham Center at Duke University, Michael Holland at the Los Angeles City Archives, and John Hannigan at the Massachusetts Archives. A very special thanks to rebel archivists Stephen Lewis, Gail Pellett, Rona Rothman, and Chris Womendez, who shared their memories and the materials they had saved. Doris Bunte, Robert diGrazia (1928–2018), Mel King, Preston Williams, and Valimore and Judith Williams contributed oral histories to chapter 4. Elizabeth Searcy did painstaking work compiling arrest data.

This book would not exist without funding provided by the William Nelson Cromwell Foundation and the American Society for Legal History, the American Council of Learned Societies, the Institute for Citizens and Scholars, the Organization of American Historians, the American Historical Association, the Center for the Study of Race and Ethnicity in America and the Pembroke Center for Teaching and Research on Women at Brown University, the Sallie Bingham Center at Duke University, the Sophia Smith Collection at Smith College, the Money for

Women/Barbara Deming Memorial Fund, the St. Botolph Club Foundation, and the Writer's Room of Boston.

This work has benefited from the rigorous and insightful engagement of smart and generous scholars at conferences, workshops, and talks: Brian Balogh, Margot Canaday, DeAnza Cook, Nancy Cott, Grace Peña Delgado, Myisha Eatmon, Max Felker-Kantor, Gil Frank, Kali Gross, Emily Hobson, Kwame Holmes, Mandy Hughett, Anna Lvovsky, Kenneth Mack, Melanie Newport, Bill Novak, Annelise Orleck, Emily Owens, Christopher Phelps, Peter Pihos, Jessica Pliley, Charlotte Rosen, Gabe Rosenberg, Lucy Salyer, Naoko Shibusawa, Michael Stauch, Timothy Stewart-Winter, Whit Strub, Carl Suddler, and Michael Willrich. Simon Balto, Heather Berg, Mindy Chateauvert, Sara Matthiessen, Emily Thuma, and Danielle Wiggins contributed their time and intellectual labor to read early (and also very late; very last-minute!) drafts, sharpen my analysis, and generally save me from myself. Many, many thanks: it is a privilege to be in conversation with all of you.

When historians get together to talk about the past, magic happens: sometimes it is the spark of a new connection and sometimes it is the revelation that a chapter needs to be scrapped entirely and rewritten. But no matter what, the magic is fellowship with people who care deeply about the past and the future. I cherish the space that was made to think together about my work in the Dallas Area Society of Historians (where Stephanie Cole gave me the idea for a prologue—thank you!), the Harvard Law School Legal History Workshop, the Intimate States workshop, the Boston Seminar on Modern American Society and Culture at the Massachusetts Historical Society, the Writing about Gender and Sex Graduate Colloquium at the Pembroke Center, the Making Market Societies Mellon Interdisciplinary Graduate Workshop, the Center for the Study of Race and Ethnicity in America seminar, and the American Society for Legal History Student Research Colloquium.

Articles drawn from chapters 3 and 4 appear in the *Journal of American History* and the *Journal of Social History*, respectively. I thank Oxford University Press for permission to use this material, and the peer reviewers and editorial staff at both journals for nurturing this work at an early stage. A very special shout-out to Sam Lebovic and Tim Lombardo, whose close reads and incisive questions for the *Journal of Social History* article sent me back to the archives, substantially improved chapter 4, and shaped the course of the argument for the entire book.

I had the ridiculously good fortune to spend a year surrounded by stacks of books, grazing deer, and the sharpest historians in the game in the little white house in Bloomington, Indiana. What a pleasure to work with Judith Allen and Peter Bailey, Hannah Alms, Stephen Andrews, Andrew Cooper, Aaron Fountain, Ben Irvin (who, along with Alison Greene and Edith Greene Irvin, made me feel so welcome and supported while I was making the donuts), Jazma Sutton, André Thompson, and the staff of the *Journal of American History*. The Indiana University faculty were amazingly supportive and offered guidance that sustains me still: Cara Caddoo, Wendy Gamber, Michael Grossberg, Michael McGerr (who went above and beyond as my faculty mentor and set me on the path to become a much better teacher), Amrita Chakrabarti Myers, Roberta Pergher, Eric Robinson, Eric Sandweiss, and Ellen Wu. Many thanks to the Center for Law, Society, and Culture at the Maurer

School of Law for giving me the opportunity to present my work. Mia Beach and Micol Seigel welcomed me into a community of care and justice. Ke-Chin Hsia and Fei-Hsien Wang made Woodlawn Avenue feel like home; Emily Prifogle and Josh Powell made us feel like Hoosiers. In an exquisite twist of fate, Joanna Niżyńska and I were reunited in Bloomington—*Joanna znała mnie gdy miałam dwadzieścia lat, a mimo to mnie kocha.* Sofia Niżyńska-Schertz will be a much better twenty-year-old than I was.

I miraculously landed beyond the limits of my own dreams, surrounded by brilliant friends, mentors, and colleagues at the University of Texas at Dallas. My job, and my life in Dallas, is meaningful because of Olivia Banner, Ashley Barnes and Jon Malesic (the best neighbors in the metroplex), Sharron Conrad, Kate Davies, Megan Gray Hering, Erin Greer (our walks nourish me) and Dan Scott, Charles Hatfield, Kimberly Hill, Pia Jakobsson, Debbie Kang, Amy Kerner and Michael Hutson, Dennis Kratz, Josef Nguyen, Jacqueline Prince, Monica Rankin, Natalie Ring and Big Jon Daniel, Mark Rosen, Andrew Scott, Erin Smith, Davis and Linda Smith-Brecheisen, Sabrina Starnaman, Whitney Nell Stewart (who always made sure I had fresh flowers on the toughest days and bubbles on the best days), Nomi Stone, Wendy Sung, Theresa Towner, Shilyh Warren, Michael Wilson, and Ben Wright (who delivered rigorous and insightful comments on the introduction in the middle of the human-made catastrophe of SNOVID 2021). Matt Brown and Nils Roemer have consistently supported my work at UTD, and Dena Davis, Desiree Johnson, and Lisa Lyles have made that work possible. What a delight to be reunited with Shifra Cohen and Ronnie Cohen, who keep my mother's memory alive in Dallas. My students give me hope for the future, and the queenmakers of the Women's Collective inspire me to keep daydreaming for a new world.

Bearing witness to and interrogating state violence is extremely painful work. I am so grateful for the joy, wisdom, and solidarity that my friends bring to my life: Claire Adams and Andrew Pope, Mary Appel and Max Felker-Kantor, Grace Cleary and Daniel Platt, Scott De Orio, Roy González, Matt Guariglia, Dennis Hogan, Ben Holtzman, Lizzie Ingleson, Alicia Maggard, and Devin McGeehan Muchmore. Many thanks to Abbie Brooks and Adam Shalvey, and Frances Tanzer and Mike Bykovski, gracious hosts who put me up and took me out when I was in New York for research. Fantastical creature Sara Matthiesen read many drafts of this work, fielded many texts, and soothed many anxieties; she deserves all the love in the universe. Amy Marcott turns ordinary days into perfect days; I'm so glad that Stace Budzko is there to join us at night. If I wrote a love letter to Boston, it would really be a love letter to Erin Casey and Chris Cota, Nora Chorover and Steve Cooley, Nate Eckstrom and Nancy Ryan, Jill Gallagher, and Vivian Meranda and Maritza Ranero who made front porch hangs on Carolina Avenue so precious. Wayne Langley was a boss and now, happily, he is a friend; the PUMA poster in his office changed my life.

Brandon Proia is *самый человечный человек*—the most humane human. Every writer should be so lucky to have an editor like Brandon: a thoughtful and compassionate advocate for the book from the first to the last. All the anxieties, and any errors, are entirely my own, because with Brandon, the publication process was careful, smooth, and incredibly fun. The Justice, Power, and Politics series, under the editorial leadership of Heather Ann Thompson and Rhonda Y. Williams, publishes the most vital and necessary histories of my generation, and I'm honored that this book shares a shelf with them. I am deeply grateful to Keona Ervin and Cheryl Hicks, who read the full manuscript, offered sharp analysis and invaluable comments, and encouraged me to make this a much stronger book. Andrea Ritchie provided important insights at a crucial stage in the process.

My family loved me through the very unexpected turns our life took. I am profoundly grateful for Paul Fischer; every time I got lost, Dad found me and welcomed me back home. I treasure my bonus mother, Sandy Jacobson; she taught me that who we are lives on in the people we love and who loved us. I am so lucky that my brother is also my best friend: many thanks to Sam Fischer and Jen Choi, who is perfect in every way, for hosting me while I was doing research in Los Angeles; and infinite thanks for Elijah Fischer, who is pure delight. Thank you to the Jacobsons and the Bleakobsons; your love made me feel whole when I was mourning the greatest loss. Judy Rosenberg hosted me when I was doing research in the Bay Area and Sacramento; we had so much fun cooking together and watching movies. Eddie Stone has asked for years when the book will be finished; I'm very pleased to finally send him a copy. Bill and Mary Kay Myers welcomed me into their family and love me like their own; they always supported me when I headed down to work in the basement bar and had a beer waiting for me when I came back up. With Laura Myers and Steven Langue, summer in Ohio is the best place to be in the world.

My husband, Will Myers, never asked for the stress and precarity that I brought into our lives when I started down this path. But from the start he shared the pain and pleasure of the work and serves as my in-house editor with care, patience, unwavering support, and an excellent sense of humor. Thank you for inspiring me daily to search for the light and beauty that surely must exist in a world that brought us together.

Finally, I want to thank the women in this book who courageously transformed their experiences of state violence into action and who remind us every day that the streets belong to all of us: Barbara, Betty, Eleanor, Emily Brow, Cherie, Julie, Patricia Lambert, Carol Lane, Gloria Lockett, Media Lewis, Janet Parlin, Gwendolyn Reddick, Treyola Terry, Lesley Weeks, Roxie Williams, Chris Womendez, and the many women whose names were disappeared from the historical record. With your help, reader, we can carry their vision forward into our unwritten future.

Notes

Abbreviations in the Notes

AARL	Auburn Avenue Research Library on African American Culture and History, Fulton County Library System, Atlanta
ACLUSC	American Civil Liberties Union of Southern California records, Charles E. Young Research Library, University of California, Los Angeles
AHC	Atlanta History Center, Atlanta
BCFB	Black Coalition Fighting Back Serial Murders, Southern California Library, Los Angeles
BMCP	Boston Municipal Court Probation Records, Massachusetts Supreme Judicial Court, Boston
BOPC	Board of Police Commissioners Agenda Packets, Los Angeles City Archives and Records Center, Los Angeles
BRA	Boston Redevelopment Authority Archives, City of Boston Archives, Boston
CAP	Central Atlanta Progress records, Atlanta History Center, Atlanta
CFNYPL	Committee of Fourteen records, New York Public Library Manuscripts and Archives Division, New York
GSA	Georgia Archives, Atlanta
KH	Collection of Kenneth Hahn, Huntington Library, San Marino, California
KW	Kevin White Papers, City of Boston Archives, Boston
LACA	Los Angeles City Archives and Records Center, Los Angeles
NACP	National Archives and Records Administration, College Park, Maryland
NU	Special Collections and Archives, Northeastern University, Boston
SCH	Schlesinger Library, Harvard Radcliffe Institute, Cambridge, Massachusetts

Introduction

1. *Cops*, season 25, episode 2, third act, aired December 22, 2012, on Fox. All *Cops* episodes can be viewed on Amazon Prime. For an excellent history and contemporary investigation of *Cops* and other law enforcement reality shows, see Dan Taberski, *Running from COPS*, podcast, Topic Studios/First Look Media, 2019. Wandick arrested the nineteen-year-old woman for underage drinking because he had no proof (beyond the woman's own account) that she had engaged in sex work

in the past. She also volunteered to officers her history of foster care and sexual abuse. The officers answered the woman's trauma with arrest.

2. "Lurking in shadows," *Cops*, season 19, episode 12, second act at 7:57, aired December 16, 2006, on Fox; "standing on the street corner," *Cops*, season 22, episode 13, third act at 14:40, aired December 10, 2009, on Fox; "loitering outside [a] business," *Cops*, season 22, episode 13, third act at 15:42, aired December 10, 2009, on Fox; "walking in the street," *Cops*, season 23, episode 10, third act, at 14:58, aired December 11, 2010, on Fox; "It's best for her," *Cops*, season 25, episode 2, third act, at 20:47, aired December 22, 2012, on Fox.

3. On gender as an ideological and historical process, see Joan W. Scott, "Gender: A Useful Category of Historical Analysis," *The American Historical Review* 91, no. 5 (December 1986): 1053–1075. On Black feminist knowledge production and its relationship to the ideological process of gender, see Patricia Hill Collins, "The Social Construction of Black Feminist Thought," *Signs* 14, no. 4 (1989): 745–73. On the construction of white womanhood in the nineteenth century, see Ariela J. Gross, "Litigating Whiteness: Trials of Racial Determination in the Nineteenth-Century South," *The Yale Law Journal* 108, no. 1 (October 1998): 109–188; and Martha Hodes, "The Sexualization of Reconstruction Politics: White Women and Black Men in the South after the Civil War," *Journal of the History of Sexuality* 3, no. 3 (January 1993): 402–417. On the production of Black and white womanhood in the Jim Crow South, see Sarah Haley, "'Like I Was a Man': Chain Gangs, Gender, and the Domestic Carceral Sphere in Jim Crow Georgia," *Signs* 39, no. 1 (2013): 53–77. On the transitive relationship between the markers of Blackness and transness, see C. Riley Snorton, *Black on Both Sides: A Racial History of Trans Identity* (Minneapolis: University of Minnesota Press, 2017).

4. As Micol Seigel argues, police work is inherently violence work. See Seigel, *Violence Work: State Power and the Limits of Police* (Durham, NC: Duke University Press, 2018). For migrant and undocumented women, morals arrests can also trigger deportation proceedings. See, for example, Melissa Gira Grant, "ICE Is Using Prostitution Diversion Courts to Stalk Immigrants," *Village Voice*, July 17, 2017. See also Andrea Ritchie and Priscilla Bustamante, "Shrouded in Silence: Police Sexual Violence: What We Know and What We Can Do About It," *Interrupting Criminalization*, n.d., https://static1.squarespace.com/static/5ee39ec764dbd7179cf1243c/t/609 bobb8fc3271012c4a93c5/1620773852750/Shrouded+in+Silence.pdf.

5. Amy Chozick and Michael Barbaro, "Hillary Clinton Laments 'Missing' Black Men as Politicians Reflect on Baltimore Unrest," *New York Times*, April 29, 2015; Sentencing Project, *Trends in U.S. Corrections* (Washington, DC: Sentencing Project, updated August 2020), 5. Of course, Hillary Clinton's reversal on mass incarceration in 2015 was notable given her vociferous support of the Violent Crime Control and Law Enforcement Act, which her husband, Bill Clinton, signed into law in 1994, accelerating the mass incarceration crisis.

The now-classic text that specifically focuses on Black men is Michelle Alexander, *The New Jim Crow: Mass Incarceration in the Age of Colorblindness* (New York: New Press, 2010), 15–16. For examples of this male-dominated discourse, see Justin Wolfers, David Leonhardt, and Kevin Quealy, "1.5 Million Missing Black Men," *New*

York Times, April 20, 2015; Keisha Lance Bottoms, "The Police Report to Me, but I Knew I Couldn't Protect My Son," *New York Times*, June 3, 2020.

Women make up the fastest-growing population of incarcerated people. See, for example, Spencer K. Beall, "'Lock Her Up!': How Women Have Become the Fastest-Growing Population in the American Carceral State," *Berkeley Journal of Criminal Law* 23, no. 2 (2018): 1–39. On Black women and mass incarceration, see Angela Y. Davis, "How Gender Structures the Prison System," *Are Prisons Obsolete?* (New York: Seven Stories Press, 2010), chap. 4; Sarah Haley, "Care Cage: Black Women, Political Symbolism, and 1970s Prison Crisis," *Souls* 20, no. 1 (January 2018): 58–85; and Beth E. Richie, *Arrested Justice: Black Women, Violence, and America's Prison Nation* (New York: New York University Press, 2012). On the relationship between Black motherhood and police violence, see Keisha N. Blain, "'We Will Overcome Whatever [it] is the System Has Become Today': Black Women's Organizing against Police Violence in New York City in the 1980s," *Souls* 20, no. 1 (January 2018): 110–121; Dorothy E. Roberts, *Killing the Black Body: Race, Reproduction, and the Meaning of Liberty* (New York: Pantheon Books, 1997); and Jennifer C. Nash, *Birthing Black Mothers* (Durham, NC: Duke University Press, 2021).

6. For articles centering Black women during the 2020 uprising, see, for example, Alisha Haridasani Gupta, "Why Aren't We All Talking about Breonna Taylor?," *New York Times*, June 4, 2020; and Jameelah Nasheed, "Breonna Taylor Received No Justice Because Black Women's Lives Aren't Valued," *Teen Vogue*, September 24, 2020. For a history of Black rebellions, see Elizabeth Hinton, *America on Fire: The Untold History of Police Violence and Black Rebellion Since the 1960s* (New York: Liveright, 2021).

7. For Black feminist interventions in the contemporary legal system, see Angela Y. Davis and Cassandra Shaylor, "Race, Gender, and the Prison Industrial Complex: California and Beyond," *Meridians* 2, no. 1 (2001): 1–25; Kimberlé Crenshaw, "Demarginalizing the Intersection of Race and Sex: A Black Feminist Critique of Antidiscrimination Doctrine, Feminist Theory and Antiracist Politics," *University of Chicago Legal Forum* 1 (1989): 139–167; Jael Miriam Silliman, Anannya Bhattacharjee, and Angela Y. Davis, *Policing the National Body: Race, Gender and Criminalization in the United States* (Boston: South End, 2002); Andrea J. Ritchie, *Invisible No More: Police Violence against Black Women and Women of Color* (Boston: Beacon, 2017); and Mariame Kaba, *We Do This 'Til We Free Us: Abolitionist Organizing and Transforming Justice* (Chicago: Haymarket Books, 2021). For Black feminist histories of the criminal legal system, see Kali N. Gross, *Colored Amazons: Crime, Violence, and Black Women in the City of Brotherly Love, 1880–1910* (Durham, NC: Duke University Press, 2006); Sarah Haley, *No Mercy Here: Gender, Punishment, and the Making of Jim Crow Modernity* (Chapel Hill: University of North Carolina Press, 2016); Cheryl D. Hicks, *Talk with You Like a Woman: African American Women, Justice, and Reform in New York, 1890–1935* (Chapel Hill: University of North Carolina Press, 2010); and Talitha L. LeFlouria, *Chained in Silence: Black Women and Convict Labor in the New South* (Chapel Hill: University of North Carolina Press, 2015). See also Keisha N. Blain, "A Short History of Black Women and Police Violence," *Conversation*, June 12, 2020, https://theconversation.com/a

-short-history-of-black-women-and-police-violence-139937; and Treva Lindsey, "Black Women Have Consistently Been Trailblazers for Social Change. Why Are They So Often Relegated to the Margins?," *Time*, July 22, 2020, https://time.com/5869662/black-women-social-change/.

8. On the antebellum and Progressive era relationship between gender, sex, and urban space, see William J. Novak, "Morals, Sex, Crime, and the Legal Origins of Modern American Social Police," in *Intimate States: Gender, Sexuality, and Governance in Modern US History*, ed. Margot Canaday, Nancy F. Cott, and Robert O. Self (Chicago: University of Chicago Press, 2021), 65–84; Sarah Deutsch, "Reconceiving the City: Women, Space, and Power in Boston, 1870–1910," *Gender and History* 6, no. 2 (August 1994): 202–223; Christine Stansell, *City of Women: Sex and Class in New York, 1789–1860* (Urbana: University of Illinois Press, 1987); Victoria E. Bynum, *Unruly Women: The Politics of Social and Sexual Control in the Old South* (Chapel Hill: University of North Carolina Press, 1992); and Timothy J. Gilfoyle, *City of Eros: New York City, Prostitution, and the Commercialization of Sex, 1790–1920* (New York: W. W. Norton, 1992). For a spatial gender analysis of urban space and an "alternative vision of the feminist city," see Leslie Kern, *Feminist City: Claiming Space in a Man-Made World* (New York: Verso Books, 2020). For an excerpt from Kern's book, discussing private security, gentrification, and the failure of police to make women "safe," see Kern, "Women, Fear, and Cities," *Verso Blog*, March 15, 2021, https://www.versobooks.com/blogs/5024-women-fear-and-cities. On social reproduction theory, see Tithi Bhattacharya, ed., *Social Reproduction Theory: Remapping Class, Recentering Oppression* (London: Pluto, 2017).

9. Peggy Pascoe named miscegenation laws and the legal institution of marriage as "factories" of race and gender in Pascoe, *What Comes Naturally: Miscegenation Law and the Making of Race in America* (New York: Oxford University Press, 2009), 11.

10. National Commission on Law Observance and Enforcement and August Vollmer, *Report on Police* (Washington, DC: U.S. Government Printing Office, 1931), 58, 17; Leonard V. Harrison, *Police Administration in Boston* (Cambridge, MA: Harvard University Press, 1934), 144, 149–152. For histories of Black sex workers before 1930, see Cynthia M. Blair, *I've Got to Make My Livin': Black Women's Sex Work in Turn-of-the-Century Chicago* (Chicago: University of Chicago Press, 2010); LaShawn Harris, *Sex Workers, Psychics, and Numbers Runners: Black Women in New York City's Underground Economy* (Urbana: University of Illinois Press, 2016); and Victoria W. Wolcott, *Remaking Respectability: African American Women in Interwar Detroit* (Chapel Hill: University of North Carolina Press, 2001).

11. For a discussion of settler colonialism and incarceration, see Kelly Lytle Hernández, *City of Inmates: Conquest, Rebellion, and the Rise of Human Caging in Los Angeles, 1771–1965* (Chapel Hill: University of North Carolina Press, 2017), introduction and chap. 1. On the centrality of sexual policing to constructing the restrictive immigration regime, see Grace Peña Delgado, "Border Control and Sexual Policing: White Slavery and Prostitution along the U.S.-Mexico Borderlands, 1903–1910," *Western Historical Quarterly* 43 (Summer 2012): 157–158.

In her research, Andrea Ritchie demonstrates that Indigenous, Latina, and Asian American women experience distinct vulnerabilities to state violence. Ritchie, *Invisible No More*. For relational Black feminist and women of color feminist analytics that could ground future histories of Black, Indigenous, Asian, and Latina women and state violence, see Grace Kyungwon Hong and Roderick A. Ferguson, ed., *Strange Affinities: The Gender and Sexual Politics of Comparative Racialization* (Durham, NC: Duke University Press, 2011); Iyko Day, Tiffany Lethabo King, Sharon Luk, and Terrion L. Williamson, "Black Feminism and Settler Colonialism Roundtable," *Environment and Planning D: Society and Space* 39, no. 1 (February 2021): 3–29; and Vanita Reddy and Anantha Sudhakar, ed., "Feminist and Queer Afro-Asian Formations," *The Scholar and Feminist Online* 14, no. 3 (2018), https://sfonline.barnard.edu/feminist-and-queer-afro-asian-formations/.

On the intersection of disability justice and sex work, see Maitresse Madeline, femi babylon, Kitty Milford, and Lorelei Lee (moderator), "Sex Work as Work and Sex Work as Anti-Work: What are People in the Sex Trades Fighting For?" Hacking//Hustling online event, April 3, 2021, transcript available online: https://hackinghustling.org/event-work-and-anti-work-what-are-people-in-the-sex-trades-fighting-for/; and Katie Tastrom, "Sex Work is a Disability Issue. So Why Doesn't the Disability Community Recognize That?" *Rooted in Rights*, January 4, 2019, https://rootedinrights.org/sex-work-is-a-disability-issue-so-why-doesnt-the-disability-community-recognize-that/.

For scholarship that discusses the sexual policing of cisgender and trans women of color, as well as histories of the police enforcement of normative gender and sexual binaries, see note 27 of this chapter.

12. California Penal Code § 653.22. As of 2021, this law's future is uncertain. In September 2021, California legislators passed SB 357, which would repeal the loitering for the purpose of prostitution law. However, SB 357 will not be sent to the California governor for a signature (or a veto) until January 2022. See Andrew Sheeler and Hannah Wiley, "California Lawmakers Vote to Decriminalization Loitering for the Purpose of Prostitution," *The Sacramento Bee*, September 10, 2021.

13. U.S. Bureau of Investigation, Federal Bureau of Investigation, *Uniform Crime Reports for the United States* (Washington, DC: U.S. Government Printing Office, 1938), 26. Laws against "drunkenness" were also routinely deployed against women at least through the first half of the twentieth century.

14. Though at times officers claimed (and still do) that sexually profiled women evaded arrest because they knew the evidence requirements for specific prostitution-related laws, the broad and interchangeable repertoire of morals laws all but ensured that police held the ultimate power in an encounter. Officers will also use this explanation to justify engaging in sexual acts with profiled women (see the epilogue of this book). For a criminological discussion of the many uses and abuses of police discretion, see Herman Goldstein, "Confronting the Complexity of the Policing Function," in *Discretion in Criminal Justice: The Tension between Individualization and Uniformity*, ed. Lloyd E. Ohlin and Frank J. Remington (Albany: State University of New York Press, 1993), 23–71.

15. Feminist criminologists have also made important interventions around the social construction of women's crime. See especially Meda Chesney-Lind, *The Female Offender: Girls, Women and Crime* (Thousand Oaks, CA: Sage, 1997).

16. Helen Reynolds, *The Economics of Prostitution* (Springfield, IL: C. C. Thomas, 1986), 75. For a feminist analysis of stop-and-frisk police practices, see Josephine Ross, *A Feminist Critique of Police Stops* (Cambridge: Cambridge University Press, 2020); and Ritchie, *Invisible No More*, 84–86. On legal contests over police discretion and vagrancy laws, see especially Risa Goluboff, *Vagrant Nation: Police Power, Constitutional Change, and the Making of the 1960s* (New York: Oxford University Press, 2016).

17. Martha Pehde and Kenneth Lauszus, "Mayor's Task Force against Street Prostitution for the City of Sacramento, Minority Opinion," July 22, 1986, 4; Melinda Chateauvert, phone conversation with the author, on or around April 8, 2017.

18. See the prologue for a longer discussion of red-light districts. For histories of red-light districts after the Civil War, see Mara Laura Keire, *For Business and Pleasure: Red-Light Districts and the Regulation of Vice in the United States, 1890–1933* (Baltimore: Johns Hopkins University Press, 2010); and Thomas C. Mackey, *Red Lights Out: A Legal History of Prostitution, Disorderly Houses, and Vice Districts, 1870–1917* (New York: Garland, 1987). See also Blair, *I've Got to Make My Livin'*; Harris, *Sex Workers, Psychics, and Numbers Runners*; and Wolcott, *Remaking Respectability*.

19. Black reformers engaged in distinct forms of rescue work for Black women, but the overwhelming preoccupation with white slavery showcases the dominance of whites in this reform movement; see the prologue for a longer discussion of white slavery and Progressive-era reform. As Kali Gross writes, "Depraved black women and endangered white females were complementary narrative constructions that advanced the emerging social discourse of race and patriarchy." Gross, *Colored Amazons*, 118. On the mutually constitutive relationship between race and the meanings of sexual deviance before World War II, see Siobhan B. Somerville, *Queering the Color Line: Race and the Invention of Homosexuality in American Culture* (Durham, NC: Duke University Press, 2000); Pippa Holloway, *Sexuality, Politics, and Social Control in Virginia, 1920–1945* (Chapel Hill: University of North Carolina Press, 2006); Haley, *No Mercy Here*; and Hicks, *Talk with You*.

20. Joseph H. Fichter and Brian Jordan, "Police Handling of Arrestees: A Research Study of Police Arrests in New Orleans," 46–47, March 1964, Box 11, Debbie Louis Collection on Civil Rights, Charles E. Young Research Library, University of California, Los Angeles. Historians Kevin Mumford and Chad Heap argue that the relocation of vice districts in early twentieth-century Black neighborhoods created racial segregation, as well as modern binaries of race, gender, and sex. Kevin J. Mumford, *Interzones: Black/White Sex Districts in Chicago and New York in the Early Twentieth Century* (New York: Columbia University Press, 1997); Chad Heap, *Slumming: Sexual and Racial Encounters in American Nightlife, 1885–1940* (Chicago: University of Chicago Press, 2009).

21. For a history of deindustrialization, see Thomas J. Sugrue, *The Origins of the Urban Crisis: Race and Inequality in Postwar Detroit* (Princeton, NJ: Princeton University Press, 2010). For the relaxation of obscenity laws and the proliferation of

urban commercial sex businesses in postwar cities, see especially Whitney Strub, *Perversion for Profit: The Politics of Pornography and the Rise of the New Right* (New York: Columbia University Press, 2010). For an excellent discussion of New York's urban sexual entertainment district, see Samuel Delany, *Times Square Red, Times Square Blue* (New York: New York University Press, 1999).

22. Goluboff, *Vagrant Nation*.

23. Eugene Robinson, "Prostitutes Return Despite Sentence," *Washington Post*, August 14, 1981. See, for example, William Bratton and Rudolph Giuliani, *Police Strategy No. 5: Reclaiming the Public Spaces of New York* (New York: New York City Police Department, July 6, 1994). Gayle Rubin wrote extensively about predatory developers and police targeting queer life in the South of Market neighborhood in San Francisco. See Gayle Rubin, "The Miracle Mile: South of Market and Gay Male Leather, 1962–1997," in *Reclaiming San Francisco: History, Politics, Culture*, ed. James Brook, Chris Carlsson, and Nancy J. Peters (San Francisco: City Light Books, 1998), 247–272.

24. George Kelling essay quoted in William Bratton and Peter Knobler, *The Turnaround: How America's Top Cop Reversed the Crime Epidemic* (New York: Random House, 1998), 87–89.

25. Patricia Hill Collins, *Black Sexual Politics: African Americans, Gender, and the New Racism* (New York: Routledge, 2005); Evelynn Hammonds, "Black (W)holes and the Geometry of Black Female Sexuality," *Differences* 6, no. 2–3 (1994): 126–145; Hortense J. Spillers, "Mama's Baby, Papa's Maybe: An American Grammar Book," *Diacritics* 17, no. 2 (1987): 65–81. On the "controlling image" of hypersexual Black womanhood, see especially Patricia Hill Collins, *Black Feminist Thought: Knowledge, Consciousness, and the Politics of Empowerment* (New York: Routledge, 1990), 174–176. For a discussion of Black-white contrasts and mass incarceration centering men, see Khalil Gibran Muhammad, "Where Did All the White Criminals Go? Reconfiguring Race and Crime on the Road to Mass Incarceration," *Souls* 13, no. 1 (2011): 72–90.

26. Sarah Haley, "'Like I Was a Man,'" 53. For histories of the experiences of Black sex workers before the 1930s, see Blair, *I've Got to Make*; Harris, *Sex Workers*; Gross, *Colored Amazons*; Haley, *No Mercy Here*; and Hicks, *Talk with You*.

27. Margot Canaday, *The Straight State: Sexuality and Citizenship in Twentieth-Century America* (Princeton, NJ: Princeton University Press, 2009); Cathy J. Cohen, "Punks, Bulldaggers, and Welfare Queens: The Radical Potential of Queer Politics?" *GLQ* 3, no. 4 (1997): 437–465; Roberts, *Killing the Black Body*; see also Snorton, *Black on Both Sides*. See the epilogue for a discussion of state violence against trans women of color. Histories of queer, trans, and nonbinary sexual policing include Melinda Chateauvert, *Sex Workers Unite: A History of the Movement from Stonewall to Slutwalk* (Boston: Beacon, 2014); Treva Ellison, "From Sanctuary to Safe Space: Gay and Lesbian Police-Reform Activism in Los Angeles," *Radical History Review* 135 (2019): 95–118; Che Gossett, Tourmaline, and AJ Lewis, "Reclaiming Our Lineage: Organized Queer, Gender-Nonconforming, and Transgender Resistance to Police Violence," *The Scholar and Feminist Online* 10, nos. 1–2 (Fall 2011–Spring 2012), https://sfonline.barnard.edu/a-new-queer-agenda/reclaiming-our-lineage-organized-queer-gender-nonconforming-and-transgender-resistance-to-police

-violence/; Christina Hanhardt, *Safe Space: Gay Neighborhood History and the Politics of Violence* (Durham, NC: Duke University Press, 2013); Emily Hobson, "Policing Gay LA: Mapping Racial Divides in the Homophile Era, 1950–1967," in *The Rising Tide of Color: Race, State Violence, and Racial Movements across the Pacific*, ed. Moon-Ho Jung (Seattle: University of Washington Press, 2014), chap. 6; Anna Lvovsky, *Vice Patrol: Cops, Courts, and the Struggle over Urban Gay Life Before Stonewall* (Chicago: University of Chicago Press, 2021); Ritchie, *Invisible No More*; Joey Mogul, Andrea Ritchie, and Kay Whitlock, *Queer (In)Justice: The Criminalization of LGBT People in the United States* (Boston: Beacon Press, 2011); Clare Sears, *Arresting Dress: Cross-Dressing, Law, and Fascination in Nineteenth-Century San Francisco* (Durham, NC: Duke University Press, 2015); and Timothy Stewart-Winter, "Queer Law and Order: Sex, Criminality, and Policing in the Late Twentieth-Century United States," *Journal of American History* 102 (June 2015): 61–72. See also Eric A. Stanley and Nat Smith, *Captive Genders: Trans Embodiment and the Prison Industrial Complex* (Oakland: AK, 2015); and Dean Spade, *Normal Life: Administrative Violence, Critical Trans Politics, and the Limits of Law* (Durham, NC: Duke University Press, 2015). Gayle Rubin provides an analytical framework for the hierarchy of sexual practices in "Thinking Sex: Notes for a Radical Theory of the Politics of Sexuality," in *Deviations: A Gayle Rubin Reader* (Durham, NC: Duke University Press, 2011), 137–181.

28. Elizabeth Hinton, *From the War on Poverty to the War on Crime: The Making of Mass Incarceration in America* (Cambridge, MA: Harvard University Press, 2016); Naomi Murakawa, *The First Civil Right: How Liberals Built Prison America* (New York: Oxford University Press, 2014); Max Felker-Kantor, *Policing Los Angeles: Race, Resistance, and the Rise of the LAPD* (Chapel Hill: University of North Carolina Press, 2018); Simon Balto, *Occupied Territory: Policing Black Chicago from Red Summer to Black Power* (Chapel Hill: University of North Carolina Press, 2019).

29. For an excellent discussion of the harmful consequences of the destruction and disappearance of police archives, see Matthew Guariglia, "What the Loss of the New York Police Museum Means for Criminal Justice Reform," *Washington Post*, May 22, 2019, https://www.washingtonpost.com/outlook/2019/05/22/what-loss-new-york-police-museum-means-criminal-justice-reform/.

30. Hernández, *City of Inmates*, 4.

31. Saidiya Hartman, *Wayward Lives, Beautiful Experiments: Intimate Histories of Riotous Black Girls, Troublesome Women, and Queer Radicals* (New York: W. W. Norton, 2019); Laura Briggs, *Reproducing Empire: Race, Sex, Science, and U.S. Imperialism in Puerto Rico* (Berkeley: University of California Press, 2002), 205–208.

Prologue

1. Edholm quoted in Jessica R. Pliley, *Policing Sexuality: The Mann Act and the Making of the FBI* (Cambridge, MA: Harvard University Press, 2014), 20. Pliley's discussion of white slavery is the gold standard. Pliley, *Policing Sexuality*, chap. 1.

For a discussion of the intersections of white slavery and immigration restrictions, see Lorelei Lee, "The Roots of 'Modern Day Slavery': The Page Act and the Mann Act," *Columbia Human Rights Law Review* 52, no. 3 (2021): 1199–1239.

2. Mark Thomas Connelly, *The Response to Prostitution in the Progressive Era* (Chapel Hill: University of North Carolina Press, 1980); Mara Laura Keire, *For Business and Pleasure: Red-Light Districts and the Regulation of Vice in the United States, 1890–1933* (Baltimore: Johns Hopkins University Press, 2010), chap. 4; Mary de Young, "Help, I'm Being Held Captive! The White Slave Fairy Tale of the Progressive Era," *Journal of American Culture* 6 (1983): 96–99.

3. Kellor and Goldman quoted in Saidiya Hartman, *Wayward Lives, Beautiful Experiments: Intimate Histories of Riotous Black Girls, Troublesome Women, and Queer Radicals* (New York: W. W. Norton, 2019), 220, 308; Joanne J. Meyerowitz, *Women Adrift: Independent Wage Earners in Chicago, 1880–1930* (Chicago: University of Chicago Press, 1991). For a discussion of Frances Kellor, see Cheryl D. Hicks, *Talk with You Like a Woman: African American Women, Justice, and Reform in New York, 1890–1935* (Chapel Hill: University of North Carolina Press, 2010), 111–121.

4. "Our City Charities: The Home for the Friendless," *New York Times*, July 20, 1860; Anya Jabour, "Prostitution Politics and Feminist Activism in Modern America: Sophonisba Breckinridge and Morals Court in Prohibition-Era Chicago," *Journal of Women's History* 25 (Fall 2013): 143; Pliley, *Policing Sexuality*, 26. On postbellum moral reform and Christianity, see Gaines M. Foster, *Moral Reconstruction: Christian Lobbyists and the Federal Legislation of Morality, 1865–1920* (Chapel Hill: University of North Carolina Press, 2002). The moral reform literature is vast. Classics and personal favorites include Mary E. Odem, *Delinquent Daughters: Protecting and Policing Adolescent Female Sexuality in the United States, 1885–1920* (Chapel Hill: University of North Carolina Press, 1995); Ruth M. Alexander, *The Girl Problem: Female Sexual Delinquency in New York, 1900–1930* (Ithaca, NY: Cornell University Press, 1998); Barbara Meil Hobson, *Uneasy Virtue: The Politics of Prostitution and the American Reform Tradition* (New York: Basic Books, 1987); Regina Kunzel, *Fallen Women, Problem Girls: Unmarried Mothers and the Professionalization of Social Work, 1890–1945* (New Haven, CT: Yale University Press, 1995); Estelle B. Freedman, *Their Sisters' Keepers: Women's Prison Reform in America, 1830–1930* (Ann Arbor: University of Michigan Press, 1984); David J. Pivar, *Purity and Hygiene: Women, Prostitution, and the "American Plan," 1900–1930* (Westport, CT: Praeger, 2001); and Sharon Wood, *The Freedom of the Streets: Work, Citizenship, and Sexuality in a Gilded Age City* (Chapel Hill: University of North Carolina Press, 2005).

5. Keire, *For Business and Pleasure*, 5; Peter C. Hennigan, "Property War: Prostitution, Red-Light Districts, and the Transformation of Public Nuisance Law in the Progressive Era," *Yale Journal of Law and the Humanities* 16, no. 1 (2004): 155; Ruth Rosen, *The Lost Sisterhood: Prostitution in America, 1900–1918* (Baltimore: Johns Hopkins University Press, 1982), 5. Despite the wide variety of urban management policies and locations, postbellum red-light districts were deliberately designed and sanctioned features of the downtown urban landscape.

6. Neil Larry Shumsky, "Tacit Acceptance: Respectable Americans and Segregated Prostitution, 1870–1910," *Journal of Social History* 19, no. 4 (Summer 1986): 666; Simon Balto, *Occupied Territory: Policing Black Chicago from Red Summer to Black Power* (Chapel Hill: University of North Carolina Press, 2019), 38–42; Khalil Gibran Muhammad, *The Condemnation of Blackness: Race, Crime, and the Making of Modern Urban America* (Cambridge, MA: Harvard University Press, 2010), 226–232.

7. Mark Wild, "Red Light Kaleidoscope: Prostitution and Ethnoracial Relations in Los Angeles, 1880–1940," *Journal of Urban History* 28, no. 6 (September 2002): 722–723n12; Thomas Mackey, "Thelma Denton and Associates: Houston's Red Light Reservation and a Question of Jim Crow," *Houston Review* 14 (1992): 139–152; Kevin J. Mumford, *Interzones: Black/White Sex Districts in Chicago and New York in the Early Twentieth Century* (New York: Columbia University Press, 1997), 28–29; Cynthia M. Blair, *I've Got to Make My Livin': Black Women's Sex Work in Turn-of-the-Century Chicago* (Chicago: University of Chicago Press, 2010), 65–66; Keire, *For Business and Pleasure*, 53; Mackey, "Thelma Denton and Associates," 152. On the racial diversity of Chicago's Levee district (1870–1904), see Blair, *I've Got to Make My Livin'*, 53–56. In the South especially, red-light districts were typically located in or bordering Black neighborhoods.

8. Rosen, *Lost Sisterhood*, chap. 2; Connelly, *Response to Prostitution*; Brian Donovan, *The White Slave Crusades: Race, Gender, and Anti-vice Activism, 1887–1917* (Urbana: University of Illinois Press, 2006); Utica Committee of Twenty report quoted in "Social Hygiene Bulletin," *Journal of Social Hygiene* 9, no. 1 (1923): 52.

9. Paul Popenoe, "Some Eugenic Aspect of Illegitimacy," *Journal of Social Hygiene* 9, no. 9 (1923): 527; "Social Hygiene Bulletin," *Journal of Social Hygiene* 9, no. 1 (1923): 55. On Black moral reform, see especially Blair, *I've Got to Make My Livin'*, chap. 6; and Hicks, *Talk with You Like a Woman*. On the intersection of "race suicide" anxieties and Progressive moral reform, see Rosen, *Lost Sisterhood*, 44–45; and Connelly, *Response to Prostitution*, 75. On the social hygiene movement, see Pivar, *Purity and Hygiene*; and Allan M. Brandt, *No Magic Bullet: A Social History of Venereal Disease in the United States since 1880* (New York: Oxford University Press, 1985). For a local case study detailing the impact of social hygiene reform on sexual policing, see Jamie Schmidt Wagman, "Women Reformers Respond during the Depression: Battling St. Louis's Disease and Immorality," *Journal of Urban History* 35, no. 5 (July 1, 2009): 698–717.

10. Wild, "Red Light Kaleidoscope," 725; "Social Hygiene Bulletin," *Journal of Social Hygiene* 9, no. 9 (1923): 509; Mary Sullivan, *My Double Life* (New York: Farrar and Rinehart, 1938), 19.

11. On the intersection of gender, sexual criminalization, and eugenics, see Susan Schweik, *The Ugly Laws: Disability in Public* (New York: New York University Press, 2009), chap. 6; and Molly Ladd-Taylor, *Fixing the Poor: Eugenic Sterilization and Child Welfare in the Twentieth Century* (Baltimore: Johns Hopkins University Press, 2017). On World War I venereal disease panics and policing, see Brandt, *No Magic Bullet*. See also Gene E. Carte and Elaine H. Carte, *Police Reform in the United States: The Era of August Vollmer, 1905–1932* (Berkeley: University of California Press, 1975), 99.

12. Eugenia Cornelia Lekkerkerker, *Reformatories for Women in the United States* (Philadelphia: J. B. Wolters, 1931), 23–25 (emphasis added). See also William J. Novak, "Morals, Sex, Crime, and the Legal Origins of Modern American Social Police," in *Intimate States: Gender, Sexuality, and Governance in Modern US History*, ed. Margot Canaday, Nancy F. Cott, and Robert O. Self (Chicago: University of Chicago Press, 2021), 65–84; and Kristin Luker, "Sex, Social Hygiene, and the State: The Double-Edged Sword of Social Reform," *Theory and Society* 27 (1998): 614. For example, Los Angeles Police Department arrest report forms included a field listing the offender's "reputation." See Box 1, Record Group 313, National Archives, Washington, DC.

13. George E. Worthington and Ruth Topping, *Specialized Courts Dealing with Sex Delinquency: A Study of the Procedure in Chicago, Boston, Philadelphia, and New York* (New York: F. H. Hitchcock, 1925), 413. On the relationship between Progressive-era moral reform and the expansion of state power, see Timothy J. Gilfoyle, "The Moral Origins of Political Surveillance: The Preventive Society in New York City, 1867–1918," *American Quarterly* 38, no. 4 (Autumn 1986): 637–652.

14. Worthington and Topping, *Specialized Courts*, 395. While Progressive moral reformers were distinct from the women whom historians typically refer to as "maternalist" reformers, Progressive moral reformers certainly appealed to their maternal authority as women: the LAPD's chief policewoman, for example, was called the "City Mother." On maternalist reformers, see Robyn Muncy, *Creating a Female Dominion in American Reform, 1890–1935* (New York: Oxford University Press, 1994). On the transition from moral benevolence to professional social work in women's reform, see Kunzel, *Fallen Women, Problem Girls*. On the establishment of the Morals Court in Chicago, see Michael Willrich, *City of Courts: Socializing Justice in Progressive Era Chicago* (Cambridge: Cambridge University Press, 2003), chap. 6. See also Janis Appier, *Policing Women: The Sexual Politics of Law Enforcement and the LAPD* (Philadelphia: Temple University Press, 1998); Odem, *Delinquent Daughters*; Alexander, *Girl Problem*; Dorothy Moses Schulz, *From Social Worker to Crimefighter: Women in United States Municipal Policing* (Greenwood, CT: Praeger, 1995); Hicks, *Talk with You*; and Estelle B. Freedman, *Maternal Justice: Miriam Van Waters and the Female Reform Tradition* (Chicago: University of Chicago Press, 1996).

15. Maude Miner, "The Individual Method of Dealing with Girls and Women Awaiting Court Action," and Martha Falconer, "The Jail as a Perverter of Womanhood," presented at the Fifty-First Congress of American Prison Association, Jacksonville, FL, 1921; "Barton Training Home of the Big Sister League of Los Angeles: Report by the Survey Division of the Los Angeles Community Welfare Federation," 1934, Box 5, Council of Social Agencies of Los Angeles Records, California Social Welfare Archives, University of Southern California; Elva Forncrook, "Probation for Women," *Journal of Criminal Law and Criminology* 14, no. 4 (1924): 608; Black probation officer quoted in Hicks, *Talk with You Like a Woman*, 163. For a discussion of the Barton Training Home, see Appier, *Policing Women*, 137. Some Black reformers fought for inclusion in the white-dominated, woman-led Progressive reforms, while others created their own protective structures with considerably less funding and fewer resources. These interventions were fraught with negotiations

to uplift Black people defined by respectability politics and white supremacist myths of Black sexual deviance, as well as class-based exclusionary policies. See especially Hicks, *Talk with You*; Blair, *I've Got to Make My Livin'*, 201–206; Christina Simmons, "African Americans and Sexual Victorianism in the Social Hygiene Movement, 1910–1940," *Journal of the History of Sexuality* 4, no. 1 (July 1993): 51–75; and Hazel Carby, "Policing the Black Woman's Body in an Urban Context," *Critical Inquiry* 18, no. 4 (Summer 1992): 738–755.

16. Nicole Hahn Rafter, *Partial Justice: Women in State Prisons, 1800–1935* (Boston: Northeastern University Press, 1985); Jabour, "Prostitution Politics," 144. See also Anya Jabour, "Claims of Protecting Sex Workers Have Long Been Used to Punish Them," *Washington Post*, August 12, 2021.

17. Emily Remus, *A Shoppers' Paradise: How the Ladies of Chicago Claimed Power and Pleasure in the New Downtown* (Cambridge, MA: Harvard University Press, 2019), chap. 5. Red-light districts in smaller cities held fast through World War II; see chapter 2.

18. Hartman, *Wayward Lives, Beautiful Experiments*, 94. See also Mumford, *Interzones*, 27. Mara Keire argues that during the Progressive era, "the conflicting mandates of racial separation and reputational segregation created significant conflict" in cities, igniting racist violence in racially mixed red-light districts. These episodes "convinced the few remaining doubters that reputational segregation did not work and that racial segregation offered a far better solution" to social order. See Keire, *For Business and Pleasure*, 52, 139.

Chapter 1

1. Staff correspondent, "Campaign against Vice Is on in St. Louis," *Chicago Defender*, October 14, 1916.

2. "Girls Are Girls: Miss Binford, Don't Be Shocked," *Chicago Defender*, February 9, 1924.

3. "Girls Are Girls."

4. On Progressive moral reforms to abolish prostitution, see the prologue. For further reading, see Mark Thomas Connelly, *The Response to Prostitution in the Progressive Era* (Chapel Hill: University of North Carolina Press, 1980); Brian Donovan, *The White Slave Crusades: Race, Gender, and Anti-vice Activism, 1887–1917* (Urbana: University of Illinois Press, 2006); Mary E. Odem, *Delinquent Daughters: Protecting and Policing Adolescent Female Sexuality in the United States, 1885–1920* (Chapel Hill: University of North Carolina Press, 1995); Ruth M. Alexander, *The Girl Problem: Female Sexual Delinquency in New York, 1900–1930* (Ithaca, NY: Cornell University Press, 1998); and Gaines M. Foster, *Moral Reconstruction: Christian Lobbyists and the Federal Legislation of Morality, 1865–1920* (Chapel Hill: University of North Carolina Press, 2002).

5. Elizabeth Alice Clement argues that Prohibition accelerated the racial stratification of the commercial sex industry in New York by expanding the opportunities for white women to engage in legal forms of sexualized labor (e.g., taxi

dancing) from which Black women were excluded. As a result, illegal commercial sex became increasingly marginalized and overrepresented with Black women, which also heightened their exposure to police action. Elizabeth Alice Clement, *Love for Sale: Courting, Treating, and Prostitution in New York City, 1900–1945* (Chapel Hill: University of North Carolina Press, 2006), chap. 6.

6. Cynthia Blair argues that the spatial relocation of the vice district and the process of "drawing the color line" in Chicago opened up "significant inroads" for white businessmen into commercial sex syndicates and significantly eroded Black women's control over their labor. Cynthia M. Blair, *I've Got to Make My Livin': Black Women's Sex Work in Turn-of-the-Century Chicago* (Chicago: University of Chicago Press, 2010), 133–142.

7. The concept of "violent neglect" is inspired by Ruth Wilson Gilmore's analytical framework of "organized abandonment." Gilmore, *Golden Gulag: Prisons, Surplus, Crisis, and Opposition in Globalizing California* (Berkeley: University of California Press, 2007), 178.

8. For a history of Prohibition enforcement, see Lisa McGirr, *The War on Alcohol: Prohibition and the Rise of the American State* (New York: W. W. Norton, 2015).

9. The FBI released the first Uniform Crime Report in 1930, but women's arrests were not published until 1932. The statistics I work with are drawn from fingerprint records and do not represent all arrests made in the United States. U.S. Bureau of Investigation, Federal Bureau of Investigation, *Uniform Crime Reports for the United States* (Washington, DC: U.S. Government Printing Office, 1932–1939). On the relationship between racism and crime data, see Khalil Gibran Muhammad, *The Condemnation of Blackness: Race, Crime, and the Making of Modern Urban America* (Cambridge, MA: Harvard University Press, 2010), chap. 1; and Tamara K. Nopper, "Counting Crime: A Lecture on the Politics of Crime Data and Its Uses," Haymarket Books webinar series, July 27, 2021. For a history of the development of the Uniform Crime Reporting system, see Lawrence Rosen, "The Creation of the Uniform Crime Report: The Role of Social Science," *Social Science History* 19, no. 2 (Summer 1995): 215–238. For a general overview of police reform during this transitional interwar period, see Robert M. Fogelson, *Big-City Police*, Urban Institute Study (Cambridge, MA: Harvard University Press, 1977); Samuel Walker, *A Critical History of Police Reform: The Emergence of Professionalism* (Lexington, MA: Lexington Books, 1977); and Samuel Walker, *Popular Justice: A History of American Criminal Justice*, 2nd ed. (New York: Oxford University Press, 1997). On the relationship between police reform and the FBI, see Walker, *Critical History*; and Claire Bond Potter, *War on Crime: Bandits, G-Men, and the Politics of Mass Culture* (New Brunswick, NJ: Rutgers University Press, 1998).

10. Walter C. Reckless, *Vice in Chicago* (Montclair, NJ: Patterson Smith, 1933), 12, 192. Kevin Mumford argues that "by . . . pushing [vice] into black neighborhoods, reformers removed prostitution from a public agenda concerned with 'white' social problems." Kevin J. Mumford, *Interzones: Black/White Sex Districts in Chicago and New York in the Early Twentieth Century* (New York: Columbia University Press, 1997), 44. See also Blair, *I've Got to Make My Livin'*, 146–148.

11. Courtney Ryley Cooper, *Ten Thousand Public Enemies* (New York: Little, Brown, 1935), 177; "Jerome Reiterates Charge Hylan Lied," *New York Times*, October 29, 1921; Lee Francis, *Ladies on Call: The Most Intimate Recollections of a Hollywood Madam* (Los Angeles: Holloway House, 1965), 49, 187; Mark Wild, "Red Light Kaleidoscope: Prostitution and Ethnoracial Relations in Los Angeles, 1880–1940," *Journal of Urban History* 28, no. 6 (September 2002): 727, 739n23; Gerald Woods, "The Progressives and the Police: Urban Reform and the Professionalization of the Los Angeles Police" (PhD diss., University of California, Los Angeles, 1973), 11, 36.

12. See also Muhammad, *The Condemnation of Blackness*, chap. 6.

13. "Chicago Tribune Aids Race Solve Problem of Vice," *Chicago Defender*, March 17, 1923; "Evening Club Hears Pastor in Vice Talk," *Chicago Defender*, September 23, 1922. While vice operations were generally directed by white bosses, draining the bulk of the profits away from the Black community, vice was nonetheless "the major industry and possibly the single largest employer," as Gerald Woods argues, in a city structured by racist hiring practices. This was true not only of women who earned wages from commercial sex but also of men and women hired as maids, valets, and messengers for gambling and prostitution establishments, who were paid at relatively higher wages than those for similarly menial positions in licit industries. Black leaders, then, were forced to untangle a knot tightly bound up with residential segregation, economic discrimination, and sexualized racism: how to protect the integrity of their neighborhood without shutting down one of the chief sources of Black people's economic security. See Woods, "Progressives and the Police," 231; LaShawn Harris, *Sex Workers, Psychics, and Numbers Runners: Black Women in New York City's Underground Economy* (Urbana: University of Illinois Press, 2016); Victoria W. Wolcott, *Remaking Respectability: African American Women in Interwar Detroit* (Chapel Hill: University of North Carolina Press, 2001); and Blair, *I've Got to Make My Livin'*, 23–25.

14. "Black Belt Vice," *Pittsburgh Courier*, October 26, 1929; "Chicago's Underworld Shaken by Vice Probe," *Chicago Defender*, August 25, 1928; report, July 13, 1927, Folder G–R, Box 36, CFNYPL; Letter to Wendell Miller, n.d., Folder 28, Box 1, Reverend Wendell Miller Papers, Special Collections and Archives, California State University, Northridge; "Black Belt Vice." An excellent history of slumming is Chad Heap, *Slumming: Sexual and Racial Encounters in American Nightlife, 1885–1940* (Chicago: University of Chicago Press, 2009).

15. Arthur Spingarn, "The War and Venereal Diseases among Negroes," *Journal of Social Hygiene* 4, no. 3 (July 1918): 340; Audrey Granneberg, "Elegant Indigence in Baltimore," *Forum and Century*, February 1940, n.p. See also Katie M. Hemphill, *Bawdy City: Commercial Sex and Regulation in Baltimore, 1790–1915* (New York: Cambridge University Press, 2020), chap. 9. On law enforcement in the south, see Amy Louise Wood and Natalie J. Ring, ed., *Crime and Punishment in the Jim Crow South* (Urbana: University of Illinois Press, 2019).

16. "White Women Must Stay Out," *New York Amsterdam News*, December 3, 1938. As historian Kevin Mumford writes, "Segregated vice was giving way to racial segregation." Mumford, *Interzones*, 27. Jennifer Fronc focuses on the enforcement of

segregation in Black-owned bars and nightclubs in "The Horns of the Dilemma: Race Mixing and the Enforcement of Jim Crow in New York City," *Journal of Urban History* 33, no. 1 (November 2006): 3–25.

17. Douglas J. Flowe, "'Fighting and Cutting and Shooting, and Carrying On': Saloons, Dives, and the Black 'Tough' in Manhattan's Tenderloin, 1890–1917," *Journal of Urban History* 45, no. 5 (2019): 926; Mary Sullivan, *My Double Life* (New York: Farrar and Rinehart, 1938), 57, 61.

18. "White Woman Is Arrested for Racial Mixing," *Baltimore Afro-American*, June 2, 1934; Frederick Whitin to Virginia Murray, Travelers Aid Society, December 29, 1925, Travelers Aid Society Folder, Box 15, CFNYPL. Whitin did add that the assumption of prostitution "had to be proven."

19. "A Just Judge," *Chicago Defender*, January 31, 1925; "Our Ultimatum," *Chicago Defender*, September 18, 1926. See Mumford, *Interzones*, 114–115.

20. Report, February 9, 1931, 1931 Brooklyn Inv. Z Folder, Box 35, CFNYPL. On the so-called badger game, which was tightly associated with Black women, see Harris, *Sex Workers*, 152; Kali N. Gross, *Colored Amazons: Crime, Violence, and Black Women in the City of Brotherly Love, 1880–1910* (Durham, NC: Duke University Press, 2006), chap. 3; and Freda L. Fair, "Surveilling Social Difference: Black Women's 'Alley Work' in Industrializing Minneapolis," *Surveillance and Society* 15, no. 5 (2017): 655–675.

21. On gender and lynching, see Crystal N. Feimster, *Southern Horrors: Women and the Politics of Rape and Lynching* (Cambridge, MA: Harvard University Press, 2011). On Black women's resistance to public punishment, see Seth Kotch, "The Making of the Modern Death Penalty," in ed., Wood and Ring, *Crime and Punishment in the Jim Crow South*, 198–200.

22. File 14397, Inmate Case Files, 1913–1973, Framingham Reformatory for Women Prison Records, Massachusetts Archives, Boston. This case file includes the woman's previous arrest and court history; her family, educational, medical, and work history; the "subject's own statement" (delivered in the words of the investigating reformatory administrator); the results of her prison psychological evaluation; excerpts from her correspondence while incarcerated; notes from her interviews with administrators; and the meeting minutes of reformatory administrators discussing her case. These records were closed when I was conducting research. I am extremely grateful to John Hannigan at the Massachusetts State Archives, who worked hard to make a sample of cases available to me. I reviewed eleven inmate case files, which Hannigan randomly selected for women with prostitution-related convictions in the interwar period. On gender and lynching, see Feimster, *Southern Horrors*.

23. File 14397. For a biography of Miriam Van Waters, see Estelle B. Freedman, *Maternal Justice: Miriam Van Waters and the Female Reform Tradition* (Chicago: University of Chicago Press, 1996). For a study of Van Waters's Progressive-era career working with delinquent young women in Los Angeles, see Odem, *Delinquent Daughters*, chap. 5.

24. "Segregation No Crime, Grand Jury Told," *Pittsburgh Courier*, July 30, 1938.

25. Staff correspondent, "Campaign against Vice"; Hattie M. Crooms, "Deep Water," *Atlanta Daily World*, August 24, 1936; Letter to Wendell Miller, n.d., Folder 28, Box 1, Miller Papers, Special Collections and Archives, California State University, Northridge; Stephen Robertson, "Harlem Undercover: Vice Investigators, Race, and Prostitution, 1910–1930," *Journal of Urban History* 35, no. 4 (May 2009): 491.

26. Sullivan, *My Double Life*, 262–263; Reckless, *Vice in Chicago*, 44–45.

27. Courtney Ryley Cooper, *Here's to Crime* (New York: Little, Brown, 1937), 246; Courtney Ryley Cooper, *Designs in Scarlet* (New York: Little, Brown, 1939), 66. See also Janis Appier, *Policing Women: The Sexual Politics of Law Enforcement and the LAPD* (Philadelphia: Temple University Press, 1998), chap. 5. AnneMarie Kooistra argues that when newspapers did use the term "white slavery" in this period, "they used it almost solely in conjunction with stories about white women having sex with men of color." AnneMarie Kooistra, "Angels for Sale: The History of Prostitution in Los Angeles, 1880–1940" (PhD diss., University of Southern California, 2003), 310. On the popular rejection of the "fallen woman," see Regina Kunzel, *Fallen Women, Problem Girls: Unmarried Mothers and the Professionalization of Social Work, 1890–1945* (New Haven, CT: Yale University Press, 1995); Alexander, *Girl Problem*; and Joanne Meyerowitz, *Women Adrift: Independent Wage Earners in Chicago, 1880–1930* (Chicago: University of Chicago Press, 1988). On the punitive turn in legal institutions, see Michael Willrich, *City of Courts: Socializing Justice in Progressive Era Chicago* (Cambridge: Cambridge University Press, 2003), esp. chap. 9.

28. N.d., 142 West 131st Street, Kewpie Doll report, Nighclubs and Speakeasies on Numbered Streets Folder, Box 37, CFNYPL.

29. "Vice in Our Communities," *Pittsburgh Courier*, September 17, 1938.

30. N.d., Eleonore Hutzel memo, Folder 417: Police Women's Manual, Jan–June 1932, Box 29, Series 3, Bureau of Social Hygiene records, Rockefeller Archive Center, Sleepy Hollow, New York; Herbert Jenkins and James Jenkins, *Presidents, Politics, and Policing: Oral History Interviews on Law Enforcement and a Career in Public Life Spanning Fifty Years* (Atlanta: Center for Research in Social Change, Emory University, 1980), 124, Herbert Jenkins Papers, AHC; Wolcott, *Remaking Respectability*, 111.

31. Letter signed "Just one of us neighbors," to Earl Warren, August 11, 1939, Folder 13, Box 219, Department of Justice and Attorney General's Office Records, Division of Criminal Identification and Investigation Records, Investigation Unit Records, California State Archives, Sacramento.

32. "Woman Fights for Honor—Sent to Jail," *Pittsburgh Courier*, April 2, 1938.

33. "Black Belt Vice"; "Cleaning Up Crime," *Pittsburgh Courier*, January 19, 1929; letter signed "Daily News Reader," Police 1930–1931 Folder, Box 13, CFNYPL; Max Bond, *The Negro in Los Angeles* (1936; Palo Alto, CA: R and E Research Associates, 1972), 136.

34. "Vice in Our Communities"; Walter White, letter to the editor, *Chicago Defender*, June 25, 1938; Sheep Club report, April 10, 1928, Sa–Su Folder, Box 36,

CFNYPL. On the role of Black male antivice investigators in Harlem, see Robertson, "Harlem Undercover."

35. Paul M. Kinsie, review of *Vice in Chicago*, by Walter Reckless, *Journal of Social Hygiene* 19, no. 6 (June 1933): 347–348; Reckless, *Vice in Chicago*, 8; Brown quoted in Kooistra, "Angels for Sale," 174.

36. Reckless, *Vice in Chicago*, 27–28; Simon Balto, *Occupied Territory: Policing Black Chicago from Red Summer to Black Power* (Chapel Hill: University of North Carolina Press, 2019), 43; Frederick Whitin to Thomas Murphy, April 14, 1926, Police Inspectors Folder, Box 12, CFNYPL. On police brutality in interwar Black women's lives and their fight against it, see Mary-Elizabeth B. Murphy, *Jim Crow Capital: Women and Black Freedom Struggles in Washington, D.C., 1920–1945* (Chapel Hill: University of North Carolina Press, 2018), chap. 3.

37. Frederick Whitin to James Hubert, May 4, 1925, Urban League Folder, Box 15, CFNYPL; Dan Burley, "Fireman Killer Faces 20 Years," *New York Amsterdam News*, October 29, 1938.

38. Kooistra, "Angels for Sale," 160; Florence Sanville, "A Forgotten Four-Hundred," *Prison Journal* 14, no. 3 (October 1934): 109.

39. I draw on this formulation of policing in flux in the interwar period from Simon Balto, who writes that in Chicago circa 1919, "the policing apparatus was not yet a fully formed instrument of antiblack repression. . . . In this moment, black people were not yet a sizable enough population to preoccupy the crafters of police policy, and there was little intentionality that guided public policy toward them. But neither was the police force an instrument that allowed black people fairness or justice." Balto, *Occupied Territory*, 29. See also Saidiya Hartman, *Wayward Lives, Beautiful Experiments: Intimate Histories of Riotous Black Girls, Troublesome Women, and Queer Radicals* (New York: W. W. Norton, 2019), 221.

40. E. Anderson, "Underworld Parlance," ca. 1934, Folder 361, RW Student Writings and Activities, Box 29, Miriam Van Waters Papers, SCH.

41. National Commission on Law Observance and Enforcement and August Vollmer, *Report on Police* (Washington, DC: U.S. Government Printing Office, 1931), 17; Ernest Jerome Hopkins, *Our Lawless Police: A Study of the Unlawful Enforcement of the Law* (New York: Viking, 1931), 34; Massachusetts Special Crime Commission and Frank Leslie Simpson, *Report of the Special Crime Commission under Chapter 54 of the Resolves of 1933* (Boston: Wright and Potter, Legislative Printers, 1933), 12–13. Brandon Jett argues that in the Jim Crow south, "police departments sought legitimacy from white southerners by appealing to their racist instincts." See Brandon T. Jett, *Race, Crime, and Policing in the Jim Crow South: African Americans and Law Enforcement in Birmingham, Memphis, and New Orleans, 1920–1945* (Baton Rouge: Louisiana State University Press, 2021), 17–18.

42. New York State and Samuel Seabury, *In the Matter of the Investigation of the Magistrates' Courts in the First Judicial Department and the Magistrates Thereof, and of Attorneys-at-Law Practicing in Said Courts: Final Report* (New York City: Lawyers Press, 1932), 82–95; Hopkins, *Our Lawless Police*, 41.

43. "Follow That Trail!," *New York Amsterdam News*, December 3, 1930; Welfare Council of New York City, "Prostitutes in New York City: Their Apprehension, Trial, and Treatment, July 1939–June 1940," 38, Reports ["Community File"] Folder, Box 7, EN 40, RG 215, NACP.

44. Welfare Council of New York City, "Prostitutes in New York City," 38–39; Frank Tannenbaum, *Crime and the Community* (Boston: Ginn, 1938), 162; "N.Y. Cops Framed House, Says Stoolie," *Baltimore Afro-American*, January 3, 1931; "Follow That Trail!" LaShawn Harris discusses how Black women were often framed for crimes they did not commit in Harris, *Sex Workers*, 132–133. See also Tannenbaum, *Crime and the Community*, esp. chaps. 5 and 6.

45. "N.Y. Cops Framed House"; "Follow That Trail!"

46. Leonard V. Harrison, *Police Administration in Boston* (Cambridge, MA: Harvard University Press, 1934), 144; Hopkins, *Our Lawless Police*, 154–155.

47. Cooper, *Here's to Crime*, 242, 274–276; "To Indict in Vice Probe," *Chicago Defender*, September 15, 1928; "Million Is Collected in Graft," *Cincinnati Enquirer*, March 17, 1937; "Grand Jury Hears Atherton Name Fifty as Grafters," *San Francisco Examiner*, April 14, 1937.

48. The grand jury investigator recommended licensing and regulating prostitution to reduce graft. Fogelson, *Big-City Police*, 120; Harrison, *Police Administration in Boston*, 149–152; "Million Is Collected."

49. Fogelson, *Big-City Police*, 146–148; minutes of special meeting, National Crime Commission, Washington, DC, May 6, 1932, Series 3, Box 26, Bureau of Social Hygiene records, Rockefeller Archive Center, Sleepy Hollow, New York.

50. Walker, *Critical History*, 160–161. On the development of "crime fighting" policing in the south, see Jett, *Race, Crime, and Policing in the Jim Crow South*, 23–33.

51. Hoover quoted in Nathan Douthit, "Police Professionalism and the War against Crime in the United States, 1920s–1930s," in *Police Forces in History*, ed. George L. Mosse (Newbury Park, CA: Sage, 1975), 333; Potter, *War on Crime*, 8, 137. On the centrality of sexual policing and conservative gender and sexual norms to FBI police practices, see Jessica R. Pliley, *Policing Sexuality: The Mann Act and the Making of the FBI* (Cambridge, MA: Harvard University Press, 2014). On the role of the FBI in the emergent "crime fighting" police movement, see Walker, *Critical History*, 151–159. For a history of the FBI and federal-local collaborations to enrich police power, see Daniel C. Richman and Sarah Seo, "How Federalism Built the FBI, Sustained Local Police, and Left Out the States," *Stanford Journal of Civil Rights and Civil Liberties* 17 (2021).

52. C. E. Gehlke and Edwin Sutherland, "Crime and Punishment," in U.S. Research Committee on Social Trends, *Recent Social Trends in the United States* (New York: McGraw-Hill, 1933), 1165, 1128; Fogelson, *Big-City Police*, 119.

53. U.S. Bureau of Investigation, Federal Bureau of Investigation, *Uniform Crime Reports for the United States* (Washington, DC: U.S. Government Printing Office, 1932–1939).

54. U.S. Bureau of Investigation, Federal Bureau of Investigation, *Uniform Crime Reports* (1935). On vagrancy and vice policing in the Depression-era south, see Jett, *Race, Crime, and Policing in the Jim Crow South*, 35–37.

55. Thelma Edna Berlack Boozer, "The Feminist Viewpoint," *New York Amsterdam News*, June 14, 1933; "The Force Scorns Them, Hence Vice Cops' Pay Rise," *New York Daily News*, June 27, 1933; "Buying Convictions from the Vice Squad," *New York Herald Tribune*, June 28, 1933; Box-Car Bertha and Ben Lewis Reitman, *Sister of the Road: The Autobiography of Box-Car Bertha as Told to Dr. Ben L. Reitman* (New York: Macaulay, 1937), 8.

56. Box-Car Bertha and Reitman, *Sister of the Road*, 8.

57. U.S. Bureau of Investigation, Federal Bureau of Investigation, *Uniform Crime Reports* (1932–1939); Kooistra, "Angels for Sale," table 13. The FBI did not consistently provide arrest statistics broken down by race and gender in the 1930s (it permanently stopped this practice by 1940 and today still does not provide race-and-gender arrest statistics). As a result, I can only talk about either gender-specific arrests or race-specific arrests when working with FBI statistics. For that reason, when I talk about race-specific arrests, I only focus on prostitution arrests since women were the overwhelming majority of people arrested on this charge. Until 1939, the Los Angeles Police Department issued annual statistics according to fiscal years, rather than calendar years. The example given in the text, then, is for fiscal years 1934–1935 and 1935–1936.

58. Blair, *I've Got to Make*, epilogue.

59. Hoover quoted in Thomas J. Deakin, *Police Professionalism: The Renaissance of American Law Enforcement* (Springfield, IL: C. C. Thomas, 1988), xi; Dorothy Moses Schulz, *From Social Worker to Crimefighter: Women in United States Municipal Policing* (Greenwood, CT: Praeger, 1995), 79.

Chapter 2

1. "Woman Judge Lectures 22 of Own Sex Arrested in Bars," *Los Angeles Times*, March 8, 1941. Because the women in the courtroom were racially unmarked, identified under a normative rubric of "American," and thought to betray their appropriate assignment to the home, I assume they were white. This chapter focuses on the sexual policing of white and Black women. For a history of Mexican American women in World War II and, in particular, the "pachuca panic," see Elizabeth Rachel Escobedo, *From Coveralls to Zoot Suits: The Lives of Mexican American Women on the World War II Home Front* (Chapel Hill: University of North Carolina Press, 2013). For a history of policing in New York during World War II, see Emily Brooks, "'A War within a War': Policing Gender and Race in New York City during World War II" (PhD diss., City University of New York, 2019).

2. Helen Pigeon, "Probation and Parole," *Prison World* 6, no. 2 (1944): 28. See also "Police War Urged on the Pick-Up Girl," *New York Times*, July 27, 1944.

3. Francis E. Merrill, *Social Problems on the Home Front* (New York: Harper and Brothers, 1948), 104; Studs Terkel, *"The Good War": An Oral History of World War II* (New York: Pantheon, 1984), 117.

4. Leisa D. Meyer writes that the war years "catalyzed popular fears about women's sexual and economic independence," in *Creating GI Jane: Sexuality and Power in the Women's Army Corps during World War II* (New York: Columbia

University Press, 1998). On the mobilization and containment of women's bodies in World War II, see Marilyn E. Hegarty, *Victory Girls, Khaki-Wackies, and Patriotutes: The Regulation of Female Sexuality during World War II* (New York: New York University Press, 2007). See also Marilyn E. Hegarty, "Patriot or Prostitute? Sexual Discourses, Print Media, and American Women during World War II," *Journal of Women's History* 10, no. 2 (1998): 112–136; Susan M. Hartmann, *The Home Front and Beyond: American Women in the 1940s* (Boston: Twayne, 1982); and Marilynn Johnson, *The Second Gold Rush: Oakland and the East Bay in World War II* (Berkeley: University of California Press, 1996).

5. Sherna Berger Gluck, *Rosie the Riveter Revisited: Women, the War, and Social Change* (Boston: Twayne, 1987), 30; Karen Anderson, *Wartime Women: Sex Roles, Family Relations, and the Status of Women during World War II* (Westport, CT: Praeger, 1981), 40. For a history of Black women in World War II, see Maureen Honey, ed., *Bitter Fruit: African American Women in World War II* (Columbia: University of Missouri Press, 1999).

6. Hegarty, *Victory Girls*, appendix 3; National Advisory Police Committee and Division of Social Protection, *Techniques of Law Enforcement against Prostitution* (Washington, DC: U.S. Government Printing Office, 1943), 52; U.S. Office of Community War Services, Division of Social Protection, *Challenge to Community Action* (Washington, DC: Social Protection Division, Office of Community War Services, Federal Security Agency, 1945), 24; Federal Bureau of Investigation and U.S. Department of Justice, *Uniform Crime Reports for the United States* (Washington, DC: U.S. Government Printing Office, 1940–1944).

7. During wartime, historian Susan Hartmann argues, "American society managed a temporary disruption of traditional social norms within a larger context of continuity in the sexual order." Hartmann, *Home Front and Beyond*, 24.

8. Amanda Littauer, *Bad Girls: Young Women, Sex, and Rebellion before the Sixties* (Chapel Hill: University of North Carolina Press, 2015), 23, 25–26; "Girls Are Different," *Cooperation in Crime Control: 1944 Yearbook, National Probation Association*, ed. Marjorie Bell (New York: National Probation Association, 1945), 81.

9. Advisory Committee on Social Protection, minutes of June 14, 1941, meeting, Social Protection Division, Committee Meetings, Box 1/3, EN 41, RG 215, NACP.

10. Advisory Committee on Social Protection, minutes of June 14, 1941, meeting, Committee Meetings, Box 1, EN 41, RG 215, NACP; lecture at VD Institute, October 31, 1944, Folder 849/04 1944, Box 2, EN 38, RG 215, NACP; Wilton Halverson, "War and the Health Department," *American Journal of Public Health* 33 (January 1943): 20–25; House Subcommittee of the Committee on Appropriations, *Department of Justice Appropriation Bill 1944*, 78th Cong., 1st sess., 1943, 226.

11. Survey of Commercialized Prostitution Conditions in Riverside, CA, December 1940, Box 1, EN 41, RG 215, NACP. See also Pippa Holloway, *Sexuality, Politics, and Social Control in Virginia, 1920–1945* (Chapel Hill: University of North Carolina Press, 2006), 159.

12. Littauer, *Bad Girls*, 33–34; Eliot Ness, "What about Girls?" 1943, 849/04.3 Jan–July 1945, Box 2, EN 38, RG 215, NACP.

13. Ernest Lion et al., *An Experiment in the Psychiatric Treatment of Promiscuous Girls* (Venereal Disease Division of the U.S. Public Health Service, 1945), 19; Mazie F. Rappaport, "Social Case Work in a Program of Social Protection," May 19, 1946, Box 11, RG 215, NACP.

14. Merrill, *Social Problems*, 102–103; minutes of the Advisory Committee on Social Protection, June 14, 1941, Box 1, EN 41, RG 215, NACP.

15. Advisory Committee on Social Protection, minutes of June 14, 1941 meeting, Box 1, EN 41, RG 215, NACP; August 13, 1945 memo, Folder 849 Region I 1946–1945, Box 5, EN 38, RG 215, NACP; Proceedings of the First Regional Conference on Social Protection, December 11, 1942, Conferences: Dec. 11, 1942, June 9, 1943, Box 2, EN 41, RG 215, NACP. Ernest Groves's biography is available online: "About," Groves Conference on Marriage and Family, accessed July 15, 2021, http://www.grovesconference.org/about.html.

16. Lion et al., *Experiment*, 12; Kearney lecture, February 1943, Folder 849, Box 2, EN 41, RG 215, NACP.

17. *Commonwealth of Massachusetts v. Emily Brow et al.*, March 24, 1945, no docket number, Old Colony History Museum, Taunton, Massachusetts. Many thanks to Taunton historian William Hanna, who provided important context on twentieth-century Portuguese communities in Taunton.

18. *Commonwealth of Massachusetts v. Emily Brow et al.* Unfortunately, this trial transcript does not include the verdict.

19. *Commonwealth of Massachusetts v. Emily Brow et al.* On the whitening of European immigrant women across the twentieth century, see, for example, Jennifer Guglielmo, *Living the Revolution: Italian Women's Resistance and Radicalism in New York City, 1880–1945* (Chapel Hill: University of North Carolina Press, 2010).

20. See, for example, Ordinance 83025, Box B-1573, City Council Records, LACA.

21. Proceedings, December 11, 1942, Box 2, EN 41, RG 215, NACP.

22. George Dunham, "The Problem from the Army Viewpoint," *Journal of Social Hygiene* 26, no. 9 (December 1940): 395–401. For World War I policy, see Hegarty, *Victory Girls*, chap. 2; Mary E. Odem, *Delinquent Daughters: Protecting and Policing Adolescent Female Sexuality in the United States, 1885–1920* (Chapel Hill: University of North Carolina Press, 1995), chap. 4; Allan M. Brandt, *No Magic Bullet: A Social History of Venereal Disease in the United States since 1880* (New York: Oxford University Press, 1985); and Scott Stern, *The Trials of Nina McCall: Sex, Surveillance, and the Decades-Long Government Plan to Imprison "Promiscuous" Women* (Boston: Beacon Press, 2018).

23. U.S. Office of Community War Services, Division of Social Protection, *Challenge to Community Action*, vi. On venereal disease politics during World War II, as well as changes in treatment regimens, see Brandt, *No Magic Bullet*.

24. Proceedings, December 11, 1942, Box 2, EN 41, RG 215, NACP.

25. Brandt, *No Magic Bullet*, 164, 168; Dunham, "Problem."

26. Proceedings of the First Regional Conference on Social Protection, December 11, 1942, Conferences: Dec 11, 1942, June 9, 1943, Box 2, EN 41, RG 215, NACP;

Eliot Ness, "Federal Government's Program in Attacking the Problem of Prostitution," *Federal Probation* 7, no. 17 (1943): 18.

27. American Social Hygiene Association memo, Policy Memoranda to FSA and Related Units, July 1941–October 1944, Box 1, EN 41, RG 215, NACP; Hegarty, *Victory Girls*, appendix 1. For a history of the American Social Hygiene Association, see David J. Pivar, *Purity and Hygiene: Women, Prostitution, and the "American Plan," 1900–1930* (Westport, CT: Praeger, 2001).

28. Research in Social Protection, 1944, Box 1, EN 38, RG 215, NACP; Survey of Commercialized Prostitution Conditions in Riverside, CA, December 1940, Box 1, EN 41, RG 215, NACP.

29. Minutes, June 14, 1941, Box 1, EN 41, RG 215, NACP. For federal support of prostitution regulation, see Hegarty, *Victory Girls*, 93, 97–99.

30. Minutes of the Interdepartmental Liaison Committee, January 22, 1942, Box 2, EN 41, RG 215, NACP; minutes of Interdepartmental Committee meeting, June 2, 1942, Box 1, EN 41, RG 215, NACP.

31. Proceedings of the National Police Advisory Committee for Social Protection, August 7, 1942, Box 1, EN 41, RG 215, NACP. For one example of federal contracts traded in exchange for prostitution repression, see Hal Rothman, *Neon Metropolis: How Las Vegas Started the Twenty-First Century* (New York: Routledge, 2003), 9–10.

32. House Committee on Military Affairs, *To Prohibit Prostitution within Reasonable Distance of Military and Naval Establishments*, 77th Cong., 1st sess., March 11, 12, and 18, 1941, 41–42; Narrative Script of Prostitution and the War, n.d., 849/04.4 1945, Box 3, EN 38, RG 215, NACP.

33. House Committee on Military Affairs, *To Prohibit Prostitution*; minutes of meeting of National Advisory Police Committee on Social Protection, June 30, 1942, Box 1, EN 41, RG 215, NACP.

34. National Advisory Police Committee and Division of Social Protection, *Techniques of Law Enforcement*, 52.

35. "Police War Urged."

36. Anderson, *Wartime Women*, 106; Ross McDonald to Board of Police Commissioners, memo, January 8, 1943, 1942–1948 packet, Box C-216, BOPC; House Subcommittee on Naval Affairs, *Investigation of Congested Areas, Part 4, Newport, R.I.*, 78th Cong., 1st sess., 1943, 1112–1114.

37. Reports, Community File, Boston, Box 5, EN 40, RG 215, NACP; Annual Reports of the Police Department, 1933–1943, City of Los Angeles, LACA; Statistics and Studies, City of San Diego, California: Record of Police Activities, Repression Exp[eriences] Region VII, Box 5, EN 43, RG 215, NACP. For an example of routine surveillance of white women in Boston, see Day Books, 1937–1963, Folder 2, Box 1, Elmer V. H. Brooks Papers, NU.

38. House Subcommittee on Naval Affairs, *Investigation of Congested Areas, Part 2, San Diego, CA*, 78th Cong., 1st sess., 1943, 414.

39. Charles Livermore to J. R. Heller, memo re: civil liberties, August 31, 1945, Folder 849 02: 1945, Box 1, EN 38, RG 215, NACP; U.S. Office of Community War

Services, Division of Social Protection, *Challenge to Community Action*, 39; File 25039, Box 48, BMCP.

40. File 26411, Box 48, BMCP. In another example, in 1942, two Boston policemen testified that they had been observing thirty-three-year-old Madeline's apartment, located near the city's Chinatown. As she approached her building, the officers followed her in and found her in the company of "a Chinaman." While the officers found "nothing at that time to warrant their arrest" on the charge of fornication, Madeline and her companion "both admitted intercourse" and they were subsequently arrested and fined. File 25281, Box 48, BMCP.

41. D'Ann Campbell, *Women at War with America: Private Lives in a Patriotic Era* (Cambridge, MA: Harvard University Press, 1984), 197; Lion et al., *Experiment*, 20; Agnes Elizabeth Ernst Meyer, *Journey through Chaos: America's Home Front* (New York: Harcourt, Brace, 1944), 293.

42. Proceedings of the Fourth Regional Conference on Social Protection, October 26–27, 1945, National Venereal Disease Committee, Box 3, EN 41, RG 215, NACP; Charles Hahn to Albert Deutsch, October 24, 1945, 849/04.3 Outside Oct. 1945, Box 3, EN 38, RG 215, NACP; Social Protection Programs in Los Angeles, April 17, 1945, 800 California 1945, Box 10, EN 38, RG 215, NACP.

43. In response to Black protests against police complicity with—and often participation in—domestic racist violence during wartime, the California Department of Justice and some local police departments initiated trainings on race relations. These programs were small in scale and focused on training sessions, lectures, and the distribution of pamphlets urging white police officers to "bring under control [their] personal sentiments and prejudices and subordinate them in a truly professional spirit." None of the so-called riot control recommendations proposed changes to everyday police practices in Black neighborhoods. Samuel Walker, "The Origins of the American Police-Community Relations Movement: The 1940s," *Criminal Justice History* 1 (1980): 235, 225–246. On the policing of Black men, and Black communities more broadly, in service to the protection of white womanhood and white communities more broadly, see Emily Brooks, "'Rumor, Vicious Innuendo, and False Reports': Policing Black Soldiers in Wartime Staten Island," *Journal of Urban History* 47, no. 5 (September 2021): 1032–1049.

44. National Venereal Disease Committee meeting, February 27, 1945, Box 2, EN 41, RG 215, NACP; Mary Lou Braly, Study of Girls Apprehended in Sumner County During 1942 Maneuvers, March 19, 1945, Special Study in Miscellaneous Data, Box 7, EN 43, RG 215, NACP; Leesville Study Summary of Case Work Interview, June 19, 1942, Box 6, EN 43, RG 215, NACP; Region VII, n.d., Repression Exp[eriences] Region VII, Box 5, EN 43, RG 215, NACP; Summary—Defense Areas, Box 2, EN 43, RG 215, NACP. On drug policing in wartime New York, see Emily Brooks, "Marijuana in La Guardia's New York City: The Mayor's Committee and Federal Policy, 1938–1945," *Journal of Policy History* 28, no. 4 (October 2016): 568–596.

45. Massachusetts Society for Social Hygiene report, 1942, Folder 246, Box 20, Maida Herman Solomon Papers, SCH; meeting minutes of VD Control, November 1, 1944, Newark, New Jersey, Box 6, EN 40, Box 6, RG 215, NACP.

46. Federal Bureau of Investigation and U.S. Department of Justice, *Uniform Crime Reports for the United States* (Washington, DC: U.S. Government Printing Office, 1940–1945); Annual Reports of the Police Department, 1941–1943, LACA; Campbell, *Women at War*, 203; Meyer, *Journey through Chaos*, 329. The FBI permanently stopped providing race- and gender-specific data during wartime (it still does not provide race and gender statistics to this day). As a result, when discussing race-specific statistics, I only work with prostitution arrest statistics since women were the overwhelming majority of people arrested on this charge during this period.

47. "The Negro Community's Share in Prevention," September 18, 1944, General Records, 1941–1946, Box 7, RG 215, NACP; Social Protection Activities newsletter, April 27, 1944, Region XII General 1943, Box 32, EN 3, RG 215, NACP.

48. Statement on the SPD, n.d., Negro Groups, General Records 1941–1946, Box 7, RG 215, NACP; Regional Letter #10 memo, February 26, 1943, Region I General 1942–1943, Box 1, EN 3, RG 215, NACP.

49. Minutes of the Interdepartmental Committee on Venereal Disease, March 13, 1942, Box 2, EN 41, RG 215, NACP.

50. Charles S. Johnson, *Patterns of Negro Segregation* (New York: Harper and Brothers, 1943), 262; John Ragland, Report on Field Trip to Region V, November 24 to December 19, 1942, Negro Community Studies, Box 2, EN 38, RG 215, NACP.

51. Research in Social Protection binder, 1944, Box 1, EN 38, RG 215, NACP.

52. File 23297, Box 48, BMCP. Many thanks to Sarah Haley for this insight on the police invasions of Black women's homes.

53. File 23297, Box 48, BMCP.

54. Negro and White VD Rates, General Records 1941–1946, Box 7, RG 215, NACP; Unsigned letter forwarded by Grace T. Willis to Leverett Saltonstall, June 9, 1941, Police 1939, Box 5, Leverett Saltonstall Papers, Massachusetts Historical Society, Boston; Berle D. Maxson to Police Commissioners, October 15, 1943 and reply, Arthur G. Baraw to Maxson, November 23, 1943, 1942–1948 packet, Box C-216, BOPC.

55. "Los Angeles Awaits Expose in Vice Probe," *Chicago Defender*, January 25, 1941; "Editorial: Political Dictatorship," *Los Angeles Sentinel*, October 17, 1940; Maurice L. Smith to Leverett Saltonstall, February 10, 1941, Boston Police—Timilty, Joseph 1941, Box 5, Leverett Saltonstall Papers, Massachusetts Historical Society, Boston.

56. Minutes of the National Advisory Police Committee, November 19, 1943, Nat'l Advisory Police Committee, Box 1, EN 41, RG 215, NACP; Nelson C. Jackson, "Community Organization Activities among Negroes for VD Control," March 31, 1944, Box 1, EN 44, RG 215, NACP; statement on the SPD, n.d., Negro Groups, General Records 1941–1946, Box 7, RG 215, NACP.

57. Rhoda J. Milliken, "The Role of the Police Woman's Bureau in Combating Prostitution," *Federal Probation* 7, no. 20 (1943): 20; U.S. Bureau of Investigation, Federal Bureau of Investigation, *Uniform Crime Reports* (1943).

Chapter 3

1. W. H. Parker, "Intra-department Correspondence," December 4, 1961, December 6, 1961 Folder, Box C-248, BOPC. Because Betty did not pursue this case after she made her initial complaint, I use only her first name. There is evidence that the police officers used force on her. She was arrested along with two other white women; the charges against all three were dismissed.

2. Parker, "Intra-department Correspondence," December 4, 1961.

3. Press release, April 13, 1964, Sheriff, Vice, 1963–1964 Folder 3, Box 143.2.18.1–3, KH; "Deputies Arrest 110 in Central Ave. Vice Raids," *Los Angeles Times*, April 12, 1964.

4. M. Keith Claybrook, Jr. argues that the Watts uprising should be renamed the "Los Angeles Rebellion." See M. Keith Claybrook, Jr., "Remembering, Rethinking, and Renaming the Watts Rebellion," *Black Perspectives*, August 13, 2021. For a history of Black rebellions, see Elizabeth Hinton, *America on Fire: The Untold History of Police Violence and Black Rebellion Since the 1960s* (New York: Liveright, 2021).

5. Los Angeles Police Department Statistical Digest, 1954–1963, LACA. After 1949, LAPD annual reports break down arrests by gender and "race": "Caucasian, Negro, Indian, Latin, Chinese, Japanese, and Other." (Previously, the categories were "White, Black, Yellow, Red, and Brown.") Black and white arrests constitute the majority of prostitution-related arrests during this period. Between 1954 and 1963, statistics are published in LAPD statistical digests, which are uniform but not available for each year. For the sake of consistency, I work exclusively with the digests. The LAPD stopped reporting morals arrests altogether after 1963.

6. In her study of postwar vice policing in Phenix City, Alabama, Tammy Ingram argues that "the decriminalization of whites was as important a function of [Jim Crow] governments as the criminalization of African Americans." Tammy Ingram, "The South's Sin City: White Crime and the Limits of Law and Order in Phenix City, Alabama," in *Crime and Punishment in the Jim Crow South*, ed. Amy Louise Wood and Natalie J. Ring (Urbana: University of Illinois Press, 2019), 82.

7. Alfred Kinsey and Institute for Sex Research, *Sexual Behavior in the Human Female* (Bloomington: Indiana University Press, 1953); Miriam Reumann, *American Sexual Character: Sex, Gender, and National Identity in the Kinsey Reports* (Berkeley: University of California Press, 2005), 1, 115. Unlike the *Human Male*, Kinsey's study of women specifically named its subject as "white American women."

8. Mabel Elliott and Francis Merrill, *Social Disorganization*, 3rd ed. (New York: Harper, 1950), 107; Pilpel quoted in Amanda H. Littauer, *Bad Girls: Young Women, Sex, and Rebellion before the Sixties* (Chapel Hill: University of North Carolina Press, 2015), 141; Christopher Gerould, *Sexual Practices of American Women* (New York: Lion Book, 1953), 133. On the contradictions and conflicts between "old" and "new" moral codes in the midcentury, see Beth Bailey, *Sex in the Heartland* (Cambridge, MA: Harvard University Press, 1999); Brett Harvey, *The Fifties: A Women's Oral History* (New York: HarperCollins, 1993); Littauer, *Bad Girls*; and Alan Petigny, *The Permissive Society: America, 1941–1965* (Cambridge: Cambridge University Press, 2009).

9. Robert Veit Sherwin, "Female Sex Crimes," in *Sex Life of the American Woman and the Kinsey Report*, ed. Albert Ellis (New York: Greenberg, 1954), 178–179. On midcentury marriage and sexual liberalism, see especially Elaine Tyler May, *Homeward Bound: American Families in the Cold War Era* (New York: Basic Books, 1988); and Beth L. Bailey, *From Front Porch to Back Seat: Courtship in Twentieth-Century America* (Baltimore: Johns Hopkins University Press, 1989).

10. John D'Emilio and Estelle B. Freedman, *Intimate Matters: A History of Sexuality in America* (Chicago: University of Chicago Press, 1998), 298.

11. Max Felker-Kantor, "Fighting the Segregation Amendment: Black and Mexican American Responses to Proposition 14 in Los Angeles," in *Black and Brown in Los Angeles: Beyond Conflict and Coalition*, ed. Josh Kun and Laura Pulido (Berkeley: University of California Press, 2013), 145–146. On race and the postwar migrations of people and capital, see Robert O. Self, *American Babylon: Race and the Struggle for Postwar Oakland* (Princeton, NJ: Princeton University Press, 2005); and Thomas J. Sugrue, *The Origins of the Urban Crisis: Race and Inequality in Postwar Detroit* (Princeton, NJ: Princeton University Press, 2010).

12. Elliott and Merrill, *Social Disorganization*, 647. Perhaps the most notorious example of the tendency in social science texts to pathologize Black behaviors produced by structural conditions is Daniel Patrick Moynihan, *The Negro Family: The Case for National Action* (Washington, DC: Office of Policy and Planning, U.S. Department of Labor, March 1965). On the midcentury presumptions of Black criminality, see Elizabeth Hinton, *From the War on Poverty to the War on Crime: The Making of Mass Incarceration in America* (Cambridge, MA: Harvard University Press, 2016), esp. chaps. 1–2. On the establishment of the linkage between race and criminality in the early twentieth century, see Khalil Gibran Muhammad, *The Condemnation of Blackness: Race, Crime, and the Making of Modern Urban America* (Cambridge, MA: Harvard University Press, 2010).

13. Arlien Johnson et al., *Final Report of the Special Crime Study Commission on Social and Economic Causes of Crime and Delinquency* (Sacramento, June 30, 1949), 12.

14. Edward Glover, "The Abnormality of Prostitution," in *Women: The Variety and Meaning of Their Sexual Experience*, ed. A. M. Krich (New York: Dell, 1953), 247–273. William Moore provides an excellent discussion of the ways that the "environmental" and "psychiatric" strains in midcentury criminology reaffirmed hierarchies of race and validated presumptions of inherent racial criminality. I draw primarily on his formulation for my argument. William Howard Moore, *The Kefauver Committee and the Politics of Crime, 1950–1952* (Columbia: University of Missouri Press, 1974), vii–viii. On the ways emerging psychological explanations for white women's sexual deviance made a legal culture of sexual permission increasingly possible, see Rickie Solinger, *Wake Up Little Susie: Single Pregnancy and Race before Roe v. Wade* (New York: Routledge, 1992), chap. 3; Bailey, *Sex in the Heartland*, chap. 2; and Rachel Devlin, *Relative Intimacy: Fathers, Adolescent Daughters, and Postwar American Culture* (Chapel Hill: University of North Carolina Press, 2005), chap. 1.

15. John M. Murtagh and Sara Harris, *Cast the First Stone* (New York: McGraw-Hill, 1957), 316.

16. Louis B. Schwartz, "Morals Offenses and the Model Penal Code," *Columbia Law Review* 63, no. 4 (April 1963): 670; Herbert Wechsler, "The Challenge of a Model Penal Code," *Harvard Law Review* 65, no. 7 (May 1952): 1112; Schwartz, "Morals Offenses," 673, 683.

17. Schwartz, "Morals Offenses," 671; Elliott and Merrill, *Social Disorganization*, 135, 137; Charlotte D. Elmott et al., Committee on the Older Girl and the Law, *Girls and Young Women in Conflict with the Law in California* (Sacramento: Governor's Advisory Committee on Children and Youth, 1958), 34.

18. Jerome H. Skolnick, *Justice without Trial: Law Enforcement in Democratic Society* (New York: Wiley, 1966), 206–207.

19. "Court Hears Carol Lane 'Sex Case,'" *Hollywood Citizen News*, April 16, 1962; "'Resorting' Ordinance in L.A. Ruled Invalid," *Los Angeles Times*, December 27, 1961; "58 District Attorneys to Meet on Vice Laws," *Los Angeles Times*, January 12, 1962; "Yorty, City Attorney Tangle on Vice Laws," *Los Angeles Times*, December 29, 1961; *In re* Carol Lane, 367 P.2d 673 (Supreme Court of California, December 21, 1961).

20. *In re* Carol Lane, 367 P.2d 673.

21. See Risa Goluboff, *Vagrant Nation: Police Power, Constitutional Change, and the Making of the 1960s* (New York: Oxford University Press, 2016), esp. chap. 5.

22. Goluboff, 71, 204.

23. Skolnick, *Justice without Trial*, 59; California Advisory Committee to the United States Commission on Civil Rights, *Report on California: Police-Minority Group Relations* (August 1963), 10.

24. William H. Parker in *Parker on Police*, ed. O. W. Wilson (Springfield, IL: Charles C. Thomas, 1957), 8. For a postwar history of the LAPD, see Max Felker-Kantor, *Policing Los Angeles: Race, Resistance, and the Rise of the LAPD* (Chapel Hill: University of North Carolina Press, 2018). Kelly Lytle Hernández writes that in the period between 1920 and 1960, Black residents became central to California's carceral regime, which was enforced through police brutality. See Hernández, *City of Inmates: Conquest, Rebellion, and the Rise of Human Caging in Los Angeles, 1771–1965* (Chapel Hill: University of North Carolina Press, 2017), chap. 6.

25. Skolnick, *Justice without Trial*, 81; William A. Westley, *Violence and the Police: A Sociological Study of Law, Custom, and Morality* (Cambridge, MA: MIT Press, 1970), 99, 104. For the historical and criminological context of Westley's midcentury work, see Jack R. Greene, "Pioneers in Police Research: William A. Westley," *Police Practice and Research* 11, no. 5 (October 2010): 454–468.

26. Howard Whitman, "Don't Go Out Alone at Night in L.A.," *Collier's*, October 28, 1950; Robert M. Fogelson, *Big-City Police*, Urban Institute Study (Cambridge, MA: Harvard University Press, 1977), 235; Herman Goldstein, "Police Policy Formulation: A Proposal for Improving Police Performance," *Michigan Law Review* 65, no. 1123 (1966): 1144; Glenn Souza, "Perspective on the LAPD: A Simple Time, in Black and White," *Los Angeles Times*, October 12, 1995; William W. Turner, *The Police Establishment* (New York: Putnam, 1968), 17. See also Mike Davis and Jon

Wiener, *Set the Night on Fire: L.A. in the Sixties* (New York: Verso, 2020), 41–42. On housing battles between police and Black residents, see Simon Balto, *Occupied Territory: Policing Black Chicago from Red Summer to Black Power* (Chapel Hill: University of North Carolina Press, 2019), chap. 3. In an indication of his personal gender and class politics, Parker believed, "It was a tragedy when the mothers of America went out of the home and became wage-earners." Donald McDonald, *The Police: An Interview* (Santa Barbara, CA: Center for the Study of Democratic Institutions, 1962), 9.

27. Goluboff, *Vagrant Nation*, 63; Kathleen J. Frydl, *The Drug Wars in America, 1940–1973* (Cambridge: Cambridge University Press, 2013), 296; Yale Kamisar, "When the Cops Were Not 'Handcuffed,'" *New York Times*, November 7, 1965; Joseph Woods, "The Progressives and the Police: Urban Reform and the Professionalization of the Los Angeles Police" (PhD diss., University of California, Los Angeles, 1973), 505. Earl Warren was no liberal usurper of the court but rather a former district attorney and attorney general with extensive law enforcement experience. See Yale Kamisar, "How Earl Warren's Twenty-Two Years in Law Enforcement Affected His Work as Chief Justice," in *Earl Warren and the Warren Court: The Legacy in American and Foreign Law*, ed. Harry N. Scheiber (Lexington, MA: Lexington Books, 2007), 91–112.

28. Paul Jacobs, *Prelude to Riot: A View of Urban America from the Bottom* (New York: Random House, 1967), 25; Alisa Sarah Kramer, "William H. Parker and the Thin Blue Line: Politics, Public Relations, and Policing in Postwar Los Angeles" (PhD diss., American University, 2007), 175–176.

29. "Western-Adams Vice Stirs Fears," *Los Angeles Times*, January 30, 1961; McDonald, *Police*, 8; Parker, *Parker on Police*, 14; Kramer, "William H. Parker," 175–176.

30. Turner, *Police Establishment*, 80; Parker, *Parker on Police*, 162; Turner, *Police Establishment*, 83. Parker's television address was after the Watts uprising.

31. Edward J. Escobar, "Bloody Christmas and the Irony of Police Professionalism: The Los Angeles Police Department, Mexican Americans, and Police Reform in the 1950s," *Pacific Historical Review* 72, no. 2 (May 2003): 173. On the history of police professionalism, see Samuel Walker, *Popular Justice: A History of American Criminal Justice*, 2nd ed. (New York: Oxford University Press, 1997), 170–174; and Fogelson, *Big-City Police*, chaps. 6, 7, 9. Escobar also notes that mobilizing the LAPD around whiteness dissolved any lingering class hostilities between the police and working-class whites. Establishing the LAPD as "the protector of the white middle and working classes against minorities ... helped the department create a constituency among groups that it had alienated by its union-busting past." Escobar, "Bloody Christmas," 178.

32. Jacobs, *Prelude to Riot*, 41; Skolnick, *Justice without Trial*, 197–198 (emphasis in original). Despite the police leaders' claims to professionalism, the stultifying occupational climate of police work turned off most aspiring professionals. The 1967 President's Commission on Law Enforcement and Administration of Justice noted that in most police departments, "personnel is closely regimented ... and initiative is not encouraged.... There is far more emphasis on making arrests and

following orders than on questioning traditional procedures or solving community problems. This is not an appealing environment for a person of professional stature." Quoted in Turner, *Police Establishment*, 24.

33. Martin Schiesl, "Behind the Badge: The Police and Social Discontent in Los Angeles since 1950," in *20th Century Los Angeles: Power, Promotion, and Social Conflict*, ed. Norman M. Klein and Martin J. Schiesl (Claremont, CA: Regina Books, 1990), 155; "Police Malpractice and the Watts Riot: A Report by the ACLU of Southern California," appendix D, Police Malpractice in Los Angeles, 1966, Box 162, ACLUSC.

34. "Police Malpractice," appendix D; McDonald, *Police*, 16.

35. James Q. Wilson, *Varieties of Police Behavior: The Management of Law and Order in Eight Communities* (Cambridge, MA: Harvard University Press, 1968), 40–41 (emphasis added); Westley, *Violence and the Police*, 126, 98, 99, 166, 164.

36. Skolnick, *Justice without Trial*, 44.

37. Jacobs, *Prelude to Riot*, 16. Criminologist Ira Reiss found that of two hundred police officers interviewed in the mid-1960s in Boston, Chicago, and Washington, DC, nearly 60 percent felt that their occupation had suffered a drop in "prestige" over the past twenty years. Fogelson, *Big-City Police*, 238–239.

38. George M. O'Connor, "The Negro and the Police in Los Angeles" (MA thesis, University of Southern California, 1955), 97; Skolnick, *Justice without Trial*, 110, 227; Wayne LaFave, "The Police and Nonenforcement of the Law, Part I," *Wisconsin Law Review*, no. 1 (1962): 104–137; Wayne LaFave, "The Police and Nonenforcement of the Law, Part II," *Wisconsin Law Review*, no. 2 (1962): 231–233.

39. W. H. Parker, "Intra-department Correspondence," February 13, 1962, February 21, 1962 Folder, Box C-249, BOPC; NAACP Los Angeles Report, n.d., February 21, 1962 Folder, Box C-249, BOPC. I use Treyola Terry's full name here because she made her complaint public. Terry was detained for an hour—during which time she remained handcuffed and was denied a phone call to her husband—and ultimately released. According to Terry, the sergeant on hand said that "he was going to let her off the hook, as it seemed she was a worthwhile citizen," though, he warned, "they could hold her and book her for what she had done." The officers in question were assigned to a felony unit, and it is unclear why they were pursuing a morals misdemeanor. Sworn statement of Mrs. Treyola Terry, n.d., February 21, 1962 Folder, Box C-249, BOPC.

40. "Police Clear in Flashlight Brutality Case," *Los Angeles Herald-Dispatch*, April 5, 1956. At Wade's trial, the judge, Ida May Adams, presumably a white woman, reasoned that Wade had filed a false report because "police wouldn't do this to a woman." "Police Clear in Flashlight Brutality Case." In a Board of Police Commissioners memo, the commissioners wrote that the NAACP's efforts to publicize LAPD abuse against Black women "clearly represents support of a movement to superimpose a police review board upon the Department." BOPC report to Mayor Yorty, re: NAACP press release, March 15, 1962, March 14, 1962 Folder, Box C-249, BOPC. On the struggle to create a civilian review board during the Tom Bradley administration, see Max Felker-Kantor, "Liberal Law-and-Order: The Politics of Police Reform in Los Angeles," *Journal of Urban History* 46, no. 5 (September 2020): 1026–1049.

On Philadelphia's Police Advisory Board, see Eric C. Schneider, Christopher Agee, and Themis Chronopoulos, "Dirty Work: Police and Community Relations and the Limits of Liberalism in Postwar Philadelphia," *Journal of Urban History* 46, no. 5 (September 2020): 961–979. See also Michael W. Flamm, "'Law and Order' at Large: The New York Civilian Review Board Referendum of 1966 and the Crisis of Liberalism," *The Historian* 64, no. 3/4 (2002): 643–665.

41. The police officers denied all but one of Terry's charges: Williams did admit that he had called Terry a "fool," and he was apparently reprimanded by his commanding officer. Commissioner Bravo memo, February 21, 1962 Folder, Box C-249, BOPC.

42. "Trend Shows Police Brutality Abuses and Terrorizing Directed to Afro-American Women," *Los Angeles Herald-Dispatch*, February 15, 1962; BOPC memo to NAACP, March 7, 1962, March 7, 1962 Folder, Box C-249, BOPC; "NAACP Claims Brutality by Police in L.A.," *Los Angeles Times*, February 17, 1962.

43. Jacobs, *Prelude to Riot*, 22.

44. Joseph Dean Lohmann et al., *The Police and Minority Groups; a Manual Prepared for Use in the Chicago Park District Police Training School* (Chicago: Chicago Park District, 1947), 101. On the twentieth-century relationship between vice, racial segregation, and police, see chap. 1; as well as Chad Heap, *Slumming: Sexual and Racial Encounters in American Nightlife, 1885–1940* (Chicago: University of Chicago Press, 2009); and Kevin J. Mumford, *Interzones: Black/White Sex Districts in Chicago and New York in the Early Twentieth Century* (New York: Columbia University Press, 1997).

45. Los Angeles Police Department Statistical Digest, 1961–1962, LACA; "Crime's Golden Egg: Sin and Glamour Pave Sunset Strip," *Los Angeles Times*, January 31, 1965; "Western-Adams Residents Seek Public Vice Action," *Los Angeles Times*, January 30, 1961; "Negro Leaders Hit Vice Probe with Bias," *Los Angeles Mirror News*, September 9, 1957.

46. "Policemanship," *Los Angeles Sentinel*, November 17, 1960; A. S. "Doc" Young, "Prostitution: It's a Recurring Problem," *Los Angeles Sentinel*, March 31, 1960; "Westside Vice War Renewed," *Los Angeles Sentinel*, January 4, 1962; Souza, "Perspective on the LAPD"; "Western-Adams Residents"; William Buchanan, "A Slice of Life," *Boston Globe*, July 18, 1965. This particular mode of Black outrage against white hunters and the discretionary police enforcement of morals laws was delivered in a patriarchal valence. In his excellent study of the "sexual cosmology of ghettoization" and the 1968 Washington, DC, riot, Kwame Holmes notes that in the 1960s-era racial politics of sexual policing in Black neighborhoods, "women's bodies are signposts in a racialized competition between heterosexual men over control and access to the city as a whole." Kwame Holmes, "Beyond the Flames: Queering the History of the 1968 D.C. Riot," in *No Tea, No Shade: New Writings in Black Queer Studies*, ed. E. Patrick Johnson (Durham, NC: Duke University Press, 2016), 310.

47. "Police Malpractice," appendix C.

48. On Black women's fraught negotiations with respectability politics to win physical safety and dignity, see especially Victoria W. Wolcott, *Remaking*

Respectability: African American Women in Interwar Detroit (Chapel Hill: University of North Carolina Press, 2001); and Darlene Clark-Hine, "Rape and the Inner Lives of Black Women in the Middle West: Preliminary Thoughts on the Culture of Dissemblance," *Signs: Journal of Women in Culture and Society* 14 (1989): 912.

49. "Westside Businessmen Organize Fight against Dope, Prostitution: Vice Council Formed," *Los Angeles Sentinel*, November 3, 1960; "Vice Hearing Set for Tonight," *Los Angeles Sentinel*, October 13, 1960.

50. "Citizens Demand Vice Cleanup: Gag Rule Throws Meeting into Uproar," *Los Angeles Sentinel*, December 8, 1960; "Policemanship." See also Edward Roybal Papers, Prostitution Folder, Box 26, UCLA.

51. "Citizens Demand Vice Cleanup"; "Policemanship"; "No Compromise with Law and Order," *Los Angeles Times*, May 1, 1964.

52. "Police Nab 20 Prostitutes in Night Raid," *Los Angeles Sentinel*, December 22, 1960; "Weekend Raids Net Large Scale Arrests," *Los Angeles Sentinel*, May 16, 1963.

53. CORE to Los Angeles County Sheriffs [sic] Department, April 11, 1964, Sheriff, Vice, 1963–1964 Folder 3, Box 143.2.18.1–3, KH; "Tensions Rises in Ghetto Areas as Cops Get Tough," *Los Angeles People's World*, April 18, 1964.

54. Paul Coates, "Vice Casts Its Shadow on West Adams District: White Men on Prowl for Negro Streetwalkers," *Los Angeles Times*, April 11, 1965; Mrs. John R. Richardson to Kenneth Hahn, April 25, 1964, Sheriff, Vice, 1963–1964 Folder, Box 1.43.2.18.3, KH. On Detroit protests against the police murder of a "Black prostitute," Saint Cynthia Scott, see Thomas J. Sugrue, *Sweet Land of Liberty: The Forgotten Struggle for Civil Rights in the North* (New York: Random House, 2008), 304–305. On the "long hot summer" of Black uprisings, see Sugrue, *Sweet Land of Liberty*, chap. 10; Michael W. Flamm, *In the Heat of the Summer: The New York Riots of 1964 and the War on Crime* (Philadelphia: University of Pennsylvania Press, 2016); and Lohmann, *Police and Minority Groups*, 101.

55. Meeting to Discuss Enforcement Problems at 68th and Central, April 9, 1964, Sheriff, Vice, 1963–1964 Folder 3, Box 143.2.18.1–3, KH.

56. Press release, April 13, 1964, Sheriff, Vice, 1963–1964 Folder 3, Box 143.2.18.1–3, KH; "Deputies Arrest 110 in Central Ave. Vice Raids," *Los Angeles Times*, April 12, 1964.

57. Sheriff's Department Supplementary Report, January 7, 1964, Sheriff, Vice, 1963–1964, Folder 2, Box 143.2.18.1–3, KH. For encouraging others to resist the police, James was charged with lynching. I use only first names here to protect the individuals' privacy.

58. "Crowds Attack Police Here for Third Time," *Los Angeles Times*, April 12, 1964; "Citizens, Police in Head-On Clash: Incidents Alarm Public," *Los Angeles Sentinel*, April 16, 1964.

59. In published essays adapted from this chapter, I intentionally used the word "riot" instead of "uprising" or "rebellion" to describe Black communal violence because I agreed with Kwame Holmes that "riot" was a way to honor the scream of Black people who "are unable to speak back to [the gratuitous violence]" of political and legal institutions in the United States. However, during the 2020 uprisings following the police murders of George Floyd and Breonna Taylor, I saw how the

word "riot" was weaponized both by liberals to police an imagined boundary between legitimate and illegitimate rebellion and by conservatives to undermine and delegitimize demands for Black justice. I acknowledge the limits of language when discussing the political complexity of Black refusal of, and resistance to, the white monopoly on armed self-defense and violence. However, I do not want to reproduce language that could be co-opted for anti-Black politics, and so, in the wake of 2020, I deliberately use "rebellion" and "uprising." See Holmes, "Beyond the Flames." For a history of the Watts Uprising, see Gerald Horne, *Fire This Time: The Watts Uprising and the 1960s* (Boston: Da Capo, 1997); and Felker-Kantor, *Policing Los Angeles*, chap. 1.

60. "Drive Opens to Place Decency Law on Ballot," *Los Angeles Times*, October 19, 1965; "Wise Action on 'Decency' Proposal," *Los Angeles Times*, January 5, 1966; "Dorn Ready to Give Up on 'Decency,'" *Los Angeles Times*, January 4, 1966; Evelle Younger correspondence, August 25, 1965, "Decency" Initiative Folder, Box 135, ACLUSC.

61. Goff, "Dorn Ready"; "Wise Action"; Ray Zeman, "Reagan Outlines 6-Step Crime War: Asks Local Ordinances to Control Sex and Public Decency Offenses," *Los Angeles Times*, January 18, 1967.

Chapter 4

1. "'Incognito' Mayor Finds Boston Nightlife Is Lively," *Boston Globe*, February 9, 1975. Images from this scene are drawn from Roswell Angier, *". . . A Kind of Life": Conversations in the Combat Zone* (Boston: Addison House, 1976); and "Boston: Combat Zone 1969–1978," Howard Yezerski Gallery, Boston, March 7–16, 2010.

2. Military servicemen on leave rerouted their destination from Scollay Square to the new entertainment district, and by the mid-1960s, the Combat Zone had gained its nickname. For a cultural analysis of the Combat Zone, see Eric Schaefer and Eithne Johnson, "Quarantined! A Case Study of Boston's Combat Zone," in *Hop on Pop: The Politics and Pleasures of Popular Culture*, ed. Henry Jenkins, Tara McPherson, and Jane Shattuc (Durham, NC: Duke University Press, 2003), 430–454. For a history of Scollay Square, see David Kruh, *Always Something Doing: Boston's Infamous Scollay Square* (Boston: Northeastern University Press, 1999). On urban renewal in Boston, see Thomas H. O'Connor, *Building a New Boston: Politics and Urban Renewal, 1950–1970* (Boston: Northeastern University Press, 1993). An essential track on the Boston urban renewal playlist is the Modern Lovers, "Government Center," *The Modern Lovers*, 1976.

3. Walter McQuade, "Boston: What Can a Sick City Do?" *Fortune*, June 1, 1964; "Boston Makes a Comeback," *U.S. News and World Report*, September 21, 1964; Kruh, *Always Something Doing*, 126. On the urban crisis, see Thomas J. Sugrue, *The Origins of the Urban Crisis: Race and Inequality in Postwar Detroit* (Princeton, NJ: Princeton University Press, 2010). On the redistribution of wealth to the suburbs and its political impact in Massachusetts, see Lily Geismer, *Don't Blame Us: Suburban Liberals and the Transformation of the Democratic Party* (Princeton, NJ: Princeton University Press, 2014).

4. "Entertainment Ills Pinpointed," *Back Bay Ledger-Beacon Hill Times*, February 24, 1972; "X-Rated District Sought in Boston," *Christian Science Monitor*, September 11, 1974. See also "'Combat Zone' Critics Speak Up," *Christian Science Monitor*, March 1, 1972.

5. "'Combat Zone' Critics Speak Up"; Ian Menzies, "Merchants Could Help Clean City," *Boston Globe*, March 16, 1972; Dan Ahern, "Semantic Renewal [Is] New Problem Solver," *Boston Herald Advertiser*, January 4, 1976.

6. "'Incognito' Mayor"; "Mayor 'Gets an Eyeful' in Combat Zone," *Boston Herald Advertiser*, February 9, 1975; "Kevin Takes a Look at the 'Bod Squad,'" *Boston Herald Advertiser*, February 16, 1975.

7. William Bratton and Peter Knobler, *Turnaround: How America's Top Cop Reversed the Crime Epidemic* (New York: Random House, 1998), 100.

8. On the relationship between liberal reform and the expansion of police power in the 1970s, see Max Felker-Kantor, "Liberal Law-and-Order: The Politics of Police Reform in Los Angeles," *Journal of Urban History* 46, no. 5 (September 2020): 1026–1049; and Christopher Lowen Agee, *The Streets of San Francisco: Policing and the Creation of a Cosmopolitan Liberal Politics, 1950–1972* (Chicago: University of Chicago Press, 2014).

9. On the realignment of interests among police, downtown business elites, and urban authorities within the context of the federal government's austerity measures for urban welfare and simultaneous funding increases to enrich urban law enforcement programs, see especially Alex Vitale and Brian Jefferson, "The Emergence of Command and Control Policing in Neoliberal New York," in *Policing the Planet: Why the Policing Crisis Led to Black Lives Matter*, ed. Jordan Camp and Christina Heatherton (New York: Verso, 2016), chap. 12; Christina Hanhardt, "Broken Windows at Blue's: A Queer History of Gentrification and Policing," in Camp and Heatherton, *Policing the Planet*, chap. 3; Christina Hanhardt, *Safe Space: Gay Neighborhood History and the Politics of Violence* (Durham, NC: Duke University Press, 2013); and Christopher Lowen Agee, "Crisis and Redemption: The History of American Police Reform since World War II," *Journal of Urban History* (Spring 2017): 951–960.

10. Geismer, *Don't Blame Us*.

11. *A Profile of Boston's Black Population* (Boston City Archives, n.d.), Minorities in Boston, Box 31, KW; "Report Says Segregation Worsens," *Boston Globe*, n.d., Police: Racism, Background Materials, Box 81, KW.

12. Sugrue, *Origins of the Urban Crisis*; "Hearings on Unemployment and Crime," Subcommittee on Crime of the Committee on the Judiciary, 95th Cong., 1st and 2nd sess., 1977–1978, 2–4.

13. "Report Says Blacks Lost Ground in '70s," *Boston Globe*, January 23, 1980; "Hearings on Unemployment and Crime," 141–144, 159; Women's Bureau, U.S. Department of Labor, "Highlights of Women's Employment and Education," n.d., Work—US Women's Bureau, Labor, Box 15, Atlanta Lesbian Feminist Alliance records, Sallie Bingham Center for Women's History and Culture, Duke University, Durham, North Carolina.

14. Paul Parks, "Proposal for the City of Boston to the National Black Caucus on National Black Priorities," n.d., Box 2, Phyllis Ryan Papers, NU; "A Summary Report

of the Congressional Black Caucus," 1972, 21, Box 2, Phyllis Ryan Papers, NU; Standards and Goals Commission meeting, November 4, 1971, San Diego Meeting, RG 423, UD, EN 4, Box 3, NACP; Robert L. Woodson, *Black Perspectives on Crime and the Criminal Justice System: A Symposium* (Boston: G. K. Hall, 1977), 20, 18. On the racialization of crime in the postwar period and the transition away from social welfare and toward law enforcement programs at multiple levels of governance, see Elizabeth Hinton, *From the War on Poverty to the War on Crime: The Making of Mass Incarceration in America* (Cambridge, MA: Harvard University Press, 2016). For an account of the racialization of criminality in the 1970s, see Woodson, *Black Perspectives on Crime*.

15. Kennedy quoted in O'Connor, *Building a New Boston*, 269–270; "BRA Chief Looks at Boston's Problems," November 3, 1969, no source, Urban Renewal Program Boston, Box 12766423, BRA.

16. Ian Menzies, "What's Good about Boston," *Boston Globe*, September 18, 1977; Walter Patten to Kevin White, February 21, 1973, Correspondence: Beacon Hill Crime, Box 1, KW.

17. J. Anthony Lukas, *Common Ground: A Turbulent Decade in the Lives of Three Families* (New York: Knopf, 1985), 634–638.

18. Gail Sheehy, *Hustling: Prostitution in Our Wide Open Society* (New York: Delacorte, 1973), 42.

19. Joan Wood to Richard Fowler, received September 17, 1974, Text Amendment Application No. 44 Advisor to the Zoning Commission Establish "E" District, Box 907278, BRA. For examples of AED debates, see "Downtown Area Study Deplores Spread of Vice," *Boston Record-American*, February 17, 1972; and "Amusement-Center Plan for Combat Zone," *Christian Science Monitor*, May 31, 1973. Many thanks to Devin McGeehan Muchmore for generously sharing his time and Combat Zone expertise for this chapter.

20. "'Boston's Red Districts' Targeted in Back Bay Report," *Christian Science Monitor*, February 18, 1972; Kathy Kilgore, "If You Can't . . . Zone It," *Yankee*, October 1975.

21. "Opposition Grows to New Bar on Warren Street," *Bay State Banner*, February 3, 1972.

22. Draft Press Release on Parrish Case (to Be Shown to Police Officers Involved before Release), n.d., Correspondence: Boston Police Department 1 of 4, Box 1, KW; police report of Ted Parrish arrest, May 8, 1969, Correspondence, Boston Police Department 3 of 4, KW; Boston City Council, "Public Hearing before the Committee on Ordinances and Resolutions, in the Matter of Streetwalking and Hitchhiking," October 2, 1969, City of Boston Archives, Boston. On the Mothers for Adequate Welfare sit-in action, see Mel King, *Chain of Change: Struggles for Black Community Development* (Boston: South End, 1981); and "Roxbury, Quiet in Past, Finally Breaks into Riot," *Harvard Crimson*, June 15, 1967. No police officer I spoke to who worked during this period was aware of the city's white hunter law. One *Boston Globe* article in 1973 claimed white hunting still "thrived" in the gentrifying South End despite the law, but this report is an exception. "'White Hunting' Thrives in Boston Despite 3-Year-Old Law against It," *Boston Globe*, May 28, 1973.

23. Charles Winick and Paul M. Kinsie, *The Lively Commerce: Prostitution in the United States* (New York: Quadrangle Books, 1971), 167; Phillip M. Vitti, *The Passage: Memoir of a Boston Undercover Cop in the '60s* (Bloomington: AuthorHouse, 2012), 170. On white hunters in Roxbury, see "Prostitution: Criminal or Social," *Bay State Banner*, January 7, 1967; and "A Mild Recession," *Bay State Banner*, January 7, 1967.

24. Vitti, *Passage*, 169; Arlene Carmen and Howard Moody, *Working Women: The Subterranean World of Street Prostitution* (New York: Harper and Row, 1985), 185. See also Melinda Chateauvert, *Sex Workers Unite: A History of the Movement from Stonewall to Slutwalk* (Boston: Beacon, 2014), 27. According to the church workers Carmen and Moody, this civic outrage was driven by "disguised racism." Carmen and Moody, *Working Women*, 185. Social scientist Jennifer James argued that white people who had "comfortably tolerated prostitution when it was in Harlem" now protested the visibility of interracial sexual commerce downtown. Jennifer James et al., *The Politics of Prostitution: Resources for Legal Change* (Seattle: Social Research Associates, 1975), 18.

25. Gail Pellett, "Prostitution in Boston," 1975, audio in author's possession; Lauri Lewin [pseud.], *Naked Is the Best Disguise: My Life as a Stripper* (New York: Morrow, 1984), 63; Sheehy, *Hustling*, 80. The two integrated bars were Rico's and Good Time Charlie's. Many thanks to Gail Pellett for sharing her recording. See also Chateauvert, *Sex Workers Unite*, 65. For an example of ongoing police neglect of Black sex workers in Philadelphia in the early 1970s, see Jonathan Rubinstein, *City Police* (New York: Farrar, Straus and Giroux, 1973), 181–182.

26. Barbara, interview by Carole, in *Sex Work: Writings by Women in the Sex Industry*, ed. Frédérique Delacoste and Pricilla Alexander (Berkeley: Cleis, 1987), 171.

27. PUMA meeting with Wages for Housework members, including Selma James and Wilmette Brown, April 12, 1978, transcript and audio in author's possession. Many thanks to Chris Womendez for saving and sharing the PUMA meeting recordings.

28. Preston Williams, interview by the author, June 6, 2017; Alan Sheehan, "Law against Prostitutes Is Upheld," *Boston Globe*, November 29, 1973; Commonwealth v. Reddick, Suffolk County Superior Court, docket numbers 70517–70519, 73435, 1973. In a well-established American pattern that held firm throughout the 1970s, white women were ineligible for preferential police treatment if they were observed associating or working with Black men. Many thanks to Preston Williams for contributing his time and oral history to this project.

29. Sheehy, *Hustling*, 9; James et al., *Politics of Prostitution*, 46, 55–56; *Commonwealth v. Reddick*. Law enforcement officials spoke broadly about street crime that targeted both people in proximity to sexually profiled women and the women themselves.

30. Sheehy, *Hustling*, 16; "New Life for the Oldest Profession," *New Republic*, July 8 and 15, 1978; Ford Foundation and Boston Redevelopment Authority, "A Study of the Interrelationship of Social Planning with Economic Development within Boston's Theater District," 1980, 25, Combat Zone, Box 12767333, BRA; B. A. Lojko,

letter to the editor, *Boston Globe*, November 25, 1975. For an analysis of the "badger game," where Black women robbed white men soliciting for sex in the late nineteenth-century, see Kali N. Gross, *Colored Amazons: Crime, Violence, and Black Women in the City of Brotherly Love, 1880–1910* (Durham, NC: Duke University Press, 2006), esp. chap. 3.

31. *Commonwealth v. Reddick*, "A Close Look at the Hub's Street Hookers," *Boston Globe*, August 26, 1979; Pellett, "Prostitution in Boston." For reasons it did not disclose, the BPD stopped reporting prostitution arrests after 1971. During a 1973 Suffolk County Superior Court trial, *Commonwealth v. Reddick*, in which a defendant appealed her conviction for common nightwalking on the grounds that prostitution-related laws were enforced with racial discrimination, the judge denied a defense motion to tabulate race statistics for prostitution-related arrests.

32. Boston City Council, "Public Hearing before the Committee on Ordinances and Resolutions, in the Matter of Streetwalking and Hitchhiking," October 2, 1969, 97–98, City of Boston Archives, Boston.

33. Boston City Council, "Public Hearing," 97–98; Folders 35550 and 44127, Box 47, BMCP. Many thanks to Libby Bouvier for heroically recovering the probation records. In my sample of 160 probation cases between 1928 and 1983, there were a total of twenty-six floaters. Sixteen, or 62 percent, were issued between 1965 and 1976. Of these, thirteen were issued to Black women. In the exceptional cases in which white women were issued floaters after 1965, they were told, for example, to "return to mother and cooperate with her." Floaters of the 1970s era represented a substantial change in police practices, which would accelerate and become institutionalized nationwide as cities transitioned away from welfare apparatus to carceral policies. For a contemporary account of carceral mechanisms of spatial banishment, see Katherine Beckett and Steve Herbert, *Banished: The New Social Control in Urban America* (New York: Oxford University Press, 2011).

34. Gloria Lockett, "What Happens When You Are Arrested," in Delacoste and Alexander, *Sex Work*, 39. For a history of the sex workers' rights movement, see Chateauvert, *Sex Workers Unite*. For a discussion of Lockett's activism in the 1980s, see chapter 6.

35. "The Oldest Profession Organizes," *Harvard Crimson*, November 16, 1977; "Report Ties Two Policemen to Kidnaping, Extortion, Rape," *Boston Globe*, November 10, 1976; Libby Cone, "Mass. Prostitutes Union Successful," *Sojourner*, February 1977.

36. *Money for Prostitutes Is Money for Black Women*, pamphlet, Black Women for Wages for Housework, ca. January 1977, in author's possession and also available online at freedomarchives.org. The authors are most likely Margaret Prescod and Wilmette Brown. For a discussion of Margaret Prescod's activism in the 1980s, see chapter 6. I am grateful to Rona Rothman for saving and sharing her extensive Wages for Housework collection.

37. William Brantley to Charles Rogovin, memo re: Law and Order Movie, July 31, 1969, RG 423, A1, EN 12, Box 3, NACP; Herman Goldstein, *Policing a Free Society* (Cambridge, MA: Ballinger, 1977), 73. *Law and Order*, directed by Frederick Wiseman, was screened at the Museum of Fine Arts, Boston, February 17, 2017. See also

Nilita Vachani, "Revisiting Wiseman's *Law and Order* (1969) in the Era of Black Lives Matter," *Film International*, October 14, 2020. Even the conservative criminologist James Q. Wilson conceded in his 1968 analysis of police that "the prevailing political culture creates a 'zone of indifference' within which the police are free to act as they see fit." Wilson noted that the zone was most contested when people were divided on discretionary policing (in this case, he was specifically referring to nineteenth-century liquor licensing debates). James Q. Wilson, *Varieties of Police Behavior: The Management of Law and Order in Eight Communities* (Cambridge, MA: Harvard University Press, 1968), 233.

38. See Chateauvert, *Sex Workers Unite*; Otto Kerner et al., *Report of the National Advisory Commission on Civil Disorders* (New York: Bantam Books, 1968); San Francisco Committee on Crime, *A Report on Non-victim Crime in San Francisco, Part 2* (Washington, DC: U.S. Department of Justice), 1971; Sheldon Krantz et al. and the Center for Criminal Justice, Boston University School of Law, *Right to Counsel in Criminal Cases: The Mandate of Argersinger v. Hamlin* (Cambridge, MA: Ballinger, 1976); and "Victimless Crime: Statement of Problem, Pros and Cons," October 17, 1972, 6, RG 423, UD, EN 4, Box 3, NACP.

39. Rory Judd Albert, *A Time for Reform: A Case Study of the Interaction between the Commissioner of the Boston Police Department and the Boston Police Patrolmen's Association* (Washington, DC: U.S. Department of Justice, Law Enforcement Assistance Administration, National Criminal Justice Reference Service, 1975), 2; Francis Sargent, "Getting the Most from Our Police," *Boston Globe*, February 21, 1977. State representatives who supported the decriminalization of prostitution included Democrats Barney Frank, Mel King, and Doris Bunte and Republican Barbara Gray.

40. Earl Marchand, "A Frank Suggestion: Hookers in the Financial District," *Boston Herald American*, November 25, 1976; memo, "Thoughts on the Entertainment District," December 4, 1974, unmarked folder, Box 13399676, BRA; Zoning Commission hearing, September 11, 1974, Box 12767333, BRA; preliminary findings report, April 16, 1974, Park Plaza—Entertainment Subcommittee—Suggested Prelim. Findings and Recommendations (Ahern), Box 13399676, BRA; "17 Women Arrested in Combat Zone Raid," *Boston Globe*, November 26, 1974.

41. "His Attire Flabbergasted the Major," *Boston Globe*, October 8, 1976; "Is the Combat Zone Going Out of Business?" *Boston Herald American*, July 30, 1978; Robert diGrazia, phone interview by the author, November 11, 2009.

42. National Advisory Commission on Criminal Justice Standards and Goals, January 23, 1973, meeting transcripts, 165, RG 423, UD, EN 4, Box 7, NACP; "Hearings on Unemployment and Crime," 465; "Crackdown on S.F. Prostitution," *San Francisco Chronicle*, December 28, 1976; "'Tough' Cop to Lead S.F. Vice War," *San Francisco Chronicle*, January 4, 1977. For the Los Angeles Police Department's position paper on the "mythical concept" of victimless crime that accompanied "the increasing permissiveness in our society," see Los Angeles Police Department, "Victimless Crimes: A Research Project," May 1972, copy in author's possession.

43. Salvatore M. Giorlandino, "The Origin, Development, and Decline of Boston's Adult Entertainment District: The Combat Zone" (MA thesis, Massachusetts Institute of Technology, 1986), 38.

44. Frank DeSario, *Badge #1: Memoirs of a Boston Cop* (Morrisville, NC: Lulu.com, 2006), 36; Albert, *Time for Reform*, 48; "Combat Zone Concept May Spread . . . to Hawaii," *Boston Herald Advertiser*, January 18, 1976. Journalist Stephanie Schorow also notes that many Combat Zone bars hired off-duty police as bouncers. Reformist commissioner diGrazia banned this practice. See Schorow, *Inside the Combat Zone: The Stripped Down Story of Boston's Most Notorious Neighborhood* (Guilford, CT: Globe Pequot, 2019), 35, 51.

45. "2 Hub Police Superintendents Want Liaison with Community," *Boston Globe*, May 2, 1973; "55 Women Face Prostitution Charges after Raids," *Boston Globe*, September 14, 1973.

46. "Hearings on Unemployment and Crime," 104–105; John Kifner, "The Men in the Middle," *New York Times*, September 12, 1976; "DiGrazia Labels Most Chiefs 'Pet Rocks, Unwilling to Grow,'" n.d., no source, Police [1/2] 1977–1978, Box 133, KW. On the relationship between liberal reform and the consolidation of police power, see Felker-Kantor, "Liberal Law-and-Order."

47. "Mr. Rogovin Gives Up[?]," *Boston Globe*, April[?] 13, 1970, News Articles, Press Releases, Etc., Box 1, A1, EN 1, RG 423, NACP; "The Police Should Do Their Job," *Bay State Banner*, December 22, 1977; "Sav-Mor Sets Up Community Patrol," *Bay State Banner*, December 31, 1970. See, for example, petition of Elaine Noble, Melvin H. King, and Doris Bunte for legislation to decriminalize prostitution, House Petition 3391, introduced during 1977 legislative session. Ruth Rosen provides one exception in which residents of a predominantly Black neighborhood in Oakland marched to remove sexually profiled women from their community, holding picket signs that read, "We are victims of prostitution." Rosen, *The Lost Sisterhood: Prostitution in America, 1900–1918* (Baltimore: Johns Hopkins University Press, 1982), 176. On Black law-and-order politics in the 1970s, see Michael Javen Fortner, *Black Silent Majority: The Rockefeller Drug Laws and the Politics of Punishment* (Cambridge, MA: Harvard University Press, 2015); and James Forman Jr., *Locking Up Our Own: Crime and Punishment in Black America* (New York: Farrar, Straus and Giroux, 2017).

48. "A Summary Report of the Congressional Black Caucus," 1972, 21, Box 2, Phyllis Ryan Papers, NU. For an overview of police reform after 1965, see Samuel Walker, *Popular Justice: A History of American Criminal Justice*, 2nd ed. (New York: Oxford University Press, 1997), esp. chap. 6. For more on Black criminologists in the 1970s, see Woodson, *Black Perspectives on Crime*.

49. King, *Chain of Change*, 215; Hubert Jones, executive director of the Roxbury Multi-service Center, to Kevin White, December 27, 1968, Correspondence: Boston Police Department 1 of 4, Box 1, KW.

50. Albert, *Time for Reform*, 96, 6.

51. Albert, 96, 6; Boston Police Department, *Annual Report of the Police Commissioner*, 1962, 1974; Albert, *Time for Reform*, 79–80.

52. "Law and Disorder III," Lawyer's Committee for Civil Rights under Law, Velde Files, RG 423, A1, EN 2, Box 15, NACP; DeSario, *Badge #1*, 83; House Select Committee on Crime, "Hearings on Street Crime in America," 93rd Cong., 1st Sess.,

1973, 376. For TPF involvement with petty morals misdemeanors in Boston, see especially Folder 36048, Box 47; Folders 41594, 41705, 42812, Box 48; and Folder 44540, Box 49, BMCP.

53. Goldstein, *Policing a Free Society*, 53–54; Kerner et al., *Report*, 304; "Blacks Protest Police Tactics," *Boston Globe*, August 17, 1975.

54. "Changing the Soul Patrol," *Boston Globe*, January 28, 1972; Black Panther Party Community Newsletter, no. 5, n.d., Black Panther Party, Malcolm X Community Information Center, Freedom House, Inc., records, Box 57, NU; Woodson, *Black Perspectives on Crime*, 102; Valimore Williams and Judith Williams, interview by the author, May 5, 2017. Many thanks to Val and Judith Williams for contributing their time and oral histories to this project. On the political mobilization of Black police officers, see Tera Agyepong, "In the Belly of the Beast: Black Policemen Combat Police Brutality in Chicago, 1968–1983," *Journal of African American History* 98, no. 2 (Spring 2013): 253–276; and Beryl Satter, "Cops, Gangs, and Revolutionaries in 1960s Chicago: What Black Police Can Tell Us about Power," *Journal of Urban History* 42, no. 6 (2016): 1110–1134; and Peter Pihos, *Black Power through Law: The Afro-American Patrolmen's League and the Struggle for Justice* (forthcoming).

55. "Roxbury Glad to Have Its New 'Soul Patrol,'" *Boston Globe*, December 8, 1971; "Dispute Grows over All-Black Patrol Force," *Boston Globe*, November 21, 1971; "Changing the Soul Patrol," *Boston Globe*, January 28, 1972; Preston Williams, interview by the author, June 6, 2017; Valimore Williams, interview by the author, May 5, 2017.

56. House Select Committee on Crime, "Hearings on Street Crime," 392.

57. Preston Williams, interview by the author, June 6, 2017.

58. Preston Williams, interview by the author, June 6, 2017; Valimore Williams, interview by the author, May 5, 2017. See also Agyepong, "In the Belly of the Beast; Satter, "Cops, Gangs, and Revolutionaries in 1960s Chicago"; and Pihos, *Black Power through Law*.

59. "Partial Text of Report on District One," *Boston Globe*, November 9, 1976; "Downtown Police Corruption Alleged: DiGrazia Ponders District 1 Report," *Boston Globe*, November 9, 1976; Dave O'Brian, "The Combat Zone: Banned in Boston Again?" *Boston Phoenix*, July 5, 1977; "Something Must Be Done," *Boston Globe*, June 13, 1977.

60. "Hub Police Report Charges District 1 Rife with 'Incompetence, Corruption,'" *Boston Globe*, November 8, 1976; "Report Ties Two Policemen to Kidnapping, Extortion, Rape," *Boston Globe*, November 10, 1976; "Partial Text of Report"; "Downtown Police Corruption Alleged."

61. "Harvard Athlete Is Stable after Combat Zone Melee," *Boston Globe*, November 17, 1976; Jeremiah V. Murphy, ". . . But Things Are the Same," *Boston Globe*, December 15, 1976; Jeremiah V. Murphy, "The Goal Is Equal Justice," *Boston Globe*, March 28, 1979; "3 Guilty in Puopolo Case Get Life Terms, No Parole," *Boston Globe*, March 25, 1977. The missing wallet that triggered the episode contained ten dollars. One of the men fighting the Harvard football players was Latino.

Journalist Stephanie Schorow writes the most thorough tick-tock account of the Puopolo stabbing. See Schorow, *Inside the Combat Zone*, 95–98.

62. Preston Williams, interview by the author, June 6, 2017; Valimore Williams, interview by the author, May 5, 2017; "Judge: 2 Deserve Contempt Charges," *Boston Globe*, November 15, 1979; Robert A. Jordan, "Perception of Justice Hurt by Puopolo," *Boston Globe*, March 29, 1977. This was, however, the narrative the defense presented in the subsequent trial: "Puopolo and his teammates attacked two Black women . . . after a night of drinking," and the three men came to the women's defense. "Community Meets to Discuss Racially Motivated Attacks," *Bay State Banner*, August 16, 1979.

63. Jordan, "Perception of Justice Hurt"; ". . . A Call for Action at Boston Rally," *Boston Globe*, December 3, 1978; Murphy, "Goal Is Equal Justice"; "The Zone Devoid of Combat as Police Replace Hookers," *Boston Globe*, November 19, 1976; "Something Must Be Done"; "Suspect in Stripper's Slaying Caught," *Boston Globe*, November 4, 1976; "A Pattern of Prostitute Slayings," *Boston Globe*, August 3, 1975. On the serial murders of Black women in Boston, see chapter 6.

64. David Rogers, "Jordan Picked to Take Over diGrazia's job," *Boston Globe*, October 6, 1976; "Jordan Wants to Give Streets Back to People," n.s., likely *Boston Globe*, November 28, 1976, 29, in author's possession; Dan Ahern, "Mobile Pimps, Hookers Poser for City," *Boston Herald American*, November 24, 1976; PUMA meeting with Wages for Housework; O'Brian, "Combat Zone"; "Boston's 'Combat Zone' Becomes Target of Police Crackdown," *New York Times*, December 3, 1976. See also "Police Had to Act Fast—and Did," *Boston Globe*, November 17, 1976.

65. "Prostitutes' Union Seeks Law Changes," *Boston Globe*, January 4, 1977; Amy Hoffman, "PUMA Reacts to Police Crackdown," *Sister Courage*, February 1977.

66. "Officials Say Concept of X-Rated Zone Failed, Plan Crackdown on Violations," *Boston Globe*, November 30, 1976; "A Zone Defense," *Real Paper*, December 11, 1976; "Something Must Be Done"; Robert Campbell, "They're Out to Get the Combat Zone!," *Boston Globe*, April 16, 1978. Historians continue to reproduce this narrative: Josh Sides argues that the zoning ordinance "was a complete failure" that produced a "wave of crime that culminated tragically in the 1976 slaying of Harvard football player Andrew Puopolo by a pick-pocketing prostitute's 'muscle men.'" See Josh Sides, "Excavating the Postwar Sex District in San Francisco," *Journal of Urban History* 32, no. 3 (March 2006): 369.

67. "Troublesome Combat Zone Here to Stay, City Planners Say," *Boston Herald American*, December 9, 1976; "Globe Readers Oppose Combat Zone by 2–1," *Boston Globe*, October 31, 1977; Terri Minsky, "Those Who Live, Work, or Hang Out in Area Feel It Serves a Need," *Boston Globe*, December 28, 1984; "Respectability Killing Boston Sex Zone," *Los Angeles Times*, June 3, 1984; William Buchanan, "Street Scene, Boston," *Boston Globe*, August 5, 1985. See also Jonathan Kaufman, "Real Estate Development Boom Threatens 'Adult Entertainment,'" *Boston Globe*, December 27, 1984.

68. Jean Dietz, "Boston Businessmen Upset over Plan for Youth Shelter," *Boston Globe*, February 6, 1983; David Farrell, "Ray Flynn's War on Combat Zone,"

Boston Globe, December 23, 1984; "Cleanup Poses Its Own Questions," *Boston Globe*, December 29, 1984.

69. Ford Foundation and Boston Redevelopment Authority, "Study of the Interrelationship," 65.

70. See also Felker-Kantor, "Liberal Law-and-Order"; and Agee, *Streets of San Francisco*.

Chapter 5

1. Dan Sweat, "Why We Can't Let Atlanta Be 'Easy City,'" *Atlanta Journal-Constitution* (Weekend Edition), September 18, 1976; Sam Hopkins, "Eaves Blasted on Prostitution," *Atlanta Constitution*, August 3, 1976. I am enormously grateful to Danielle Wiggins, whose expertise on law enforcement and Black politics in Atlanta considerably improved this chapter. See Danielle Wiggins, "Crime Capital: Public Safety, Urban Development, and Post-Civil Rights Black Politics in Atlanta" (PhD diss., Emory University, 2018).

2. "Evil Lurketh Not in Downtown, Thanks to Mobile Action Unit," *What's Up in Atlanta*, Atlanta Convention and Visitors Bureau newsletter, September/October 1978, 1, 2, 1973–1979 Crime Task Force 1 Folder, Box 170, CAP; "Report of the Criminal Justice Coordinating Council's Committee on Special Police Protection," June 19, 1975, Metropolitan Atlanta Crime Commission Folder, Box 169, CAP.

3. Clarence N. Stone, "Partnership New South Style: Central Atlanta Progress," in *Public-Private Partnerships: Improving Urban Life, Proceedings of the Academy of Political Science*, ed. Perry Davis (New York: Academy of Political Science, 1986), 100; Richard Stormont, general manager of Marriott Hotel Atlanta, to Carl Ware, president of the Atlanta City Council, April 11, 1979, 1979 Crime Task Force #1 Folder, Box 171, CAP; Susan R. Braido to Pete Woodham, Atlanta Chamber of Commerce, November 22, 1978, 1977–1978 Crime Task Force #1 Folder, Box 170, CAP. For a discussion of the "convention center boom" in Atlanta, see Heywood T. Sanders, *Convention Center Follies: Politics, Power, and Public Investment in American Cities* (Philadelphia: University of Pennsylvania Press, 2014), esp. chap. 7.

4. DeWitt Rogers, "Revitalizing of 'Strip' Planned," *Atlanta Constitution*, September 2, 1976; Joe Brown and Frederick Allen, "Embargo on Sin Trade Is Expensive to Enforce," *Atlanta Constitution*, June 29, 1976.

5. Hank Ezell, "Prostitution Study Urged," *Atlanta Journal*, January 14, 1976; Reginald Eaves, "Police May Be Wasting Time Chasing Hookers," *Atlanta Constitution*, September 18, 1976; Sharon Bailey, "Eaves: Revise 'Victimless Crime' Laws," *Atlanta Constitution*, January 15, 1976; Brown and Allen, "Embargo on Sin Trade"; "Study of the Control and Regulation of Adult Entertainment," draft, 1976, 5, 6, Adult Entertainment 1976 Folder, Box 167, CAP. Eaves did claim that society was victimized by this "victimless crime," linking prostitution with the usual suspects, including the drug trade, sexually transmitted infections, robbery, and organized crime. But rather than arguing that prostitution enforcement should be escalated in order to prevent larger-order crimes, in some interviews he favored Dutch-style

legalization and argued that Boston's model did not go far enough in "de-emphasiz[ing] enforcement." Brown and Allen, "Embargo on Sin Trade;" Bailey, "Eaves: Revise 'Victimless Crime' Laws."

6. Ed Jahn and Ron Taylor, "Peachtree Porn Area Alive and . . . Well . . . ," *Atlanta Constitution*, October 5, 1975; "Study of the Control," 5, 6. CAP possibly studied the ostensibly liberal solution to morals policing because it had already tried and failed to implement a strategy of intensified morals policing: the organization's early efforts in 1973 to design a program to aggressively police disorder on downtown streets in the broadly unpopular Corner Cop program was "sabotaged by disgruntled policemen and press," according to internal CAP memos. Public Safety Task Force meeting minutes, June 11, 1981, Public Safety Task Force 1981 Folder, Box 176, CAP.

7. For histories of the role of Black residents in supporting punitive policies, see Michael Javen Fortner, *Black Silent Majority: The Rockefeller Drug Laws and the Politics of Punishment* (Cambridge, MA: Harvard University Press, 2015); and James Forman, Jr., *Locking Up Our Own: Crime and Punishment in Black America* (New York: Farrar, Straus, and Giroux, 2017). See also Jordan T. Camp and Christina Heatherton, "How Liberals Legitimate Broken Windows: An Interview with Naomi Murakawa," in *Policing the Planet: Why the Policing Crisis Led to Black Lives Matter*, ed. Jordan T. Camp and Christina Heatherton (New York: Verso, 2016), chap. 17.

8. Maurice J. Hobson, *The Legend of the Black Mecca: Politics and Class in the Making of Modern Atlanta* (Chapel Hill: University of North Carolina Press, 2017), 66; Gary M. Pomerantz, *Where Peachtree Meets Sweet Auburn: The Saga of Two Families and the Making of Atlanta* (New York: Scribner, 1996), 407.

9. Mack H. Jones, "Black Political Empowerment in Atlanta: Myth and Reality," *Annals of the American Academy of Political and Social Sciences* 39 (September 1978): 104–105; Stone, "Partnership New South Style," 106, 104. See also Hobson, *Legend of the Black Mecca*, chap. 2. On the history of Atlanta politics, see Floyd Hunter, *Community Power Structure: A Study of Decision Makers* (Chapel Hill: University of North Carolina Press, 1953); and Clarence N. Stone, *Regime Politics: Governing Atlanta, 1946–1988* (Lawrence: University Press of Kansas, 1989).

10. Stone, "Partnership New South Style," 107, 108; Francis Kent, "Atlanta Hurt by Racism, Bitterness," *Los Angeles Times*, September 30, 1974; Wayne King, "Atlanta's Confident Hope Is Faltering," *New York Times*, October 7, 1974; "Atlanta: Business Wary of City Area," *Baltimore Afro-American*, October 12, 1974; Francis Kent, "Atlanta Mayor, Eaves Pitted against Businessmen, Police in Racial Squabble," *Boston Globe*, October 2, 1974; "Maynard Jackson Denies Conflict with Atlanta Business Community," *Baltimore Afro-American*, December 7, 1974. The rabid national media interest in the "racial squabble" between Jackson and the Atlanta business elites reflects the white panic that erupted after the election of the first Black, big-city mayor in the South.

11. Kent, "Atlanta Mayor"; Kent, "Atlanta Hurt by Racism"; Walter Haynes, "Ousted Eaves Is Still a Rallying Point," *Boston Globe*, April 1, 1978. The *Boston Globe* nursed an obsession with Eaves because he had served as a rare Black prison

official in Boston (and had been pilloried throughout his tenure there) before joining Jackson's administration in Atlanta.

12. "Visitors Bureau Joins Blast at Prostitution," *Atlanta Daily World*, August 13, 1976; Joe Brown and Frederick Allen, "Sex for Sale—and City's Paying Price," *Atlanta Constitution*, June 27, 1976, A1; Joe Brown and Frederick Allen, "Sex for Sale: Loopholes and Laxity Aid 'X-Rated' Shops," *Atlanta Constitution*, June 28, 1976, A1; Brown and Allen, "Embargo on Sin Trade."

13. Brown and Allen, "Sex for Sale."

14. Brown and Allen, "Embargo on Sin Trade." Many thanks to Danielle Wiggins for raising this important point about the Afro-American Patrolmen's League.

15. Jessie Carney Smith, *Black Firsts: 4,000 Ground-Breaking and Pioneering Historical Events* (Canton, MI: Visible Ink, 2003), 360; "Ms. Welcome Explains War on Local Vice," *Atlanta Daily World*, April 15, 1977; Sasha Futran, "Some Are Calling Her 'Wild Mary' Welcome," *Baltimore Afro-American*, April 9, 1977. Welcome served as lead defense in the trial of Wayne Williams, convicted for the Atlanta child murders; Williams maintains his innocence. On Welcome's departure from the Jackson administration and her role in the trial, see Bernard D. Headley, *The Atlanta Youth Murders and the Politics of Race* (Carbondale: Southern Illinois University Press, 1998).

16. "Eaves Scolded for Hiring Black Cops," *Baltimore Afro-American*, March 13, 1976; B. Drummond Ayres, "Mayor of Atlanta Suspends Police Head, Giving the City's Image a Blow," *New York Times*, March 11, 1978; Haynes, "Ousted Eaves."

17. Dan Sweat to James Hurst, ACVB, December 5, 1978, 1978–1978 Crime Task Force 1 Folder, Box 170, CAP; "Atlanta's Crime Task Force," n.d., 1973–1979 Crime Task Force 1 Folder, Box 170, CAP.

18. "Atlanta's Crime Task Force"; "Evil Lurketh Not." The Crime Task Force wanted a "super saturation" of police downtown "without giving the impression of an 'armed camp,'" which would presumably frighten the very whites they were trying to reassure.

19. "Atlanta's Crime Task Force."

20. Wiggins, "Crime Capital," chap. 3; Joe Ledlie, "Summer Murder Wave Has Atlantans on Edge," *Washington Post*, August 5, 1979; Barry King and Angelo Lewis, "Stranger Kills Secretary on Peachtree Street," *Atlanta Constitution*, October 18, 1979; Hobson, *Legend of the Black Mecca*, 121 and chap. 3. James Baldwin traveled to Atlanta and published a book about the Atlanta child murders, which he referred to as the "terror." See James Baldwin, *The Evidence of Things Not Seen* (New York: Holt, 1985). For a critical analysis of the Atlanta child murders and the true crime genre, see Terrion L. Williamson, "Of Serial Murder and True Crime: Some Preliminary Thoughts on Black Feminist Research Praxis and the Implications of Settler Colonialism." *Environment and Planning D: Society and Space* 39, no. 1 (February 2021): 22–29.

21. Central Atlanta Progress, "Atlanta's Crime Task Force: Planning for Police Effectiveness in Downtown Atlanta," ca. 1977–1978, 1973–1979 Crime Task Force 1 Folder, Box 170, CAP; Wiggins, "Crime Capital," chap. 3.

22. George Kelling and James Q. Wilson, "Broken Windows," *Atlantic*, March 1982. For a rich and extensive analysis of broken windows policing, see Bernard E.

Harcourt, *Illusion of Order: The False Promise of Broken Windows Policing* (Cambridge, MA: Harvard University Press, 2001). See also Bench Ansfield, "The Broken Windows of the Bronx: Putting the Theory in Its Place," *American Quarterly* 72, no. 1 (March 2020): 103–127.

23. Kelling and Wilson, "Broken Windows"; George Kelling essay quoted at length in William Bratton and Peter Knobler, *The Turnaround: How America's Top Cop Reversed the Crime Epidemic* (New York: Random House, 1998), 87–89. See also Samuel Walker, "Broken Windows and Fractured History: The Use and Misuse of History in Recent Police Patrol Analysis," *Justice Quarterly* 1, no. 1 (1984): 75–90. Many thanks to Stuart Schrader for bringing this article to my attention.

24. Kelling and Wilson, "Broken Windows." The concept of the "redistribution of fear" comes from Themis Chronopoulos, "The Making of the Orderly City: New York since the 1980s," *Journal of Urban History* 46, no. 5 (September 2020): 1085–1116.

25. Kelling essay quoted in Bratton and Knobler, *Turnaround*, 87–89; Kelling and Wilson, "Broken Windows."

26. Kelling and Wilson, "Broken Windows." See also Mason B. Williams, "How the Rockefeller Laws Hit the Streets: Drug Policing and the Politics of State Competence in New York City, 1973–1989," *Modern American History* 4, no. 1 (2021): 67–90.

27. Frederick Allen, *Atlanta Rising: The Invention of an International City, 1946–1996* (Lanham, MD: Taylor Trade, 1996), 200.

28. Richard Stormont to Carl Ware, president of the Atlanta city council, April 11, 1979, 1979 Crime Task Force Folder, Box 171, CAP; "Crime in Atlanta: Review and Analysis," August 30, 1979, 28, 1979 Crime in Atlanta: Review and Analysis Folder, Box 169, CAP.

29. Dan Sweat to James Hurst, ACVB, December 5, 1978, 1978–1978 Crime Task Force 1 Folder, Box 170, CAP; "It's the Mayor's Job," *Atlanta Constitution*, October 19, 1979; Joe Dolman, "Police Have Anti-prostitute 'Plan' for Strip," *Atlanta Journal*, February 22, 1979. See, for example, the flurry of correspondence related to prostitution between the city council president, the general manager of Marriott, and Corbin Davis, vice president of corporate marketing for Blue Bird Body Company, 1979 Crime Task Force 1 Folder, Box 171, CAP; or that between the Atlanta Chamber of Commerce and a Fulton County State Court judge, April 10, 1979, 1979 Crime Task Force 2 Folder, Box 171, CAP.

30. "Atlanta Anti-crime Action Plan," November 21, 1979, 1, 47–48, Department of Public Safety Folder, Box 213, NAACP Atlanta records, AARL; "A Strategy for Crime Control in Atlanta," memo and report from Lee Brown to Maynard Jackson, July 26, 1979, Statements Concerning Crime in Atlanta Folder, Box 56, Research Atlanta records, AHC.

31. On vagrancy law's journey to the Supreme Court and *Papachristou*, see Risa Goluboff, *Vagrant Nation: Police Power, Constitutional Change, and the Making of the 1960s* (New York: Oxford University Press, 2016), esp. chap. 9.

32. Leigh Ann Wheeler, *How Sex Became a Civil Liberty* (New York: Oxford University Press, 2013), 162–165; People v. Smith, 393 N.Y.S.2d 239, 240 (1977);

Commonwealth v. King, 374 Mass. 5 (1977); Lambert v. City of Atlanta, 250 S.E.2d 456, 457 (Ga. 1978). See also Daniel E. Wade, "Prostitution and the Law: Emerging Attacks on the Women's Crime," *UMKC Law Review* 43, no. 3 (Spring 1975): 413–428; and Marilyn Haft, "Hustling for Rights," *Civil Liberties Review* 1, no. 2 (Winter/Spring 1974): 8–26. Many thanks to Marilyn Haft for her contributions to an earlier version of this project. Marilyn Haft, phone interview by the author, September 17, 2009.

33. Anna Lvovsky, "The Judicial Presumption of Police Expertise," *Harvard Law Review* 130, no. 8 (June 2017): 2041.

34. People v. Smith, 393 N.Y.S.2d 239, 240 (1977); Lvovsky, "Judicial Presumption," 2042. This loitering law—finally repealed in 2021—served as one of the key mechanisms in the major spike in New York prostitution-related arrests through the 1980s. For a history of New York prostitution laws, see Pamela Roby, "Politics and Prostitution: A Case Study of the Formulation, Enforcement and Judicial Administration of the New York State Penal Laws on Prostitution, 1870–1970" (PhD diss., New York University, 1971). On the loitering law and LGBTQ policing, see Karen Struening, "Walking While Wearing a Dress: Prostitution Loitering Ordinances and the Policing of Christopher Street," *Stanford Journal of Criminal Law and Policy* 3, no. 16 (2016): 16–54. For a further discussion of contemporary prostitution-related laws, see the epilogue.

35. People v. Smith, 393 N.Y.S.2d 239, 240 (1977); Lvovsky, "Judicial Presumption."

36. Lvovsky, "Judicial Presumption," 2050; "'Ladies Day': Discretion in Municipal Court, Department One," Box 16, COYOTE records, SCH. As lawyer William Trosch has written, "Lawmakers responded to the Supreme Court's admonition by requiring a specific intent to engage in an unlawful activity. By adding a *mens rea* element, legislators hoped to wrap the same unconstitutional law in a prettier package that was more likely to receive judicial sanction. The first of these laws to gain popularity sought to lessen the standard for arresting prostitutes by criminalizing 'loitering with the intent to solicit prostitution.'" William Trosch, "The Third Generation of Loitering Laws Goes to Court: Do Laws That Criminalize Loitering with the Intent to Sell Drugs Pass Constitutional Muster?" *North Carolina Law Review* 71, no. 2 (1993): 517.

37. Lambert v. City of Atlanta, 250 S.E.2d 456, 457 (Ga. 1978); Atlanta City Code Section 17-2004(d). The Atlanta City Council passed this 1974 law "due to the demands made by CAP." Annie R. Johnson, "The City of Atlanta's Responses to Prostitution" (MA thesis, Atlanta University, 1981), 16. This law also "affords such person an opportunity to explain this conduct, and no one shall be convicted of violating this subsection if it appears at trial that the explanation given was true and disclosed a lawful purpose," which Lambert charged was a violation of her due process rights and empowered police officers to act as street-level judges. Code and Ordinances of Atlanta, Section 20-23(d). Gay activists mobilized to repeal this law, gathering signatures for a petition, direct action, court watching, and organizing with the Atlanta Community Relations Commission. See "Atlanta CRC Urges Repeal of Idling and Loitering Law," *The Barb*, October 1975; "Fowler Rejects Petition," *The Barb*, February 1976.

38. *City of Atlanta v. Patricia Lambert,* Case #33655, Georgia Supreme Court Case Files, GSA.

39. *City of Atlanta v. Patricia Lambert; Lambert v. City of Atlanta;* Brief of Appellant, September 7, 1977, Case #33655, Georgia Supreme Court Case Files, GSA. For another such case, which also hinged on state preemption, see *Charles Pace and Sharon Louise DeLima v. City of Atlanta,* 135 Ga. App. 399 (Court of Appeals of Georgia, Division No. 3, 1975).

40. *City of Atlanta v. Patricia Lambert;* Brief of Appellant, Case #33655.

41. Appellee's Brief in Response to Appellant's Enumerations of Error, June 19, 1978, Case #33655, Georgia Supreme Court Case Files, GSA; Application for Rehearing, December 1, 1978, Case #33655, Georgia Supreme Court Case Files, GSA; Brief of Amicus Curiae on Motion for Rehearing, n.d., Case #33655, Georgia Supreme Court Case Files, GSA.

42. *Lambert v. City of Atlanta;* Appellee's Brief in Response.

43. T. L. Wells, "Hookers Operate Openly: Court Ruling Bars Arrests," *Atlanta Constitution,* December 11, 1978, C1; Orville Gaines and Susan Wells, "32 More Arrested as Police Continue Prostitution War," *Atlanta Constitution,* March 4, 1979.

44. Thomas K. Hamall, Atlanta Chamber of Commerce, to Judge Nick Lambros, April 10, 1979, 1979 Crime Task Force 2 Folder, Box 171, CAP; Richard Beene, "'Shocked' by Local Prostitutes, Gov. Busbee Acts by Signing Law," *Atlanta Daily World,* February 22, 1979. The Georgia State Legislature also passed loitering laws of increasingly dubious constitutionality. See, for example, Fran Hesser, "Antiloitering Bill Easily Passes House Despite Opposition," *Atlanta Constitution,* February 28, 1980.

45. Alexis Scott Reeves, "Anti-prostitution Law Reinstated by Council," *Atlanta Constitution,* March 20, 1979; George Rodrigue, "Plans Readied to Aid Mayor in Hooker War," *Atlanta Constitution,* December 25, 1978; Dan Sweat to Marie Nygren, August 15, 1984, Folder 9, Box 175, AHC; city council minutes, 1981, City of Atlanta records, AHC.

46. Trosch, "Third Generation"; "Atlanta Acts to Save Peachy Image," *Chicago Tribune,* August 28, 1979; Special Investigative Grand Jury presentment, May 22, 1980, 21, Grand Jury Reports Folder, Box 53, Research Atlanta records, AHC; Wesley Smith, "Don't Stand So Close to Me," *Policy Review,* no. 70 (Fall 1994): 48. As a result of the drug-loitering law in Saint Petersburg, police had arrested "several thousand people for drug dealing alone" between 1989, when the law was passed, and 1994, when a study was conducted. Smith, "Don't Stand So Close," 48. See also Richard Danielson, "Court Rules against Loitering Ordinance," *Tampa Bay Times,* October 9, 2005.

47. Completed forms in the 1981 Harassment Folder and 1982–1984 Harassment Folder, Box 172, CAP; Dennis Ilgen to Maynard Jackson, January 15, 1980, Harassment Folder, Box 172, CAP; Dan Sweat to Captain Jim Mullins, June 8, 1981, 1981 Harassment Folder, Box 172, CAP; Dan Sweat to George Napper, February 4, 1980, Harassment Folder, Box 172, CAP. CAP was building on (presumably) white women's efforts. After the murder of Patricia Barry in October 1979, "women working in downtown Atlanta" organized an anticrime rally featuring a white National

Organization for Women speaker. "Do you know that your rights are being violated every day?" the event's flyer asked. "Women and men have the right to walk down the streets of Atlanta without being MUGGED, RAPED, SHOT, HARASSED BY OBSCENE LANGUAGE, MOLESTED, STABBED!!!" These organizers, however, did not demonstrate consideration of the ways in which poor Black women were harmed by police officers. Flyer, ca. November 1979, Public Safety 1979 Aug–Nov Crime Folder, Box 167, CAP. On predominantly white women's antiviolence activism and their alliance with law enforcement, see chapter 6.

48. Atlanta City Council memo on twenty-one-point plan, December 4, 1979, Harassment Folder, Box 172, CAP; CAP Public Safety Task Force Liaison Subcommittee meeting minutes, August 11, 1981, 1981 Public Safety Task Force Folder, Box 176, CAP; John H. Parker Jr. to Dan Sweat, June 1, 1981, 1981 Harassment Folder, Box 172, CAP.

49. "Businessmen Seeking Downtown Protection," *Atlanta Daily World*, September 22, 1981; Allen, *Atlanta Rising*, 214–215.

50. Barry Bearak, "Atlanta Mayor Young a Healer to White Leaders," *Los Angeles Times*, December 25, 1982.

51. Comprehensive Development Plan report, 1986, 2, Department of Community Development Folder, Box 269, Andrew Young Papers, AARL.

52. Comprehensive Development Plan report, 3; David L. Sjoquist, "The Economic Status of Black Atlantans," 1988, 1–2, Economic Status of Black Atlantans Folder, Box 270, Andrew Young Papers, AARL; Hobson, *Legend of the Black Mecca*, 144–145, 167, 185. On the deinstitutionalization movement and its entanglements with incarceration, see Anne E. Parsons, *From Asylum to Prison: Deinstitutionalization and the Rise of Mass Incarceration after 1945* (Chapel Hill: University of North Carolina Press, 2018).

53. Jane Hansen, "Growing Up with Crack," *Atlanta Journal and Constitution*, September 27, 1998; Sally Jacobs, "Captives of Crack," *Boston Globe*, December 13, 1989; John Kifner, "As Crack Moves Inland, Ohio City Fights Back," *New York Times*, August 29, 1989. On the multiple forms of violent victimization that Black women confronted in the context of crack use, and the ways in which the stigma of being a female crack smoker sustains "the social legitimacy of violence against women," see Lisa Maher and Richard Curtis, "Women on the Edge of Crime: Crack Cocaine and the Changing Contexts of Street-Level Sex Work in New York City," *Crime, Law, and Social Change* 18 (1992): 221–258. On the scapegoating and criminalization of Black women's reproduction during this period, see Dorothy E. Roberts, *Killing the Black Body: Race, Reproduction, and the Meaning of Liberty* (New York: Pantheon Books, 1997). For historical context on gender and drug addiction, see Mara L. Keire, "Dope Fiends and Degenerates: The Gendering of Addiction in the Early Twentieth Century," *Journal of Social History* 31, no. 4 (Summer 1998): 809–822.

54. Jeff Dickerson, "Self-Respect: The Scarcest of Ghetto Commodities," *Atlanta Journal-Constitution*, April 7, 1989.

55. Donna M. Hartman and Andrew Golub, "The Social Construction of the Crack Epidemic in the Print Media," *Journal of Psychoactive Drugs* 31, no. 4 (October–December 1999): 424, 429.

56. James A. Inciardi, Dorothy Lockwood, and Anne E. Pottieger, *Women and Crack-Cocaine* (New York: Macmillan, 1993), 13; Atlanta Drug Use Forecasting Project, City of Atlanta Office of Corrections, Department of Public Safety, 1991–1992 Folder, Box 46, Maynard Jackson Third Term Series, Robert W. Woodruff Library, Atlanta University Center, Atlanta. It is worth noting that in Atlanta (and cities elsewhere), the war on drugs coincided with a predictable rise in police corruption. Nationwide, see, for example, Philip Shenon, "Enemy Within: Drug Money Is Corrupting the Enforcers," *New York Times*, April 11, 1988; and in Atlanta, see Ronald Smothers, "Atlanta Holds Six Policemen in Crackdown," *New York Times*, September 7, 1995.

57. Samuel Walker, "The Origins of the American Police-Community Relations Movement: The 1940s," *Criminal Justice History* 1 (1980): 225–246. See also Elizabeth Hinton, *From the War on Poverty to the War on Crime: The Making of Mass Incarceration in America* (Cambridge, MA: Harvard University Press, 2016), 113–114, 188–189. Many thanks to Cheryl Hicks for raising this important point. See also Michael Stauch, *The Age of Community Policing* (Philadelphia: University of Pennsylvania Press, forthcoming).

58. George Kelling et al., *The Newark Foot Patrol Experiment* (Washington, DC: Police Foundation, 1981); Kelling and Wilson, "Broken Windows." For a discussion of police-community relations in Atlanta, see Stone, *Regime Politics*, 156–158.

59. "Police Community Action Agreement Finalized," Department of Public Safety news release, June 14, 1982, Atlanta Business Coalition 3 Folder, Box 167, CAP; Police/Community Action Agreement (signed), June 14, 1982, Atlanta Business Coalition 3 Folder, Box 167, CAP; Tony Cooper, "74 Netted in Crime and Vice Roundup," *Atlanta Constitution*, April 28, 1981; Department of Public Safety biennial report, 1984–1985, Folder 9, Box 56, Research Atlanta records, AHC; Partnership against Crime brochure, ca. 1985, Folder 4, Box 70, CAP; Comprehensive Development Plan report, 2. Shortly after the city-business Police/Community Action Agreement was formalized, the Bureau of Police Services unveiled Central Atlanta Patrol, a foot-patrol program featuring an "aggressive approach to policing in the downtown area." See Department of Public Safety biennial report, 1984–1985.

60. As legal scholar Dorothy Roberts writes, neighborhood associations that supported aggressive police action were more likely to gain "legitimacy and visibility because of their alliance with the police and city officials." Dorothy E. Roberts, "Race, Vagueness, and the Social Meaning of Order-Maintenance Policing," *Journal of Criminal Law and Criminology* 89, no. 3 (Spring 1999): 826. See Hobson, *Legend of the Black Mecca*, chap. 3 and esp. 117–122, for a discussion of the Bat Patrol, which was also called the Ron Carter Patrol. See also Benjamin Holtzman, "Expanding the Thin Blue Line: Resident Patrols and Private Security in Late Twentieth-Century New York," *Modern American History* 3, no. 1 (March 2020): 47–67.

61. Mark E. Johnson Jr., "Prostitution Is at a Crisis Stage," *Atlanta Constitution*, September 9, 1984; Keith Graham, "Midtowners Begin New Drive against Area's Prostitution," *Atlanta Constitution*, May 28, 1981; Lyn Martin, "Midtown Rallies to Fight Hookers," *Atlanta Constitution*, October 31, 1978; Dolores French and Linda Lee, *Working: My Life as a Prostitute* (New York: E. P. Dutton, 1988), 162.

62. Alan Boyer, "New War on Old Problem: Group Charts Fight against Prostitution," *Atlanta Constitution*, June 18, 1981, A35; David Secrest, "Prostitution Foes Say They're Victims," *Atlanta Constitution*, June 25, 1981, D6; Mark Barnette, "Neighborhoods Press Drive against Hookers," *Atlanta Constitution*, July 23, 1981, E6; "United against Prostitution," *Atlanta Constitution*, August 31, 1984, A17; Tony Cooper, "Young Wants Crackdown on Prostitution," *Atlanta Constitution*, October 6, 1982, A10; Carole Ashkinaze, "In Broad Daylight: Prostitutes Changing Method of Operations," *Atlanta Constitution*, May 22, 1980. For a history of the residents' antiprostitution mobilization, see Keith L. Thomas, "Neighborhoods against Crime, Part 3," *Atlanta Journal-Constitution*, July 8, 1987, B1.

63. Michael Moss, "Both Sides Join Prostitution Protest," *Atlanta Journal-Constitution*, March 1, 1985; John Lancaster, "A War of Wills Mounts, Pits Midtown against [title incomplete]," *Atlanta Journal-Constitution*, March 11, 1985; Michael Moss, "Midtown Rally Set for Protest of Prostitution," *Atlanta Journal-Constitution*, February 27, 1985; Thomas S. Woodward, "Letter to the Editor: Press and Mayor Muddle Midtown Hooker [title incomplete]," *Atlanta Journal-Constitution*, March 20, 1985; Gale Mull et al., "The Mayor's Task Force on Prostitution Findings and Recommendations," March 1986, 1, Folder 8, Box 175, CAP. For Dolores French's memoir, see French and Lee, *Working*.

64. The MTFOP also recommended "police sensitivity training" and wider circulation of "AIDS and STD" information, counseling, and "voluntary" testing. Mull et al., "Mayor's Task Force," 6–7.

65. CAP's special resolution is appended to the end of the MTFOP recommendation. Mull et al., "Mayor's Task Force."

66. Larry D. Thompson, "Conservatives Fight Black-on-Black Crime," *Atlanta Journal-Constitution*, June 24, 1987; Larry D. Thompson, "Dealing with Black-on-Black Crime," *Atlanta Daily World*, March 15, 1990; Jim Galloway, "Greater Trust in Police Underlies Shift in [title incomplete]," *Atlanta Journal-Constitution*, March 22, 1987; Eunice Palmer to Police Chief Eldrin Bell, August 31, 1992, Department of Public Safety, 1991–1992 [folder 6 of 8], Box 46, Maynard Jackson Third Term Series, Robert W. Woodruff Library, Atlanta University Center, Atlanta. Danielle Wiggins provides an important account of Black middle-class mobilization for broken windows policing in Atlanta in "'Order as Well as Decency': The Development of Order Maintenance Policing in Black Atlanta," *Journal of Urban History* 46, no. 4 (July 2020): 711–727. See also Fortner, *Black Silent Majority*; and Forman, Jr., *Locking Up Our Own*.

67. Kelling and Wilson, "Broken Windows"; Kelling essay quoted at length in Bratton and Knobler, *Turnaround*, 87–89; Tracey L. Meares and Dan M. Kahan quoted in Harcourt, *Illusion of Order*, 44–45. See also Tracey L. Meares and Dan M. Kahan, "When Rights Are Wrong: The Paradox of Unwanted Rights," in *Urgent Times: Policing and Rights in Inner-City Communities*, ed. Joshua Cohen and Joel Rogers (Boston: Beacon, 1999), 3–32.

68. Charles G. Steffen, "The Corporate Campaign against Homelessness: Class Power and Urban Governance in Neoliberal Atlanta, 1973–1988," *Journal of Social*

History 46, no. 1 (Fall 2012): 184. For a discussion of CAS II public safety recommendations, see Stone, *Regime Politics*, 143–144.

69. CAS II final report, February 17, 1988, Box 5.37 (ovs), CAP; Central Area Study II Public Safety Issue Paper, n.d., 6–7, Folder 5, Box 69, CAP; CAS II Atlanta Bureau of Police Services Improvement and Support Needs, Section Two, n.d., Public Safety Police Effectiveness Sub-Task Force 6 Folder, Box 74, CAP.

70. Central Area Study II Public Safety Issue Paper, n.d., 6–7.

71. CAS II Public Safety Task Force Police Effectiveness Sub-Task Force meeting minutes, September 9, 1986, Folder 6, Box 74, CAP; "A Strategy for a Safe Atlanta Central Area Including a 'Safeguard Zone,'" draft, November 1986, 17–20, 9, appendix 4, Folder 4, Box 72, CAP; William Wyatt Holland, "Who Is My Neighbor? Framing Atlanta's Movement to End Homelessness, 1900–2005" (PhD diss., Georgia State University, 2009), 259. See also Michael S. Foley, *Front Porch Politics: The Forgotten Heyday of American Activism in the 1970s and 1980s* (New York: Farrar, Straus and Giroux, 2013), 275–276.

72. "Strategy for a Safe Atlanta," 1.

73. Donna Williams Lewis, "Homeless Advocates Protest 'Safeguard' Zone," *Atlanta Journal-Constitution*, December 26, 1986; Holland, "Who Is My Neighbor?," 261. Other critiques of the Safeguard Zone were more self-interested: the Buckhead Business Association, representing the white, wealthy neighborhood on the northern border of the city limits, was concerned that the Safeguard Zone would drain police resources away from its neighborhood, while residents in Piedmont Park and Ansley Park, neighborhoods adjacent to downtown, worried that they would be subject to the "enforcement saturation contemplated for the 'Peachtree Spine.'" See CAS II Public Safety Task Force Police Effectiveness Sub-Task Force meeting minutes, October 14, 1986; and "Rationale for New Safeguard Zone Proposal," n.d., Folder 6, Box 74, CAP.

74. CAS II Public Safety Task Force meeting minutes notes, n.d., ca. 1986, 3, Folder 6, Box 71, CAP; CAS II Public Safety Task Force meeting minutes notes, October 21, 1986, Folder 6, Box 71, CAP. See also Jim Galloway, "Task Force Continues to Push for Downtown Police Zone," *Atlanta Journal-Constitution*, December 8, 1986.

75. Steffen, "Corporate Campaign against Homelessness," 187–188.

76. CAS II final report, February 17, 1988, 55, 54, Box 5.37 (ovs), CAP; Holland, "Who Is My Neighbor?," 278–279; CAS II Public Safety Task Force meeting minutes notes, March 30, 1987, 2, Folder 6, Box 71, CAP; Fran Hesser, "Downtown Study Seeks Expanded 'Safeguard Zone,'" *Atlanta Journal-Constitution*, March 24, 1987; Jim Galloway, "Add Police, Oust Vendors, Panel Urges," *Atlanta Journal-Constitution*, May 28, 1987; Jim Galloway, "Downtown District for Police Is Proposed," *Atlanta Journal-Constitution*, May 28, 1987; Frederick Allen, "Crime Isn't Task Force's Real Worry," *Atlanta Journal-Constitution*, May 31, 1987; Jim Galloway, "$50 Million Plan for Downtown Safety Offered," *Atlanta Journal-Constitution*, July 30, 1987; Marvin Arrington, "Bond Issue Would Let Citizens Decide on Public [title incomplete]," *Atlanta Journal-Constitution*, February 1, 1988. When Atlanta was named the site of the 1988 Democratic National Convention, CAP leaders, police officials, and allied

politicians renewed their calls for the Safeguard Zone. See Hal Straus, Sam Hopkins, and Jim Galloway, "Local Officials Cheer Decision by Democrats," *Atlanta Journal-Constitution*, February 10, 1987.

77. Lorri Denise Booker, "Public Safety Bond Election Draws Support, but [title incomplete]," *Atlanta Journal-Constitution*, July 31, 1987; Cynthia Tucker, "The Reality of Downtown Crime," *Atlanta Journal-Constitution*, August 3, 1987; Jim Galloway and Nathan McCall, "Young Blames 'Demagoguery' for Bond Defeat," *Atlanta Journal-Constitution*, May 4, 1988; Lorri Denise Booker, "Council President Marvin Arrington Angered by [title incomplete]," *Atlanta Journal-Constitution*, February 16, 1988; Mark Sherman, "Proposal to Bump Homeless from Downtown Not [title incomplete]," *Atlanta Journal-Constitution*, December 7, 1989.

78. Lorri Denise Booker, "Council President Marvin Arrington Angered by [title incomplete]," *Atlanta Journal-Constitution*, February 16, 1988.

79. CAS II final report, February 17, 1988, esp. illustrations on 16–18, 20, Box 5.37 (ovs), CAP.

80. Harcourt, *Illusion of Order*, 158.

81. Federal Bureau of Investigation and U.S. Department of Justice, *Uniform Crime Reports for the United States* (Washington, DC: U.S. Government Printing Office, 1980–1989); Minouche Kandel, "Whores in Court: Judicial Processing of Prostitutes in the Boston Municipal Court in 1990," *Yale Journal of Law and Feminism* 4 (1992): 330; New York State Bar Association Criminal Law Hearings on Prostitution, Box 17, COYOTE records, SCH; Miles Corwin, "Arrests Make Little Impact: Battling Prostitution: Just 'Keeping Lid On,'" *Los Angeles Times*, December 8, 1985; Philippa Levine, *Prostitution in Florida: A Report Presented to the Gender Bias Study Commission of the Supreme Court of Florida* (Tallahassee: Policy Studies, Florida State University College of Law, 1988), 112; "Sex and Race of Persons Arrested," August 1983, Atlanta Municipal Court Docket, 1982–1983, Box 53, Research Atlanta records, AHC.

82. *Uniform Crime Reports*, 1974–1991; Levine, *Prostitution in Florida*, 138.

83. Lee Walburn, "Sweetpea's Woe: There's No Justice for the Hookers," *Atlanta Journal-Constitution*, September 18, 1986, C1; Barry King and Robert Lamb, "The Night People," *The Atlanta Journal–The Atlanta Constitution (Weekend Edition)*, November 12, 1977, A1; "U.S. High Court Denies Appeals of 2 Ga. Killers," *The Atlanta Journal and Constitution*, April 4, 1989, B6. See also George Rodrigue, "Atlanta Police Officer Goes to Court on Rape Charge," *Atlanta Constitution*, April 10, 1980, C3; "City Detective Indicted on Bribery Charge," *Atlanta Daily World*, September 2, 1983, 1; Al Kamen and Benjamin Weiser, "Jury Acquits Men Charged with Raping Prostitute," *Washington Post*, September 29, 1981, B3.

Chapter 6

1. Andrea Dworkin, "The Night and Danger," *Letters from a War Zone* (New York: Lawrence Hill Books, 1988), 13–18. Dominance feminists are also referred to as radical feminists. I use "dominance feminism" for two reasons: first, this label specifies the feminist legal politics I focus on in this chapter, which are closely

associated with the legal analysis of Catharine MacKinnon; and second, this particular lineage of feminist activists did not work to uproot prevailing state and political structures, and therefore I consider "radical feminism" to be a misnomer. On TBTN marches in the 1970s, see Elizabeth Currans, *Marching Dykes, Liberated Sluts, and Concerned Mothers: Women Transforming Public Space* (Urbana: University of Illinois Press, 2017); Anne Valk, "Remembering Together: Take Back the Night and the Public Memory of Feminism," in *U.S. Women's History: Untangling the Threads of Sisterhood*, ed. Leslie Brown, Jacqueline Castledine, and Anne Valk (New Brunswick, NJ: Rutgers University Press, 2017), chap. 10; and Maria Bevacqua, *Rape on the Public Agenda: Feminism and the Politics of Sexual Assault* (Lebanon, NH: University Press of New England, 2000). Many thanks to Melinda Chateauvert for providing the inspiration for this chapter.

2. For a history of anticarceral feminist mobilizations against violence during this period, see Emily Thuma, *All Our Trials: Prisons, Policing, and the Feminist Fight to End Violence* (Urbana: University of Illinois Press, 2019). On the Combahee River Collective, see Keeanga-Yamahtta Taylor, ed., *How We Get Free: Black Feminism and the Combahee River Collective* (Chicago: Haymarket Books, 2017). On WfH, see Silvia Federici, *Wages for Housework* (New York: Autonomedia, 2017); Selma James, *Sex, Race and Class, the Perspective of Winning: A Selection of Writings, 1952–2011* (Oakland: PM, 2012); Louise Toupin, *Wages for Housework: A History of an International Feminist Movement, 1972–1977* (London: Pluto, 2018); Beth Capper and Arlen Austin, "'Wages for Housework Means Wages *against* Heterosexuality': On the Archives of Black Women for Wages for Housework and Wages Due Lesbians," *GLQ* 24, no. 4 (2018): 445–466; and Selma James and Wilmette Brown, interview by Terry Gross, *Fresh Air*, February 21, 1980. On sex worker activism, see Melinda Chateauvert, *Sex Workers Unite: A History of the Movement from Stonewall to Slutwalk* (Boston: Beacon, 2014). On sex worker labor negotiations and activisms, see Heather Berg, *Porn Work: Sex, Labor, and Late Capitalism* (Chapel Hill: University of North Carolina Press, 2021).

3. Kenna Quinet, "Prostitutes as Victims of Serial Homicide: Trends and Case Characteristics, 1970–2009," *Homicide Studies* 15, no. 1 (2011): 74–100; Black Coalition Fighting Back Serial Murders statement, n.d., BCFB. In 1985 the *Los Angeles Times* reported that "usually one prostitute a month is murdered in Los Angeles County—twice as many as ten years ago." Miles Corwin, "Life on the Street," *Los Angeles Times*, December 8, 1985. In 2015 Terrion Williamson counted more than sixty serial murder cases "in which Black women were the sole or primary targets" since the mid-1970s. Terrion Williamson, "In the Life: Black Women and Serial Murder," *Social Text* 33, no. 1 (March 2015): 95–114. Between 1970 and 2009, over one-third of all serial murder victims were women marked as "prostitutes." However, Williamson refuses to replicate the social scientific preoccupation with "numbers, data, and data collection" in serial murder research and instead works with this material "to index serial murder as a gendered form of premature black death that is continuous and ongoing and is irreducible to the specific locations or circumstances in which individual deaths occur." Terrion L. Williamson, "Of Serial Murder and True Crime: Some Preliminary Thoughts on Black Feminist Research

Praxis and the Implications of Settler Colonialism," *Environment and Planning D: Society and Space* 39, no. 1 (February 2021): 22–29. See also John Fountain and journalism students at Roosevelt University, "Unforgotten: The Untold Story of Murdered Chicago Women," accessed July 29, 2021, https://www.unforgotten51.com.

4. Lou Cannon, "Los Angeles Lives in Fear of Strangler," *Washington Post*, January 8, 1978; Black Coalition Fighting Back Serial Murders statement, n.d., BCFB; Rachel West, "U.S. PROStitutes Collective," in *Sex Work: Writings by Women in the Sex Industry*, ed. Frédérique Delacoste and Pricilla Alexander (Berkeley: Cleis, 1987), 287–289.

5. This is work that Black feminists in Black Women for Wages for Housework had been advancing since the mid-1970s. Margaret Prescod and Wilmette Brown were the likely coauthors of *Money for Prostitutes Is Money for Black Women*, a pamphlet quoted in chapter 4. Pamphlet, Black Women for Wages for Housework, ca. January 1977, in author's possession, also available online at freedomarchives.org.

6. International Prostitutes Collective and Nina Lopez-Jones, eds., *Some Mother's Daughter: The Hidden Movement of Prostitute Women against Violence* (London: Crossroads Books, 1999), 157; statement by U.S. PROStitutes Collective, February 1, 1989, BCFB. For a Black feminist analysis of the multiplicative effect of law enforcement on the "male violence matrix," see Beth E. Richie, *Arrested Justice: Black Women, Violence, and America's Prison Nation* (New York: New York University Press, 2012).

7. On the sex wars, see especially Whitney Strub, *Perversion for Profit: The Politics of Pornography and the Rise of the New Right* (New York: Columbia University Press, 2010), chap. 7; Lorna N. Bracewell, *Why We Lost the Sex Wars: Sexual Freedom in the #MeToo Era* (Minneapolis: University of Minnesota Press, 2021); and Lisa Duggan and Nan D. Hunter, *Sex Wars: Sexual Dissent and Political Culture* (New York: Routledge, 1996). See also "Coming Apart: Feminists and the Conflict over Pornography," *Off Our Backs* (special issue) 15, no. 6 (June 1985): 6–14.

8. Combahee River Collective, "Why Did They Die? A Document of Black Feminism," *Radical America* 13, no. 6 (December 1979): 41; Cheryl Devall and Margaret Tarter, "Multiple Murders Provoke Shock, Fear in Community," *Bay State Banner*, February 8, 1979; Nancy McMillan, "The Murders in Roxbury," *Boston Phoenix*, March 27, 1979; Gayle Pollard, Carmen Fields, and Viola Osgood, "Six Slain Women, and Those Who Loved Them," *Boston Globe*, April 1, 1979. See also *Since January, Twelve Black Women . . .* , pamphlet, Women Defending Women, n.d., in author's possession. Many thanks to Melinda Chateauvert for sharing this source. In other accounts, Ricketts's and Foye's bodies were found in garbage bags and a bedspread.

9. Jaime Grant, "Who's Killing Us?," in *Femicide: The Politics of Woman Killing*, ed. Jill Radford and Diana E. H. Russell (Boston: Twayne, 1992), 145–160.

10. Terrion L. Williamson, "Who Is Killing Us," in *Ain't Gonna Let Nobody Turn Me Around: Forty Years of Movement Building with Barbara Smith*, ed. Alethia Jones and Virginia Eubanks (Albany: State University of New York Press, 2014), 65–70; Barbara Smith, interview by Kimberly Springer, in Jones, *Ain't Gonna Let Nobody*, 72. On Black feminism and the Combahee River Collective, see especially

Combahee River Collective, "A Black Feminist Statement," in *Words of Fire: An Anthology of African-American Feminist Thought*, ed. Beverly Guy-Sheftall (New York: New Press, 1995), 231–240; Barbara Smith, ed., *Home Girls: A Black Feminist Anthology* (New York: Kitchen Table, Women of Color Press, 1983); and Taylor, ed., *How We Get Free*.

11. Combahee River Collective, "Why Did They Die?," 44–45 (emphasis in original). See also Terrion L. Williamson, "Why Did They Die? On Combahee and the Serialization of Black Death," *Souls* 19, no. 3 (2017): 328–341; Christina Hanhardt, *Safe Space: Gay Neighborhood History and the Politics of Violence* (Durham, NC: Duke University Press, 2013), 126; Grace Kyungwon Hong and Roderick A. Ferguson, ed., *Strange Affinities: The Gender and Sexual Politics of Comparative Racialization* (Durham, NC: Duke University Press), 14–16; and Thuma, *All Our Trials*, 128.

12. Combahee River Collective, "Why Did They Die?," 44, 46–47.

13. "Take Back the Night History," 2, n.d., Take Back the Night, Box 2, Sondra Gayle Stein Papers, Special Collections and Archives, Northeastern University, Boston; Combahee River Collective, "Why Did They Die?," 43. See also Thuma, *All Our Trials*, 137. One such coalition, the Coalition for Women's Safety, participated in the efforts to fight the police brutality case of Bellana Borde, a student at Northeastern University who was assaulted by a white police officer and charged with battery of an officer. See Thuma, *All Our Trials*, 133.

14. Grant, "Who's Killing Us?," 89–90.

15. Rape Action Project press release, July 27, 1979, in author's possession. Many thanks to Rona Rothman for saving and sharing her materials from this action. Many thanks, as well, to Sue Kaufman for sharing her experiences and memories of this activism during our interview on July 27, 2009.

16. Rape Action Project press release; "Public Street Trial: Women vs Governor King," flyer and handout, in author's possession; "Join with All Women to Fight Rape!," petition, n.d., in author's possession; Kathy MacDonald, "King 'on Trial' for Rape in Women's Street Court," *Gay Community News*, August 11, 1979; "Women Charge King and Accomplices," *Equal Times*, August 12, 1979.

17. The New York Prostitutes' Union is also referred to elsewhere as the New York Prostitutes Collective. See Margaret Prescod, "Outlaw Poverty, Not Prostitutes," *Wages for Housework International Campaign Journal* (Spring 1982): 6. For more on Prescod's analysis and perspective as an Afro-Caribbean woman, see Margaret Prescod-Roberts, *Black Women: Bringing It All Back Home* (Bristol: Falling Wall, 1980).

18. Canon texts on Black women's sexuality and silence include Hortense J. Spillers, "Interstices: A Small Drama of Words," in *Pleasure and Danger: Exploring Female Sexuality*, ed. Carole Vance (New York: Routledge, 1984), 73–100; Evelyn Hammonds, "Black (W)holes and the Geometry of Black Female Sexuality," *Differences: A Journal of Feminist Cultural Studies* 6, nos. 2/3 (1994): 126–142; Darlene Clark-Hine, "Rape and the Inner Lives of Black Women in the Middle West: Preliminary Thoughts on the Culture of Dissemblance," *Signs: Journal of Women in Culture and Society* 14 (1989): 912; Cathy J. Cohen, "Punks, Bulldaggers, and Welfare Queens: The Radical Potential of Queer Politics?" *GLQ* 3, no. 4 (1997): 437; and

Patricia Hill Collins, *Black Sexual Politics: African Americans, Gender, and the New Racism* (New York: Routledge, 2005). On Black women's sexuality and sex work, see Linda Rae's oral history in Tricia Rose, *Longing to Tell: Black Women Talk about Sexuality and Intimacy* (New York: Farrar, Straus and Giroux, 2004), 95–120; Mireille Miller-Young, *A Taste for Brown Sugar: Black Women in Pornography* (Durham, NC: Duke University Press, 2014); and Siobhan Brooks, *Unequal Desires: Race and Erotic Capital in the Stripping Industry* (Albany: State University of New York Press, 2010). Histories include Cynthia M. Blair, *I've Got to Make My Livin': Black Women's Sex Work in Turn-of-the-Century Chicago* (Chicago: University of Chicago Press, 2010); Cheryl D. Hicks, *Talk with You like a Woman: African American Women, Justice, and Reform in New York, 1890–1935* (Chapel Hill: University of North Carolina Press, 2010); Victoria W. Wolcott, *Remaking Respectability: African American Women in Interwar Detroit* (Chapel Hill: University of North Carolina Press, 2001); and Saidiya Hartman, *Wayward Lives, Beautiful Experiments: Intimate Histories of Riotous Black Girls, Troublesome Women, and Queer Radicals* (New York: W. W. Norton, 2019).

19. "Working the Streets: Gloria Lockett's Story," interview by Siobhan Brooks, n.d., Sin City Alternative Professionals' Association website, accessed December 13, 2013, archived webpage in author's possession. On the California Prostitutes' Education Project, which was also called the California Prevention Education Project, see Nancy E. Stoller, *Lessons from the Damned: Queers, Whores and Junkies Respond to AIDS* (New York: Routledge, 1997), esp. chap. 4. Lockett's writing appears in multiple essays in Delacoste and Alexander, *Sex Work*.

20. Gloria Lockett testimony, New York State Bar Association Committee on the Review of Criminal Law Hearings on Prostitution, 1985–1986, Box 17, COYOTE records, SCH.

21. Black Coalition Fighting Back Serial Murders, "Women Count—Count Women's Lives," statement to the Los Angeles Police Commission, February 21, 1989, BCFB. See also Thuma, *All Our Trials*; Chateauvert, *Sex Workers Unite*. For an example of contemporary human rights analysis, see Catherine Murphy, "Sex Workers' Rights Are Human Rights," Amnesty International, August 14, 2015, https://www.amnesty.org/en/latest/news/2015/08/sex-workers-rights-are-human-rights.

22. Scott Harris, "Impressed Council Oks More Police Overtime," *Los Angeles Times*, March 25, 1987.

23. Prescod, "Outlaw Poverty, Not Prostitutes"; "Counting Women's Lives," May 19, 1987, BCFB.

24. Sarah Wynter, "Whisper: Women Hurts in Systems of Prostitution Engaged in Revolt," in Delacoste and Alexander, *Sex Work*, 268–269. Giobbe formerly wrote as Sarah Wynter. Giobbe went on to state, "We reject the false hierarchy imposed on women by men which claims that 'call girls' are inherently better off than 'street walkers,' when the only real difference between the two is the private abuse of women juxtaposed to the public abuse of women." Wynter, 269.

25. Vednita Nelson, "Prostitution: Where Racism and Sexism Intersect," *Michigan Journal of Gender and Law* 1, no. 1 (1993): 81–89. "Prostitution: From Academia to Activism" was held on October 31, 1992. This symposium was the scene of the

organizers' controversial shutdown of a video art installation curated by Carol Jacobsen and exhibited in conjunction with the symposium. The video, which featured testimony from sex workers, allegedly threatened the safety of symposium attendees. See Tamar Lewin, "Furor on Exhibit at Law School Splits Feminists," *New York Times*, November 13, 1992; and Chateauvert, *Sex Workers Unite*, 185–199.

26. Nelson, "Prostitution," 81, 87. See also Vednita Carter and Evelina Giobbe, "Duet: Prostitution, Racism, and Feminist Discourse," *Hastings Women's Law Journal* 10, no. 1 (1999): 37–57.

27. Nelson, 89. For MacKinnon's policy recommendations for contemporary sex work, see Catharine A. MacKinnon, "OnlyFans is Not a Safe Platform for 'Sex Work.' It is a Pimp," *New York Times*, September 6, 2021.

28. Crenshaw and MacKinnon have since collaborated on drafting a new constitutional amendment for equal rights. See Catharine A. MacKinnon and Kimberlé W. Crenshaw, "Reconstituting the Future: An Equality Amendment," *Yale Law Journal* 129 (December 26, 2019): 343–364. For Crenshaw on MacKinnon, see Kimberlé W. Crenshaw, "Close Encounters of Three Kinds: On Teaching Dominance Feminism and Intersectionality," *Tulsa Law Review* 46, no. 1 (2010): 151–189. See also Cheryl Nelson Butler, "A Critical Race Feminist Perspective on Prostitution & Sex Trafficking in America," *Yale Journal of Law and Feminism* 27, no. 1 (2015): 95–139.

29. Kathleen Lahey, "Women and Civil Liberties," in *The Sexual Liberals and the Attack on Feminism*, ed. Dorchen Leidholdt and Janice G. Raymond (New York: Pergamon, 1990), 201. On the power of the state to create social meaning, see Dorothy E. Roberts, "Race, Vagueness, and the Social Meaning of Order-Maintenance Policing," *Journal of Criminal Law and Criminology* 89, no. 3 (Spring 1999): 775–836; and Bernard E. Harcourt, *Illusion of Order: The False Promise of Broken Windows Policing* (Cambridge, MA: Harvard University Press, 2001).

30. Catharine MacKinnon, "Prostitution and Civil Rights," *Michigan Journal of Gender and Law* 1, no. 1 (1993): 21.

31. At the Michigan Law conference, one speaker, identified only as an anonymous "call girl," called for the legalization of prostitution and the abolition of prostitution-related laws. Anonymous, "Prostitution: A Narrative by a Former 'Call Girl,'" *Michigan Journal of Gender and Law* 1, no. 1 (1993): 105–106.

32. Levine's report was originally published in British English. I have changed the language to the U.S. spelling for consistency. Philippa Levine, *Prostitution in Florida: A Report Presented to the Gender Bias Study Commission of the Supreme Court of Florida* (Tallahassee: Policy Studies, Florida State University College of Law, 1988), 205.

33. Margaret Baldwin, "Public Women and the Feminist State," *Harvard Women's Law Journal* 20 (1997): 124–125.

34. Baldwin, 125.

35. Baldwin, 139–140; Levine, *Prostitution in Florida*, 37, 206–207. Levine not only recognized the danger of sexual policing; she would also go on to publish a deeply researched study on the violent and harmful matrix of colonialism, racism, and sexual policing. Philippa Levine, *Prostitution, Race, and Politics: Policing Venereal Disease in the British Empire* (New York: Routledge, 2003).

36. The Florida statute is 796.09; in Minnesota, it is 611A.81. Over thirty-five states and Washington, DC, currently have such civil remedies in place. See the documentary Kate Nace Day, dir., *A Civil Remedy* (2014); and Regina Austin, "'A Civil Remedy' Backstory: How Law Professor Kate Nace Day Came to Make a Documentary Short about Domestic Sex Trafficking," *Docs and the Law Blog*, July 17, 2015, https://www.law.upenn.edu/live/news/5689-a-civil-remedy-backstory-how-law-professor-kate. The Trafficking Victims Protection Reauthorization Act of 2008 included a provision for civil remedies in federal court. Melissa Farley, Kenneth Franzblau, and M. Alexis Kennedy, "Online Prostitution and Trafficking," *Albany Law Review* 77, no. 3 (2013–2014): 1083. On the antipornography ordinance campaign, see Duggan and Hunter, *Sex Wars*; and Catharine A. MacKinnon and Andrea Dworkin, *In Harm's Way: The Pornography Civil Rights Hearings* (Cambridge, MA: Harvard University Press, 1997). For a discussion of the civil prostitution-damages laws, see Beverly Balos and Mary Louise Fellows, "A Matter of Prostitution: Becoming Respectable," *New York University Law Review* 74 (1999): 1220–1303. On the ordinance campaign in Minnesota, see Kirsten Delegard, "Contested Geography: The Campaign against Pornography and the Battle for Urban Space in Minneapolis," in *U.S. Women's History: Untangling the Threads of Sisterhood*, ed. Leslie Brown, Jacqueline Castledine, and Anne Valk (New Brunswick, NJ: Rutgers University Press, 2017), chap. 9.

37. MacKinnon, "Prostitution and Civil Rights," 13–31; Kathleen Barry, *Female Sexual Slavery* (New York: Prentice-Hall, 1979), chap. 2; MacKinnon, "Prostitution and Civil Rights," 22; Judy Klemesrud, "A Personal Crusade against Prostitution," *New York Times*, June 24, 1985; Dorchen Leidholdt, "When Women Defend Pornography," in Leidholdt and Raymond, *Sexual Liberals*, 129.

38. MacKinnon, "Prostitution and Civil Rights," 30. Perhaps these civil remedies did not address women's right to sue police officers who entrapped, extorted, or abused them because other civil remedies were available, such as Section 1983 of Title 42 of the United States Code, which granted individuals the right to sue state employees operating "under color of state law." However, Section 1983 delivered mixed results that were not improved or remedied by the dominance feminists' civil rights legislation. See, for example, Sarah Eschholz and Michael S. Vaughn, "Police Sexual Violence and Rape Myths: Civil Liability under Section 1983," *Journal of Criminal Justice* 29, no. 5 (September–October 2001): 389–405.

39. E. Walter Terne, "Report of the Florida Supreme Court Gender Bias Study Commission," *Florida Law Review* 42 (1990): 898, 908. In 1993, buoyed by the victory in Florida, a coalition of WHISPER activists and University of Minnesota Law School faculty and students convened a conference to develop antiprostitution legislation with a number of state authorities, including members of the state legislature, representatives from the city attorney's office and the public defender's office, and police officers. Five months later, Minnesota's version of the bill passed. Balos and Fellows, "Matter of Prostitution."

40. Balas v. Ruzzo, 703 So. 2d 1076 (Fla. Dist. Ct. App. 1998); Shay-Ann M. Heiser Singh, "Comment: The Predator Accountability Act: Empowering Women in Prostitution to Pursue Their Own Justice," *DePaul Law Review* 56 (2007): 1035.

41. *Balas v. Ruzzo*, 703 So. 2d 1076.

42. *Balas v. Ruzzo*, 703 So. 2d 1076.

43. Balos and Fellows, "Matter of Prostitution," 1299. For an analysis of civil remedies within a racial context, see Melissa Milewski, *Litigating across the Color Line: Civil Cases between Black and White Southerners from the End of Slavery to Civil Rights* (New York: Oxford University Press, 2017). Many thanks to Myisha Eatmon for bringing this insight to my attention.

44. *WHISPER Newsletter*, Winter/Spring 1992, Box 19, COYOTE records, SCH; Holly Fechner, "Three Stories of Prostitution in the West: Prostitutes' Groups, Law and Feminist 'Truth,'" *Columbia Journal of Gender and Law* 4 (1994): 26–72. On the "carceral turn in feminist advocacy movements," see Elizabeth Bernstein, "Carceral Politics as Gender Justice? The 'Traffic in Women' and Neoliberal Circuits of Crime, Sex, and Rights," *Theory and Society* 41, no. 3 (May 2012): 233–259. On "john schools," see Elizabeth Bernstein, *Temporarily Yours: Intimacy, Authenticity, and the Commerce* (Chicago: University of Chicago Press, 2007), 134–141.

45. *WHISPER Newsletter*, Winter/Spring 1992, 3–6, 4, Box 19, COYOTE records, SCH (emphasis added).

46. See Sandra Moser, "Anti-prostitution Zones: Justifications for Abolition," *Journal of Criminal Law and Criminology* 91, no. 4 (Summer 2001): 1101–1126; Lisa Sanchez, "Enclosure Acts and Exclusionary Practices: Neighborhood Associations, Community Police, and the Expulsion of the Sexual Outlaw," in *Between Law and Culture: Relocating Legal Studies*, ed. David Theo Goldberg, Michael Musheno, and Lisa C. Bower (Minneapolis: University of Minnesota Press, 2001), 122–140; Lisa Sanchez, "The Global E-rotic Subject, the Ban, and the Prostitute-Free Zone: Sex Work and the Theory of Differential Exclusion," *Environment and Planning D: Society and Space* 22 (2004): 861–883; and Katherine Beckett and Steve Herbert, *Banished: The New Social Control in Urban America* (New York: Oxford University Press, 2011).

47. Sanchez, "Global E-rotic Subject," 871 (emphasis in original); Beckett and Herbert, *Banished*, 14. For a discussion of the contemporary impact of, and activism against, these spatial banishment measure, see the epilogue.

48. Michael Shively et al., *An Overview of Exclusion Zones ("SOAP Orders") for Sex Buyers in the United States* (Cambridge, MA: Abt Associates and the National Institute of Justice, 2013). See also Beckett and Herbert, *Banished*. The city-commissioned report on exclusion zones in Portland only researched racial disparities in Drug-Free Zones, not Prostitution-Free Zones. See David Ashton, "Life after Prostitution-Free Zones," *East Portland News*, n.d, 2007, https://eastpdxnews.com/fire-and-police/street-sex-part-3-life-after-prostitution-free-zones/; and Gay and Lesbian Activists Alliance of Washington, D.C., "Testimony on Bill 19-567," January 24, 2012, Gay and Lesbian Activists Alliance of Washington, D.C., http://glaa.org/archive/2012/glaaonpfzso124.htm.

49. Sandra Minor, *"Prostitution": 1997 Herman Goldstein Excellence in Problem Solving Award* (Saint Petersburg, FL: Saint Petersburg Police Department, 1997), 2, 3, 6–7. In 1996 Sandra Minor was involved in the murder of TyRon Lewis, a Black youth. This violence triggered two separate uprisings in Saint Petersburg, one after

the murder and one after the county grand jury ruled the murder "justifiable homicide." Minor and her partner, James Knight, remained on the force. "2 Officers Shot after White Officer Is Cleared in Black Man's Death," *New York Times*, November 14, 1996, A20; "Riot Erupts in St. Petersburg, Florida after White Cop Shoots and Kills Black Motorist," *Jet*, November 11, 1996, 12.

50. Skogan quoted in Tanya Erzen, "Turnstile Jumpers and Broken Windows: Policing Disorder in New York City," in *Zero Tolerance: Quality of Life and the New Police Brutality in New York City*, ed. Andrea McArdle and Tanya Erzen (New York: New York University Press, 2001), 21.

51. Kenneth Conboy testimony, New York State Bar Association Committee on the Review of Criminal Law Hearings on Prostitution, 1985–1986, Box 17, COYOTE records, SCH.

52. Linda Fairstein testimony, New York State Bar Association Committee on the Review of Criminal Law Hearings on Prostitution, 1985–1986, Box 17, COYOTE records, SCH; David Giacopassi and Jerry Sparger, "Cognitive Dissonance in Vice Enforcement," *American Journal of Police* 10, no. 2 (1991): 49, 48.

53. Nina Lopez-Jones, "Workers: Introducing the English Collective of Prostitutes," in Delacoste and Alexander, *Sex Work*, 274–275; "Violence against Women in the Sex Industry," *Network: News from the English Collective of Prostitutes*, July 1983 (emphasis in original); Fechner, "Three Stories of Prostitution," 46.

54. Michael Massing, "The Blue Revolution," *New York Review of Books*, November 19, 1998.

55. Levine, *Prostitution in Florida*, 187, 210; Harcourt, *Illusion of Order*, 207.

56. Crenshaw, "Close Encounters of Three Kinds," 163.

57. "Women Count—Count Women's Lives." See especially Laura McTighe and Deon Haywood, "Front Porch Revolution: Resilience Space, Demonic Grounds, and the Horizons of a Black Feminist Otherwise," *Signs: Journal of Women in Culture and Society* 44, no. 1 (Autumn 2018): 25–52; INCITE! Women of Color Against Violence, ed., *Color of Violence: The INCITE! Anthology* (Durham, NC: Duke University Press, 2016); Kimberlé Williams Crenshaw and Andrea J. Ritchie, *Say Her Name: Resisting Police Brutality against Black Women* (New York: African American Policy Forum and the Center for Intersectionality and Social Policy Studies at Columbia Law School, July 2015). Andrea J. Ritchie provides an essential study of police abuses and women of color activisms in *Invisible No More: Police Violence against Black Women and Women of Color* (Boston: Beacon, 2017).

Epilogue

1. Throughout this epilogue, "woman" is fully inclusive of trans women and all people who identify as women. Sexually profiled migrant women are especially vulnerable to police abuse, in addition to deportation. See, for example, Laura María Agustín, *Sex at the Margins: Migration, Labour Markets and the Rescue Industry* (London: Zed Books, 2007); and Molly Smith and Juno Mac, *Revolting Prostitutes: The Fight for Sex Workers' Rights* (New York: Verso, 2018), chap. 3. On Black women's vulnerability to police violence, see Michelle S. Jacobs, "The Violent State: Black

Women's Invisible Struggle against Police Violence," *William and Mary Journal of Women and the Law* 24 (2017): 39–100.

2. Lisa Rayam and Russ Spencer with Morse Diggs, Fox News, "Atlanta Prostitution," YouTube video, 3:10, aired January 28, 2013, posted by Michael Julian Bond on July 15, 2015, https://www.youtube.com/watch?v=Ing6AeOh7q8; Bill Torpy, "Often Vilified, Midtown Crime Fighter Moves On," *Atlanta Journal-Constitution*, June 4, 2014. Trans women were singled out for demonization in this particular battle. It is also worth noting that a gay man later took over the Midtown Ponce Security Alliance and continued the work of vilifying and harassing trans sex workers. Dyana Bagby, "Midtown Ponce Security Alliance Brings Back That Ol' Tired Complaint of Violent Trans Prostitutes," *Georgia Voice*, September 23, 2014. For a history of how white middle-class gay men and women developed punishing crime politics targeting trans people of color, see Christina Hanhardt, *Safe Space: Gay Neighborhood History and the Politics of Violence* (Durham, NC: Duke University Press, 2013).

3. Michael Shively et al., *An Overview of Exclusion Zones ("SOAP Orders") for Sex Buyers in the United States* (Cambridge, MA: Abt Associates and the National Institute of Justice, 2013), 25; Lisa Sanchez, "The Global E-rotic Subject, the Ban, and the Prostitute-Free Zone: Sex Work and the Theory of Differential Exclusion," *Environment and Planning D: Society and Space* 22 (2004): 871; Manny Diaz, *Miami Transformed: Rebuilding America One Neighborhood, One City at a Time* (Philadelphia: University of Pennsylvania Press, 2012), 140–141. As discussed in chapter 6, spatial exclusion orders can take many forms. In some cities, police officers had the authority to impose spatial restrictions on women in lieu of arrest, before they had been convicted of a crime. However, exclusion orders were more often appended as a condition of probation.

4. See chapter 5 for a discussion of loitering with intent laws and chapter 4 for a discussion of "floaters," the predecessor to banishment laws. For the earliest test case of banishment laws, see *In re White*, 97 Cal. App. 3d 144 (1979); and Joseph Whitaker, "Plan to Restrict Prostitutes, Drug Figures Drafted," *Washington Post*, February 28, 1980. For the Illinois banishment law history and test case, see Rana Sampson and Michael Scott, *Tackling Crime and Other Public-Safety Problems: Case Studies in Problem-Solving* (Washington, DC: U.S. Department of Justice, Office of Community Oriented Policing Services, 1999), 155–157; Chase Leonhard, "Roadblocks to Crime: Travel Restrictions for Convicted Prostitutes," *FBI Law Enforcement Bulletin*, June 1, 1994; and *People v. Pickens* 186 Ill. App. 3d 456 (1989). For more literature on prostitution banishment orders, see Sandra Moser, "Anti-prostitution Zones: Justifications for Abolition," *Journal of Criminal Law and Criminology* 91, no. 4 (Summer 2001): 1101–1126; William Garth Snider, "Banishment: The History of Its Use and a Proposal for Its Abolition under the First Amendment," *New England Journal on Criminal and Civil Confinement* 24 (1998): 455–509; Karen Bancroft, "Zones of Exclusion: Urban Spatial Policies, Social Justice, and Social Services," *Journal of Sociology and Social Welfare* 39, no. 3 (2012); Lisa Sanchez, "Enclosure Acts and Exclusionary Practices: Neighborhood Associations, Community Police,

and the Expulsion of the Sexual Outlaw," in *Between Law and Culture: Relocating Legal Studies*, ed. David Theo Goldberg, Michael Musheno, and Lisa C. Bower (Minneapolis: University of Minnesota Press, 2001), 122–140; and Katherine Beckett and Steve Herbert, *Banished: The New Social Control in Urban America* (New York: Oxford University Press, 2011), 45.

5. Clare Sears, *Arresting Dress: Cross-Dressing, Law, and Fascination in Nineteenth-Century San Francisco* (Durham, NC: Duke University Press, 2015); Mogulescu quoted in Andrea J. Ritchie, *Invisible No More: Police Violence against Black Women and Women of Color* (Boston: Beacon, 2017), 149; American Friends Service Committee, *Struggle for Justice: A Report on Crime and Punishment in America, Prepared for the American Friends Service Committee,* quoted in David Garland, *The Culture of Control: Crime and Social Order in Contemporary Society* (New York: Oxford University Press, 2001), 56; George Kelling and James Q. Wilson, "Broken Windows," *Atlantic*, March 1982.

6. Juhu Thukral and Melissa Ditmore, *Revolving Door: An Analysis of Street-Based Prostitution in New York City* (New York: Sex Workers Project at the Urban Justice Center, 2003), 35–36, https://sexworkersproject.org/downloads/RevolvingDoor.pdf; Complaint and Demand for a Jury Trial, D.H., N.H., K.H. f/k/a/ J.H., Natasha Martin, Tiffaney Grissom, R.G., A.B. and Sarah Marchando, individually and on behalf of a class of all others similarly situated against the City of New York, United States District Court Southern District of New York, 16 CV 7698, https://lawprofessors.typepad.com/files/stamped_complaint.pdf; Meredith Dank, Jennifer Yahner, and Lilly Yu, *Consequences of Policing Prostitution: An Analysis of Individuals Arrested and Prosecuted for Commercial Sex in New York City* (Washington, DC: Urban Institute Justice Police Center, 2017), 30, https://www.urban.org/sites/default/files/publication/89451/legal_aid_final_0.pdf; Thukral and Ditmore, *Revolving Door*, 35, 36, 37. The website policeprostitutionandpolitics.com maintains an exhaustive list of receipts of police violence against sexually profiled women.

7. Yolande M. S. Tomlinson and Black Women's Blueprint, "Invisible Betrayal: Police Violence and the Rapes of Black Women in the United States," *Women's All Points Bulletin*, September 22, 2014, https://tbinternet.ohchr.org/Treaties/CAT/Shared%20Documents/USA/INT_CAT_CSS_USA_18555_E.pdf; Thukral and Ditmore, *Revolving Door*, 37, 38; Alliance for a Safe and Diverse DC, *Move Along*, 54, 53; Matthias Gafni, "Oakland Police Scandal: How Often Are Cops Having Sex with Prostitutes?" *Mercury News*, July 2, 2016, https://www.mercurynews.com/2016/07/02/oakland-police-scandal-how-often-are-cops-having-sex-with-prostitutes/. See also Dank, Yahner, and Yu, *Consequences of Policing Prostitution*, 28–29; Ethan Brown, "What the DOJ's Report on Baltimore Teaches Us about Cops, Sex Workers, and Corruption," *Marshall Project*, August 16, 2016, https://www.themarshallproject.org/2016/08/16/what-the-doj-s-report-on-baltimore-teaches-us-about-cops-sex-workers-and-corruption; James Barron, "Ex-Detective Admits Running Brothels in the Worst NYPD Scandal in Years," *New York Times*, May 22, 2019, https://www.nytimes.com/2019/05/22/nyregion/nypd-detective-brothel.html; Ian Duncan, "Former Baltimore Officer Pleads Guilty to Pimping Teenage Wife," *Baltimore Sun*,

January 22, 2014, https://www.baltimoresun.com/news/crime/bs-xpm-2014-01-22-bs-md-ci-officer-prostitution-plea-20140122-story.html; Peter B. Kraska and Victor E. Kappeler, "To Serve and Pursue: Exploring Police Sexual Violence against Women," *Justice Quarterly* 12, no. 1 (1995): 85–111; and Andrea Ritchie and Priscilla Bustamante, "Shrouded in Silence: Police Sexual Violence: What We Know and What We Can Do About It," Interrupting Criminalization, n.d, https://static1.squarespace.com/static/5ee39ec764dbd7179cf1243c/t/609b0bb8fc3271012c4a93c5/1620773852750/Shrouded+in+Silence.pdf.

8. Jenavieve Hatch, "Sex Workers in Alaska Say Cops Are Abusing Their Power to Solicit Sex Acts," *HuffPost*, August 17, 2017, https://www.huffpost.com/entry/sex-workers-in-alaska-say-cops-are-abusing-their-power-to-solicit-sex_n_596e1d26e4b010d77673e488; Emily Lawler, "Undercover Michigan Police Officers Can No Longer Legally Have Sex with Prostitutes," MLive, December 13, 2017, https://www.mlive.com/news/2017/12/undercover_michigan_police_off.html; Albert Samaha, "An 18-Year-Old Said She Was Raped While in Police Custody. The Officers Say She Consented," BuzzFeed News, February 7, 2019, https://www.buzzfeednews.com/article/albertsamaha/this-teenager-accused-two-on-duty-cops-of-rape-she-had-no; Lily Dancyger, "Alaska Cops Defend Their 'Right' to Sexual Contact with Sex Workers before Arresting Them," *Glamour*, July 10, 2017, https://www.glamour.com/story/alaska-cops-defend-sexual-contact-sex-workers-arrests; Tracy Clark-Flory, "Alaska Police: We Need to Have 'Sexual Contact' with Sex Workers," *Vocativ*, May 10, 2017, https://www.vocativ.com/428218/alaska-police-sexual-contact-sex-workers/index.html; and Kate Goldberg, "Time's Up: A Call to Ban the Use of Sex as an Investigatory Tactic in Alaska," *Alaska Law Review* 38, no. 1 (2021): 65–91; Dave Philipps, "Former Oklahoma City Police Officer Found Guilty of Rapes," *New York Times*, December 10, 2015, https://www.nytimes.com/2015/12/11/us/former-oklahoma-city-police-officer-found-guilty-of-rapes.html; Danny Monteverde, "New Orleans Police Officer Henry Hollins Sentenced to 45 Years for Kidnapping and Attempted Rape," *The Times-Picayune*, March 5, 2011, https://www.nola.com/news/crime_police/article_09bb7e29-d39b-5ad8-bd8a-30fe11d4bb5a.html; Joshua Kaplan and Joaquin Sapien, "NYPD Cops Cash in on Sex Trade Arrests with Little Evidence, While Black and Brown New Yorkers Pay the Price," *ProPublica*, December 7, 2020, https://www.propublica.org/article/nypd-cops-cash-in-on-sex-trade-arrests-with-little-evidence-while-black-and-brown-new-yorkers-pay-the-price; African American Policy Forum email, "The Status of Black Women and State Violence," March 25, 2021.

The woman whose apartment was raided was charged with prostitution and child endangerment; she lost custody of her children for two months after this raid. See Kaplan and Sapien, "NYPD Cops Cash In." The Michigan bills are now Public Acts 194–195 of 2017. Hawaii passed its ban on police engaging in penetrative sex in 2014: Eliana Dockterman, "Hawaii Police Won't Get to Have Sex with Prostitutes Anymore," *Time*, March 26, 2014, https://time.com/33333/hawaii-law-police-prostitutes/.

Police sexual violence is an ongoing issue. See, for example, Melissa Gira Grant and Emma Whitford, "Family, Former Attorney of Queens Woman Who Fell to Her

Death in Vice Sting Say She Was Sexually Assaulted, Pressured to Become an Informant," *Appeal*, December 15, 2017, https://theappeal.org/family-former-attorney-of-queens-woman-who-fell-to-her-death-in-vice-sting-say-she-was-sexually-d67461a12f1/; and Dylan Segelbaum and Sam Ruland, "Tactics in Prostitution Stings Raise Questions," *York Daily Record*, May 25, 2019, https://www.ydr.com/story/news/watchdog/2019/05/06/investigation-undercover-prostitution-sting-cases-pennsylvania-police/3344293002/. See also Phillip Walters, "Would a Cop Do This: Ending the Practice of Sexual Sampling in Prostitution Stings," *Law and Inequality: A Journal of Theory and Practice* 29 (2011): 451–476; and Anne Gray Fischer, "Police Sexual Violence is Hidden in Plain Sight," *Boston Review*, July 20, 2020, http://bostonreview.net/law-justice/anne-gray-fischer-reform-wont-end-police-violence.

9. Martin D. Schwartz, *National Institute of Justice Visiting Fellowship: Police Investigation of Rape—Roadblocks and Solutions* (Washington, DC: National Institute of Justice, December 2010), 23, 46; Kevin Ellis, "Woman Claims Rape, Police Arrest for Prostitution," *Gaston Gazette*, February 19, 2020, https://www.gastongazette.com/news/20200219/woman-claims-rape-police-arrest-for-prostitution; Lisa Rathke, "Bill in Vermont Would Decriminalize Prostitution," Associated Press, February 6, 2020, https://apnews.com/article/2f92fad4f8154f934183eb84b8048d39. On feminist proposals and collaborations with police, see, for example, Marie Gottschalk, *The Prison and the Gallows: The Politics of Mass Incarceration in America* (Cambridge: Cambridge University Press, 2006), chap. 5; Beth E. Richie, *Arrested Justice: Black Women, Violence, and America's Prison Nation* (New York: New York University Press, 2012); Aya Gruber, *The Feminist War on Crime: The Unexpected Role of Women's Liberation in Mass Incarceration* (Berkeley: University of California Press, 2020); Mary Ellen Gale, "Calling in the Girl Scouts: Feminist Legal Theory and Police Misconduct," *Loyola of Los Angeles Law Review* 34 (2001): 691–746; and Jane Sadusky, *Working Effectively with the Police: A Guide for Battered Women's Advocates* (Minneapolis: Battered Women's Justice Project, August 2001).

10. Survey cited in Ritchie, *Invisible No More*, 137–138. On trans people's experiences of carceral violence and resistance to it, see especially Eric A. Stanley and Nat Smith, *Captive Genders: Trans Embodiment and the Prison Industrial Complex* (Oakland: AK, 2015).

11. Karina Piser, "The Walking While Trans Ban Is 'Stop and Frisk 2.0,'" *Nation*, February 19, 2020, https://www.thenation.com/article/activism/walking-while-trans-repeal/; Graham Rayman, "NYPD Changes How It Applies Loitering Law as It Settles Legal Aid Lawsuit over Arrests of Transgender People, Women Accused of Prostitution," *New York Daily News*, June 5, 2019, https://www.nydailynews.com/new-york/nyc-crime/ny-nypd-settles-legal-aid-lawsuit-loitering-prostitution-transgender-20190605-exywzz6t6jdwrnngz3k26c3gaa-story.html; Complaint and Demand for a Jury Trial, 24; Anna North, "The Movement to Decriminalize Sex Work, Explained," Vox, August 2, 2019, https://www.vox.com/2019/8/2/20692327/sex-work-decriminalization-prostitution-new-york-dc; Jesse McKinley and Luis Ferré-Sadurní, "N.Y. Repeals Law That Critics Say Criminalized 'Walking While Trans,'" *New York Times*, February 3, 2021, https://www.nytimes.com/2021/02/03/nyregion/walking-while-trans-ban.html; Michael Gold and Sean Piccoli, "After a

Transgender Woman's Death at Rikers, Calls for Justice and Answers," *New York Times*, June 11, 2019, https://www.nytimes.com/2019/06/11/nyregion/layleen-polanco-xtravaganza-death-rikers-island.html; Katelyn Burns, "Why Police Often Single Out Trans People for Violence," *Vox*, June 23, 2020, https://www.vox.com/identities/2020/6/23/21295432/police-black-trans-people-violence.

12. Rick Rojas and Vanessa Swales, "18 Transgender Killings This Year Raise Fears of an 'Epidemic,'" *New York Times*, September 27, 2019, https://www.nytimes.com/2019/09/27/us/transgender-women-deaths.html; Lauren McGaughy, "Texas Leads the Nation in Transgender Murders. After the Latest Attack, the Dallas Trans Community Asks Why," *Dallas Morning News*, September 30, 2019, https://www.dallasnews.com/news/2019/09/30/texas-leads-nation-transgender-murders-according-national-lgbtq-organization/; "Fatal Violence against the Transgender and Gender Non-conforming Community in 2020," Human Rights Campaign, accessed July 30, 2021, https://www.hrc.org/resources/violence-against-the-trans-and-gender-non-conforming-community-in-2020; Alliance for a Safe and Diverse DC, *Move Along*, 41. See chapter 6 for a discussion of the serial murders of Black women.

13. Alliance for a Safe and Diverse DC, *Move Along*, 39.

14. Marko Robinson, "Activists Block Atlanta Prostitution Banishment Plan, Propose Alternatives," *Atlanta Progressive News*, July 21, 2013, https://atlantaprogressivenews.com/2013/07/21/activists-block-atlanta-prostitution-banishment-plan-propose-alternatives-update-1/; "Prostitution Free Zones Repealed in the District of Columbia," Global Network of Sex Work Projects press release, October 16, 2014, https://www.nswp.org/news/prostitution-free-zones-repealed-the-district-columbia; "Drug- and Prostitution-Free Zone Ordinances to Expire," *Portland Business Journal*, September 26, 2007, https://www.bizjournals.com/portland/stories/2007/09/24/daily18.html; Agustín, *Sex at the Margins*; Smith and Mac, *Revolting Prostitutes*; "Win! San Francisco Stops Using Condoms as Evidence," Transgender Law Center, April 16, 2013, https://transgenderlawcenter.org/archives/5402; "Condoms as Evidence," St. James Infirmary, https://www.stjamesinfirmary.org/wordpress/?page_id=2083; Barbara, interview by Carole, in *Sex Work: Writings by Women in the Sex Industry*, ed. Frédérique Delacoste and Pricilla Alexander (Berkeley: Cleis, 1987), 174. For more on the Solutions Not Punishment Collaborative, see snap4freedom.org.

15. Catherine Murphy, "Sex Workers' Rights Are Human Rights," Amnesty International, August 14, 2015, https://www.amnesty.org/en/latest/news/2015/08/sex-workers-rights-are-human-rights/; North, "Movement to Decriminalize"; Rathke, "Bill in Vermont"; Jess McKinley, "Bills to Decriminalize Prostitution Are Introduced. Is New York Ready?" *New York Times*, June 11, 2019, https://www.nytimes.com/2019/06/11/nyregion/prostitution-legal-ny.html; Timothy Williams, "In Washington, a Fight to Decriminalize Prostitution Divides Allies," *New York Times*, October 17, 2019, https://www.nytimes.com/2019/10/17/us/washington-legal-prostitution.html; Abigail Higgins, D.C. Could Be the First U.S. City to Decriminalize Sex Work," *The Lily*, October 27, 2019, https://www.thelily.com/dc-could-be-the-first-us-city-to-decriminalize-sex-work-here-are-arguments-from-both-sides-of-the

-debate/; Barbara Rodriguez, "What is the Future of Prostitution and Sex Work? Two States Preview Diverging Paths," *The 19th*, July 29, 2021, https://19thnews.org/2021/07/future-of-prostitution-and-sex-work-two-states-preview-diverging-paths/; Staff, "Seattle City Council Repeals 'Problematic' Prostitution Loitering Law Affecting Minorities," *KOMO News*, June 22, 2020, https://komonews.com/news/local/seattle-city-council-repeals-problematic-prostitution-loitering-law-affecting-minorities; Staff, "Burlington City Council Approves Decriminalizing Prostitution," *The Sun*, July 13, 2021, https://suncommunitynews.com/news/90509/burlington-city-council-approves-decriminalizing-prostitution/.

16. Men of color are just as vulnerable to wrongful arrest and police discrimination in gender-reversed sexual policing programs. See, for example, Kaplan and Sapien, "NYPD Cops Cash In." For a thorough discussion of the "Nordic Model" that carceral feminists support, which criminalizes the buyers of sex, see Alex Nielsen, "On the 'Nordic Model': The Ongoing Criminalization of Sex Workers," *Pulp*, July 1, 2018, https://medium.com/pulpmag/nordic-model-the-ongoing-criminalization-of-sex-workers-in-northern-europe-c1df02ba94ae; Melissa Gira Grant, *Playing the Whore: The Work of Sex Work* (New York: Verso, 2014), 73–74; Maggie McNeill, "Are You a Pimp?," *Honest Courtesan* (blog), December 9, 2019, https://maggiemcneill.com/2019/12/09/are-you-a-pimp; Manuel Gamiz Jr., "Woman Charged with Pimping after Online Sex Sting at Lehigh County Motel," *Morning Call*, December 30, 2015, https://www.mcall.com/news/breaking/mc-c-woman-charged-with-promoting-prostitution-in-lehigh-county-motel-20151230-story.html; Jeanette Lach, "Five Women Charged with Prostitution, Pimping," *Northwest Indiana Times*, September 6, 2013, https://www.nwitimes.com/news/local/lake/hammond/five-women-charged-with-prostitution-pimping/article_3e82106c-860d-5335-889d-705c9047ca8f.html; and Anna Spoerre, "Illinois Woman Charged with Human Trafficking, Pimping at Des Moines-Area Hotel," *Des Moines Register*, July 29, 2019, https://www.desmoinesregister.com/story/news/crime-and-courts/2019/07/29/illinois-woman-charged-human-trafficking-pimping-ankeny-east-dubuque-felony-quality-inn-suites-iowa/1855660001/. Many thanks to Mindy Chateauvert for locating and sharing these news sources.

17. Few quoted in Melinda Chateauvert, *Sex Workers Unite: A History of the Movement from Stonewall to Slutwalk* (Boston: Beacon, 2014), 4; Yannick Marshall, "'We'll Hold the Police Accountable!': The Useful Meaninglessness of Liberal-Speak," *Black Perspectives*, April 27, 2020, https://www.aaihs.org/well-hold-the-police-accountable-the-useful-meaninglessnesses-of-liberal-speak/.

18. The image of the race and gender "factory" comes from Peggy Pascoe, *What Comes Naturally: Miscengenation Law and the Making of Race in America* (New York: Oxford University Press, 2009), 11. "Invisible barriers" is inspired by Sara Ahmed, who uses this image to discuss inequity in higher education. Sara Ahmed, *On Being Included: Racism and Diversity in Institutional Life* (Durham, NC: Duke University Press), 175.

19. Mariame Kaba, *We Do This 'Til We Free Us: Abolitionist Organizing and Transforming Justice* (Chicago: Haymarket Books, 2021); Margaret Prescod, "Outlaw Poverty, Not Prostitutes," *Wages for Housework International Campaign Journal* (Spring

1982): 6. I was unable to find what percentage of the FBI's $9.3 billion budget in 2020 was dedicated to prostitution stings, or what percentage of the $115 billion that cities and states spent on police in 2017 went to prostitution-related misdemeanor enforcement, according to "State and Local Finance Initiative," Urban Institute, accessed July 30, 2021, https://www.urban.org/policy-centers/cross-center-initiatives/state-and-local-finance-initiative/state-and-local-backgrounders/police-and-corrections-expenditures. A 1987 study calculated that sixteen cities spent $7.5 million in 1985 (which at the time was more than some cities spent on all healthcare services). Julie Pearl, "The Highest Paying Customers: America's Cities and the Costs of Prostitution Control," *Hastings Law Journal* 38 (1987): 772. The costs of morals policing do not include the millions of dollars of taxpayer money spent to settle lawsuits brought by those falsely arrested on morals charges. See, for example, Kaplan and Sapien, "NYPD Cops Cash In."

Index

Page numbers in italics refer to illustrations and maps.

abortion, 123, 181
ACLU (American Civil Liberties Union), 92, 98, 100, 151
Acuna, Chile, 43
Adams, Ida May, 243n40
Adams, Joanna, 167
adult entertainment districts: in Atlanta, 139–141, 142; in Boston, 109, 114, 115, 116, 123, 124, 125, 131, 135, 139–140. *See also* Combat Zone (Boston)
Afro-American Patrolmen's League (Atlanta), 143
AIDS epidemic, 158, 164, 263n64
Alaska, 204
alcohol: criminalization of consuming, 156; drunkenness arrests, 72; Prohibition-era, police profits from, 29, 32, 38, 39, 42; underage drinking, 1, 215–216n1
American Civil Liberties Union (ACLU), 92, 98, 100, 151
American Legal Institute, 83
American Social Hygiene Association, 61, 62, 236n27
Amnesty International, 206
Amsterdam News (New York), 43
Amy, 173
Anchorage Police Department, 204
Ansa, J. P. (Atlanta), 153, 154
antiprostitution efforts: banishment programs, 195, 196, 201–202, 206; Progressive-era reforms, 18–25. *See also* morals laws; prostitution laws
Antiuk, Stephen, 204

antiviolence feminism, 174–186, 198–200. *See also names of people and organizations*
archives, 14–15
arrests: in the 1970s, soaring rates of, 172; Black women targeted for, 1–2, 113; cleared cases, 92; Depression-era escalation of, 46–48; and drug use, 159; economic incentives for, 124–125; in postwar Los Angeles, 77–78, 91–92, 97, 172, 239n5; racial disparities of, 28, 48–49, 52, 65, 69, 71–73, 77–78, 97, 106, 120, 172; repercussions of, 2; and serial murders, 176; statistics, 28, 48–49, 64, 65, 69, 227n9, 233n57, 239n5; World War II period mass arrests, 52, 64–67, 75
Arrington, Marvin, 164
Asian women, 7, 201
Atlanta, 14, 16, 35, 37, 137, 138–173; banishment laws in, 201–202, 206; Black leadership, 141–146, 157–158; broken windows policing, 17, 141, 148, 158–173; Bureau of Police Services, 165, 166; Central Area Study (CAS), 165–171, *170*; Central Atlanta Progress (CAP), 138–146, 148–151, 155–158, 159, 163, 165–171, *170*; Central Police Zone, 168; commercial sex trade, 139–141, 143, 144–145, 149–151; community partnerships, 160–165; Comprehensive Development Plan, 158; economic inequality in, 158; *Lambert v. City of Atlanta,* 151–155; map, *140*; Mayor's Task Force on

Atlanta *(continued)*
  Prostitution (MTFOP), 162–163, 166; Midtown Ponce Security Alliance, 201; misdemeanor policing in, 149, 150, 164, 169, *170*; Neighborhood Planning Unit Prostitution Task Force, 162; Partnership against Crime program, 161, 166; Police/Community Action Agreement, 160; protests in, 162, *163*; Public Safety Task Force, 157, 168; "Safeguard Zone," 166–171; serial murders of Black children, 145–146, 149, 161, 257n15, 2577n20; violent crime in, 139, 145–146, 169
Atlanta Business Coalition, 160
Atlanta Chamber of Commerce, 155, 160
Atlanta City Council, 168, 169
Atlanta Constitution, 143, 150, 155, 161
Atlanta Convention and Visitors Bureau (ACVB), 138, 143, 145
Atlanta Department of Community Development, 161
Atlanta Department of Public Safety, 139, 142, 160, 161
Atlanta Journal-Constitution, 159, 167, 168, 173, 201
Atlanta Police Department, 143, 156–157; Anticrime Action Plan, 150; Mobile Action Unit, 138, 145; racial conflict in, 138, 142–145
Atlanta Regional Commission, 142
The Atlantic, 146, 160
Axel, Naomi, 132, 133

Back Bay (Boston), 114
Back Bay Ledger-Beacon Hill Times, 109
badger game, 33, 229n20, 250n30
Balas, Kimberly, 192–193
Baldwin, James, 257n20
Baldwin, Margaret, 189–190
Balos, Beverly, 194
Baltimore, 32
Baltimore Afro-American, 144

Balto, Simon, 14, 231n39
banishment laws targeting prostitution, 11, 12, 111, 120–121,136, 173, 191, 195, 196, 197, 200, 201–202, 206, 250n33,
Barbara, 117
Barry, Kathleen, 191, 194
Barry, Patricia, 145–146, 156
Barton, Minnie, 23
Bates, George, 65
Bates, Sanford, 56
Bat Patrol (Atlanta, also known as the Ron Carter Patrol), 161
Bay State Banner, 115
Beacon Hill (Boston), 114
Beckerman, Debra, 115
Betty (Los Angeles), 76
Binford, Jessie, 26
Black Coalition Fighting Back Serial Murders, 175, 176, 182, 184, 185, 200
Black community activists: in Atlanta, 146; in Boston, 115, 121–122, 126–127; in Los Angeles, 95–96, 101–102, 104; Progressive-era, 21
Black community relations: in Atlanta, 138, 142–143, 161, 164; in Boston, 127–131
Black deviance myth, 13, 18, 37; and broken windows theory, 147, 156, 158–160, 164–165, 167, 171; and LAPD, 96–97, 106; media depictions, 158–159; and police professionalism, 87–97; postwar criminology on, 81–82, 240n12. *See also* Black women, deviance presumed of
Black feminists: in antiviolence activism, 4, 174–186, 198–200; contesting police power, 17; in dominance activism, 186–187; on gender and racial binaries, 14, 216n3; intellectual framework of, 4. *See also names of people and organizations*
Black men: interracial socialization, 7, 27, 34, 35, 36–37, 66; mass incarcera-

tion of, 3, 216–217n5; targeting of, 171, 207, 279n16
Black middle class: in Atlanta, 158, 161–162; respectability politics, 100–103
Black neighborhoods: in Atlanta, 146, 159, 161, 164–165; in Boston, 111–112, 115, 116, 126, 127; community relations, 127–131, 161; postwar attitudes of, 81–82, 88, 90; postwar unequal policing in, 92–93, 96–106; postwar urbanization patterns, 81–82; red-light districts' proximity to, 20; red-light districts' relocation to, 10–11, 16, 25, 27; repressive World War II policing in, 67–75; sexual policing in, 5, 13; vice districts' impact on, 30, 37. *See also* Black vice districts; *specific neighborhoods*
Blackness, criminalization of, 101, 113, 133, 139, 171
Black police officers and leaders, 111, 127, 129–131, 132–133, 136, 138, 142–145
Black press: archives, 15; on Boston's racist planning, 115; on postwar Los Angeles policing, 74, 95–96, 97, 101; on Prohibition-era policing, 26, 31–32, 35, 38–39, 43
Black segregation. *See* racial segregation
Black self-defense: community patrol, 115, 126, 161; Black feminist strategies of, 178–179
Black sexuality, 81–83, 178, 183, 185
Black urban uprisings, 16; of 2020, 3, 217n6, 245–246n59; in Harlem (1964), 116; in postwar Los Angeles, 100–106; and racial inequities of morals enforcement, 77, 78, 96–106; Roxbury (1967), 116, 129; Watts (1965), 77, 85, 105; against white vice, 34–35; use of term "uprising," 245–246n59

Black vice districts: employment in, 30, 2228n13; neighborhood degradation from, 30, 37; and political corruption, 29, 39; in postwar Los Angeles, 96–106; Prohibition-era segregationist policing in, 10, 13, 26–41; white invasions in, 26, 30–31, 35, 38, 70, 97–98, 115–116
Black women: antiviolence feminist activists on, 175–186, 198, 199, 200; in Atlanta, sexual profiling of, 138, 139, 158–159, 163, 169, 171; in Boston, serial murders of, 177–182; and Boston redevelopment, 109–111, 116–122, 132–133, 136–137; and broken windows policing, 11, 148, 163; and carceral feminist positions, 207; deviance presumed of, 13, 18, 37, 82–83, 119–120, 148, 158–159, 171, 178, 182–183; employment of, 54, 112; historical shifts in sexual policing, 2, 3–7, 10, 11–12, 49; interracial sexuality of, 70–71, 97–98, 115–116; and mass incarceration, 3, 216–217n5; and police tactics, 1–2, 3, 4; postwar discretionary policing of, 11–12, 13, 16, 76–87, 94–106, 99; and Progressive era reform, 10, 19, 23–24; serial murders of, 175–186, 200; sex work and presumed criminality, 119–120, 171, 172, 183–184; violent neglect of, 28, 37–41, 68–75, 175–186, 187, 201, 227n7; World War II period policing of, 51, 52, 67–70
Black Women for Wages for Housework, 122, 181–182, 198, 250n36
Black youth: Atlanta child murders, 146, 149, 161; media depictions, 159
Blair, Cynthia, 227n6
Blue Revolution, 17, 199
Board of Police Commissioners, Los Angeles (BOPC), 95–96
Bolan, James S., 48
Bolden, Eva and Ike, 38
Borde, Bellana, 268n13

Index 283

Boston, 14, 16–17, 66, 69, 71–72, 74, 107–137; Combat Zone, 107–110, *108*, 114–121, 124–125, 130–136, 177; crime policies, 113–115, 128–131; downtown development, 107–112, 135–136; feminist activisms in, 175, 177–182; map, *108*; postwar demographics, 111–112; Puopolo murder, 132–135; racist and sexist policing in, 115–121, *118*, 135 (*see also* Boston Police Department); segregationist policies in, 111–115
Boston Area Rape Crisis Center, 181
Boston Council of Social Agencies, 65
Boston Globe, 109, 113, 120, 122, 123, 133, 135, 136
Boston Herald, 134
Boston Municipal Court, 120
Boston Police Department (BPD), 43, 110–111, 122–137, 177; Black officers with, 111, 129–131, 132–133, 136; rifts among leaders and rank-and-file, 124–125, 127–128; Special Investigation Unit (SIU) report, 131–134; Tactical Patrol Force (TPF), 128–131
Boston Redevelopment Authority (BRA), 109, 112, 114, 115, 123, 124
Bowron, Fletcher, 74
Box-Car Bertha, 48
Bradley, Tom, 185
Bratton, William, 110
Briggs, Laura, 15
broken windows policing: in Atlanta, 17, 141, 148, 158–173, 201–202; and Black men, 12; Black women profiled in, 11, 148, 163; and community policing, 160–165; dominance feminists' support for, 176, 185, 186, 188–189, 196–200; effect on urban planning and policy making, 5–6, 12, 16; and exclusion orders, 195–196, 201–202; gender-specific harms of, 173; legal foundations for, 150–157, 202–203; and loitering with intent, 155–156; in New York, 197–198; postwar Los Angeles policing foundational for, 106; and sexual policing, 12, 173; theory, 146–149
Brooklyn, 38–39
Brooklyn Law School, Criminal Defense and Advocacy Clinic, 203
Brown, George, 39
Brown, Lee, 150, 159–160
Brown, Pat, 86
Bunte, Doris, 126–127
Burgoon, Janet, 61
Burlington, Vermont, 207
business, law enforcement, and political alliances. *See* political, law enforcement, and business alliances

California Department of Justice, 237n43
California morals laws, 77, 85–87, 97, 105, 106, 155
California Prostitutes' Education Project (later known as the California Prostitutes' Education Project), 183
California Special Crime Commission, 82
California Supreme Court, 85–86, 105
Canaday, Margot, 14
capitalism. *See* gentrification; political, law enforcement, and business alliances; real estate developers
carceral feminist policies, 185, 207, 208. *See also* dominance feminism
Cast the First Stone (Murtagh and Harris), 83
Central Area Study (CAS), 165–171, *170*
Central Atlanta Progress (CAP), 138, 139–146, 148–151, 155–158, 159, 163, 165–171, *170*, 256n6
Chandler, Otis, 90
Charlotte, North Carolina, 34
Chateauvert, Melinda, 9
Chicago, Prohibition-era policing in, 24, 26, 27, 39, 40, 44, 227n6, 228n13, 231n39
Chicago Defender, 26, 30, 32, 39
Chinatowns, red-light districts' proximity to, 20
civil law, 190–194, 271n38

civil rights: activism, 4, 21, 87, 93, 164; and broken windows policing, 147, 148, 164–165; legislation of dominance feminism, 190–194, 271n38; postwar support for, 87; World War II period, 65–66, 74
Clapp, Raymond, 74
Clement, Elizabeth Alice, 226–227n5
clergy, radical, 123
Clinton, Bill, 216n5
Clinton, Hillary, 3, 216n5
Coalition against Trafficking in Women, 191, 194
Coalition for Women's Safety, 268n13
Cohen, Cathy, 14
Collins, Patricia Hill, 13
Combahee River Collective, 174, 178, 179, *179*, 185
Combat Zone (Boston): Adult Entertainment District (AED) concept, 109, 114, 115, 116, 123, 124, 125, 131, 135, 139–140; Black women policed in, 116–121, 132–133, 177; development of, 107–110, *108*, 114–115; police reform efforts in, 122–125, 130–131, 177; Puopolo murder, 132–134
commercial sex industry: in Atlanta's business district, 139–141, 143, 144–145, 149–150; dominance feminists' stance on, 192–193, 207; FBI's 1938 Uniform Crime Report on, 7–8; legal forms of, 226–227n5; police corruption and, 5, 38, 39, 42; street vs. indoor, 11, 163; violent crimes tied to, 149, 150
Committee of Fourteen (New York), 21, 32, 36, 40
common nightwalking, 7, 34, 119
community policing programs, 160–165, 171
condoms, 1, 60, 206
Conference of State and Territorial Health Authorities, 63
Congress of Racial Equality (Los Angeles), 102
convention and tourism industry, 139, 141, 143, 144–145, 150
Cooper, Courtney Ryley, 36, 44
Cops (television show), 1, 2, 215–216nn1–2
Council of Organizations against Vice (COAV), 100–102, 103
COYOTE (Call Off Your Old Tired Ethics), 121, 183. *See also* sex workers rights movement
crack cocaine addiction, 158–159, 183
Crenshaw, Kimberlé, 4, 187, 200
"crime-fighting" policing, 28, 42–49, 61
Crime Task Force (Atlanta), 144–145, 146, 148
Crooms, Hattie, 35

Davis, Angela, 4
Davis, Ed, 124
Debro, Julius, 167
decriminalization campaigns: ACLU on, 151; in Atlanta, 140; in Boston, 123–127; and broken windows theory, 147; dominance feminists' stance on, 188, 194–195, 199, 207; twenty-first century activism, 206–208
D'Emilio, John, 81
Democratic National Convention: in Atlanta, 168; in New York City, 151
Depression era, 28, 46–49
DeSario, Frank, 125
Detroit, 38, 175
Diaz, Manny, 202
Dickerson, Jeff, 159
diGrazia, Robert, 124, 126, 127, 128, 130, 131, 134
discretionary police authority, 7–8, 9, 32, 41; and broken windows policing, 147–148, 164–165, 203, 205; efforts to counter, 150–157, 208–209; postwar racial disparities in, 84–87, 96–106, 176; postwar threats to, 89; and Progressive-era misdemeanor laws, 22–23; during Prohibition, 27

Index 285

disorder and disorderly conduct, 7, 8, 22, 47, 52, 58, 64, 72, 79, 128; and broken windows policing, 146–149, 171, 189; racism and sexism of arrests for, 172
Diver, Colin, and Joan, 113–114
dominance feminism, 174, 176, 186–200, 207, 265–266n1. *See also names of people and organizations*
Dorchester (Boston), 112
Dorn, Warren, 105, 106
Dorothy (Boston), 66
Dossey, V. C. (Los Angeles), 76
downtown commercial districts: postwar tolerance for sex work in, 11; red-light districts in, 10, 11, 19–20; red-light districts' move from, 10–11, 16, 25, 27, 31. *See also names of cities and specific districts*
Doyle, John, 124
Dragnet (television show), 88
drug addiction, 158–159, 164, 183
drug laws, 155–156
drug selling, 184, 195, 202
Dunham, George, 59, 60
Dworkin, Andrea, 174, 190

Eaves, Reginald, 138, 139, 142, 143, 144, 255–256n5
economic conditions: in Atlanta, 158, 164, 171; Boston redevelopment, 110–113; of Boston's Black population, 112–113; and crime, 166; feminist activists on, 176, 180–182, 183, 185, 189; police justifications for sexual policing, 2, 12; poor and marginalized women's vulnerability, 201, 204–209; pornography as a hindrance to growth, 139
Edholm, Charlton, 18
Eight-Point Agreement, 61
Eleanor (Massachusetts), 41
election slush funds, 29, 44
Emily (Taunton), 57
Emma (Boston), 71–73

employment, women's: access to workplaces, 4; Black rates of, 54, 112; job loss from sexual policing, 2; Progressive-era, 18; racist hierarchies of, 54; urbanization and, 53; in the vice industry, 30, 228n13; World War II increase in, 50–51, 53, 54
English Collective of Prostitutes, 198
entrapment, 42–43, 44, 104, 128, 184, 201, 204, 271n38
environmental criminology, postwar, 81–82
Escobar, Edward, 91
Escobedo v. Illinois, 89
eugenics, 4, 21, 22, 23
European immigrant women, 18, 23, 24, 57–58
evangelicals, 19
evidence collection, 42–43
The Evidence of Things Not Seen (Baldwin), 257n20
exclusion orders, 195–196, 201–202, 206
extortion, 3, 8, 28, 44, 173, 203–204. *See also* police corruption
extramarital sexuality, 79. *See also* nonmarital straight sexuality, women's

Fairstein, Linda, 197–198
FBI (Federal Bureau of Investigation): arrest statistics, 48–49, 69; under Hoover's crime-fighting leadership, 28, 46; *Uniform Crime Reports*, 7–8, 113, 233n57
federal police: cooperation from local forces, 75; Depression-era empowerment of, 46; and World War II period morals policing, 58–67
Federal Security Agency, 52, 61
feeble-mindedness, 21, 22
Felker-Kantor, Max, 14
Female Sexual Slavery (Barry), 191

feminist activisms, 17, 174–200; antiviolence activists, 174–186, 198; Black Women for Wages for Housework, 122, 181–182, 198, 250n36, 267n5; in Boston, 123, 134, 177–182; carceral feminist policies, 185, 207, 208; dominance feminists, 174, 176, 186–200; in Los Angeles, 177, 184–185; Progressive era, 19; "sex wars" debate, 176–177, 198–200; Take Back the Night Coalition rally, 179–180, 182; Wages for Housework, 174, 175, 176, 181, 198; Women's Court (Boston), 180–182. *See also* prostitutes' rights movement
Few, Robyn, 207
finger-print records, statistics drawn from, 227n9
floaters (court rulings), 120–121, 195, 250n33. *See also* banishment laws targeting prostitution
Florida, 172, 192–193
Florida Supreme Court, Gender Bias Study Commission, 189, 190, 192
Flowe, Douglas, 32
Floyd, George, 3, 245–246n59
Flynn, Raymond, 136
Fogelson, Robert, 46
forced sterilization, 21
Ford Foundation, 112
Foye, Andrea Lorraine, 177
Frank, Barney, 123, 124, 127
Franklin, Shirley, 168
Freedman, Estelle, 81
French, Dolores, 162

Gain, Charles, 124
gambling, 5, 19, 29, 38, 39, 42, 44, 96, 123
gang membership, 155, 184, 195, 202
Gates, Daryl, 184
Gay Community News, 134, *181*
gender: Black feminists' positioning of, 4; and broken-windows policing, 173; conformity, 14; Depression-era arrests by, 47–48; dominance feminists' focus on, 174, 176, 186–200; as a historical process, 2, 216n3; and misdemeanor arrests, 172; and police power, 3–7; and racialized crime, 171
Gender Bias Study Commission (Supreme Court of Florida), 189, 190, 192
gentrification: in Atlanta, 162, 201–202; Boston's early efforts in, 111, 135–136; and broken windows policing, 16; harm from, 201; and sexual policing, 5, 12–13
Georgia Supreme Court, 153–155
Germany, Tim, 115, 126
Gerould, Christopher, 79
"ghettos," 25, 82, 92, 116, 126
Gilmore, Ruth Wilson, 227n7
Ginsburg, Ruth Bader, 151
Ginzberg, Eli, 112
Giobbe, Evelina, 186, 194
global human rights campaigns, 184, 206
Gloria (Los Angeles), 104
Glueck, Sheldon, 54, 62
Goldman, Emma, 18
Goldstein, Herman, 89, 122
graft. *See* police corruption
Grant, Jaime, 177, 180
Gross, Kali, 4
Groves, Ernest, 56

Haft, Marilyn, 151
Hahn, Charles, 67
Hahn, Kenneth, 77, 103–105
Haley, Sarah, 4, 13
Hamer, Fannie Lou, 4
Hammonds, Evelynn, 13
Harcourt, Bernard, 171
Harlem, 32, 36–37, 39, 43, 116
Hartman, Saidiya, 15, 25
Harvard Crimson, 121
healthcare, 6, 185, 188, 209, 280n19
Heritage Foundation, 164
Hernández, Kelly Lytle, 15, 241n24
heteropatriarchy, 6

heterosexual marriage, 80, 81
Hicks, Cheryl, 4
Hill, Fanny Christina, 51
Hinton, Elizabeth, 14
Hobson, Maurice J., 141
Hoffman, Amy, 134
Holloman, Laynard, 100
Holmes, Kwame, 244n46, 245n59
Holtzclaw, Daniel, 204
homelessness, 155, 158, 167, 168, 195, 202
Hooking Is Real Employment (HIRE), 162
Hoover, Herbert, 42
Hoover, J. Edgar, 28, 36, 46, 47, 49, 54
Hopkins, Ernest, 42, 44
housing: in Atlanta, 158; and Reaganomics, 185; and sexual policing, 2; of single women during World War II, 66–67; social support for, 209. *See also* racial segregation
Houston, red-light district in, 20
Howard, Abbie, 139
Hull House, 26
Human Rights Campaign, 206
human trafficking, 203

Illinois, 202
INCITE! 200
Indianapolis, 190
Indigenous women, 7, 201, 205
Ingram, Tammy, 239n6
Inman, John, 142
In re Lane ruling, 85–86, 87, 90, 97, 100, 105, 106, 155
Institute for the Control of Syphilis, 58
International Association of Chiefs of Police, 64, 90
interracial socialization and sexuality: in Boston, 34, 110, 115–116; and police raids, 43; Prohibition-era policing of, 27, 31–37, 43; in red-light districts, 20, 27; and "white slavery," 36; white "slumming," 26, 30–31, 38, 70, 78, 96, 97–98, 99, 115–116; during World War II, 66, 70–71
intersectionality, 187, 199–200

Jabour, Anya, 24
Jackson, Maynard, 141–146, 150, 155, 156, 157, 161, 167, 169
Jacobs, Paul, 93, 96
James (Los Angeles), 104
Jeanette (Boston), 66
Jett, Brandon, 231
Jim Crow, 13, 23, 31–35
Johnson, Bascom, 62
Johnson, Charles, 71
Jones, Kenneth, 104
Jones, Mack, 141
Jordan, Joseph, 134, 135
Journal of Social Hygiene, 21
juvenile delinquency, 69
Juvenile Protective Association, 26

Kaba, Mariame, 4
Kansas City Police Department, 122
Kearney, Fred, 56
Keire, Mara, 19, 226n18
Kelling, George, 12, 146–149, 160, 164, 169, 171, 189, 199, 203
Kellor, Frances, 18
Kerner Commission (National Advisory Commission on Civil Disorders), 128–129
Kewpie Doll (Harlem bar), 36–37
King, Edward, 180, 181, *181*
King, Mel, 126–127
Kinsey, Alfred, 79, 80
Kinsie, Paul, 39
Kooistra, AnneMarie, 230n27

LaFave, Wayne, 94
Lahey, Kathleen, 187–188
Lamb, Roger, 113
Lambert, Patricia, 153–155
Lambert v. City of Atlanta, 153–155
Lamoreaux, A. L. (Los Angeles), 94
Lane, Carol (*In re Lane* ruling), 85–86, 87, 90, 97, 100, 105, 106, 155
Las Vegas, 1, 236n1
LAPD (Los Angeles Police Department), 76, 87, 89, 90, 91, 94–96, 98, 101, 124

LAPD Board of Police Commissioners (BOPC), 95–96
lasciviousness laws, 7
Latinx community, 7, 41, 184, 201, 205–206, 233n1
Law and Order (documentary film), 122
law enforcement: Black collaboration with, 100–103; Black women targeted by, 11–12, 27; citizen alliances with, 160–165, 171; discretionary nature of (*see* discretionary police authority); and dominance feminism, 188–190, 194–198; federal-local relationship, 75; political and business alliances (*see* political, law enforcement, and business alliances); post-Prohibition rescue of authority of, 46, 49; postwar professionalism and status, 87–96; as preservers of white moral order, 50; Reagan-era, 184–185; white supremacy of, 34, 50, 87–88, 90, 187, 188, 193; World War II period nationalization of, 58–67. *See also* morals law enforcement; police power; sexual policing
Law Enforcement Assistance Administration (LEAA), 113, 122, 126, 128, 156, 160
laws and legislation. *See* morals laws; prostitution laws
League of Women Voters, 114
LeFlouria, Talitha, 4
Leidholdt, Dorchen, 191, 194
Lekkerkerker, Eugenia, 22
Levine, Philippa, 189, 190, 199, 270n35
"lewdness," 7, 22, 34, 58, 63
Lewin, Lauri, 117
Lewis, TyRon, 272n49
LGBT community: activism, 123, 134; targeting and violence against, 7, 14, 205–206
Littauer, Amanda, 53
Lockett, Gloria, 121, 183–184, 185
Lois (Boston), 133

loitering laws, 1, 7, 86, 202, 205, 207; and broken windows policing, 7, 14, 155–156; in California, 7, 219n12; challenges to, 151–156
Lopez-Jones, Nina, 198
Los Angeles, 14, 16, 76–78, 81, 82, 85–106; Black confrontations with police, 103–105; Black feminist activism in, 175, 176. 184–186; Black protest in, 96–106; demographics, 81, 90; Depression-era, 48–49; map, 78; morals law reform in, 85–87; and police professionalism, 87–97; Progressive-era, 23, 35; Prohibition-era, 39, 40–41; racial disparities in morals enforcement, 76–87, 96–106, 175; vice raids, 102–105; Watts uprising, 77, 105; 'World War II period, 38, 64, 65, 69, 73–74
Los Angeles City Council, 184
Los Angeles Herald-Dispatch, 95–96
Los Angeles People's World, 102
Los Angeles Police Department (LAPD), 76, 87, 89, 90, 91, 94–96, 98, 101, 124, 184–185, 239n5
Los Angeles Sentinel, 74, 97, 101, 104, 105
Los Angeles Times, 50, 90, 96, 102, 104, 135, 185
Lukas, J. Anthony, 113–114
Lvovsky, Anna, 151

Mackey, Thomas, 20
MacKinnon, Catharine, 186, 187, 188, 190–191, 265–266n1, 271n38
Madeline (Boston), 237n40
Mallory v. United States, 89
"map area restrictions," 195, 202. *See also* banishment laws targeting prostitution
Marcus, Sidney, 157
marginalized and poor women, 167–168, 201, 204–209
Marin, Nancy, 120
Marjorie (Boston), 34

Index 289

Marriott Hotel, 149
Massachusetts Association of Afro-American Police, 129
Massachusetts Black Caucus, 127
Massachusetts government, feminist charges against, 180–182
Massachusetts Society for Social Hygiene, 69
Massachusetts Special Crime Commission, 42
mass incarceration, 3, 216–217n5
Mattapan (Boston), 112
Maxson, Berle, 73
May, Geoffrey, 70
May Act, 63–64
McChristie, Mary Edna, 53
McCormack, Arthur, 63
McIntyre, Cassandra, 132–133
Media (Taunton), 57–58
Meikle, Theresa, 50
mental health deinstitutionalization, 158
Merrill, Francis, 56
Meyer, Agnes, 67, 69
Miami, 128, 202
Michigan, 204
migrant women, 201, 273n1
Milliken, Rhoda, 75
Minneapolis, 190
Minnesota Department of Corrections, 194
Minnie Barton Training Home, 23
Minor, Sandra, 196, 272n49
Miranda v. Arizona, 89
miscegenation laws, 32, 34
misdemeanor policing. *See* broken windows policing; morals law enforcement; sexual policing
Mobile Action Unit (Atlanta), 138, 145
Model Penal Code (MPC), 83–84
Mogulescu, Kate, 203, 205
Money for Prostitutes Is Money for Black Women (pamphlet), 250n36
morals law enforcement: and arrest rates, 172; Depression-era arrests from, 47–49; discretionary nature of (*see* discretionary police authority); failure of, 43–44, 45; gender differences in, 172; and police authority, 8–9; and police corruption, 123, 124, 126; police sexual violence as a tactic of, 204; and postwar professionalization of police, 93–96; Progressive era, 16, 18–25, 27, 37; Prohibition-era, 5–6, 27, 39–41, 42, 43–44; racial inequity of, 10–12, 76–87, 96–106, 99, 162, 172, 175, 208; and racial segregation, 40–41, 49; sexual policing as a form of, 7–8, 9; World War II period repression campaign, 16, 52–53, 59–67, 75. *See also* law enforcement; sexual policing
morals laws: of California, 77, 85–87, 97, 105, 106, 155; and liberalized sexuality, 56–57, 79–83; liberal reforms of, 83–87, 89; *Papachristou v. Jacksonville*, 150–151; *People v. Smith*, 151–155; Progressive-era, 19; racial inequities of, 3–4, 35–37, 56–57, 79–87; state violence legitimatized by, 205–206. *See also* decriminalization campaigns; prostitution laws
Morgan, Woods, 35
Morrissey, Francis X., 121
Morrissey, Michael, 64
Mott, James, 65
Moynihan, Daniel Patrick, 240n12
multiracial antiviolence feminists, 17, 174, 177–178, 180, 200
Mumford, Kevin, 228–229n16
Murakawa, Naomi, 14
murders: Boston's Puopolo murder, 132–135; serial murders of Black Atlanta children, 145–146, 149, 161, 257n15, 2577n20; serial murders of Black women, 175–176, 177–186, 200; of transgender people, 206
Murphy, John, 119
Murrell, Cecil B., 100

NAACP (National Association for the Advancement of Colored People), 31, 39, 95–96, 98, 100, 101, 129
The Nation, 67
National Advisory Commission on Civil Disorders (Kerner Commission), 128–129
National Advisory Commission on Criminal Justice Standards and Goals, 124
National Advisory Police Committee, 64, 74
National Commission on Law Observance and Enforcement, 42, 44
National Conference on Women and the Law, 191
National Crime Commission conference (1932), 46
National Police Advisory Committee for Social Protection, 63
National Sheriffs Association, 67
National Urban League, 112, 113
National Venereal Disease Committee, 68
"The Negro and the Police in Los Angeles," 93
Negro Conference, 74
The Negro Family: The Case for National Action (Moynihan), 240n12
Nelson, Vednita, 186–187
Ness, Eliot, 52, 61, 62, 63, 70, 74
Neusom, Thomas, 101–102
Newark, 69, 160, 175
New Deal, 46
New Orleans, 204
Newport, Rhode Island, 64–65
New York City: police bonuses for prostitution convictions, 48; broken windows policing in, 197–198; Harlem, 32, 36–37, 39, 43, 116; marginalized women targeted in, 205; racism and segregationist policing in, 27, 32, 36–37, 39, 40, 43, 117, 205, 226–227n5; Seabury investigation, 42; sex-offense arrests in, 172

New York Prostitutes Union (also known as the New York Prostitutes Collective), *181*, 182, 268n17. See also sex workers rights movement
New York State Bar Association, 183, 197
New York Times, 64, 126, 134, 144, 159
New York University Law School conference, 187–188
"The Night and Danger" (Dworkin), 174
nonbinary people, 7, 14
nonmarital straight sexuality, women's: postwar legal liberalization, 11, 76, 77, 79–83, 97; Progressive-era, 22; racial disparities in criminalizing, 76–83, 97; during World War II, 53, 57–58
normativity, enforcement of, 6, 7
North Carolina, 34, 205
Northern cities: postwar problems of, 107, 112; segregationist sexual policing in, 26–31, 33–34

Oakland, California, 175, 183, 202, 252n47
O'Brien, Michael, 72
Office of Defense Health and Welfare Services, 70
Oklahoma City, 204
Omelia (Boston), 121
Omnibus Crime Bill, 46
Oregon, 175, 195–196, 202, 206, 207

Palmer, Eunice, 164
Papachristou v. Jacksonville, 150–151
Parker, Kathleen, 85
Parker, William, 87, 88, 89–90, 91, 94, 95, 241–242n26
Parks, Paul, 113
Parlin, Janet, 134
Parrish, Ted, 115–116
Partnership against Crime program (Atlanta), 161, 166
patriarchy, 174, 176, 186–200
Pellett, Gail, 117

Pennington, L. R., 61
Pennsylvania, 41
Pensacola, Florida, 175
People United for Freedom, 146
People v. Smith (New York State), 151–152, 154, 155, 156
Phenix City, Alabama, 239n6
Pilpel, Harriet, 79
pimps, legal action against, 191–194
Pittsburgh, 38, 175
Pittsburgh Courier, 30, 38, 39
Playboy Foundation, 151
Polanco, Layleen, 205
police corruption, 6, 24–25, 27, 39; bribery, 20, 44; extortion, 3, 8, 28, 44, 173, 203–204; and morals policing, 123, 124, 126, 172–173; postwar strategies of, 11; during Prohibition, 5–6, 20, 25, 28, 38–39, 41, 42, 44; scandals of, 41, 42, 43–44, 49, 131–132; in World War II period, 73–74
police harassment of sexually profiled women, 8, 68, 105, 122, 128, 134, 143, 175, 190, 203, 205
police power: archival records of, 14–15; arrest rates and, 28–29; and banishment laws, 202; and broken windows policing, 147; crime-fighting transition, 28, 46; harms of and remedies for, 208–209; history of, women's place within, 3–8; local and national policies, 14; and morals arrests, 8–9; post-Prohibition expansion of, 46, 49; and postwar professionalism, 87–96, 127; Progressive-era effect on, 22–25; repressive policies during World War II, 58–67; sexual policing as key to, 2–9; violence of, 2–4, 6–7. *See also* discretionary police authority; state violence
police professionalism, 78, 87–96, 127, 242n32
police raids: in Boston, 132; in postwar Los Angeles, 102–105; during World War II, 57, 72

police reform: community policing programs, 160–166, 171; racially inclusive hiring, 111, 127, 129, 136, 143
police sexual violence, 2–3, 42, 121–122, 132, 173, 203–204, 208
police surveillance, 4, 11, 12, 28, 46, 59, 62
policewomen, 23–24, 32
political, law enforcement, and business alliances, 5–6, 8, 10, 11–12, 20; in Atlanta, 138–145, 148–150, 155, 160–161, 165–166, 173, 201–202 (*see also* Central Area Study; Central Atlanta Progress); and banishment programs, 202; in Boston, 107–111, 113, 135–36; early 20th century, 10, 24–25, 27, 29, 37–39, 48–49; wartime, 73–74
poor and marginalized women, 167–168, 201, 204–209
pornography: antipornography ordinances, 190; feminists' debates on, 176, 186, 199; and urban economics, in Atlanta, 139, 176
Portland, Oregon, 175, 195–196, 202, 206
postwar period: police professionalism in, 87–96; racial disparities in morals law enforcement, 10–12, 76–87, 96–106; sexual liberalism in, 79–83; urban white flight, 11, 81, 88–89
Potter, Claire, 46
Prescod, Margaret, 175, *181*, 182, 184, 185, 188, 209
President's Research Committee on Social Trends, 47
profiling, 9, 15–16. *See also* sexual policing; status policing
Progressive era: morals legal infrastructure established, 22–24, 27, 37; police power escalation in, 18–25; red-light districts targeted during, 10–11, 16
Prohibition era: Black women's harm and arrests during, 37–41; crime-

292 Index

fighting as a fallout from, 28, 42–49; legalized sexual policing established in, 24, 25; police corruption in, 5–6, 20, 25, 28, 38–39, 41, 42–44; segregationist policing in, 26–37

promiscuity, women's: postwar decriminalization of, 84; Progressive-era criminalization of, 22; racial differences in policing, 10, 11; state anxieties about, 4, 7, 54, 55, 58–59; venereal disease tied to, 58–59

prostitutes rights movement. *See* sex workers rights movement

Prostitutes Union of Massachusetts (PUMA), 117, 121, 123, 134, 180–181. *See also* sex workers rights movement

"prostitution-free zones," 195, 196, 201–202. *See also* banishment laws targeting prostitution

"Prostitution: From Academia to Activism" (University of Michigan Law School symposium), 186–187, 188

prostitution laws, 7–8, 9, 22, 58, 63–64, 123–127; antiviolence feminists on, 174–186; banishment programs, 195–196, 201–202, 206; civil remedies, 190–194, 271n38; dominance feminists on, 174, 176, 186–200; and loitering with intent, 151–156; and Progressive-era reforms, 18–25; prostitution-related misdemeanors, 181, 182, 203, 206–207; racist enforcement of, 176; repressive federal World War II policy, 61–67; and vagrancy, 150–151. *See also* decriminalization campaigns; morals laws

"Prostitution: Where Racism and Sexism Intersect" (Nelson), 186–187

psychiatry, postwar, 80, 82

public order policing. *See* morals law enforcement

Public Safety Task Force (Atlanta), 157, 168

public space. *See* urban space, women's rights to

Puopolo, Andrew, murder, 132–135

"quality of life initiatives," 167. *See also* broken windows policing

queer community: activism, 123, 124; targeting of, 7, 14, 205–206

racial segregation, 5, 12–13; in Boston, 110–112; intensification of, 49; and postwar policing, 50, 87, 88–89, 90, 187, 193; Progressive-era "segregated" sex districts, 19–25; and Prohibition-era sexual policing, 26–37; in red-light districts and establishments, 20, 226n18; and World War II policing, 66

racism and racial discrimination: in Boston policing, 110, 116–122; of broken windows theory, 12–13, 148; of dominance feminist positions, 186–187, 188, 191, 198; of hierarchies of working women, 54; in Los Angeles policing, 76–87, 96–106; and misdemeanor morals arrests, 172; and police power, 3, 4, 5, 6, 13, 88, 208; in postwar morals enforcement, 10–12, 76–87, 96–106, 99; of Progressive-era reformers, 10, 18, 23, 26; of Prohibition-era policing, 41; of Puopolo murder narratives, 133–134; in urban development, 12–13, 115

"radical feminism," use of term, 265–266n1. *See also* dominance feminism

Ragland, John, 71

rape: feminist activists on, 180–182, 181; of sex workers as false reports, 204–205; of sex workers by police, 42, 121–122, 132, 173, 203–204, 208

Rape Action Project, 181

Rappaport, Mazie, 55

Reagan, Ronald, 106

Reagan era: broken windows theory in, 171, 184; economics, 184, 185

Index   293

real estate developers: in Boston's Combat Zone, 109, 135–136; and gentrification, 12; and red-light districts, 19. *See also* political, law enforcement, and business alliances
"rebel archive," 15
"rebellion," use of term, 245–246n59
Reckless, Walter, 29, 36, 39, 40
Reconstruction era aftermath, 4
red-light districts: creation of, 19; political functions of, 10, 20, 29; Progressive-era campaigns against, 10, 16, 18–25, 27; relocation of, to Black neighborhoods, 10–11, 16, 25, 27, 31; "segregated" sex districts, 18–25; support for, 24
Reed, Kasim, 201
Reformatory for Women in Massachusetts, 34, 41
reformers, Progressive-era, 18–25
Remus, Emily, 24
respectability politics, 100–103
restricted areas, 195. *See also* banishment laws targeting prostitution
Reumann, Miriam, 79
Reyes, Raquita, 1
Richardson, Mrs. John, 103
Ricketts, Christine Renee, 177
"riot," use of term, 245–246n59
Ritchie, Andrea, 4, 205
robberies, 131, 132, 135, 139, 145, 149, 155, 164
Roberts, Dorothy, 14
Robertson, Stephen, 35
Robinson, H. A., 51
Rochester, New York, 175
Roosevelt, Franklin, 46
Roxbury (Boston), 112, 115, 116, 126, 127, 129, 177
Ruzzo, Marjorie, 192, 193

Saint Louis, 35
Saint Petersburg, Florida, 155–156, 196, 272n49
Salcedo, Bamby, 205–206
San Diego, 65, 175
San Francisco, 44, 50, 124, 183
Sargent, Francis, 123
Say Her Name campaign, 200
Schiesl, Martin, 91
Schmitz, Bob, 168
Schulz, Dorothy Moses, 49
Schwartz, Louis, 84
Schwiezer, Officer, 98
Seabury investigation, 42
Sears, Clare, 202
Seattle, 175, 202, 207
segregation. *See* racial segregation
service industry workers, 55
sex industry. *See* commercial sex industry
Sexual Behavior in the Human Female (Kinsey), 79
sexual criminalization. *See* morals laws; prostitution laws
sexual entertainment districts. *See* adult entertainment districts; Black vice districts; Combat Zone (Boston); red-light districts
sexual liberalism: in Atlanta, 141, 162–164; in Boston, 111, 115, 125, 134, 136; in Los Angeles, racial disparities in policing, 76–83, 87, 89; of white men during World War II, 59–61, 62; of white women during World War II, 50, 51, 52–53, 54, 55–61, 75. *See also* morals laws; nonmarital straight sexuality, women's
sexual policing: defined, 2, 6; discretionary power of (*see* discretionary police authority); effect on urban planning and policies, 5–6; financial costs of, 209, 279–280n19; gender and sexual binaries enforced by, 14; harms of, 208; historical shifts in, 2–7, 11, 12–13 (*see also* Depression era; postwar period; Progressive era; Prohibition era; World War II period); as key to police power, 2–8; and morals law enforcement (*see* morals

law enforcement); nationalization of, 58–67; queer, trans and non-binary resistance to, 14; racial power dynamics of, 13, 208 (*see also* Black women; white women); social, political, and economic roots of, 8; unreformability of, 207–208; violence of, 2, 3–4 (*see also* state violence). *See also* morals law enforcement; morals laws; prostitution laws

Sexual Privacy Project, 151

"sex wars," 17, 176–177, 190, 198,

Sex Workers Outreach Project-USA, 207

sex workers' rights activists, 121, 123, 134; and antiviolence feminism, 174; archives, 15; in Atlanta, 162, *163*; feminist alliances, 182

sex workers rights movement, 15, 117, 119, 121, 123, 134, 174, 180, *181*, 182, 183, 205, 206, 207

Shange, Ntozake, 178

Sheehy, Gail, 114

Sheep Club, 39

Sherwin, Robert Veit, 80

Shumate, Teresa, 192

SIU, Boston Police Department (Special Investigation Unit), 131, 134

Six Black Women: Why Did They Die? (Combahee River Collective), 178–179

Skogan, Wesley, 197

Skolnick, Jerome, 87, 91, 94

slavery, 18, 191. *See also* "white slavery"

"slumming," 26, 30–31, 38, 70, 78, 96, 97–98, *99*, 115–116

"slums," 82, 88

Small, Sara, 177

Smith, Barbara, 178, *179,* 185

Smith, Maurice, 74

Smith, Toni, 151

Social Disorganization, 79, 82, 84

Social Problems on the Home Front (Merrill), 56

Social Protection Division (SPD): on Black neighborhood policing, 68–69, 70, 71, 73; establishment of, 51–52; and repressive wartime policing, 59, 61, 62, 63, 64, 65–66, 67, 75; on sexual liberalization, 53–54, 55, 56, 59

social welfare: feminists on, 181–182, 184–185, 209; police justifications for, 1, 5; Progressive-era, 23

Society for the Scientific Study of Sexuality, 80

sociology, postwar, 81–82

Sojourner, 177, 180

Solutions Not Punishment Collaborative, 206

Soul Patrol (Boston Police Department), 129

South End (Boston), 112, 113, 115–116, 127

Southern cities and towns, 31, 34–35, 68

South Los Angeles. *See* Los Angeles

spatial exclusion programs, 195–196, 201–202, 206. *See also* banishment laws targeting prostitution

Special Investigation Unit, Boston Police Department (SIU), 131–134

Spillers, Hortense, 13

Spingarn, Arthur, 31

state violence: Black women's violent neglect, 4, 7, 27–28, 37–41, 184, 227n7; in Boston, 121–122, 126, 131–134; in crime-fighting policing, 46; feminist activisms on, 174–176, 179–183, 189–190, 200, 205; historical lessons of, 17; against marginalized and poor women, 204–209; police harassment, 8, 203, 205; and police professionalism, 94–96; police sexual violence, 2–3, 121–122, 132, 173, 203–205; in sexual policing, 2, 3, 4, 8, 216n4; in twenty-first century cities, 201–202, 203

status policing, 12, 57–58, 94–96, 205; efforts to counter, 151–156; and *Papachristou v. Jacksonville*, 150–151; prostitution as a testing ground for, 171

Index 295

Stay Out of Areas with Prostitution orders (SOAP orders), 195, 196, 201–202. See also banishment laws targeting prostitution
Stay Out of Drug Area orders (SODA orders), 202
stigma of prostitution, 182, 184
Stokes, John, 58
"stool pigeons," 43, 44
"straight state," 14
street crime: in Atlanta, 138–139, 144–145, 156–157, 162–164, 165–167; in Boston, 113–115, 119, 128–131; legal banishment programs targeting, 195, 196, 201–202; in Los Angeles, 184–185; and public safety, 162–163; and sex work, 119–120, 163. See also broken windows policing; morals law enforcement
street walking, 65, 67, 126
Struggle for Justice, 203
suburbs, postwar, 11, 81, 88–89, 111, 138–139, 158
Sullivan, Edward, 64–65
Sullivan, Mary, 21–22, 32, 35–36
suspicion, arrests due to, 22, 57–58, 72, 84–86
Sweat, Dan, 138, 139, 142–143, 144, 150, 156, 157, 167–169
Sweetpea (Atlanta), 173
Swissair Associated Companies, 136

Tactical Patrol Force (TPF, Boston Police Department), 128–131
Taft, Charles, 63–64, 70
Take Back the Night (TBTN), 174, 175, 176 179–182
Taunton, Massachusetts, 57–58
Taylor, Breonna, 3, 245–246n59
Techniques of Law Enforcement against Prostitution (National Advisory Police Committee), 64
Terry, Treyola, 94–95, 96, 98, 243n39
Tetalman, Marc, 145–146, 156
Thirteenth Amendment, 191

Thompson, Larry, 164
Times Square, 116
Topping, Ruth, 22–23
TPF (Tactical Patrol Force, Boston Police Department), 128–131
Trans Latina Coalition, 205
trans women, 201, 205–206; activism of, 123; targeting and violence against, 7, 14, 123, 201, 205–206; use of term "woman," 273n1
Trosch, William, 259n36
Tuck, Bennett F., 143
Turner, George, 201
Turner, Thomas, 70
Turner, William, 89

undercover policing, 42–43, 94–95, 104, 116, 204
Underground Atlanta, 168
"Underworld Parlance" (E. Anderson), 41
"undesirable" people, 189
undocumented women, 201, 216n4, 273n1
Uniform Crime Reports (FBI), 7–8, 113, 233n57
United Nations Working Group on Contemporary Forms of Slavery, 194
University of Michigan Law School symposium, "Prostitution: From Academia to Activism," 186–187, 188
"uprising," use of term, 245–246n59
"urban apartheid," 112. See also racial segregation
urban criminality: Black people associated with, 112–113
urban crisis, 11, 16, 110, 111, 113, 136
urban development and policy, 5–6, 44
urban politics. See political, law enforcement, and business alliances
urban space, women's rights to: and banishment laws, 202; historical shifts in, 2, 4–5, 12; police as state arbiters of, 3–4; and postwar arrests, 98; racial stratification in, 117, *118*

U.S. Department of Justice, 113, 165, 175
U.S. Prostitutes Collective (U.S. PROS), 176
U.S. Supreme Court, 107, 150
U.S. Transgender Survey, 205

vagrancy laws, 7, 8, 22, 47, 50, 52, 58, 64, 79, 128; and *Papachristou v. Jacksonville*, 150–151; postwar legal reforms for, 86–87, 89, 97
Van Waters, Miriam, 34
venereal disease control: racial disparities in policing of, 59, 68, 69–71; and repressive morality, 52, 53, 54, 58–67, 68; World War II public service poster, 59, *60*
Vermont, 205, 207
vice control. *See* morals law enforcement
vice districts. *See* Black vice districts; red-light districts
victimless crime, decriminalization of, 122–127. *See also* decriminalization campaigns
violent crime, 132–135; in Atlanta, 139, 145–149, 169; Black sex workers association with, 119–120; commercial sex associated with, 149, 150; male violence against women, 174, 176, 186–200; racialization of, 112–113, 119–120, 161. *See also* murders; police sexual violence; rape; state violence
Violent Crime Control and Law Enforcement Act, 216n5
Vitti, Phillip, 116
Volstead Act, 24

Wade, Marie, 95
Wages Due Lesbians, 181
Wages for Housework (WfH), 174, 175, 176, 181, 198. *See also* Black Women for Wages for Housework
Walker, Samuel, 46
Wandick, Calvin, 1

War Department, 61
Warren, Earl, 38, 89, 242n27
Washington, D.C., 12, 175, 202, 204, 206, 207
Watson, C. H. (Los Angeles), 76
Watts Chamber of Commerce, 73
Watts Uprising of 1965, 77, 105
weaponry: crime-fighting focus on, 46
Weeks, Lesley, 121
Weirnamont, Tita, *181*
Welcome, Mary, 144, 154, 257n15
Welfare Island, 39
Wells, Ida B., 4
Westley, William, 88, 93
White, Kevin, 107, 108, 109, 110, 124
White, Walter, 39
white family, moral concerns over, 55–56
"white hunters," 26, 30–31, 38, 70, 78, 96, 97–98, *99*, 115–116
white men: dominance of, in red-light districts, 20; interracial sexuality of, 70–71, 97–98; sexual license of, 59–61, 62; "slumming," 26, 30–31, 38, 70, 78, 96, 97–98, *99*, 115–116
white middle class: Atlanta's focus on, 161–162, 169, *170*; Boston's redevelopment efforts for, 113–115, 135; culture of, 88–89; and urban crime, 148–149, 156; urban flight, 11, 81, 88–89, 111
white purity myth, 35; and Progressive reform, 18–25; and racial segregation, 10, 16, 17; red-light districts used to protect, 10, 16, 19; sexual policing as enforcing and protecting, 6, 16, 52–53, 156
"white slavery," 10, 16; abandonment of, 35–37, 46; dominance feminists' revival of, 191; Progressive-era, 18–25, 35–36, *45*
white supremacy, 34, 50, 87, 88–89, 90 187, 188, 193
white women: Black women as counterparts to, 13; in Boston's adult entertainment industry, 107, 109, 117,

white women *(continued)*
118, 119; criminality of, 35–36; Depression-era focus on, 47, 48; and dominance feminism, 174, 186–187, 194–195; interracial socialization, 7, 27, 33, 34, 35, 36–37, 66, 237n40; middle-class, during World War II, 55, 59, *60*, 62; and police power, 4, 5, 6; treatment of, 18–25, 34, 47, 48, 55, 82; postwar decriminalization of, 5, 10, 12, 13, 16, 76–83, 97, 106; postwar psychological views, 80, 82–83, 106; Progressive era reform efforts targeted to, 18–25, 26; Prohibition-era protection and targeting of, 26–37, 40–41, 42; purity presumed of, 13 (*see also* white purity myth); reformers, 17, 23, 34; sexual liberalization of, 2, 16, 50, 51, 52–53, 54, 55–61, 75, 79; and sexual policing, 6, 12, 172; workforce participation, 50–51, 53, 54, 75; World War II period targeting of, 65–67, 75
Whitin, Frederick, 21
Wichita, Kansas, 196
Wickersham Commission, 42, 44
Wild, Mark, 20
Wilkins, Baron, 32
Wilkins, Roy, 96
Williams, J. L. (Los Angeles), 94
Williams, Preston, 117, 118, 122, 129, 130, 131
Williams, Roxie, 98

Williams, Valimore, 122, 129, 131
Williams, Wayne, 257n15
Williamson, Terrion, 266–267n3
Wilson, James Q., 12, 92, 146–149, 160, 164, 169, 171, 189, 199, 203, 250–251n37
Women Against Rape (WAR), 198
Women Hurt in Systems of Prostitution Engaged in Revolt (WHISPER), 186, 188, 194–195
Women's Bureau (WB), 112
Women's Christian Temperance Union, 21
Women's Court (Boston), 180–182
Women's Rights Project, 151
Women With A Vision, 200
Wood, Joan, 114
Woods, Gerald, 228n13
World War II period: Black neighborhood policing, 67–75; repressive federal policies during, 58–67; sexual policing during, 16; white women's sexual liberalization, 50, 52–53, 54, 55–61; white women's workforce participation, 50–51, 53, 54
Worthington, George, 22–23

Young, Andrew, 157–158, 162, 165, 168
Younger, Evelle, 105

Zell, Glenn, 153–154
zoning. *See* adult entertainment districts